The Abutia Ewe of West Africa

Studies in the
Social Sciences *Anthropology*
38

The Abutia Ewe
of West Africa

A Chiefdom that Never Was

Michel Verdon

Mouton Publishers
Berlin · New York · Amsterdam

For Diane

Library of Congress Cataloging in Publication Data

Verdon, Michel.
   The Abutia Ewe of West Africa.

   (Studies in the social sciences (Berlin, Germany) ;
38. Anthropology)
   Bibliography: p.
   Includes index.
   1. Ewe (African people)—Social life and customs.
2. Ewe (African people)—Politics and government.
I. Title.   II. Series: Studies in the social sciences
(Berlin, Germany) ; 38.   III. Series: Studies in the
social sciences (Berlin, Germany).   Anthropology.
DT510.43.E94V47   1983   306'.089963   83-864
ISBN 90-279-3410-X

Printing Druckerei Hildebrand, Berlin. – Binding: Lüderitz & Bauer Buchgewerbe GmbH, Berlin. – Cover illustration: K. Lothar Hildebrand, Berlin.   Printed in Germany.

Preface

Many doctoral dissertations remain dormant on the shelves of University libraries and should not be disturbed from their peaceful slumber. This was the fate that I had chosen for my own thesis; for five years it lay buried in the University archives, but I then decided to resurrect it. What prompted me to do so is the subject of this preface. Whether or not it was a wise step to take should be answered by this book.

I came to Cambridge to escape the American and French anthropology which had dominated my undergraduate years at the Université de Montréal. A keen admirer of British social anthropology, I desperately wanted a first-hand acquaintance with the 'no-nonsense' tradition of British empiricism and happily accepted Professor Fortes' guidance in this new direction. He suggested that I study the Ewe-speaking peoples of southeastern Ghana, and I took his advice. Since the coastal Ewe had already been studied by an Ewe anthropologist, I turned my attention to the inland Ewe. After a series of decisions influenced more by chance and necessity than rational considerations, I settled in Abutia Kloe, a village of the Abutia Division, an administrative unit embracing groups of villages sharing this common name and acknowledging a common 'chief'.

There are only three Abutia villages, in close proximity to one another. Although I settled in Kloe, I came to know the two others quite well.

Life in Kloe was so much like life in the French-Canadian village that I had studied before that I came to take their social organization for granted. At first sight, there was little 'exotic' about their institutions and when I discovered their elaborate funeral rites, I immediately and almost instinctively dedicated most of my fieldwork to their investigation. Back in Cambridge, however, Professor Fortes wanted a sketch of their social organization, not their rituals. Eager to receive the

ultimate accolade from the greatest representative of the
Great Tradition I complied again, unaware of the direction
in which this decision would take me.

The Abutia social organization was to impose a
rethinking. Its very lack of exotic features proved
indeed to be its most challenging facet. This was a
society without divine kings, warrior chiefs or revered
elders, without inordinately polygynous men, without
elderly men exploiting female labour and appropriating
their products, without bridewealth or initiation rites,
without extended families, without..., without..., and
without! And yet Abutia was undeniably an African
society, an African society without the features that we
have come to expect after four decades of segmentary
lineage systems, of village headmen or proto-states. More
than that; the very institutions that it possessed
challenged the 'African orthodoxy'. It had descent
groups, but with properties more reminiscent of Melanesia
and the Middle East than sub-Saharan Africa. With shallow
genealogies and numerous matrifiliants, their **agnatic**
descent groups allow in-marriage and combine with a
cognatic system of kinship behaviour!

Initially blind to this uncommon association of
features when I was in the field, I realized their
uniqueness when I came to write a coherent account of
Abutia social organization. I also realized that what I
had come to get in Cambridge was now failing me. Indeed,
nothing in the Great Tradition could help me bring
coherence to this incongruous medley.

Like all monistic explanatory models, however,
'classical descent theory' was not without safety valves
which enabled it to cope with instances like Abutia. It
would invoke anomie, disruption of the old normative
order, or the amorphous structure of village life
disrupted by one hundred years of foreign influence. On
both intellectual and aesthetic grounds, however, I could
not bring myself to adopt this view; it would have
amounted to betraying both myself and the Abutia. The
Abutia social organization had certainly changed since the
precolonial days, but it deserved to be treated on its own
terms; I could not discard it as some form of degenerate
remnant of a once coherent and well-lubricated traditional
society.

I also sought inspiration from other paradigms,
marxist, structuralist, transactionalist, and so on, but
to no avail. None of them enabled me to describe and
analyze Abutia social organization in terms which were

adequate to the reality I had observed. Quite frustrated, I produced an intellectually hybrid and eclectic doctoral dissertation which earned me the title I coveted, but I buried the monster in my personal files as soon as it had been examined.

The restlessness, however, lingered on. I was convinced that the Abutia presented unique organizational features to which the current paradigms could not do justice. One option remained open. It was a foolhardy and most pretentious one, I confess, but the only one I could honestly face, short of distorting the facts to fit the Procrustean bed of conventional approaches. I could indeed try to understand why the conventional models failed to make sense of the Abutia data, and excogitate a new approach which would live up to their full richness and complexity.

I returned to the classics and, with some inspiration from the history of science, I started elaborating this new model; to contrast it to previous ones, I labelled it 'operational'. Its details have been spelled out elsewhere (Verdon 1980a, 1980b, 1981, and especially n.d.1), and the reader will be spared a book on theory. With this operational model in hand I could then return to the original ethnography, re-analyze the data and present it in a form which no longer suffered from my previous eclecticism. The result is this monograph.

For these reasons, I do not regard this monograph as a run-of-the-mill, conventional ethnography. I present it as the first and only full-fledged application of an operational approach to a study of social organization; more pompously, I would call it a 'paradigmatic application' of an operational model.

To set the ethnography in its proper theoretical perspective, I must nonetheless say something about operationalism. But I do wish to keep this presentation to a minimum, because I have already dedicated a full book to its theoretical elaboration (Verdon n.d.1). If the reader can bear the concentrated and highly selective exposition that follows, he may gain a better insight into the deep motivations which drove me to bring back to life an ethnography which, without an operational perspective, would have at best remained concealed in the obscurity of the University archives.

Contents

x.   Contents

List of Tables

List of Illustrations

MAPS

1. Eweland
2. The sub-ethnics Divisions of the Ewe part of the Volta Region
3. Abutia and its neighbouring Divisions
4. A road map of the Abutia area

DIAGRAMS

Operationalism: its basic concepts
I. Synchronic representation of a **fhome**
II. Minimal lineage reproduction in ideal demographic conditions
III. Minimal lineage reproduction in more realistic conditions
IV. Synchronic representation of a Type I lineage
V. Synchronic representation of a Type II lineage
VI. Simplified representation of a Type III lineage
VII. Diagrammatic representation of the bi-dimensional aspect of **fia**-ship
VIII. Pictograms of some common residential groups in Abutia
IX. Marriage preferences
X. Causal linkages between village sovereignty, descent and the various features of Abutia matrimonial practices
XI. Residential growth and reproduction: two case histories
XII. Edited version of the Nkubia lineage, with the residential distribution of its members
XIII. Age pyramid of the resident Kloe population, collected in census
XIV. Age pyramid of all the members of a minimal lineage of a Type I lineage

xvii.

Acknowledgements

I carried out fieldwork in Eweland between March 1971 and October 1973, with a two-month interruption in April-May 1973. Professor Meyer Fortes, my supervisor at Cambridge, suggested that I study the northern Ewe. I am immensely grateful to him for this suggestion, and for challenging me to understand their social organization. I am also thankful to Professor Jack Goody for his advice and encouragement during my doctoral work.

Above all, I am forever thankful to the people of Abutia, and particularly Kloe, where I settled. They patiently and kindly gave their time to answer interminable questionaires and interviews and, during the two years that I lived in Kloe, they showed a friendliness and understanding that made these two years two of the most pleasant ones in my life.

The research was financed by generous grants from the Canada Council and the Quebec Ministry of Education. Their financial support made possible my long stay in the field and ultimately enabled me to collect sufficient data to make some sense of the Abutia social organization.

More personally, I wish to thank Dza Kwasi and Daniel Doh, my closest assistants in Kloe; their friendship gave me a privileged insight into Kloe life. The unwavering moral and financial support of my brother Jean and his wife Nicole have also helped me find the time necessary to write this monograph. Dr Peter Sutton kindly accepted to copy-edit the manuscript. They, but above all my wife, Diane, to whom this book is dedicated, have made this book possible.

Parts of this book have already appeared in print. The Abutia political organization has already been examined in some detail in three articles in Africa: "The structure of titled offices among the Abutia Ewe" (49:159-71), "Redefining precolonial Ewe polities: the case of Abutia" (50:280-92) and "Political sovereignty, village reproduction and legends of origin: a comparative hypothesis" (51:465-76). In another paper, "Sleeping together: the dynamics of residence among the Abutia Ewe" (Journal of Anthropological Research 35:401-425), I have presented part of my analysis on residence whereas the study of the Abutia matrionial practices has already been broached in a number of publications: "Agnatic descent and endogamy: a note" (Journal of Anthropological Research 37:247-255), "Of mathematics and comparison: Pende and Abutia marriages" (L'Homme 22: 75-88), "Divorce in Abutia" (Africa 52 (4)) and "Polygyny, descent, and local fission: a comparative hypothesis" (Journal of Comparative Family Studies, forthcoming). The theoretical part of the book, as mentioned in the Introduction, has been elaborated in greater detail in three main articles: "Shaking off the domestic yoke, or the sociological significance of residence" (Comparative Studies in Society and History 22:109-32), "Descent: an operational view" (Man (n.s.) 15:129-50), and "Kinship, marriage and the family: an operational approach" (American Journal of Sociology 86:796-818).

Note on Ewe Orthography

ã, ɔ̃ and ẽ are all nasalized vowels, like the
      French 'an' (in 'plan'), 'on' (in 'mon') and 'ain'
      (in 'pain') respectively

'fh'   (phi in international phonetic alphabet) is a
      voiceless bilabial fricative

'vh'   (beta in international phonetic alphabet) is a
      voiced bilabial fricative

ḍ   is a voiced retroflex (apico-domal) stop

ŋ   is a strongly nasalized 'ng' (as in 'sing')

x   is a voiceless dorso-velar fricative, as the 'ch'
      in Lochness

ɔ   is an open 'o', like the 'o' in 'order'.

The General Problem

I. INTRODUCING OPERATIONALISM

Up to the 1970s, when marxism first invaded British social anthropology, two main traditions dominated the British scene; one, a 'social action' model, originated from the work of Malinowski whereas the other, a 'social structure' model, emanated from the work of Rivers. Rivers defined social organization as the manner in which individuals form groups, and groups as associations of individuals with (1) rules of entry and exit (let us conveniently call them 'criteria of membership') and, (2) rules of internal **organization** which (a) regulated interpersonal behaviour within the group and, possibly (although it is not explicitly stated in the text) (b) distributed activities to the various members (division of labour) (Rivers 1924:9). **Descent,** which Rivers construed as a criterion of membership in unilateral groups, clearly fell under (1) and did not serve to regulate interpersonal behaviour; this was achieved by **sibship** (in the context of unilineal groups) and **kinship** (in the context of families) (for further elaboration, see Verdon 1980c and n.d.1).

Radcliffe-Brown believed he was improving upon Rivers' theory by representing groups as 'corporations' which owned an 'estate' composed of the statuses of their members (Radcliffe-Brown 1935). Statuses, he defined as the sum of rights and duties characteristic of a position (or role) in a reciprocal relationship. 'Rights and duties', however, are nothing but ideas about what people ought to do; in short, they are **normative mental representations** which regulate interpersonal behaviour (**2a** in Rivers' definition).

According to this 'corporatist' model of group, individuals gain membership of groups by acquiring a status, a sum of rights and duties which also determine the manner in which they ought to relate to other members.

Radcliffe-Brown's notion of 'status' thus denoted both criteria of group membership and rules regulating interpersonal behaviour, thereby confusing conceptually what Rivers had distinguished.

Fortes and Evans-Pritchard further innovated upon Radcliffe-Brown's model by separating analytically relationships between discrete, 'corporate' groups - relations which they regarded as 'political' - from relationships between individuals (Fortes and Evans-Pritchard 1940, Evans-Pritchard 1940, 1951, Fortes 1945, 1949a). They used 'descent' to refer either to a charter or to an ideology which reflected (charter) or regulated (ideology) relationships **between** corporate groups. By the 1940's, therefore, 'descent' had already come to designate three different entities, namely (a) a criterion of membership of unilineal groups, (b) a system of normative mental representations ordering interaction within descent groups and (c) the mechanism responsible for the regulation of relationships between corporate groups.

'Classical descent theory' was built on these foundations [1]. By this locution, I will mean a particular set of assumptions, both conceptual and analytical, premised upon 'corporatist' and 'segmentary' representations of groups.

The corporatist model posits that groups, as corporations, must possess their members exclusively in order to persist over time (Radcliffe-Brown 1935). To achieve that they endow some facts, like agnatic or uterine descent, with a centripetal force that pulls some individuals together, thereby separating them from others and delineating the boundaries around diverse corporations. In addition, the segmentary model asserts that corporate groups define their identity in contradistinction, or, complementary opposition, to corporate groups of co-ordinate genealogical level, a process viewed as 'political'. In other words, the element which defines these corporate groups, namely descent, also serves as the blueprint for political relationships.

By 'classical descent theory' I will also mean an **explanatory** model rooted in the conviction that kinship (or ascribed criteria) dictates group membership in 'primitive' societies. In those societies which have evolved beyond the hunting-and-gathering stage and value some forms of property, such as cattle or land, unilineal descent (a sub-set of kinship) allegedly serves for group recruitment (Fortes 1953). In view of these assumptions, political organization and 'descent system' practically coincide in societies with unilineal descent groups which have not yet developed into proto-states (Fortes and Evans-Pritchard 1940) and one ought to be able to deduce most of the features of 'descent-based' societies from their type of descent.

Most of the peculiarities of their marriage system, for instance - such as the amount of bridewealth, the levirate, widow-inheritance, ghost-marriage, marriage stability (or divorce frequencies) - have indeed been accounted for in terms of 'descent systems' (Radcliffe-Brown 1950, Gluckman 1950, Schneider 1961), as have the features of their 'family system' or residential arrangements (Richards 1950, Fortes 1949b). The 'descent system' also made sense of the types of relationships between spouses, siblings, parents and children, mother's brother and sister's son and other kinship ties (Fortes 1949a, Richards 1950, Schneider 1961) and of the essential features of kinship terminologies (Murdock 1949, Gluckman 1950). Religious practices (ancestor worship, burial rites or witchcraft) also had their place in this all-encompassing scheme where kinship, marriage, residence, politics and religion (economics being the neglected relation) could all be logically derived from the mechanism of descent.

Classical descent theory thus separated the study of groups from that of social relationships and provided a set of concepts for identifying the various 'principles of social organization' and the diverse types of grouping in society (an analytical and conceptual model). It further assumed that descent was the most important principle of social organisation in the majority of societies studied by ethnographers and that it could therefore **explain** other aspects of social organization by virtue of the fact that society was defined as a system of interconnected parts; it thus presented itself as an explanatory model as well.

Classical descent theory enjoyed a remarkable success but it failed to create a consensus among social anthropologists. When descent theorists tried to link descent to the question of marital stability, the edifice started to crumble. Sharp observers soon asked embarassing questions: does 'strong agnatic descent' mean that fathers can keep their daughters in their own descent group, or that husbands can assimilate their wives to theirs (Leach 1957, Schneider 1965, Barnes 1967a)? No satisfactory reply was offered. Ethnographers working in the Middle East and North Africa also joined the chorus of discordant voices, claiming that individuals in 'agnatic segmentary societies' do not automatically align themselves with their agnates (Barth 1959, Peters 1967).

Since the theory postulated that corporate groups have to possess their members **exclusively**, classical descent theorists concluded that only discontinuous elements could exclude properly. Unilineal descent served this purpose admirably, clearly separating agnates from non-agnates, and uterine kin from non-uterine kin. Cognatic descent, on the other hand, lacked this power of discrimination; cognatic descent groups, it was concluded, are therefore a contradiction in terms! Davenport, Firth, and other ethnographers working in the Pacific protested vigorously (Davenport 1959, Firth 1957).   They were studying societies composed of groups which exhibited all the characteristics of corporateness, and yet recruited on the basis of cognatic descent. On the basis of one of the classical definitions of descent (as a criterion of group membership), these groups were cognatic descent groups. These Oceanian groups, replied the classicists, do not derive their corporateness from descent, but from the occupation of a common locality; they are therefore 'territorial corporate groups'!

This casuistry, however, soon reached its limit.   In Melanesia, ethnographers discovered **agnatic** descent groups whose features, however, departed significantly from the 'segmentary' societies of the 'African model' because of their shallow genealogies, their lack of segmentation, their assimilation of non-agnates and their use of residence as a criterion of membership in descent groups. The time had come for a major rethinking and, to account for such departures from the classical model, Scheffler proposed a new approach.

Scheffler separated conceptually the 'genealogical constructs' - i.e., the fact that individuals have a picture of their genealogical connections in their head - from 'actual groups' - i.e., the collection of individuals actually engaged in specific 'processes' (or activities) (Scheffler 1965, 1966).   These individuals sometimes invoke their genealogical connections to regulate their interpersonal behaviour when involved in a given process; they then form descent groups. In other places, however, individuals can be aware of their relatedness without ever doing anything together; in this instance they form a descent **category**, and not a descent group (Keesing

1971). A specialist of North Africa, Robert F. Murphy (1971) had reached a similar conclusion, and the Schefflerian model bounced back into African ethnography in the 1970s. The 'social structure' model which had inspired the pioneering works of Evans-Pritchard and Fortes has now given way to a new variant of a 'social action' perspective.

Recent ethnographers of Africa have indeed realized that individual strategies and actions are dictated not by individuals' positions within a system of corporate groups but by a larger set of principles, many of which are more 'achieved' or optative than lineage membership. This has led Webster, for instance, to describe African polities as more ego-centric than socio-centric (Webster 1977) and has encouraged the new generation of Africanists to focus upon individuals engaged in activities (or 'processes') rather than structures, and to conclude that 'descent' is only one of the many cultural (or 'ideological' - many writers seem to equate the two) elements which individuals can manipulate in defining their social position (Jackson 1977a, 1977b, Karp 1978).

The movement has culminated in Holy's 'transactional model' (Holy 1979) which re-emphasizes the distinction between the way in which social actors represent their society, and what they actually choose to do in concrete situations. Two models thus coexist in their heads: a 'representational model' of the society, coupled with an 'operational model' of whom to join and whom to shun in specific circumstances; the two models, however, do not necessarily coincide.

Despite their revolutionary claims, these recent theoretical developments were somewhat anticipated by classical descent theory itself insofar as it held descent to mean a set of rules regulating interpersonal behaviour, among other things. The transactionalists can therefore be credited with one major innovation, namely, their claim that descent does not operate alone in the regulation of interpersonal behaviour even within descent groups.

The new 'social action' theorists have thus abstracted one meaning of descent (as a behaviour regulator) from the other two meanings (as a criterion of group membership and a charter of intergroup relations) and have ignored Fortes and Evans-Pritchard's point of departure: the analytical distinction between groups and interpersonal relationships.

To state matters differently, let us say that Fortes's and Evans-Pritchard's group-centred (or 'structuralist') approach contained an implicit ego-centred one. Descent, in addition to denoting group membership and inter-group relations (hence, a group referent), also referred to rules, beliefs or values influencing the behaviour of agnates or uterine kin (hence a submerged 'social action' referent). Firth and Davenport, in their attempt to demonstrate the existence of cognatic descent groups, stressed the structural (or group) coefficient of descent; the transactionalists, on the other hand, have emphasized its interpersonal, or psychological, referent. They have therefore inverted Fortes's and Evans-Pritchard's premises by viewing descent as a mechanism of behaviour regulation and treating the constitution of groups as either derivative, or the environment within which individuals operate. Have they improved matters? To answer this question, I must first explain my own misgivings about classical descent theory.

Classical descent theory evolved in the wake of a debate which reached back to the nineteenth-century, and revolved around the ontological and analytical primacy of group ties or individual ties (for elaboration, see Verdon 1980c, 1980d, or n.d. 1). In this long tradition, Fortes and Evans-Pritchard sought to distinguish **analytically** and to reconcile the levels of groups and interpersonal relationships; their effort did not fulfill its original 'scientific' promises because it failed to posit the same distinction at the **conceptual** level[2]. To elaborate a set of concepts which would have tallied with their analytical postulates, they would have had to define groups and interpersonal relations in mutually exclusive ways. In other words, neither of the two terms should have been a part of the definition of the other. This, unfortunately, is precisely what happened. By holding on to Radcliffe-Brown's corporatist definition of group (and indirectly, on to Rivers's) they implicitly shared their Hobbesian assumption that interpersonal behaviour must be regulated for individuals to associate and form groups (i.e., to form an ordered society). This amounted to postulating that interpersonal relationships are intrinsic to the very definition of group.

By rooting groups in the regulation of interpersonal behaviour, they deprived them of any independent, autonomous ontological status. To use a Durkheimian idiom, they failed to treat groups as phenomena **sui generis** but reduced them to epiphenomena of behaviour regulation. Without a mechanism to order interpersonal behaviour, they assume, interaction would be anarchic and the ordered association of individuals impossible. There are groups, therefore, only insofar as there are mechanisms to regulate and therefore order interaction.

Why should these views be problematical? Because only normative mental representations can regulate inter-personal behaviour. Since behaviour and norms never coincide perfectly (always leaving an uncomfortable gap between ideal and actual), the groups made possible by this regulation are doomed to 'vary ontologically'.

To illustrate this thesis, let us return to our cherished 'agnatic descent'. To classical descent theorists it is a 'principle of social organization', that is, a system of normative mental representations which pulls agnates together and orders their interpersonal behaviour, thus forming corporate agnatic descent groups[3]. Some ethnographers, however, noted that Melanesian agnatic descent groups often include individuals excluded by the 'principle of agnatic descent'. Descent theorists then retorted that the 'principle' operated with varying strength, generating agnatic descent groups which varied along a continuum from very weak to very strong. In the end, therefore, descent groups appeared to **vary in degrees**, i.e., to be 'more or less' agnatic descent groups. This is what I mean by the groups' 'ontological variability'. I would further submit that this ontological variability of groups, in classical descent theory, stems directly from the fact that the regulation of interpersonal behaviour is an intrinsic part in the definition of groups; it also accounts, in my opinion, for the relative failure of classical descent theory. No rigorous comparative study of social organization can indeed be erected upon ontologically variable groups.

The line of criticism followed by Firth and Davenport revolved around the problem of group membership, but they did not redefine their concepts within the larger perspective inherited from Rivers, Radcliffe-Brown, Fortes and Evans-Pritchard. Their critique shook the foundations of the corporatist model and forced a rethinking which eventually climaxed in the social action takeover, but it died without direct heirs. It remains paradoxical that their effort to establish the legitimacy of cognatic descent groups ultimately inspired an ego-centred, transactionalist perspective.

The social action writers preoccupied with the question of descent, I wish to re-emphasize, have selected the one meaning of descent (as behaviour regulator) and ignored the others. If, as I contend, descent groups vary ontologically because anthropologists have defined descent as a rule regulating behaviour, and in fact the only rule serving in the formation of descent groups, descent groups will vary all the more if they are regulated by many rules!   In other words, transactionalists or social action theorists have never questioned the implicit Hobbesian postulate of classical descent theory.   They also assume that groups presuppose ordered interaction, and that ordered interaction cannot be achieved without regulation, i.e., the operation of rules.   They differ from the classical descent theorists by acknowledging that people can be conscious of genealogical relatedness without translating this into a rule of social action and by recognizing that social action, in any given activity, results from the operation of many rules.   On the more fundamental question of defining groups as ontologically separate entities, however, they have taken us backwards, by neglecting descent as a criterion of group membership. I would thus conclude that the models proposed by Scheffler, Keesing or Holy simply reinforce the basic weakness of classical descent theory and almost preclude the rigorous comparative study of groups [4].

Fortes and Evans-Pritchard did open up the right path, but espoused the wrong conceptual framework to carry out their task.   If we wish to succeed where two of the greatest anthropologists of this century have not been completely successful, our task seems relatively clear. We want to distinguish analytically (a) the study of groups, i.e., the manner in which individuals form groups, the properties of these groups, as well as the manner in which they combine, from (b) the study of interpersonal relationships, i.e., the manner in which individuals interact, the behavioural regularities in social interaction as well as the various ways of manipulating social relations.   To carry out this programme, we must also separate the two levels **conceptually**, that is, we must define groups as phenomena **sui generis**, not reducible to another level of social reality (namely, interpersonal behaviour) so as to rid them of their ontological variability.

To this point, we have identified one source of this ontological variability, but it is not the only one.   The fact that groups are also defined as 'multi-functional' (i.e., as involved in many different types of activities) also exacerbates this variability.   In the wake of Durkheim, many social anthropologists have indeed written as if solidarity increased proportionally to the quantity and quality of interaction so that some activities (or 'functions' [5]) appear more important than others because of their greater contribution to social life (see, for instance, Murdock 1949, or Scheffler 1965). If activities vary in importance and groups are multi-functional, groups will also display varying degrees of 'corporateness' (or solidarity) according to the number and importance of their functions. Such premises, I believe, only amplify their ontological variability and make comparison more formidable still (for fuller elaboration, see particularly Verdon 1980a).

If this diagnosis is right, we will render groups ontologically invariable if, and only if, (a) we divorce groups from the question of regulation of interpersonal behaviour and, (b) we separate analytically the different types of activities (or 'functions') in which groups are involved.

In other words, we will assume that solidarity, or sociability - i.e., the regular and predictable occurrence of ordered interaction - does not need explanation. We simply take it as given, and will not try to account for the formation of groups in terms of constraints (cognitive, normative or other), exercised on individual behaviour in social contexts. Also, we will posit groups **analytically** 'uni-functional' (i.e., one activity - one group) and speak of 'group overlapping' when different activities are performed by the same group (this idea, to my knowledge, was first formulated by Goody, 1958). In accordance with these two stipulations, I have redefined groups and labelled this new representation 'operational'. I hasten to add, however, that 'operational' as I use it has nothing to do with the concept as it appears in Firth and Holy (Firth 1957; Holy 1979)[6]. On the basis of an operational definition of group, it is then possible to redefine operationally the key concepts that we need in the study of groups. Let us then start with the operational definition of group.

First of all, I concur with the great majority of social anthropologists in rooting groups in activities. In the performance of a given type of activity (such as production, distribution, legislation, warfare, residence, and so on) an individual may allow anybody to join him or her. The resulting collection of individuals, in this instance, would form a **crowd**. On the other hand, where the individual(s) involved in an activity use(s) specific criteria (such as sex, type of filiation, age, etc.) to discriminate between the individuals who can join and those who cannot, we will call the resulting unit a **group** if the criteria of membership are defined with respect to the individual(s) already involved in the activity.   Where discriminating criteria are employed which are defined with respect to individual(s) not involved in the activity, the resulting association of individuals will be called an **exo-group** (for the pertinence of this distinction, see below, Chapter 2).

In other words, a group presupposes one type of activity (and only one) and at least one criterion of membership.   Ideas of 'corporateness' and ownership are therefore set aside in the definition of group.   If corporateness denotes collective action and solidarity, as it does with many authors, it is simply taken for granted. If it designates 'ownership of an estate', as it does with others, it then calls for a different definition, that of **corporation**.

When individuals do use specific criteria to distinguish themselves from the rest of the world but are **not** engaged in any type of activity, they form a **category**, as already suggested by Scheffler and Keesing.   But when members of a category **qua** members of that category differentiate themselves from the rest of the world with reference to the ownership of jurally bounded resources (man-made or natural, tangible or incorporeal; jurally-bounded resources, by this definition, form an estate – for further elaboration, see Verdon and Jorion 1981), they form a **corporation**[7].   When they differentiate themselves with reference to resources which are not jurally bounded, they form a **quasi-corporation** (see Verdon 1983 for illustration).

Analytically speaking, a corporation is not a group; the members of a corporation **qua** members of a corporation are not involved in any activity, but in ownership.   Similarly, groups are not corporations, although the two may overlap in membership. Operationally defined corporations, moreover, are quite distinct from the protean 'corporate groups' of social anthropology. There is no room for 'corporate groups' in an operational perspective.   Corporations do have a corporate identity, do persist over time, but so do many other types of collectivities.   They normally have a representative (or representatives) but, again, so do many other types of collectivities.   To lump together the most disparate entities under the umbrella concept of 'corporate group' because they have a corporate identity, a feeling of solidarity, a representative or continuity over time is only begging for analytical imbroglios.

It is therefore the involvement in activities or ownership, as well as **criteria** (and not 'rules') of membership which, operationally speaking, distinguish analytically between the various collections of individuals: crowds, groups, exo-groups, categories, corporations and quasi-corporations (see following Diagram for summary).

What Rivers and Radcliffe-Brown could have viewed as criteria of membership (as other authors have done), they represented in fact as 'rules' of group membership. Radcliffe-Brown, furthermore, merged conceptually these 'rules' of group membership with the rules ordering interpersonal behaviour within corporate groups. But rules, by their very definition, imply regulation of behaviour, whereas criteria do not. In fact, criteria of group membership may be represented like axioms defining subsets in mathematics. They function like a franchise delineating, among the 'world outside', the subset of individuals who can gain membership from those who cannot. They imply nothing about the behaviour expected of the group's members. Whether the eligible members activate their membership or not, and how they behave once members, are relevant but analytically separate problems.

Groups often choose their criteria of membership because of the value attached to such criteria but this, once again, does not influence the groups' ontological status. A mathematician may select axioms because they highlight problems in which he is interested, but the value he attaches to these axioms does not in any way affect the ontological status of the subsets they define. Moreover, the number of axioms selected does not change anything in the set's ontological status; whether one or ten axioms are applied, the subset is not 'more or less' of a subset (as our descent groups vary with the strength of unilineal descent!). The subset will certainly display different properties according to the axioms chosen, but it will not vary in degree.

Defined operationally, groups are endowed with an independent ontological status and are rid of their ontological variability. They are no longer epiphenomena of the regulation of interpersonal behaviour; they simply **are.** Ontologically speaking, all types of activities are equal, as are the criteria. There are no 'degrees' of activities or criteria, nor any degree of conformity to them. Collections of individuals defined for every separate type of activity, in terms of criteria of membership, cannot vary in degree [8]. They can be

CRITERIA OF MEMBERSHIP

	Absent	Defined with respect to individual(s) involved in the activity	Defined with respect to individual(s) NOT involved in the activity
ACTIVITY Present	crowd	group	exo-group
Absent	–	category	?
OWNERSHIP Estate (jurally bounded)	–	Corporation	?
Resources not jurally bounded	Collective (non-corporate) ownership	Quasi-corporation	?

Groups, corporations, categories: individual membership

Criteria:

Filiation, matrifiliation, patrifiliation, cognatic kinship, uterine kinship, agnatic kinship, gender, age, marital status, and so on.

Mechanisms

Above groups

Criteria:

Agnatic descent, uterine descent, cognatic descent, generational level of ancestors, territoriality, and so on.

Mechanisms

1) group aggregation

2) group alliance

Ritual collaboration, economic collaboration, military coalitions, and so on.

OPERATIONALISM ITS BASIC CONCEPTS.

short- or long-lived, large or small; they may use one or many different criteria, overlap with other groups, categories or corporations in various ways and display radically different properties. Vary they will, mostly in their various demographic properties, but not in their 'being' as groups 9.

If all groups are ontologically equal and no activity is considered more important than another on aprioristic grounds, there is no need for 'privileged groups of reference' (such as the family and descent groups in descent theory, groups of production and reproduction in marxist theory, and so on) around which to organize ethnographic analysis. As a result, although an operational approach does posit some analytical distinctions and redefines concepts accordingly, it does not present itself as an explanatory model. The factors which influence group formation, growth, combination and reproduction in a given society will have to be discovered through research; they cannot be postulated a priori.

Once the question of interpersonal adjustment is set aside, the notion of 'group structure' takes on a different meaning. In an operational perspective, a group is structured only when different interconnected activities (as in production, for instance) are performed by different individuals of the same group, that is, when there is a division of labour. Since some groups do not have any division of labour, insofar as all their members perform the same activity, the notion of structure is consequently not intrinsic to the notion of group.

To put this operational definition of group into a wider perspective, let us briefly contrast it to Rivers's. Where Rivers defined groups in terms of (1) rules of entry and, (2) rules regulating (a) the interpersonal behaviour of the group's members and, possibly, (b) the distribution of activities, we only retain (1) in an operational definition. Furthermore, what to Rivers were 'rules of entry and exit' are translated as criteria of group membership.   2a now completely vanishes from the definition of group and 2b is extrinsic to it; it is sometimes found in a group, but not necessarily so.

Maine and Morgan, however, had introduced a further dimension neglected by Rivers and resurrected in a different guise by Fortes and Evans-Pritchard; this was the notion of 'groups of groups', a topic which takes us out of the definition of group into the field of descent.

Groups, categories and corporations, in fact do not encompass all types of collectivities. In certain types of activities certain units emerge which are not groups, but compound groups, so to speak. For the adjudication of certain offences, for instance, a Canadian province is not a group of individuals (although it may be defined as such in the context of other activities, such as tax collection) but a conglomeration of counties. In fact, **territorial** groups (such as provinces) are not defined by the membership of individuals, but by the mechanism used to aggregate (or merge) smaller groups into more inclusive ones. In this particular context, a province is therefore a 'group of groups' or an **aggregated** group using 'territoriality' (Maine's 'local contiguity' to aggregate or coalesce counties.

I believe that **descent groups** belong to the same category as territorial groups; they are 'groups of groups' utilizing the fact of descent (putative or real) to coalesce smaller groups. We can speak of individual membership (and therefore of criteria of membership) of the elementary or simple groups only; above the lowest level, we are no longer dealing with membership, but with group **aggregation**.

If we distinguish analytically between group formation and group aggregation the same concept, namely descent, cannot be used to denote both levels of reality. Barnes has already suggested a distinction along similar lines (1962), although he treated descent as a system of beliefs. If a person gains membership of a group through his or her parents, one can thus write of patrifiliation, matrifiliation or filiation as being the criterion of membership, depending upon the case. If he or she gains membership because (s)he is descended from one of his or her father's ancestors through males only, or one of his or her mother's ancestresses through females only, or through either ancestors or ancestresses of both parents, we can then speak of agnatic, uterine or cognatic **kinship**.

Kinship is therefore a criterion of group membership, whereas descent is a mechanism of group aggregation. Operationally speaking, kinship is simply the fact of consanguinity used as a discriminating criterion in the formation of groups, categories or corporations. It does not regulate behaviour, nor does it carry with it specific rights and duties (defining statuses). It simply operates like an axiom defining a subset.

Descent, therefore, differs radically from kinship. In an operational perspective, descent escapes any of its previous definitions. It is neither (a) a criterion (or rule) of group membership, nor (b) a system of values, beliefs or norms ordering interaction within descent groups, nor (c) a charter or ideology of inter-group relations. Furthermore, my definition differs still more radically from new meanings that descent has acquired in recent years, either as an ideology of group solidarity and continuity, or as symbolic filiation. Descent is the mechanism used for the aggregation of groups, and descent groups are therefore groups aggregated on the basis of descent. An 'agnatic descent group', for instance, is an entity distinct from a 'patrifiliative' or even 'agnatic' group or corporation (i.e., groups or corporations using patrifiliation or agnatic kinship as their predominant criterion of membership). The lowest level (i.e., elementary group) in a descent group will be called a 'minimal lineage' and a lineage (or 'maximal lineage' if there are many intermediate levels of aggregation) is a descent group in which descent, whether real or fictitious, is actually remembered in terms of specific genealogical connections. Where collectivities (either groups or groups of groups) are aggregated on the basis of purely putative descent, we shall speak of a 'clan'.

If descent is a mechanism of group aggregation, what then is aggregation? Elementary groups are aggregated when they are merged into more inclusive units, thereby losing their separate identity and representation and acting as one group under the new representative(s) of the wider group. Admittedly, they retain their identity in the contexts in which they emerge as elementary groups and lose it only in the performance of activities in which the aggregated group only is relevant.

This definition, however, would not enable us to distinguish certain types of alliances from aggregation. We can very well imagine autonomous Trade Unions allying themselves and sending a delegation (of perhaps only one representative) to speak to the government on their common behalf, without implying that the Trade Unions are aggregated (i.e., lose their autonomy). To achieve aggregation, other conditions must be fulfilled, and the following ones seem common to aggregated groups: (1) specific criteria of eligibility (and procedures if there is selection or election, or both) must define accession to the role(s) of group representative(s). (2) The group representative(s) must be empowered either to perform by himself or herself (or themselves) the activity over which the group has jurisdiction (such as legislation, or adjudication, or ritual performance) or to convene a sub-group which has the authority to perform the activity. Since the group representative(s) hold(s) tenure of office for a given period of time (a new one does not surface for every new case encountered), aggregated groups normally act as frames of reference in recurrent activities.

When these features accompany the 'merging under one representative', we can truly speak of aggregation. In other words, there are numerous ways in which groups which perceive themselves as being related genealogically can associate or form alliances, **without at all being aggregated**, and the segmentary definition of descent as a charter or ideology of intergroup relations does not enable us to make the distinction. As Scheffler indicated long ago, it takes more than genealogical charters to produce descent groups (Scheffler 1966).

Alliances, on the other hand, vary greatly in their organization, from the loose type without any common representative(s) to the more organized type with features resembling somewhat those of aggregated groups. There are also coalitions, such as the Delian League, which threaten the very sovereignty of their participating groups. Since partners in military (or other) alliances are rarely equal in strength (witness the Warsaw Pact or NATO), the more powerful use the alliance to their own benefit. Despite Russia's overpowering role in the Warsaw Pact, however, the participating countries have retained their sovereignty (although perhaps only nominally) so that we cannot speak of aggregation, but of an alliance.

Alliances, moreover, do vary in degrees, in that some are literally more binding than others; aggregation, on the contrary, is 'discontinuous'. Groups are either aggregated or not, but cannot be more or less so. Aggregation does not represent a locus on a continuum from weak to strong alliances, but a completely different organizational mechanism.

Finally, how are descent groups as aggregated groups different from the 'segmentary lineages' of Fortes and Evans-Pritchard? To answer this question, we must make a long diversion into the meaning of segmentation, and my own reinterpretation of segmentary lineages (Verdon 1982a, 1982b, 1983).

Evans-Pritchard depicted anarchic and egalitarian Nuer territorial segments which emerged in action only, and which lacked any permanence or reality except in opposition to segments of co-ordinate status. Fortes also read the same relativity in the Tallensi lineage segments but, in reality, every level of segmentation among the Tallensi is clearly identified at all times. The problem was solved by assuming that all segments emerged in complementary opposition, but that some were corporate (Tallensi) and others not (Nuer, Tiv).

Corporateness implied perpetuity; and since corporate groups were therefore endowed with the attributes of permanence   (a   name,   a   representative,   recurrent activities, and so on) the segmentary lineage model became a contradiction in itself. If the groups formed through the merging of lower groups (the lineage segments) were essentially relative, gaining substance in complementary opposition only, they could not be corporate. Thus, either lineages could never be corporate (because of their essential relativity) or they could not be segmentary (because of their corporateness). Either assumption could legitimately be selected, but not both simultaneously; unfortunately, the notion of corporateness was added to that of segmentary lineage to save the original 'family resemblance' and keep the Tallensi, Nuer and Tiv in the same category of segmentary lineage system.

This lumping together of diverse polities in the same hybrid   category   was   facilitated   by   the   semantic proliferation   which   surrounded   the   concept   of segmentation. As early as 1954, Barnes had remarked that 'segmentation' denoted three different realities, namely (a) 'nesting', or the fact that 'descent groups' appear graphically as a system of group inclusion, where groups at one level are subdivided into more groups at a lower level,   (b)   the   process   of   'complementary   opposition', whereby descent groups allegedly define their identity in contradistinction   to   groups   of   coordinate   genealogical status only, and, finally, (c) the process of formation of new 'segments' ('segments' referring to the component groups   'nested'   in   a   more   inclusive   unit)   (Barnes 1954:45-49, Middleton and Tait 1970:7).

To remedy this situation, we must rid ourselves of the concept of 'corporate group' and restrict 'segmentation' to one process only. Using the operational definition of descent group to re-analyze the Tallensi ethnography, one finds that the Tallensi do have descent groups (i.e., aggregated   groups)   which,   however,   do   not   define themselves in complementary opposition (Verdon 1982a. 1983).   The   Tallensi   lineages   have   permanent representatives empowered to act at any moment within the sphere of activities for which the group is relevant; the Tallensi lineages are thus aggregated, and do not emerge in opposition to groups of coordinate genealogical status, or to any groups.

If we turn our attention to the Nuer and Tiv, on the other hand (Verdon 1982b, 1983), we do find groups which emerge in complementary opposition only, but these are not descent groups. They are allied groups. From this, I conclude that where there are true lineages, or descent groups, there is no complementary opposition. Where there is complementary opposition, on the other hand, one does not find group aggregation, but group alliance.

Moreover, our operational reinterpretation of the Tallensi revealed interesting variations in the constitution of descent groups. Among the Namoos, for instance, one finds an intermediate level of aggregation between minimal and maximal lineages, so that their lineages could be described as 'multi-level'. Among the Hill Talis, on the other hand, no such intermediate level of aggregation is to be found, so that minimal lineages are directly aggregated into (maximal) lineages, a situation which we shall witness with Abutia descent groups.

Also, where minimal lineages are directly aggregated into a lineage without any intermediate level, descent alone suffices to achieve aggregation. Where there are intermediate levels of aggregation, however, the generational level of ancestors must also operate, together with the recollection of common descent, to aggregate groups. Descent groups thus vary (a) in the number of their levels of aggregation, and (b) in the number of elements or mechanisms used to aggregate. Because of these differences and of other ones which shall emerge in the course of ethnographic analysis, they further vary (c) in the manner in which they reproduce themselves.

In fact, the view that 'segmentary lineages' reproduce themselves through the creation of new segments 'at the bottom', so to speak, through the natural proliferation of polygynous families, appears to be erroneous in the cases that I have reviewed. I am convinced, for instance, that group reproduction among the Namoos takes place at the intermediate level, where genealogical connections can be easily manipulated and distorted and not at the bottom, with every new polygynous family potentially creating a segment. Among the Nuer, I have argued, the model of the 'polygynous family' is a folk model without any analytical usefulness for the understanding of group reproduction.

Since it is far from clear which societies, if any, do reproduce themselves through 'segmentation' as understood by classical descent theorists, it seems more appropriate to abandon this meaning of the term and to replace it with the more neutral 'group reproduction', while specifying the level of grouping at which reproduction takes place (whether minimal, intermediate or maximal level).

Furthermore, the traditional category of 'segmentary lineage systems' has lumped together instances of (a) **alliances** between groups, expressed genealogically, (b) of group **aggregation** by means of descent but without any intermediate level of aggregation ('simple' or 'uni-level' lineages), (c) of group aggregation by means of descent and the generational level of ancestors, with an intermediate level (or levels) of aggregation (i.e. 'multi-level lineages') and, (d) of simple cognitive mapping of the social environment in terms of progressively inclusive frames of reference. Since 'nesting' is a feature of every one of these various entities, to equate 'segmentation' with 'nesting' would simply perpetuate the present state of confusion.

We are left with one alternative: either to abandon the term altogether, or to restrict it to the process of 'complementary opposition'. I have adopted this latter solution but with the major qualification that lineages, as aggregated groups, cannot emerge in complementary opposition. 'Segmentary lineages' is therefore a contradiction in terms, and segmentation, defined in this restricted way, is a feature of some types of **alliances.** We now find segmentary alliances, but no segmentary descent groups or lineages. This, in brief, explicates the main differences between operationally defined descent groups, on the one hand, and segmentary lineages, on the other.

At the end of this conceptual revision (we are not dealing with simple redefinitions, I would like to stress, but with the formulation of a new conceptual framework - see Verdon n.d.1), I would like to add that I will here call **social organization** the manner in which individuals form groups, categories, corporations and the like, the manner in which groups form aggregated groups, and the manner in which all of them grow, reproduce themselves, combine and overlap. I have indulged in this lengthy introduction, moreover, because I have applied this new conceptual model to the ethnography that I have myself collected, that of the Abutia Ewe.

I have contrasted my own conceptual endeavour to classical descent theory and transactionalism, moreover, not to demean them by questioning their fundamental assumptions but to propose a new approach to the study of social organization which would revive a basic creed of classical descent theory, namely, a belief in the possibility of rigorous comparisons of social organization. In fact, this much one must admit: classical descent theory outdid all its rivals by the richness of the ethnography it inspired, and by the great number of comparative hypotheses it generated. Some of these proved to be wrong and led to the new formulations of the 'culturalists' and the 'transactionalists' whose frameworks, unfortunately, have not engendered any serious comparative hypotheses beyond those of classical descent theorists. I must emphasize, however, that this monograph **is not comparative in design**, dedicated as it is to the analysis of the social organization of one population. In spirit, however, it has been written with a set of concepts redefined so as to provide more universal, more etic definitions of emic institutions in order to enhance the comparability of our ethnographic data.

Finally, I wish to re-emphasize that an operational approach, unlike many contemporary ones (but, in this instance, in the wake of the transactionalist approach) is essentially pluralist, and not monistic. Unlike 'cultural materialism', 'historical materialism', 'descent theory' or 'alliance theory', it does not seek to explain or derive all the organizational features of a society from one privileged or key element, such as the environment, production, descent or alliance. In this respect, operationalism is not an 'explanatory' model. Therefore, if the reader confuses this conceptual and analytical effort with the all-encompassing models which presently encumber anthropological analyses, he may perceive discrepancies between the theoretical guidelines and the ethnographic analysis itself. But to those who understand the distinction between conceptual-analytical models, on the one hand, and explanatory models, on the other, the unity between the theory and its execution will be evident.

II. GENERAL ORIENTATION OF THE WORK

The conceptual aspect, however, formed only part of the general problem of studying Abutia. As I have mentioned earlier, the Abutia Ewe form a group of three linked Ewe villages acknowledging a common **fiagā** (translated as 'Paramount Chief' in administrative English), and located some sixty miles from the Ghanaian coast, as the crow flies. These Ewe 'groups of villages' under a common Paramount Chief were labelled **Divisions** or **Traditional Areas** by the colonial administrators, and Rattray identified one hundred and twenty Ewe-speaking Divisions conglomerated in the southern part of the Volta Region, Ghana (then Gold Coast) and in southern Togo, between the Volta and Mono Rivers (Rattray 1915). This global territory, often referred to as Eweland, is a linguistically homogeneous area of over 8,000 square miles, with a population exceeding one million inhabitants (see map 1). The Ewe share common legends of origin and a common language of which the local variations are mutually intelligible throughout the area. They claim to have migrated from Ketu, in Yorubaland, but their migrations never took them west of the Volta. Their western neighbours comprise groups of Ga-Adangme origins in the south, and of Akan origin in the north (west). To the East, they were bordered by the kingdom of Dahomey. The fact that Ewe and Fon (the language of southern Benin) are linguistically cognate, whereas Ewe and Akan are only very remotely related, as members of the Kwa group, tends to support their theory of migration from the East. Some of the Ewe groups settled in the south, on the coast, whereas others took refuge in the mountain ridges north of the coastal plain, where they mingled with pockets of other refugee groups of various ethnic origins - the Avatime (studied by Brydon 1976), Lolobi, Akpafu, etc.

Because of the Ewe's community of origin and language, their ethnographers have tended to depict them as one homogeneous sociocultural system. Some differences have been noted, but their systematic occurrence has not been seriously investigated. Spieth, for instance, treated Eweland as one large 'tribal area' (1906, 1911). Ward and Manoukian reported some diversity; both contrasted northern to southern Ewe, but as variations around the same theme (Ward 1949, Manoukian 1952). Nukunya, a southern Ewe, implicitly adopted a similar view, writing of the "Ewe society' as if it was socially and culturally uniform (Nukunya 1969). Neither Asamoa (a northern Ewe)

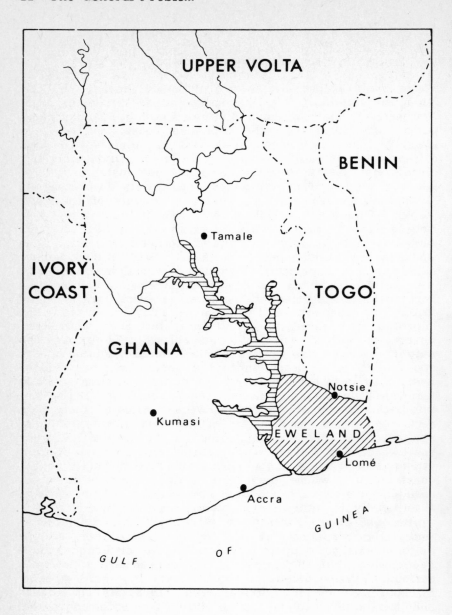

Map 1. Eweland.

nor Bukh even hinted at the existence of variations between Ewe regions, in their recent monographs (Asamoa 1972, Bukh 1979).

Kludze confined his exposition of Ewe law of property to the northern Ewe but did not elaborate on the differences between north and south (1973). Marianne Friedländer, an East German marxist analyst, made the fullest appraisal of the disparity between the two regions, but I believe her evaluation to have been couched in the wrong idiom. She did recognize that southern and northern Divisions represented different levels of political integration, but she analyzed them in terms of the 'formation of classes', thereby misinterpreting the ethnography [10] (Friedländer 1962).

Having worked in seven Divisions throughout both Ghanaian and Togolese Eweland, I came to recognize that the three ecological and geographical regions of Eweland (see map 2) concealed deep dissimilarities in social and cultural organization. These regions are:

1) the **coastal** region (and its people), known as Aŋlɔ (transliterated as Anlo) occupy the coast, the lagoons and the coastal savanna some forty miles inland, to their borders with Abutia and Agotime. The name 'Anlo', however, refers both to the largest and most important Division of the coastal region (henceforth designated as 'Anlo proper'), and to all the Divisions occupying this coastal zone.

2) the **riverine** region (and its people), known as Tɔŋu (transliterated as Tonu) are found along the shores of the River Volta up to Akuse, where the River bends, and a few miles north of the River to the borders of the Abutia, Adaklu and Avenor Divisions.

3) the **inland** region (and its people), known as **Ewedome**, is located north of both Anlo and Tonu, in the transitional area of savanna and woodland, and also in the mountain ridges which run parallel from the Akwamu area, near the Volta, to the north-east of Togo. I will use alternatively Ewe-dome, northern Ewe or inland Ewe to designate the Ewe Divisions which are neither of Anlo nor of Tonu extraction[11].

The social organization of Tonu Divisions has never been properly studied (Huber 1957, 1965, Fiawoo 1961 and Lawson 1972 fail to treat it adequately), and they have often been assimilated to the Anlo. In fact, Anlo proper has implicitly served as a paradigm in the study of Ewe social organization. From my fieldwork, however, I gained firm impression that southern and northern Divisions

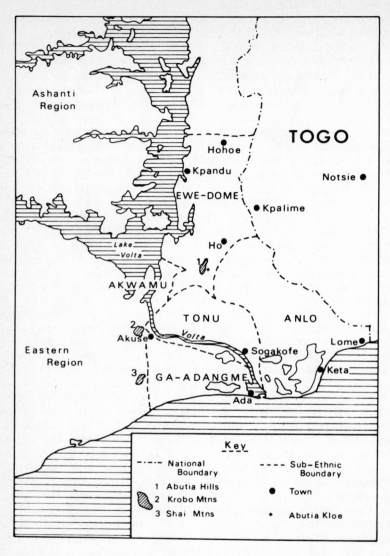

Map 2. The subethnic Divisions of the Ewe part of the Volta Region.

differ as much from one another as both do from the Akan.
Some of these differences will be investigated more
closely in the course of the analysis, and it will suffice
here to point out the more glaring dissimilarities.

The Ewe-dome, for instance, occupy areas of woodland
savanna and forest hills whereas the Anlo are settled in
the plain, the grass savanna and on the coast. This is
reflected economically in the crops cultivated. The
southern Ewe grow maize above all (except on the coast
itself, where they also fish and grow shallots), which
they use for subsistence, whereas the northern Ewe grow
yams and cassava for subsistence, and maize as a cash
crop. Interestingly enough, this is the main level of
differentiation which finds expression in the manner in
which northern and southern Ewe perceive one another. In
contrast to their southern brethren, the Ewe-dome describe
themselves as **fufu**-eaters (**fufu** is a dish made of
pounded yams, cassava or plantain). The southern groups
correspondingly view themselves and are described by the
inland people as '**akple**-eaters' (**akple** is a dish
made of ground and boiled maize).

Deeper contrasts are also noticeable in the political
organization. The southern areas appear more
'centralized', with a Yoruba-type 'divine' kingship, in
contrast to the more 'decentralized' or 'federated'
northern Divisions, with a type of chiefly paraphernalia
reminiscent of the Ashanti chiefship. The very size of
northern and southern Divisions bears further testimony
to that; southern Divisions can number up to thirty and
more villages (Anlo proper has 116), with towns exceeding
5,000 inhabitants (on the coast) whereas northern
Traditional Areas never surpass five villages, the biggest
of which do not boast of more than 1,500 inhabitants.

These political and demographic disparities are further
rooted in geographical and historical divergences. The
Danes established their forts on the coast and, under the
influence of European traders, the southern Divisions
engaged in slave-raiding. In the north, trade flowed with
the Volta and only the few Divisions actually bordering
the Volta (such as Kpeki or Kpandu) reached a degree of
political centralization almost comparable to the south.
Most of the other inland groups were somewhat cut off from
the main trading routes and were also victims of southern
and western (Akwamu) slave raids.

Northern and southern lineages and clans, as well as
legends of origin, also vary significantly, as do their

matrimonial practices.   The clans of Anlo proper are
dispersed and its exogamous lineages thrive on high rates
of polygyny; divorce is hardly tolerated.   The localized
and non-exogamous northern clans and lineages hardly
tolerate plural marriage, and their divorce rates are
soaring.   Finally, the religious practices of the two
regions are equally discrepant.   Their respective **rites
de passage** are patently dissimilar but more significant
still is the absence of spirit-mediumship in the south
where ancestral cults and secret societies flourish, and
the total absence of these two institutions in the
northern religious system which completely revolves around
spirit-mediumship.   And these are but a **few** of the
ways in which coastal and inland areas vary.

I would not suggest, however, that the northern
Divisions are entirely homogeneous; I am nevertheless
inclined, in their case, to speak of variations around the
same theme.   I therefore believe Abutia to be somewhat
representative of Ewe-dome Divisions, if one excepts the
northern groups which claim Anlo ancestry (such as Klefe,
Taviefe, Kpedze, Kpele and some others) and those
bordering the Volta (Kpeki and Kpandu especially) which
have emulated coastal areas in their political style.   It
is this complete lack of convergence between southern and
northern Divisions which ruled out the adoption of the
'Anlo paradigm' to understand inland Divisions, as I had
originally believed possible, and which prompted me to
study Abutia on its own.   I resided for two years in one
of its villages, Abutia Kloe, where I collected the main
bulk of my data.   My familiarity with Abutia's three
villages, however, enables me to claim that the features
of Kloe social organization are also characteristic of
those of the other two villages, with minor variations
only.

In the first part of my analysis I wished to describe
the 'traditional' political organization but the
contradictory statements of Abutia elders on matters
political made it methodologically impossible to
'reconstruct' the precolonial polity in a naive inductive
manner.   Abutia Kloe, for instance, had been deprived of a
chief for twenty years because of chieftaincy disputes,
and the Paramount Chief of Abutia was also opposed, and
finally 'destooled' during my stay.   Any question about
the division of labour between village chiefs and
Paramount Chiefs, or between the various office-holders
within the villages, only elicited conflicting
information, depending upon the various candidates' stakes

in the political game.   Some assured me that the
precolonial Paramount Chiefs had very little power indeed,
whereas others swore that he wielded the power of an
Ashanti **omanhene.**   Disappointed with these political
manipulations of the alleged tradition, I opted for an
indirect, 'deductive' route, using the 'level of
sovereignty' as my guiding hypothesis.

Ethnographers of Eweland have concurred on one point,
namely that the 'group of villages acknowledging a common
fiagā or otherwise-titled Paramount Chief' (i.e., the
Divisions) constituted the sovereign political entity in
precolonial Eweland.   This, in my opinion, applied
accurately to Anlo proper as it has been described in the
literature (Amenumey 1964, Nukunya 1969), but I considered
this assumption to be completely unwarranted in the case
of Abutia.   There, I rather assumed that it was the
villages that were sovereign in precolonial times.   I then
demonstrated that this new hypothesis of precolonial
village sovereignty does account for an important number
of features, both political and 'demographic', and that it
permitted a plausible reconstruction of the precolonial
Abutia polity.   Furthermore, by assuming that the whole
Division was sovereign in Anlo proper, I could also
explain some of the important differences between the two
societies.   In the strongly empiricist Anglo-Saxon world
to which this book is addressed, I ought to feel
apologetic for this rather deductive and conjectural
approach to Abutia political organization, but I can
assure the reader that contradictory sets of statements
recorded from the actors themselves made this type of
approach necessary.

In the second and third parts of the monograph, the
'facts' were less fractious to classical ethnographic
investigation.   I did not have to deduce the residential
arrangements or matrimonial alliances from a certain
hypothesis (although it remained difficult to elicit what
they were in the past) because they could be observed more
directly.   However, this methodological advantage did not
simplify the analysis because residence and marriage in
Abutia are not easily accounted for.   At a first glance,
Abutia residential groups seem capable of any composition
and, like those observed by Fortes in Ashanti (1949b), men
and women live in separate dwelling units, with their
children sometimes scattered over yet other houses.   In
trying to disentangle this problem, I remained faithful to
my operational premises.   On strictly theoretical grounds,
I could argue that the association between descent and

residence (Fortes 1949a, 1949b, Richards 1950) is at best indirect, if at all possible, but I chose rather to substantiate my position with empirical data.   On the basis of an operational definition of residence, and of a classification better suited for my purpose, I showed that Abutia residential groups are influenced, not by descent, but by the mode of devolution of houses and by labour migrations.   To account for the neolocal trend in Abutia residence, furthermore, I looked into production and land tenure while avoiding, however, writing a complete account of Abutia economic organization.

The study of residence led into that of marriage although Abutia 'marriages', according to existing 'anthropological definitions', do not exist (like the Carribbean marriages).   Faced with this paradox, one either has to postulate a state of 'social breakdown' conducive to general promiscuity, or to re-define marriage in a way which suits the facts.   In the tradition of Anglo-Saxon empiricism, I respect facts over concepts..., and therefore altered the definition of marriage to include the type of unions found in Abutia (as well as in the Caribbean).   This operational analysis of Abutia matrimonial unions demonstrated further that descent does not influence marriage in the manner predicted by classical descent theory, but in ways which have been somewhat overlooked.

This third part of the book, dealing with matrimonial practices, concludes the analysis of <u>some</u> aspects of Abutia social organization.   I underline 'some' to avoid raising false expectations because this study does **not** cover the whole of Abutia social organization.   Fieldworkers consciously or subconsciously select problems which they deem more relevant, so that certain aspects are emphasized while others are neglected.   I cannot confess to a dearth of material on economic and religious topics since most of my fieldwork was devoted to the collection of such data.   Because detailed analyses of the activities of production and worship would have filled a monograph each, I have included only the minimum of relevant information on these two aspects of social organization, as the investigation of politics, residence and marriage required.   The reader should therefore regard this study as an analysis of politics, residence and marriage among the Abutia Ewe, with ritual and economics as ancillary topics supporting the main themes.

Finally, the need for clarity and conciseness in an ethnographic work which strives to be amenable to comparative analysis has also affected the style of presentation. I openly confess to a complete lack of literary inclination, dangerously aggravated by the theoretical perspective adopted, with its emphasis on numerical aspects (where numerical analysis is both possible and pertinent, admittedly). I have tried to confine myself to the minimum of information necessary to understanding the manner in which the groups analyzed are formed, grow, reproduce and combine themselves, deliberately relegating 'ethnographic details' to footnotes and appendices to make the reading more 'fluent'. Many will protest that the real 'flesh' or 'juice' has been squeezed out to the periphery, but such an accusation would wilfully distort the basic ambitions of this monograph. Once the criteria used in the formation of groups and in succession to group headship have been isolated, once their social organizational implications are well understood, and once the absence of some eligible members is accounted for, it does leave me completely indifferent to know about the psychological disposition or idiosyncratic deeds of the particular chiefs who were in office at the time of fieldwork (unless, obviously, some of these psychological ingredients affected the social organization), and this ethnography aims to live up to operational expectations of clarity, precision and parsimony.

III.   ABUTIA: LOCATION AND POSITION

The Abutia people occupy an area extending approximately ten miles south of the 6°35' latitude, and ten miles between the 0°20' and the 0°30' longitude north of the Equator. This territory lies well within the Equatorial Climatic zone, characterized by its two rainy seasons every year. The heavier rains start in March and last until June-July, followed by a shorter rainy season which begins in September and ends in early November.

The three villages were built at the foot of the Abutia Hills in the northern part of the Ho-Keta plain which receives, on average, annual rainfalls ranging from 810 mm for 73 days of rain to 1270 mm for 100 days of rain. The temperature is very hot and humid, and the soils have been described as follows:

"The great soils group classification of Ghana soils assigns the Kolor area to the Tropical Black Earth of the Coastal Savanna Zone.   Those are dark couloured heavy alkaline, cracking clays.   They occur on gentle savanna topography over the main basic gneiss crossing the Ho-Keta plains." (Volta 1972:12)

The peneplain around the Hills is covered with typical savanna woodland, where perennial grasses predominate, and is dotted here and there with thickets.   On the Hills and in some of the thickets, however, the vegetation is more akin to secondary forest.   One can thus look upon Abutia as straddling two ecological zones - the woodland savanna in the plain, and the secondary forest on the Hills and in some places in the plain.

Parts of this large area consist of hunting grounds, and the actual portion claimed as farmlands does not exceed 60 to 70 square miles, yielding a population density of approximately 40-50 people to the square mile. Although it may seem high for a savanna area, this density is low for this part of Eweland [12].   The local inhabitants see their lands as rich and plentiful and they do not recall having ever suffered from either famine or land shortages.   Considering their farming methods and the portion of land actually farmed (see Section 2),   their claim that the land can support much more than the present population does seem plausible.   In fact, Abutia's location in Eweland is somewhat unique, occupying as it does the southermost tip of Ewe-dome, and half-surrounded by southern Divisions (map 3).   This particular situation may account for the vastness of Abutia land, in contrast to the much smaller territories of most other northern Divisions.   The southern half of Abutia land probably remained unoccupied in the early years of settlement to serve as a buffer zone against possible invasions from the south.

The Abutias began selling their land to their southern Tonu neighbours more than a century ago, a fact which explains the puzzling presence of an immigrant village (Abutia Kpota) and of foreign hamlets on Abutia soil, some of which have been allegedly inhabited since 1860.   Kpota and its neighbouring hamlets are completely independent from the three autochthonous villages and are only linked to them through their geographical situation.   This is true to such an extent that Ewland's north-south separation is reduplicated within Aubtia's boundaries itself.   The immigrants purchased their land and therefore

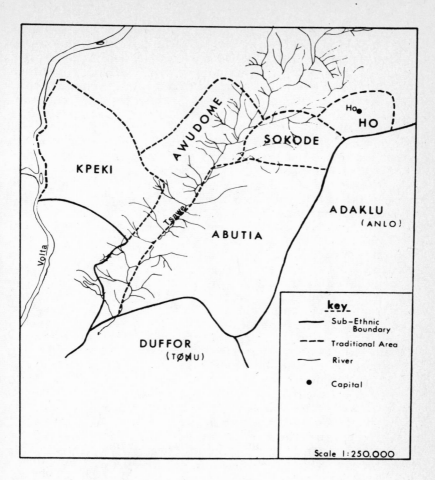

Map 3.   Abutia and its neighbouring Divisions.

do not owe anything to the autochthons. Their settlements were never integrated in the traditional (or precolonial) Abutia political organization and are only indirectly integrated nowadays, through the national political organization. Immigrants and autochthons exchange very little, be it of goods or wives. Despite the fact that the former specialize in the production of groundnuts and charcoal, the latter do not buy from these Tonu settlements but procure these same goods from the Ho market instead. Immigrants and autochthons thus gravitate around different poles. The southern immigrants prefer to market their products in the south, especially in Akuse whereas the Abutia are economically dependent upon Ho. Abutia's dependence upon Ho, in fact, is not coincidental, since the Anlo and Ewe-dome Divisions also diverge in their historical experiences.

From 1734 onward, the Ewe-dome were ruled by the Akwamu, who delegated to Kpeki the task of administering the conquered territories. In 1833 the Kpekis, with the help of surrounding northern groups, rebelled and overthrew their Akan rulers. In the course of those 100 years (1734-1834), the Anlo never suffered any foreign African domination, but rather connived with the Akwamus in their expansionist and slaving policies. In 1869, in a last effort to reconquer their lost colonies, the Akwamus invited the Ashanti to help them crush the Kpekis and Ewe-dome. In this last fully-fledged war, known as the 'Ashanti wars' in Eweland, the Anlo proper and the southern Ewe Divisions joined forces with the Ashanti, thus giving the best evidence of their closer political association with the raiding empires, and their estrangement from their own etchnic brethren.

Confronted with such formidable opposition, the Ewe-dome solicited British assistance, with the result that they later showed little or no resistance to European colonial expansion. This stands in sharp contrast to the Anlo who resisted and rebelled. The ensuing 'scramble for Africa' further widened the gap between southern and northern groups. First conquered in 1874, the south remained under British rule until Ghana's independence in 1957. The northern Ewe, on the other hand, were colonized by the Germans who occupied most of the northern and south-eastern Divisions in their colony of Togoland. When they were ousted in 1914, the colony was divided into an eastern and a western part. The eastern section became a mandated area under French trusteeship, later to become (in 1960) the independent Republic of Togo. The western section fell under British trusteeship, and called British Togoland. In 1957, British Togoland voted to join the newly-independent Ghana, when it became Ghana's Volta Region. During the German occupation, Abutia was part of the German colony whereas its immediate southwestern and southern neighbours (Awudome, Kpeki, Duffor - see map 3) belonged to the Gold Coast.

These twenty-five years of German colonial occupation had forged much closer links between French and British Togoland than between British Togoland and the Gold Coast, with which it was later to unite to form Ghana. On the other hand, Anlo's resistance had compelled the British to make their presence felt much more strongly in the south than in the mandated areas. This hastened Anlo's integration into the Gold Coast, whereas British Togoland remained very much a separate and distinct entity. In contemporary Ghanaian politics, this is directly expressed in the fact that the Anlo play the role of strong integrationists, whereas the Ewe-dome, during the period of my fieldwork, still cherished the dream of joining Togo.

IV. THE THREE VILLAGES

Teti, Agove and Kloe are the only three autochthonous Abutia villages, nestled at the foot of the Abutia Hills. A second-class road, linking Sokode Etoe to Juapong, runs centrally through all three villages, stringing them together on an almost straight line. Few vehicles travel the full length of this road. Most of the lorries coming from Ho stop at Kpota and go back to Ho, and very few of them continue to the southern portion of the road, to the Duffor area. In order to reach Accra, people from Abutia take a loory to Ho, and from Ho to Accra, instead of travelling directly to Juapong, and from Juapong to Accra (map 4).

Unlike other Ewe-dome villages in the mountains to the north, the Abutias never settled on their Hills (although they lived on the Agbenu Hills in earlier times - see map 4). Their three villages are densely nucleated, the houses being built very close to one another; no fences separate the houses, and no farming is practiced on the village site. The farms are spread around the settlements, sometimes miles away. All three settlements have been extremely sedentary, since they are still located on the very sites where the first German

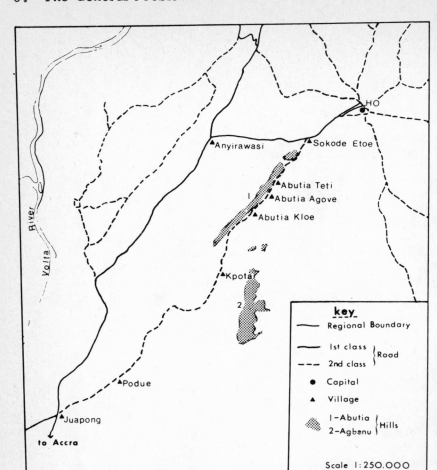

Map 4. A road map of the Abutia area.

missionaries found them in 1888. Apart from the dissecting main road, the villages are also divided by streets, one of them parallel to the Sokode-Juapong road, the other one transversal. These streets also serve to delineate clan areas.

Three or four vast open spaces, shaded by an enormous tree, also serve to 'open up' the settlement. These shaded public places are used for daily trading or as an assembly point for important village meetings. The streets are also dotted with specially designed stones which serve as chairs, and are used by men in their evening rest. Every village also has one (the larger ones two) main store and a palm-wine bar, both of which serve as rallying-points for youths and men.

The northernmost village and the 'Paramount Chief's' village, Teti numbered 1300 inhabitants in the 1960 census, and was then the second largest village in Abutia. Teti also harbours Abutia's main marketplace, where women traders convene from neighbouring Divisions every four days. The market-place, the Evangelical-Presbyterian church and both the Primary and Middle Schools are built outside the main settlement, at the periphery of the village (as in the other villages). The Abutia show a preference for building their schools and churches on the Hills.

Three quarters of a mile south of Teti lies the village of Agove, the smallest of the three Abutia villages in the 1960 census, with a population then of slightly less than 1000. Agove has neither church nor Post Office, but it does have a dispensary with a resident midwife, as well as Primary and Middle Schools. It also boasts of the shrine of the Abutia High God, a privilege which gives it a paramount role in traditional religious affairs.

Kloe is located one and a half miles south of Agove. This is the village where I settled and carried out most of the fieldwork. It comprised 1500 inhabitants in the 1960 census but had declined to 1200 by the early 1970s. As I did not have time to take censuses of Teti and Agove during fieldwork, I am unable to say if it declined more than the others, and which one was then the largest. Geographically more separate than the other two villages, Kloe also enjoys the largest number of services. Apart from a church, a Post Office, two schools and a dispensary (without a midwife, however), it also had the dubious privilege of having a Police Post which grew into a full-fledged Police Station in 1973, with three resident officers.

These three villages form a separate Division, deriving their unity from a common myth of origin.   It is the manner of their political association, together with some details of their social organization, which form the subject of this monograph.

Politics

I. NATIONAL AND TRADITIONAL

Many anthropologists view politics in terms of power relations between individuals (social action model); since power pervades every type of social relationship, political relations are then almost impossible to isolate and politics thus applies indiscriminately to a wide range of phenomena. By focusing upon the groups formed in specific activities, on the other hand, we can more easily circumscribe a set of activities which may be termed 'political'. In a celebrated article, Goody demonstrated that 'domestic groups' conceal many different units engaged in various activities (reproduction and production, the latter including production proper, distribution of products, food processing and consumption), all of which overlapped in membership and were related to a dwelling-place (Goody 1958).

The same could be said about politics; there are no 'political groups' but various activities, namely legislation, administration, adjudication, defence (and offence), as well as competition for accession to office, and the groups formed in their performance also overlap in membership. They may also overlap further with the groups active in production, trade or the worship of certain gods (to name but a few); on the other hand, they may not coincide with any of those groups so that, analytically speaking, the distinction is justified. In this first part, we will therefore examine the groups formed around those 'political' activities in contemporary Abutia, in order to opine later about the political organization in precolonial times.

A. The contemporary judiciary organization

Our three Abutia villages form part of a national judiciary organization not easily distinguishable from the 'traditional' one because of the many grey areas of uncertain jurisdictions and of the conflicting testimonies of 'traditional leaders'.   Some minor cases involving land disputes, minor theft or transgressions of the kinship ethics can be arbitrated without any appeal to the national system of courts, but there are no automatic rules.   Much depends upon the individuals' satisfaction with the manner in which they have been treated by the village authorities, since they can always appeal to the magistrate's court.

The particular court called upon for arbitration is normally decided on the basis of (a) the nature of the offence and, in certain instances, of (b) the groups of origin of the persons involved.   Despite a lack of consensus about the customary classification of offences, the following categories have been observed to emerge in action:

(1) simple disputes involving conflicting claims over fallow land or boundaries between farms, matrimonial quarrels, insults, abuses or offensive behaviour, breach of the kinship ethics, and so on (offences known as yiāwo, sing. yiā);

(2) transgressions of sexual prohibitions, such as incest or love-making in the 'bush';

(3) transgressions of other prohibitions of a semi-religious nature (known as **guwo**, sing. **gu**);

(4) adultery, theft, debt and divorce (classified together as **nuvɔ**);

(5) **trɔyiawo**, or cases taken to Togbe Atando, the Abutia High God;

(6) witchcraft and manslaughter (there is no Ewe term to designate them together, as a category);

(7) breaches of national laws and local by-laws[13]. Different penalties attach to these different types of offences, and various levels of grouping come into operation in the adjudication.

1. In the case of **yiāwo**, the guilt has to be established.   Elders called upon to settle a **yiā** cross-examine plaintiff and defendant, as well as the relevant witnesses, to reach a judgment about the sharing of liability.   Their sentences normally consist in fines (of money, alcohol or sheep) which partly serve as remuneration for their judiciary services.   Restitution is demanded whenever necessary.

In domestic disputes, the plaintiff will take the case to the head of his/her fhome (minimal lineage [14]) who will invite the guilty spouse for a friendly word of

advice.   If this fails, the head of the plaintiff's
fhome will consult the head of the defendant's minimal
lineage, and a council of the two minimal lineages may
then be necessary to adjudicate the case.   A simple breach
of kinship ethics between two individuals of the same
minimal lineage, for instance, will be dealt with by their
fhome-metsitsi (minimal lineage head [15]);   a more
serious assault might have to be adjudged by higher
authorities.   The 'group of reference'[16] in the
adjudication of **yìāwo** is thus partly determined by the
seriousness of the offence, but more importantly by the
groups of origin of the disputants.   Two disputants from
the   same **fhome** will solicit the **fhome-tsitsi's**
assistance;   plaintiff and defendant from different
fhomewo (sign. **fhome**) of the same **agbanu** (or
dzotinu; both are synonyms, and will be translated as
lineages) will seek help from the lineage head; litigants
from different **agbenuwo** (sing. **agbenu**) of the same
sāme (to be translated as clan) will take their case
to the representative of their clan; individuals from
different clans of the same **du** (village) will take
their case to the **dufia** (village 'chief').

When plaintiff and defendant hail from different
duwo (sing. **du**) but within Abutia, there is no
superior authority to which the **yìā** can be brought.
Elders from the villages concerned will meet in order to
settle it amicably.   If the litigants are domiciled in
villages of different Divisions, the case has to be taken
to the magistrate's court.

2.   In instances of sexual deviance the guilty parties
will conceal their deeds but any serious sickness or
abnormal occurrence will bring them to confess.   Their
guilt is automatically established, and no tribunal is
needed to adjudicate.   Because their breach of sexual
mores represents a sin against the earth, they have to be
dealt with ritually by elders of the culprits' clans,
together with the priest of the Earth.   A detailed study
of these sexual infractions and their ritual cleansing
would take us into the realm of symbolism, and lies
outside the scope of this chapter.

3.   The   notion   of **gu** defies any attempt at
translation.   The **guwo** are divided into **xɔmeguwo**
(literally 'bedroom-**guwo**') and **xìxeguwo** (literally
'outdoor-**guwo**').   The first revolve around sex, while
the latter pertain to the spheres of cooking, eating, and
the education of children.

All forms of gestures of anger which involve the misuse of sex, of things related to food and the kitchen, and of household utensils in general, are described as **guwo**. If the wife hits the husband with her loin-cloth, if she pulls his penis or pulls the mat from under him, she is guilty of **xɔmegu**. Beating a child for having defecated in town, refusing a person's food only to eat it later, throwing food at someone, breaking a hearth in anger, hitting somebody with a broomstick, pointing a knife or a sharp instrument at someone with intent to harm, all these constitute **xixeguwo**. Such transgressions have to be ritually cleansed with different medicinal herbs, although no god is involved.

Although I was unable to collect any information on the basic elements comprised in the definition of **guwo** (apart from the mere listing), I would nonetheless be tempted to regard them as an overlapping of symbolic categories which ought to be kept apart. Objects belonging to the house and to the activities performed in its precincts do not tolerate any violence or aggression. These are both categories of behaviour which should be directed towards the outside, that is, towards enemies. Quarrels are reprehensible, but quarrels in which domestic utensils are utilized as weapons somehow disrupt a symbolic order which calls for ritual atonement. Indeed, domestic conflict or conjugal aggression in matters of sex disturb the natural process of reproduction, as its very sequels intimate. The victim of a **gu** who remains deprived of ritual curing will in fact swell and die. In nature, reproduction entails a swelling (pregnancy) which normally culminates in the emergence of life. A lethal swelling, therefore, can be construed as the symbolic expression of an abnormal process of reproduction.

When victim and perpetrator of a **gu** originate from the same **sāme**, regardless of their lineage or minimal lineage of origin, the responsibility of cleansing the **gu** ritually falls on their **sāme** elders. If the victim and his or her **gu**-aggressor come from different **sāmewo**, the ritual is performed by elders from the two clans.

4. **Nuvɔ** as a category also eludes easy definition, although some parallels with the **guwo** can be detected. The word **vɔ**, by itself, can be translated as 'to fear'; when repeted (**vɔvɔ**) it denotes the substantive 'fear'. When suffixed to other words, it consequently denotes something 'bad', or 'to be feared'. **Kuvɔ** (**ku** = to die) is a 'bad death', or a death that

results from a violent and brutal violation of the normal process of growth and ageing (i.e., an accidental death). When suffixed to **nu**, therefore (which by itself means 'thing'), **-vɔ̃** may designate those infringements to the natural process of growth and reproduction. One may believe, for instance, that children develop into responsible adults as a result of durable conjugal relationships, or that money multiplies through diligent work. When marriages break up (divorce), or when people are despoiled of their wealth (theft), someone is deprived of what should naturally accrue to him/her, and the natural process of growth is thereby hampered. Reparations are then called for, either to the person robbed of his/her money (in instances of theft and debt), to the man deprived of exclusive sexual access to his wife (adultery) or to the person deprived of a spouse (divorce). The **nuvɔ̃** thus share this one element, that they all involve repayment. Because of this monetary component, all of these cases (and especially theft) can now be taken directly to the magistrate's court, so that elders do not agree on former practices. Some claim that **nuvɔ̃** were formerly matters for **sāme** representatives to arbitrate, and others contend that they fell under the jurisdiction of the **agbanu-metsisti**. In the instances that I have witnessed, theft cases were taken directly to the Police Station and from there to the magistrate's court, and divorce cases were dealt with by the lineage representative.

5. When dealing with accusations without evidence, the case can ultimately be withdrawn from secular courts and taken directly to Togbe Atando (the Abutia High God), by either plaintiff or defendant. Someone robbed of his money, for instance, will voice his complaint to the Abutia High Priest (in Agove) who will beseech his god to strike the culprit. They claim that the thief will so fear Togbe Atando's retribution that he/she will confess his/her crime. The case would subsequently be tried at the High Priest's court. On the other hand, people wrongfully accused of misdeeds on the basis of mere suspicion can also 'swear the fetish oath' as a testimony of their innocence. Should mishaps start befalling them or their family, they will be accused more directly and the incident will be investigated at the High Priest's Court.

6. Witchcraft and manslaughter obviously share one common element, their lethal effect. Both, fortunately, are extremely rare occurrences in Abutia. Some elders

claim that witches only started infiltrating their area
when villagers began working in Ashanti. Only women can
be witches, and the evil is not transmitted. As in many
other African societies, witches are allegedly recognized
by the light they emit when flying at night. They are
also believed to form covens and kill children, sometimes
their own. Accusations of witchcraft are made when the
soul of someone who has died from an accidental death (and
not from sickness or infected wounds) possesses one of his
or her relatives, revealing that he or she has been struck
down by the evil action of a witch. The Abutias, however,
have no means of testing the veracity of the accusation.
Divination is almost completely absent and, to determine
whether the accused is a witch, they have to take her to a
witch-finder outside Abutia. These witch-finders are
usually non-Ewe, or have learnt their trade outside
Eweland. If he reports that the woman is indeed a witch,
she is then brought back to Abutia where she is tried and
sentenced.

Only one case occurred during my fieldwork, and in the
village of Agove. As the Agove chief was too ill to
attend, the trial was presided over by the priest of the
Abutia High God. He invited chiefs, elders and religious
leaders of other villages, but only a few attended; since
the **fiagā** was then disputed and not recognized outside
his own clan, the Teti **tsiame** (chief's herald)
represented him. The accused woman was found guilty by
the witch-finder, but his evidence was still debated by
the council present. They finally concurred with his
conclusion, and the Teti **tsiame** cleansed her ritually
by shaving her head and washing her with urine. In Kloe,
I only knew of one woman who had been accused of
witchcraft ten or fifteen years earlier. In fact,
witchcraft accusations cannot be made lightly; although
they are made 'under possession', the accuser can be sued
for libel if the witch-finder declares the accused
innocent, and the penalty is quite heavy. The accuser
would indeed be fined a sheep, alcohol, and a certain
amount of money (unknown to me).

Togbe Atando prohibits the shedding of blood on Abutia
soil, and murder is practically unknown. I have in fact
not recorded any special concept to express the notion of
homicide. Only one elder in Abutia could recall a
voluntary killing, by natural means (i.e., not by witchcraft) of one Abutia citizen by another; this occurred
some seventy years ago, and the man murdered his wife's
lover (crime passionnel!). All other occurrences of

individuals killed by human agents, using natural weapons, are in fact treated as manslaughter. Such mishaps only occur during communal animal hunts and are automatically construed as accidents; the slayer's motivation does not seem to be questioned. Nowadays, however, manslaughter has to be reported to the Police Station, and the case has to be examined in court. If the verdict of accident is upheld, and I have not heard of a case where it has not, the case is then treated ritually by the Abutia authorities.

7. Finally, the new categories of offences which correspond to national laws and Local Authority by-laws (i.e., offences against community property or against the smooth running of the administration, such as refusal to pay taxes) fall under the exclusive jurisdiction of magistrate's courts, divided into 'district court' or 'circuit court'. These national courts are not characterized by the type of offences they can arbitrate, but by the severity of the penalty they can impose. The more serious the penalty advocated, the higher the court to which it must be referred.

In contemporary Abutia, a number of groups of reference thus emerge in the adjudication of 'traditional' offences, namely the **fhome, agbanu, sãme, du,** and the whole Division. The courts responsible for the settlement of these offences, however, form the lowest, almost informal level in the national organization. Individuals dissatisfied with their judgment may, in most instances, appeal to a magistrate's court outside Abutia.

B. The contemporary administrative and legislative organization

In administrative activities, no group is formed below the level of the **du** (village). As the Local Government agency within the village, the Village Development Committee represents the local community in administrative matters. It implements decisions taken by the Local Councils and formulates policies regarding public services, such as public health, education, roads, water maintenance and agricultural extension. It also organizes communal labour once a week, on a 'company' basis; all able-bodied adult men and women are divided into four 'companies' which perform the weekly communal labour in turn. They are responsible for the construction of public facilities, namely dispensaries, schools, post office, police station, nurses' quarters, and so on. In fact, the

Village Development Committee exerts a narrowly executive role, since it lacks any legislative power. Only higher councils are empowered to legislate.

Local Councils draw together the Development Committees of many Divisions, and are themselves merged into District Councils. The latter have been granted authority to pass by-laws, but they are further aggregated into Regional Councils. The heads of the country's eight Regional Councils are directly answerable to the Minister of the Interior, in Accra. Abutia is thus part of the Anyirawasi Local Council, one of the many such councils which compose the Ho District Council, itself part of the Volta Region. The Regional Council has its headquarters in Ho, which therefore acts as administrative capital of the Volta Region, and of the Ho District Council.

A third organization also deals with traditional constitutional matters (i.e., those pertaining to traditional chiefs) - the House of Chiefs. A regional 'House of Chiefs' assembles all 'Divisional chiefs' (such as the Abutia fiagā), but is itself part of the 'national House of Chiefs'.

In administrative, legislative and judiciary activities, northern Ewe villages or Divisions are aggregated into larger entities which ultimately encompass the whole Ghanaian nation. This I describe as the 'national' level of organization. The manner in which Local Authorities, magistrate's courts and Houses of Chiefs are organized does not vary much throughout Ghana, and this aspect has received adequate coverage in many books on Ghana (see for instance Nsarko 1964, or Area Handbook for Ghana 1971). 'Traditional' and 'national' zones, however, are not clearly delineated and sometimes overlap; as a result, individuals can take different courses of action, and play one organization off against the other. Since one's own co-villagers are often members of District, Regional or National groups, the manipulations are infinitely complex. In this monograph, however, as the Preface should have made clear, I have not aimed at investigating the different strategies of political action and manipulation, nor at studying the ever-changing networks and factions which have taken shape around the numerous issues which polarize village life, such as the building of a road, the uses of money gained through communal labour, the distribution of Local Council funds, the aggregation into this or that Local Council, the election of this or that chairman, the disputes over chieftaincy and so on. To understand these phenomena, on the contrary, a preliminary understanding of the more permanent ways in which individuals are grouped within the village seems required.

In the greater part of their daily life, Abutia citizens solve their own problems or take them to their 'traditional authorities'. What I witnessed between 1971 and 1973, however, was anything but the exercise of 'traditional authority'. Like so many other things, 'tradition' was manipulated to promote the interests of particular individuals or groups. Different 'traditions' were invoked by various individuals in different contexts with the aim of winning approval, not of keeping intact a body of customs. As a result, the observer can hardly rely on actors' reports but must contextualize every statement and surmise what the informant was trying to achieve. I will therefore cast aside any naive and substantive definition of 'tradition' and 'traditional'. The actors' references to 'traditional' rarely indicate what was really practiced in the past; it rather says something about the kind of representation of the past which is useful for present-day politicking. With this caveat in mind, I would nevertheless like to suggest a negative definition of 'tradition' and 'traditional'. The manner in which Divisions, Local Councils, Districts and Regions are defined is fairly well documented and relatively easy to comprehend. What is meant by **fhome, agbanu, sāme** or **du**, however, is not well understood at all, even by the Abutia themselves. Whether these groups resemble those which existed one or two hundred years ago is a different problem. In the present time, they are the groups which 'escape' direct inclusion in the national organization and, to that extent, I will designate them as 'traditional'. This use of 'traditional' thus eschews any reference to chronology. 'Tradition' is what remains when the national organization is 'abstracted'. When actual chronology becomes relevant, I will write about the precolonial society between 1870–1890, or before 1870, or whatever. In this monograph, 'traditional' is a contemporaty category, whereas 'precolonial' is not.

Insofar as a 'contemporary tradition' exists and is manipulated in the context of Local Government, the Church or magistrate's courts, it deserves to be studied on its own and explicated. The first part will consequently be dedicated to understanding the composition and organization of the **fhome, agbanu, sāme** and **du** as they were observed between 1971 and 1973, and not as lingering evidence of a narrowing past.

II.   THE 'TRADITIONAL' BODY POLITIC

A.   *The fhome*

In judiciary matters, the **fhome** constitutes the lowest group of reference in the adjudication of **yiāwo**. Most children are automatically members of their father's **fhome** but, in special circumstances, a person may gain membership through matrifiliation and even marriage. A child without a recognized genitor, for instance, will belong to its mother's **fhome**. When women marry outside their own village, furthermore, they often get divorced and raise their children in their natal village. These children can choose to remain members of their mother's **fhome** if they elect to live in their mother's village upon reaching maturity; if they choose to return to their father's village, they will automatically activate their membership of his **fhome**. Marriages between individuals of different villages do not always culminate in coresidence; when they result in coresidence, however, the incoming spouse will become a honorary member of his/her spouse's **fhome**. Since men rarely move into their wife's residential group (I counted only five instances of uxorilocal residence in Kloe in 1972), this mostly applies to women, who nevertheless retain full membership of their father's **fhome** (no individual whose paternity has been acknowledged can ever lose membership of his/her genitor's **fhome**). Therefore, if incoming wives are dissatisfied with the manner in which their affines treat them, they will return and complain to their people. Moreover, most inter-village marriages used to take place within the framework of pre-existing genealogical connections, so that an incoming wife was always more than a simple honorary member of her husband's **fhome** because of her genealogical connection to its apical ancestor.

Nowadays, matrifiliation serves very often to determine **fhome** membership, as the number of matrifiliants testifies (Table 1). This situation resembles the Melanesian one, where alleged 'agnatic groups' include a large percentage of matrifiliants, so that genealogical diagrams of contemporary **fhomewo** (See Diagram I) also display a 'cognatic' composition. However, if we use descent to denote aggregation and speak of matrifiliation and patrifiliation as criteria of membership in elementary groups, there is no paradox in speaking of 'agnatic descent groups' composed of minimal lineages somewhat

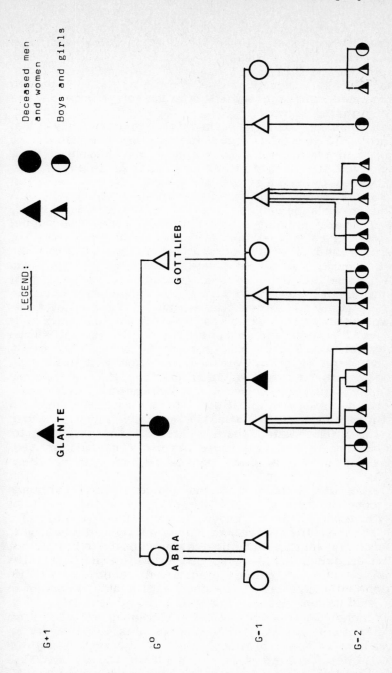

DIAGRAM I. Synchronic representation of a fhome.

cognatic in membership. The Abutia **fhomewo**, like many Melanesian minimal lineages, are predominantly patrifiliative groups using also matrifiliation and marriage (or affinity or cognatic kinship, or other criteria) as additional criteria in specific circumstances, **but aggregated into larger groups on the basis of agnatic descent.**

The problem of the **fhome**'s upper genealogical boundary, and that of its reproduction, are somewhat more complex. In ideal demographic conditions, namely, (1) if all men lived to seventy years of age, (2) if every man was survived by at least one son who also sired children and, (3) if there was complete village endogamy with coresidence of spouses and clear knowledge of genitors, hence if there existed no 'special circumstances' which call for the operation of additional criteria of membership and if every person belonged to his or her father's **fhome**, we could state categorically that the Abutia **fhome** is bounded genealogically in G+1, that is, that it is descended from an apical ancestor in G+1[17]. It would then necessarily follow that new **fhomewo** would be created as one generation dies out (i.e., as G$^\bullet$ becomes G+1), and the process of **fhome** reproduction would then look graphically as in Diagram II. It is this type of graphical representation which has led anthropologists to speak of segmentation; if one imagines graphically the development of **fhomewo** over many generations, everything looks as if **fhomewo** derived from the same ancestor would eventually form a larger group (an intermediate lineage) which would over a longer period of time form a yet larger group (a maximal lineage, for instance). As we shall see the reality does not bear this out.

In real Abutia life divorces are frequent, spouses rarely coreside and genitors are often unknown, so that many **fhomewo** comprise numerous matrifiliants. Men also die at all ages, many are not survived by a fertile son, and polygyny further complicates the picture (though not as much as expected, because of its low frequency). Let us then simulate an exaggerated model including real life conditions to appreciate some of the problems involved in **fhome** delineation and reproduction (Diagram III). At Time 1, one finds a crystallized **fhome** descended from Z and headed by No. 3. Individual No. 2 is survived by an infertile son and his brother, no. 3, by only daughter whose children are absorbed in his own **fhome**. At Time 2, three years later, No. 3 is dead and ought to be

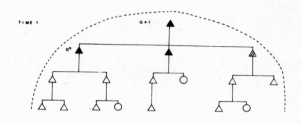

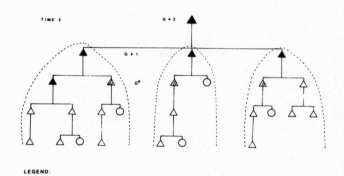

LEGEND:

- - - - -   minimal lineage

   minimal lineage heads

DIAGRAM II. Minimal lineage reproduction in ideal

demographic conditions.

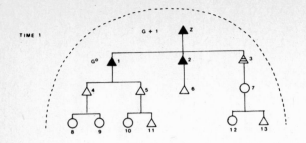

TIME 1

TIME 2   3 dies but 4 is too young and without sufficient influence to assume the headship of the minimal lineage. The minimal lineage thus disappears, absorbed in a more distant one through genealogical connections in G+3.

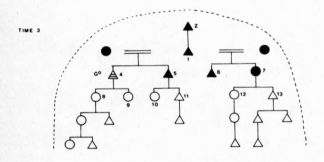

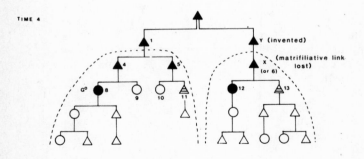

DIAGRAM III. Minimal lineage reproduction in more realistic conditions.

succeeded by the oldest of the following generation but all of them are in their mid-thirties and relatively poor (and possibly on labour migrations). Because of this, none of them can really act as **fhome-metsitsi** and, should a dispute arise in their midst, the case would have to be arbitrated by the **ametsitsi** of the closest collateral **fhome** to which they are linked in G+3. They would not be able to assert their separate identity as a **fhome**. No. 4 may rebel and try to impose his authority but Nos 5, 6 and 7, and their dependants do not seek his arbitration, and he will remain politically isolated. He may then leave on labour migrations never to return again, or live in a maverick style, as individuals in those particular circumstances are known to have done and still do.

Let us imagine that No. 4 accepted his fate. Twenty-five or more years later, Nos 6 and 7 have died and No. 4 is now a respected elder who has succeeded in asserting the separate identity of his **fhome** and acts as its **ametsitsi**. Nos 6 and 7 being dead, No. 4 has a freer hand and he is quite likely to present a radically new genealogical picture of former connections (see Time 3). In this new representation his father has two wives, from whom he and Nos 5, 6 and 7 all issued; Nos 2 and 3 have simply vanished. No. 7's descendants, moreover, will not claim separate **fhome** status because of their connection through a woman; had No. 7 been a man, his progeny would have already formed a new **fhome** by Time 3. At Time 4, finally, No. 4 has died, and the matrifiliative connection through No. 7 is forgotten and replaced by a patrifiliative (but fictitious) one. The creation of a **fhome** is thus delayed by one generation because the apex was a woman. At Time 4, No. 11 has assumed the headship of the now separate **fhome** A, descended from an apical ancestor in G+2. Note that the second **fhome** (B), is descended from an ancestor in G+1, so that A and B are linked in G+3. Ancestor No. 1, recollected earlier as a polygynist, now appears as a monogynist with a patri-sibling, the fictitious Y. From Time 1 to Time 4, 50 years may have elapsed and, during this period, two **fhomewo** have been created out of one. On the basis of the Princeton Regional Life Tables, I have calculated that the population of Kloe has increased approximately four times in the last eighty years (see Appendix 1) so that, since the imposition of the Pax Germanica and later Brittanica, the rate of growth of **fhomewo** might have been slightly faster than suggested.

Minimal Lineage

From this model incorporating some of the real life circumstances (and far from all), some important conclusions emerge:

1. Because of the extreme variability of demographic conditions, Abutia **fhomewo** are actually bounded genealogically between G+1 and G+3. Our real life model was exaggerated because it was plagued by many of the most extreme situations; on the ground, we find extremely few **fhomewo** bounded in G+3, and the greatest majority bounded in G+1. But the variability exists, and it can be derived from the experimental model; Terray has shown similar variations for the Dida minimal lineages, seeing them, however, in terms of developmental phases (Terray 1966: 105, 110, 115).

2. Because of its shallow genealogical depth and narrow genealogical span, the **fhomewo** tend to be relatively small (median size 31, average size 34.41, see Table 2), and therefore the most sensitive to variations in demographic factors. This is directly visible in the extremes between their sizes, which vary from a minimum of 14 (including children) to a maximum of 104 (a 7.5:1 ratio). In fact, the **fhomewo** must have a minimum size in order to emerge as separate entities, and I would suspect that minimum size to be 4-5 adults (and their children). Smaller **fhomewo** are in fact absorbed by their larger collateral **fhomewo**. The factor of size should therefore be added to the 'real life' demographic conditions which influence the reproduction of **fhomewo**, as Lewis and Meggitt have demonstrated for other levels of grouping among the Somalis and Mae Enga respectively (Lewis 1961: 149-51; Meggitt 1965).

The variations in size also influence the sensitivity of groups to random distribution of sex ratios, so that some of the smaller **fhomewo** are composed almost exclusively of individuals of the same gender (see age pyramids for illustration, Diagrams XIII to XVII in Appendix 11).

3. In other words, **fhomewo** can reproduce themselves (i.e., a new one can assert its independent identity) only if (a) it has reached a minimal acceptable size and, (b) if it can have a representative (i.e., if there is an 'elder' in the group). Because these conditions are not always met, and because the individuals involved may contest their dependent position (see their number as sufficient, or themselves as elders), it is impossible to delineate perfectly all **fhomewo**. Most

have crystallized but some are in a state of transition. Despite these obstacles, I have numbered between 50 and 60 **fhomewo** in Kloe in 1972, the real number being probably towards the lower figure.

4. This model also highlights some of the mechanisms by which genealogies are distorted and transformed to reflect conditions on the ground. The fact has been observed many times and has led Iona Mayer to conclude that we should distinguish **ascendants** from **ancestors**. "**Ascendants** could be used for forebears . . . whom ego places in known, strictly consecutive generations. This is to say that he demonstrates kinship with them . . ." (1965; 377) and "**Ancestors** could be used for all other lineal forebears – those whose exact generation relative to ego are no longer demonstrable ..." (377). From this, she separates 'kin lineages' (involving ascendants) from 'ancestor lineages' (involving ancestors) (1965:380), a distinction which parallels in some respects the one I advocate between **fhome** as a group, and one within which all genealogical relationships are remembered and exact, because of its shallow depth, and the **agbanu** as an aggregated group (Mayer's ancestor lineage, so to speak), using genealogical relationships which are partly real and partly fictitious. The parallel does not go all the way, because the distinctions I propose are not made on the basis of genealogical 'correctness', and one does find distortion in **fhomewo** bounded genealogically in G+3, and even in G+2.

For Abutia, I am utterly convinced that, all kinds of distortions are taking place from G+2 upward: ancestresses are transmogrified into ancestors, full-siblings split into half-siblings (and, consequently, dead monogynists emerge as polygynists) and vice versa, fictitious ancestors are introduced, the infertile are made fertile, generational levels are inverted, and so on. This appeared very clearly from the manner in which elders argued about the respective genealogical positions of their ancestors during the collection of genealogies, and how some of these elders called me back to offer me various versions of their genealogies.

Having examined the **fhome**'s composition and reproduction, let us look at its other features. **Fhomewo** are designated as 'the **fhome** of the apical ancestor in G+1/G+2' (such as Glante **fhome**) and they are represented by an **ametsitsi** whose position is achieved through physical and genealogical seniority (the oldest of the oldest living generation), by eldership (**ametsitsime**), male gender, a sufficient number of dependants and membership of the previous **fhome** through patrifiliation. A man who belongs to his mother's **fhome** will not be able to create a new **fhome** when his mother's generation dies out unless he is an extremely powerful elder; his son, however, will achieve it by transmuting his ancestress into an ancestor (this is not automatic, however, since some **fhomewo** are openly descended from ancestresses in G+2 and even G+3).

The criteria of eligibility to the position of **fhometsitsi** have two important implications. First of all, once gained, the position remains the incumbent's until his death. Moreover, this quasi-automatic succession rules out competition for succession to office, although the imprecision of **fhome** boundaries in the transition phase (when the successor is too young) leaves room for political conflicts, as budding elders wish to establish the separate identity of their **fhome**. Paradoxically enough, this very imprecision makes the **fhomewo** politically the most dynamic of Abutia traditional groups! Above this level, as we shall see, the question of boundaries never arises.

The **fhome**, furthermore, does not overlap with any other group or corporation, although a few **fhomewo** are also land-owning corporations, for reasons unknown to me. None of them, however, owns any 'religious estate', such as a shrine, a god, a stool, a special ritual, and so on. This seems to account for the complete absence of para-phernalia attached to the position of **fhome-metsitsi**, and the lack of any ceremony to accompany the accession. As Kludze also pointed out (1973: 91), the various positions of representatives of traditional groups in northern Eweland never brought any substantial profits, so that very few gained anything by acceding to any position (except that of **fiagā** in the national organization). The fact that the set of closest agnates is not involved either as a group or a group of reference in any other activities, seems to me to go a long way towards accounting for the tremendous individualism that one encounters in Abutia.

To conclude, then, the **fhome**, in the context of traditional judiciary activities, emerges as a group (of reference) represented by a man whose position is defined according to specific criteria. The **fhome**, consequently, is neither an agnatic descent group, nor even an agnatic group, but a predominantly patrifiliative group of reference in judiciary activities, which also

uses matrifiliation and marriage as criteria of membership
in specific circumstances. This group is the most
elementary, lowest-level group in the traditional
judiciary organization. In anticipation of later
conclusions, I have dubbed it a 'minimal lineage'.

B. The *agbanû*

In the same context of judiciary activities, two or more
minimal lineages form one **agbanu** when the apical
ancestors of the minimal lineages are descended from a
common male ancestor in G+2, or from a common ancestor in
G+3 or G+4, but through males only. In this context the
agbanu (or **dzotinu**; the two words are synonymous
in Abutia) is therefore a group of **fhomewo**, or a
'group of groups' (see Section 1.I.) with a representative
and all the organizational features which evince
aggregation.

Indeed, the **agbanu** is named, and designated as 'the
children of the apical ancestor' (if the latter is Dza,
then they are **Dza-viwo**). It is represented by a man,
the **agbanu-metsitsi**, whose eligibility to the position
of group representative is defined by precise criteria,
namely male gender, membership of one of the **agbanu's**
constituent minimal lineages through patrifiliation, as
well as physical and genealogical seniority (the oldest
man of the oldest generation). Within the **agbanu**,
however, genealogical knowledge is imprecise beyond G+2
and cannot serve to ascertain seniority. It is rather the
kinship terminology and the system of address which
indicate the relative age and generational level of all
villagers vis-à-vis Ego, making it always possible to
resolve the question of seniority in the absence of
correct genealogical representations. Within the
agbanu, the person who fulfills these criteria is
almost always an elder, so that the problems encountered
with the minimal lineages do not surface within the
agbanu. **Agbanu** boundaries, moreover, are always
clearly delineated; there is one, and only one, **agbanu**
to which a minimal lineage can belong and, whatever its
size (and we witness important variations here, the
smallest **agbanu** numbering 23 individuals whereas the
largest boasts of 370, i.e., a ratio of 16:1 - Table 3)
the **agbanu** acts independently. Finally, the **agbanu-
metsitsi** has the authority to convene a group for
adjudication when cases fall within the **agbanu's**
jurisdiction. The **agbanu** thus possesses all the
features of an aggregated group in which agnatic descent

(remembered as real, but mostly fictitious above G+2) is used to merge **fhomewo** into one aggregated entity; it is therefore an **agnatic descent group**. Since no genealogical connections are remembered (i.e., named) above the **agbanu**, it is therefore a 'maximal' lineage. There is no intermediate level of aggregation between the **fhomewo** and the **agbanu**, however, so that we will designate it simply as a lineage, and not a 'maximal lineage'. By implication, the **fhomewo** are 'minimal lineages'.

The most intriguing and important feature of the Abutia lineages is that their number is ideally fixed (namely, always three per clan) so that, by implication, they are not expected to proliferate. Bukh notes that the three lineages of every Tsito clan (Tsito is a village in the Awudome Division, the territory of which Division borders Abutia's south-western boundary) were created from time immemorial (1979:25). Kludze, reflecting the local ideology, also writes:

> "Empirically it is not known that any **dzotinu** has ever disappeared or disintegrated . . . The other aspect is that a family as understood among the Northern Ewe (by which Kludze means a **dzotinu**, translated in this monograph as 'lineage') cannot be created today. All the families have existed from time immemorial and new ones cannot be created today by a fission or fusion of families. The number of families in any community is, therefore, fixed and unalterable."
> (1973:79)

Admittedly, the reality departs somewhat from the native model. In Kloe, for instance, two clans comprise five lineages but the elders were quick to point out that this is a recent development which grew out of 'greed' over the sale of land. Bukh also admits as much; the prospect of selling land has hastened its fragmentation (1979:30). Whereas all land was formerly owned by **agbanuwo** (i.e., the same individuals which were included in the **agbanu** as a judiciary group of reference also formed a land-owning corporation, so that the head of the **agbanu** also acted as trustee of this corporation [18]), the peculiarities of land tenure have led some minimal lineages to claim separate rights to land and, in some instances, to split and form new corporations (on land tenure, see below, Appendix 2 and especially Kludze 1973). Some minimal lineages have achieved this in Kloe where land is more abundant and land sales more frequent than in the other two villages, but none have done so in Teti or Agove. Of the twenty Abutia clans, therefore, 17 have retained their three lineages, one has only two because one of its lineages has died out, and only two clans (both from Kloe) number five lineages.

This lack of lineage proliferation has some interesting consequences. Since accession to the position of lineage representative is completely automatic and since lineages cannot hope to split and assert independent identities, there is absolutely no competition to become **agbanu-metsitsi**. The fixed number of lineages also explains the mode of minimal lineage reproduction and the distortions inflicted on genealogical representations above G+2. Indeed, lineages can avoid fission (i.e., proliferation) only if they can maintain a high rate of proliferation among their constituent groups, the minimal lineages. If the minimal lineages were bounded in G+2 or above in ideal demographic conditions, they would then be larger, and the largest among them would be more likely to assert their independence and eventually grow into new lineages. In other words, minimal lineages have to be relatively small not to threaten to form budding lineages, and this is achieved by giving them a shallow genealogical depth (their upper genealogical boundary being 'ideally' in G+1)[19]. New minimal lineages are indeed created as one generation dies out, but they do not form the new ground from which budding lineages would grow into fully-fledged lineages over time. On the contrary, genealogical representations are distorted, telescoped[20], and condensed so that minimal lineages may multiply within the same lineages. Abutia minimal lineages do not therefore 'segment', but increase in number within the framework of a fixed number of lineages which, theoretically, do not proliferate. The shallow genealogical depth of the minimal lineage thus ensures the rapidity of its proliferation, gives it a relatively small size, and genealogical connections are distorted to keep the minimal lineages within the same lineages. As a result, the lineages themselves do not multiply but remain three in number within each clan. To put it differently, the 'ban' on lineage proliferation seems to determine the mode of minimal lineage reproduction.

The same 'ban' on lineage proliferation helps to account for a second feature of Abutia lineages, notably their lack of homogeneity. We can indeed distinguish three different types of lineages from their genealogical representations:

1.   In a first type (Type I, Diagram IV   ), two or more minimal lineages are aggregated into one lineage through one male ancestor in G+2.   These are demographically the smallest lineages, varying in size between 30 and 55 individuals (children included).

2.   Type II lineages (Diagram V   ) are more complex. Typically, they consist of more than two minimal lineages aggregated to an ancestor in G+3 or G+4 through intermediate ancestors placed at different generational levels. Type II lineages look graphically like a series of Type I lineages aggregated one or two generations above, but there is strictly no aggregation between the minimal lineages (**fhomewo**) and the complete lineage.   Type II lineages vary in size from 50 to 190 members[21].

3.   Type III lineages (Diagram VI   ) are by far the largest, and look graphically as if Type II lineages were further aggregated through a male ancestor and his wives in G+5, but there is no intermediate level of aggregation in Type III lineages either.   Such lineages number close to 400 individuals.

It would thus seem that the absence of lineage proliferation has a further implication: it thwarts the formation of an intermediate level of aggregation between minimal lineages and maximal lineages.   If it allowed it, it would invite large intermediate lineages to assert their autonomy outside the lineage framework and eventually grow into separate lineages.   Since minimal lineages are directly aggregated into a 'maximal' lineage without any intermediate levels, the various generations of ancestors do not serve to differentiate various levels of aggregation (as they do among the Namoos, for instance; see Fortes 1945, Verdon 1982a).   Whether a minimal lineage is linked to the apical lineage ancestor through two, three or four generations does not affect its status or relative rank in any way.   Only the fact of common agnatic descent is relevant to aggregating the various minimal lineages into one single **agbanu**.   This is what I mean when I write that descent alone produces aggregation in Abutia.

The lack of proliferation of lineages would thus account for the lineages' differences in size and genealogical configuration.   Lineages which grew inordinately large, unable to split, would display a much more complex genealogical record, and we could therefore read a 'developmental cycle' of lineage growth in this typology: Type I lineages would develop into Type II, which would grow into Type III, without splitting.

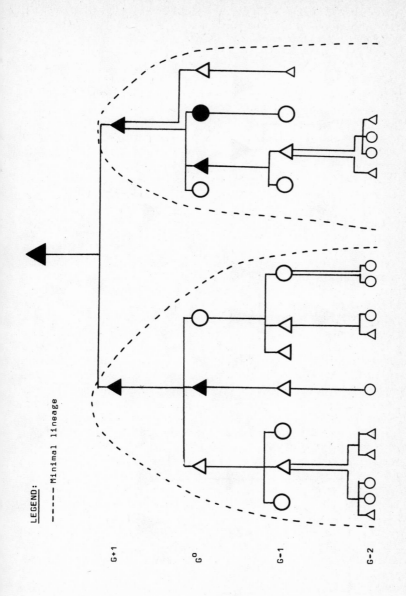

LEGEND:

------ Minimal lineage

G+1

G⁰

G-1

G-2

DIAGRAM IV. Synchronic representation of a Type I lineage.

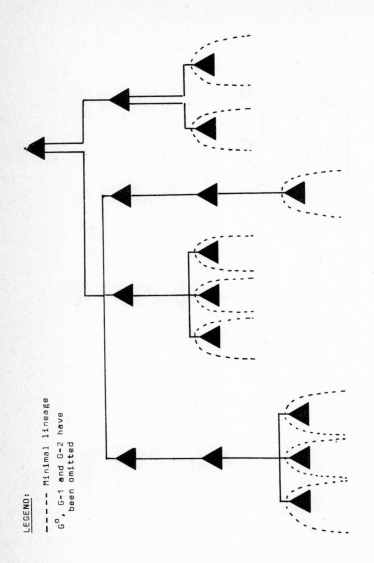

LEGEND:

------ Minimal lineage

G^0, G-1 and G-2 have
been omitted

DIAGRAM V. Synchronic representation of a Type II lineage.

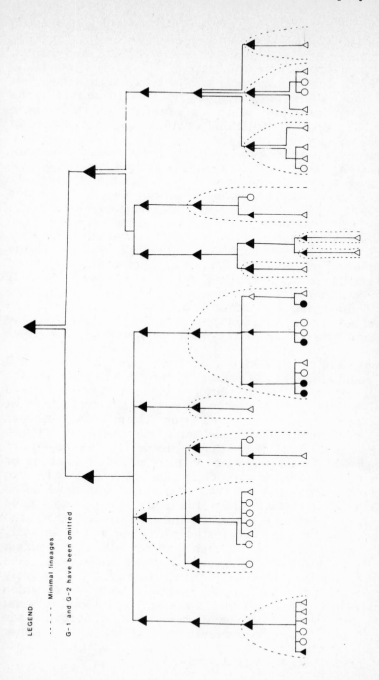

LEGEND

- - - - Minimal lineages

G-1 and G-2 have been omitted.

DIAGRAM VI. Simplified representation of a Type III lineage.

Admittedly, some would grow and then dwindle in size while other would eventually split, after many generations (in reality, lineage proliferation is so incredibly slow as to **appear** impossible). Moreover, a Type III lineage is as likely to secede and form a new clan, with three new lineages, as to create a new lineage; if it achieved the latter alternative, it would create a fourth lineage within the clan, a situation which could not exist in precolonial times.

There is, however, one disquieting fact which does not completely square with this interpretation, namely that the various types of lineage are not distributed randomly within the clans, as one might expect. Table 3 indicates clan sizes in Kloe: Akpokli and Gulegbe stand apart, with 600 and 800 members respectively; Wome numbers 200 individuals, whereas Etsri and Atsadome have approximately 150 each. Strangely enough, neither of the two large clans have any Type I lineages, all ten of which are found in the smaller clans, whereas six of the seven Type II lineages are in the two larger clans only, as are the two Type III lineages. In other words, the small clans are composed of small lineages only (Type I), whereas the large clans are composed of large lineages only (Types II and III).

Because of the complete opacity of the historical record regarding the formation of traditional groups, one can only guess at the conditions which promoted such a state of affairs. The reason may be historical, in that some clans may have arrived much later than others, despite their unanimous disclaimer of such a fact. There is indeed evidence that Etsri is partly composed of strangers who would have moved in from Teti a century or so ago. The two largest clans are also the only two stool-owning clans in Kloe, and this fact might have acted to retard their fission (unfortunately, I do not have comparable data from Agove and Teti, so that the hypothesis could not be tested. I know for a fact, however, that the **fiagā's** clan in Teti is the smallest of the Teti clans). I will later suggest that clans have had unequal access to the 'means of reproduction', namely the means of acquiring women and also slaves (a fact which may not be unrelated to their ownership of stools, in that stool-owning clans may have been the richest in the distant past). But the complete ban on mentioning either slave or stranger ancestry has made it impossible to clarify this situation satisfactorily.

As mentioned earlier, **agbanu** is also a term used to designate land-owning corporations whose membership coincides exactly with the **agbanu** defined as a descent group in judiciary activities. This topic will be examined in more detail below (Appendix 2) but one aspect of ownership is pertinent here. Among the lands an **agbanu** (as a corporation) owns, are tracts of land located on the village sites. Kludze asserts that "usually it is one family (i.e., **dzotinu**) that releases its lands for occupation by the whole community as a town land" (1973:167), implying that possession of that town land then passes on to the various corporations (**dzotinuwo**, or **agbanuwo**). Such a formula seems to have been adopted in Teti, where one **agbanu-metsitsi** is designated as the **anyigba-tɔ**, or 'owner of the land' and plays a small ritual part in the chiefly rituals (he inspects the ears of the sheep to be slaughtered to the Teti 'stool' to certify that the animal is good enough for the sacrifice). In Kloe, on the other hand, I was told that the various **agbanuwo** had purchased their own tracts of land, and nobody acted as **anyigba-tɔ**. Whatever the variations, the result is the same, namely that parts of village land are owned by corporations whose membership coincides absolutely with that of the lineage. Adult men and women of the corporation (and hence of the lineage) can build their houses on this tract of land only, so that houses of adult men (and, increasingly, those of adult women) of the same lineage are localized. These houses, on the other hand, are occupied by various people who do not all belong to the same **agbanu**, while other lineage members live elsewhere. It is therefore inaccurate to state that the **agbanu** is localized; only the houses owned by its members are, so that house-owners and their dependants can be said to be localized to the extent that they are domiciled on that parcel of land. The collection of individuals occupying houses built on a given **agbanu**-site in the village, one can call a 'local category'. It would form a group (a local group) if its members were engaged in a common activity, or if it emerged as a group of reference in a given activity, but it does not.

As a corporation, the **agbanu** does not own any other estate (especially religious estate). This, in my opinion, would partly account for the fact that no ceremony marks the accession of the **agbanu-metsitsi** to his position, and that the **agbanu**'s corporate identity is not culturally expressed through the ownership of any paraphernalia, which would be attached to the position of lineage representative.

In sum, Abutia lineages are almost incapable of proliferation and are left no room for political competition for the position of lineage/corporation representative. This statics, I submit, accounts for the genealogical depth and mode of reproduction of minimal lineages, for the absence of intermediate levels of aggregation, and for the fact that descent alone operates in aggregation. We will later try to isolate the conditions which favour such lineage statics.

C. The sāme

In theory (and the practice is hardly discrepant if we take the whole of Abutia), three and only three lineages form one sāme when they claim to be descended from three different wives from one unnamed, putative ancestor. The sāme is therefore a 'group of lineages' with a representative supported by all the organizational features which accompany aggregation [22].

First of all, the sāmewo are named. The names used to designate the Kloe sāmewo in this monograph are fictitious; some of the real sāmewo names, in Kloe, have a 'totemic' aspect. One clan is know as the 'hawk', and another by the name of a species of bird which I have been unable to identify. As to the other sāmewo names in Kloe, they cannot be called totemic; one could be translated as 'the metal-breakers' (but they are not blacksmiths...), another as 'those who sleep awake', and a third one defies translation. Those with totemic names do not observe any taboos with reference to their 'totemic' animal, nor do they practice any cult involving it. Only the name is totemic. All clans, however, prohibit some foods, although different clans can share the same prohibitions[23]. The sāmewo's corporate identity is also culturally expressed by a set of paraphernalia[24].

Secondly, the sāme is represented by one man, although Abutia sāmewo differ in the type of representatives they have, whether sāme-metsitsi, sāme-fia, tsiame or mankraḍo. The sāme-metsitsiwo are found in clans without 'stools', or without titled office related to the 'village stool' (such as tsiame and mankraḍo). In Kloe, Etsri alone falls in this category, and eligibility to the position of sāme-metsitsi is defined by the same criteria which delineate eligibility to the position of lineage **ametsitsi**; the **sãme-metsitsi** is the oldest man in the oldest generation of all three lineages within the clan. Only one man fulfills these criteria, and succession is therefore automatic, ruling out competition. Furthermore, clan boundaries (in membership) are clearly demarcated since a lineage can only belong to one clan.

The **sãmewo** are also 'religious corporations' which 'own' certain gods (i.e., they have the exclusive ritual responsibility for their cults), and whose membership is coterminous with that of **sãmewo** in judiciary activities. There are three types of gods that can be 'owned' by a **sãme**, namely chthonic gods (**togbetrɔwo**, literally 'ancestors' gods'), gods of the hunt (**adewo**) and 'stools' (**zikpuiwo**). All five Kloe **sãmewo** own the first two types, but their priest is not necessarily the **sãme**-representative; in the clans which do not own stools or titled offices related to the stool, therefore, the **sãme**-representative is not the priest of any god (if he is, it is a coincidence) so that no ceremony marks his accession to office. Such representatives are simply **sãme-metsitsiwo**.

In **sãmewo** with stools, however, it is the priest of the stool, known as **fia** (which missionaries, administrators and ethnographers alike have translated as 'Chief'), who acts as representative of the **sãme**. The criteria of eligibility to **fia**-ship (**fiadudu**) differ from those of **ametsitsime**, as they include membership, through either father or mother[25], of one of the clan's component **agbanuwo** from which the two previous chiefs did not originate (in other words, the **fia**-ship must rotate between the three lineages of a clan), youth, bodily perfection, character appropriate for the task (which implies humility, obedience, respect for the people, wisdom) and a sufficient degree of literacy to be able to read, speak and write English adequately. Unlike criteria for **ametsitsime**, which only one individual can fulfill, these criteria delineate a set of potential candidates. The new **fia** is therefore selected (but not elected) by the elders of his **sãme**. The candidates do not compete because the name of the chief-designate must remain secret; if he knew of his impending fate, the chief-to-be would flee to avoid incumbency. The Abutias, like the Ashanti and other West African people, regard chiefship as an onerous task, not to be desired by any sane man (these ideological statements, however, do not bear any correspondence to reality...). Whatever politicking takes place does not occur publicly, but in private, among the elders whose task it is to reach a consensus on the choice of a candidate. When a decision has been reached by the **sāme** elders, they convene a general assembly of the clan some time ahead and, on the appointed day, they 'seize' the chief-designate and 'enstool' him ritually (see Appendix 3 for details). The chief is then presented to the people and he pledges to obey and respect them; the youth of the clan, however, have no right of veto. Because they are 'enstooled', i.e., selected and ritually installed by the 'stool-father' (the **zikpui-tɔ**, who is the **ametsitsi** of the lineage from which the chief is selected) chiefs can also be 'destooled' if they incur public displeasure, as the Teti **fiagā** experienced during my stay. The length of a **fia**'s tenure of office thus depends upon his good behaviour.

In Kloe the two largest clans only, namely Akpokli and Gulegbe, possess stools which were 'carved' before 1890 (the latter date marking approximately the arrival of the Germans; some **sāme** representatives have since carved new stools in order to promote themselves in the eyes of the administration. Since the administrators treated **fiawo** as 'chiefs', these **sāme**-representatives decided to acquire the status by obtaining the stool itself!). Teti, with eight clans, has three stool-owning ones, and Agove two out of seven. Only these clans are represented by a **fia**. Why some clans have stools while others have not is the result of historical circumstances, the obscurity of which has made it unintelligible to contemporary actors and observers.

Clans not represented by either a **sāme-metsitsi** or a **sāme-fia** are represented by titled office-holders, namely **mankraḍo** (or Regent) and **tsiame** (or 'linguist'), whose position in the political organization is defined with reference to the 'village stool'. The Kloe **mankraḍo** hails from Wome, and the **tsiame** from Atsadome. The 'linguist' is selected and invested like a **fia**, whereas the **mankraḍo** acceeds to the position like a **sāme-metsitsi**[26].

These various representatives of the **sāme** all wield the power to convene a group for the adjudication of offences which fall within the **sāme**'s jurisdiction. The **sāme**, like the **agbanu**, displays all the features of an aggregated group in which descent from the various wives of a common male ancestor is used to coalesce lineages into one embracing entity. It is therefore an **agnatic descent group** but not a lineage since it uses putative descent from an unknown, unnamed ancestor to aggregate lineages. This type of group I call a 'clan'.

There are twenty clans in Abutia (five in Kloe, seven in Agove and eight in Teti) but, unlike the lineages, the Abutia clans all share the same pattern despite their varying sizes (from 142 to 800 in Kloe, or a ratio of 5.5:1)[27]. Because of the unique property of their component lineages, the clan also are not expected to proliferate. I have been able to record evidence of the creation of a new clan in Teti only, where two separate clans acknowledge a former unity. All other Abutia clans claim to have existed since the very beginning of the Ewe people, in Notsie. Akpokli, nevertheless, looks very much like a clan that averted fission through diplomacy.

Agbanu houses, we mentioned earlier, are localized on the corporation's land. The lands of **agbanuwo** from the same clan are moreover adjacent and well distinguished from the lands of the corporations of other clans by wide streets. Again, it is inaccurate to speak of the clan as being localized since its members can be scattered all over Ghana. The various lineage-sites are merged into a clearly delineated and visible clan-site, on which clan members build their houses (although within the clan-site, they can only build on their lineage site). These clan sites are also occupied by house-owners from the clan, as well as by residents from other clans so that we find another 'local category' although this one has more of a separate identity. These clan sites are indeed named by some feature of their geographical location, so that Kloe's five clan sites, for instance, are known as (1) Anyigbe, or 'the down-side', a part occupied by house owners from Akpokli and their dependants, (2) Dzigbe, or 'the up-side', a section of the village occupied by Gulegbe house-owners and their various dependants, (3) Dome, or 'the middle section', occupied by Etsri house-owners and their various dependants, (4) Kloe-tia, or 'the one at Kloe's periphery', occupied by Wome house-owners and their dependants and (5) the fifth area is known by the very name of its clan, namely Atsadome. There is no precise correspondence between the number of clans and such named geographical sections of the village, however. Indeed, members of Etsri who could no longer build on the old clan site because of overcrowding opened up a new area, now known as Gboyiyiame, or 'new town'. Anyigbe,

moreover, is divided into Adeyime and Hihladzi, two
separate areas which reflect Akpokli's internal division.

Young men and women from Dzigbe and Anyigbe form
'singing groups' which, however do not have a fixed
membership and also recruit members from the sites on
their side of the village. This is a far cry, however,
from claiming that the local categories are engaged in an
activity, or that they emerge as groups of reference in an
activity, since they do not. That they do not form local
groups, however, does not mean that they are not relevant
for social action; on the contrary, most of the social
categorizations are done in those geographical terms,
since it is in those areas that one lives, that one has
one's closest friends, and that one spends most of the
time of day. The perspectives of social action,
nevertheless, do not coincide necessarily with those of
social organization; in organizational terms, the people
occupying those areas only form local categories.

The fact that people can only build on their
corporation's village land (except in very unusual
circumstances), and that the tracts of land belonging to
lineages of the same clan are contiguous, does practically
entail that people can virtually not build outside their
clan site. In other words, nobody in Abutia can build and
settle permanently outside his native village, and create
a new outgrowth of a clan in a new settlement. In a
simplified, but inaccurate way, we could say that the
Abutia clans are not dispersed, a most interesting feature
when one considers that authors like Service regard clans
as inherently dispersed because, in most societies, clan
members can build and settle outside their native
settlements, that is, their houses are spread over many
settlements (Service 1962:116).

Now, if lineages were to proliferate with relative
ease, the largest would 'spill over' new or other old
settlements, where new lineages would grow but retain
their putative common descent with the lineages of the
mother-settlement. Alternatively, smaller lineages might
escape the hegemony of larger ones by moving out. In
other words, if lineages were allowed to disperse they
would multiply at a faster rate, and the clans would
thereby be also dispersed. I will thus assume that it is
the factors which operate against lineage dispersal which
thwart their proliferation and, by implication, stop clan
dispersal and proliferation. I will try to isolate these
factors when more evidence has been presented.

D. The *du*

The clans which have settled in the same locality form a **du**. The **du** thus emerges as a 'group of groups' with a representative and supported by all the organizational features which accompany aggregation.

Every **du** is indeed named, although I have been unable to find any meaningful etymology behind these names (Kloe, Agove and Teti), and it is represented by one man, the **du-fia**. In all villages but Kloe one clan, whose ancestor allegedly led the clans in their migrations to the present settlements, owns a 'stool' which is regarded as the 'village stool' in addition to being a clan stool, and whose priest (the **sãme-fia**) acts as the **du-fia** (i.e., as representative of the village) as priest of the village stool. The selection and enstoolment of a **du-fia** are consequently those of a **sãme-fia**, although on a larger scale because the whole village is involved. In Kloe only are the positions of **sãme-fia** and **dufia** dissociated; Akpokli is unique in owning two stools, namely a clan stool and a separate village stool so that the Kloe **dufia**, although selected and enstooled like other **dufiawo**, is not at the same time the representative of Akpokli. This idiosyncratic division may be attributed to Akpoli's extreme size (600 individuals). I would be tempted to believe that its dominant Type III lineage (with 370 individuals) once threatened to split and form a separate clan (or even village), although no such event is recollected. To avert this calamity, the clan elders would have allowed members of this gigantic lineage to 'carve their own stool' and behave as if they constituted a clan within the clan[28]. Akpokli's Type III lineage is indeed internally differentiated into two entities which take turn in providing a priest for the clan stool, whereas a separate village stool rotates between Akpokli's other two lineages. Most of the politicking in Kloe in the last twenty years (date of reference 1972) has revolved around this office of village chief, disputed since 1950. During fieldwork, the Chairman of the Kloe Village Development Committee acted as **dufia**, the Teti **mankraḍo** acted in the place of the destooled Teti **dufia** (and Abutia **fiagã**), and the Agove High Priest represented the Agove chief who was bed-ridden for the better part of two years! Wherever **dufiawo** are not disputed, however, they have the power to convene groups to adjudicate offences which are deemed a village responsibility. The du, therefore, also displays the features of an aggregated group but, the real question is, what kind of aggregated group?

The Abutia villages are composed of clans, the members of which are in fact dispersed, despite the localization of their houses. They are aggregated into a du, however, on the basis of their occupation of a common settlement, or local contiguity. If by 'territoriality' we denote the fact of local contiguity used to aggregate groups, the Abutia villages are therefore territorial groups. Their component groups, however, are descent groups and not local groups. Tonu (i.e., riverine) towns, however, are divided into **towo** (sing. **to**) or wards, which emerge as groups of reference in judiciary (and formerly military) activities. To that extent, a Tonu town is a territorial group composed of local groups (the wards) which, in turn, aggregate descent groups[29]. Many polities of the forest belt and even savanna of West Africa share this feature of Abutia villages; one is immediately reminded of some Cross River societies (the Mbembe especially), or indeed the Ashanti, or other populations of south-western Ivory Coast and south-eastern Liberia (such as the Dida, for instance).

E. The Division: Abutia

As the clans migrated together, led by a man whose clan now provides the chief, the three villages migrated together, led by a man whose village provides the Paramount Chief (**fiagā**, literally 'great **fia**'). The Three villages also share a common name (Abutia; etymology obscure) and are represented by the **fiagā**, whose criteria of eligibility and procedures of enstoolment are those of a **dufia** (and, therefore, of a **sāmefia**), although on a more elaborate scale still. The **fiagā** is indeed the **sāmefia** of the chiefly clan of Teti, and automatically Teti's **dufia**. The three Abutia villages thus have a common representative but are they aggregated? In the national and judiciary organization, the three villages are definitely aggregated into one Division, and the **fiagā** has the authority to convene a council to arbitrate certain types of offences. But can we speak of aggregation at the Division level in the 'traditional' judiciary organization? The problem is almost impossible to solve on the basis of contemporary evidence because the Division emerges as a traditional group of reference in the adjudication of witchcraft only,

an extremely rare offence, and because there was not
fiagā accepted by the 'traditional authorities' during
my stay. Moreover, villages and Division are the two
levels of grouping overlapping with the national
administrative and judiciary organization, and displaying
the greatest discrepancy between theory and practice. The
councils convened by acting chiefs attract only a tiny
fraction of those eligible, as factions backing the
disputed chiefs do not recognize their authority.
Dissatisfied individuals can always sidestep their
decisions by referring their case to a magistrate's court.
The traditional judiciary organization has suffered its
greatest disruption at the village and Division levels and
this leaves completely open the question of whether the
Division is an aggregated group in the contemporary
traditional judiciary organization. The question can only
be answered indirectly, as will be done below, through a
reconstruction of the precolonial political organization.

We have only mentioned disruptions of the traditional
judiciary organization. In legislative and executive
matters, the havoc is still more complete, since the
traditional groups have lost all such powers. Village
Development Committees and Local Councils have supplanted
village councils and the Police Force has superseded
gerontocratic authority. The Police Station in Kloe is
manned by three officers, none of whom originates from
Abutia. It is under the authority of a District and
Regional police force which works in close liaison with
local government agencies. Its recruitment is regulated
by the national authorities. All legislative authority,
finally, has been withdrawn from traditional leaders and
placed in the hands of local and national governments
(i.e., Local Authorities and the central government).
Local Government (directed from the Ministry of the
Interior, despite its deceptive name...) promotes the
formation of Village Development Committees which recruit
'traditional authorities'. In this perspective, one may
be led to believe that they are simply a re-named and re-
fashioned version of the village 'council of elders'.
This, however, is far from being the case. The Village
Development Committee is the minimal group in the national
administrative organization; its criteria of membership
and internal structure are determined from above, and it
has little in common with the "Council of Elders" which
allegedly ruled Abutia villages in the distant past.

But nothing has yet been said about these 'councils of
elders'. In line with our programme, we have investigated

the 'traditional' political organization, examining the composition of minimal groups and their mode of aggregation, as well as the mode of reproduction of the groups at all levels.   We have enquired into the criteria which define eligibility to office and seen that the group representatives were empowered to convene groups for adjudication.   We will now study the criteria of membership of the judiciary groups and look at their internal structure.

In judicial matters, both heads (**ametsitsiwo**) and chiefs (**fiawo**) have authority only to convene a council (court) and to preside over it.   Up to the clan level, these councils bring together elders who are cognates of the parties involved in the dispute, and who possess the appropriate wisdom and knowledge for its adjudication.   Younger individuals may also be invited if their knowledge as witnesses is relevant to the deliberations.   The actual arbitration is not marked by any specific division of labour, save for the 'presidential' role played by the head or chief. Deliberations are not ordered, despite the chairman's attempt to channel the discussion.   Those who have something to say express their opinion freely, and naturally the most skilful orators exert the greatest influence.   The elders only pass their judgment when they have reached a consensus about the verdict, and the privilege of pronouncing the sentence is reserved for the group's representative.   Sentences are traditional, and a head who departs from a traditional sentence will arouse a flurry of further deliberations which may become a case in itself!

Apart from a core of resident elders from the minimal lineage, lineage or clan who derive pleasure from such reunions, the composition of a court varies from one occasion to the next.   These councils are nevertheless the main arenas for many of the 'political games', and convenient stepping-stones for the advancement of personal power and influence.   Assiduous elders learn more about the 'tradition'; they also discover how to manipulate it to convince their audience of the validity of their statements (and interpretation of the tradition...).   An individual's wisdom and general judgment, his quality as a convincing orator or a formidable cross-examiner, is developed and recognized in such judiciary debates.   The judiciary courts thus function as the main channels for the transmission of the 'tradition'.   An individual learns from his peers, as there is no custom of parents passing on a body of 'traditional lore' to their children; the tradition is learned in action, as it is involved in the settlement of various disputes. Those who fail to attend councils thus miss out on the tradition and their ignorance keeps them away from councils, and thus from the main source of influence in Abutia society.

Above the clan, cases reported to the village chief are tried by a council composed of the village elders, when village chieftancies are not disputed. Eldership, **amegā**-ship and domicile in the village are the only criteria which confer membership of this council of elders, or **du-tɔwo** (literally, 'fathers of the village'). The council has an embryonic structure, because of the specific tasks filled by the **mankradọ** and the **tsiame**. Nowadays, few lawsuits are submitted to the village council, because of the chieftaincy disputes; most are dealt with at the clan level, in the presence of village elders.

The entanglement of local-traditional with national politics is partly to be blamed for the chieftaincy disputes, which further account for the conflicting interpretations of the 'tradition'. Present-day Paramount Chiefs (i.e., in the period 1971-1973), for instance, belong to the Regional House of Chiefs and are paid a salary by the State. Destooled by his own people, the Abutia Paramount Chief still retained his 'official' Paramountcy because of the politicking that went on at the regional level (more specifically, because of his nepotistic connnections with an influential member of the Regional House of Chiefs). In fact, all chiefship matters were further complicated by 'party' nominations during the Nkrumah regime. One individual from Kloe used to work as Discrict Commissioner during this period and has been accused of supporting a candidate from his own lineage (as he himself came from the chiefly clan). During the Nkrumah regime, chiefs who stood against the C.P.P. (Nkrumah's party) were deposed and pro-C.P.P. rivals were enstooled. When the military ousted Nkrumah in 1966, the C.P.P.-nominated chiefs were deposed, regardless of rightful succession, and their opponents were invested. Consequently, Abutia and even the whole of Ewe-Dome chieftaincy is in a state of constant turmoil. Two commissions have already been formed to investigate the topic without really uprooting the evil.

Good eye for little ethnographic detail. history -

This survey of traditional judiciary groups altogether much too brief, suggests a lack of internal structure and a 'diffuse power base'. Adjudication in Kloe was a very private affair (and presumably still is...) so that I was not invited to attend such meetings; the more public ones are normally those conducted by the village chief, but none of those took place. I only witnessed arbitration at burials, when unsettled cases with the deceased have to be resolved, so that I openly confess the paucity of my data on legal processes. I thus gained most of my information on this topic from interrogation, and not observation.

It is not lack of knowledge of Abutia legal processes, however, which impeded me from elucidating the relationships between the various positions of authority, as well as the relationships between the citizenry as a whole and their group representatives. I met with such a mass of conflicting and contradictory information on these matters that the conventional empirico-inductive approach failed. Because of the disruptions brought about by colonial and national politics, the traditional office-holders have mostly become meaningless political agents; if they play any significant role (like the Teti **mankraḍo**), it is because of their own personality, or because of the manner in which they have intrigued to control the 'national' posts in the Village Development Committee, the Church, or the Local Councils. To make any sense of the deeds of contemporary traditional office-holders I had to understand something of the precolonial political organization and, to achieve the greatest part of this, I was compelled to resort to a rather conjectural and deductive approach.

III. RECONSTRUCTING THE PRECOLONIAL POLITY: 1870-1890

A. *Political sovereignty*

To tackle these questions, it appeared fruitful to start the enquiry with the question of political sovereignty. But what is political sovereignty? Since Radcliffe-Brown's Introduction to African Political Systems and Evans-Pritchard's book on the Nuer (Radcliffe-Brown 1940, Evans-Pritchard 1940), many social anthropologists have defined the 'political community' as that community within which conflicts are resolved peacefully, and war therefore almost impossible. The operation of legal processes, and the point where they break down, thus demarcated the boundaries of that 'political community' or, in other words, of the politically 'sovereign' entity. The definition did not square too well with certain ethnographic facts, such as the modes of aggression among the Tiv themselves, or the Yanomamo, for instance, where one observes gradients of violence matching the 'structural distance' between disputants.

I would beg to disagree with this definition of the politically sovereign entity as a political community bounded by the reign of law. Indeed, the 'community' within which there is an explicit effort to resolve conflicts peacefully does not have to be sovereign. We find the nations of Western Europe, since the Second World War, keen on settling their differences through mediation without assuming Western Europe to be a politically sovereign group. Allied groups seek peace every bit as much as aggregated ones, so that the 'moral obligation' (Middleton and Tait 1958: 9) to settle disputes through arbitration cannot serve as an indication of either alliance or aggregation.

I define as sovereign the political groups beyond which no aggregation takes place; admittedly, the component groups of this sovereign community try to avoid war, but so do allied sovereign groups. In fact, allied groups are sometimes more strongly 'morally obliged' or committed to peaceful relations (witness the Hill Talis, for instance - Fortes 1945) than aggregated groups. The Basque country, although aggregated within Spain, would blithely declare war against the latter if it had any chance of winning it! A commitment to peace cannot therefore be interpreted as an indication of political sovereignty (i.e., maximal aggregation).

Political sovereignty, moreover, only applies to political activities. One can indeed find sovereign nations associated for economic matters (the EEC being the most obvious illustration) without surrendering their political sovereignty. Similarly, many national states may have a predominantly (or even exclusively) Roman Catholic population grouped into parishes aggregated into dioceses, which are themselves aggregated under the Vatican, without for that reason losing their political sovereignty to the Vatican[31]. In other words, communities which are sovereign politically may, in the context of economic or religious activities, be aggregated into more encompassing groups without thereby relinquishing their political sovereignty[32].

These few definitions thus enable us to look at the matter from a different angle, and ask which of the precolonial Abutia groups was sovereign or, in other words, at which level did aggregation stop?

B. Political sovereignty in precolonial Abutia

Students of Ewe social organization have differed widely in their identification of the precolonial type of Ewe government. The early German missionaries wrote of the Ewe **Stämme** (tribes) when discussing the component sovereign groups (the administrative Divisions), a usage taken over by Rattray (Spieth 1906, 1911, Westermann 1935, Rattray 1915). Subsequent English ethnographers have used 'sub-tribe' to refer to the same entities, implicitly assuming that the Ewe people as a whole formed one large 'tribe' (Manoukian 1952, Ward 1949). Nukunya, who hails from Anlo proper, uses alternatively 'kingdom', 'chiefdom' and 'tribe' (Nukynya 1969). Friedländer calls them 'states' (**Staat**) and Asamoa, an inland Ewe himself (although from a group of Anlo extraction) compares the Ewe-dome Divisions to the Akan **oman**, a political group which shares many of the features of 'chiefdoms' as defined by Service (Friedländer 1962, Asamoa 1972, Service 1962). Bukh writes of 'chieftaincies' (1979:15) while Kludze insists on the overlordship and paramountcy of the **fiagã** (1973:16).

All of them agree, however, in treating the 'group of villages acknowledging a common **fiagã**, or otherwise-titled Paramount Chief' as the precolonial sovereign political group, a usage deeply rooted in administrative thinking since Rattray's report on the 'tribal history' of the inland Ewe (1915). However, the whole debate surrounding the report at the time it was written has unfortunately been ignored. After ousting their Akwamu oppressors in 1833 the Abutias, together with many other northern groups, acknowledged the 'overlordship' (the term is Rattray's) of the Kpekis who led them during their rebellion. In view of these historical events, the Kpeki chief claimed the role of the traditional ruler of all the inland Divisions, and demanded that the British colonial officers treat him accordingly. The nature of this overlordship was very nebulous, but the claim was serious enough to raise a difficult question: which level of grouping were the administrators going to identify as the traditionally sovereign one - the Division (or group of villages), or the group of Divisions united under Kpeki?

Rattray mustered sufficient evidence to demonstrate that Kpeki never 'ruled' over northern Eweland, but was simply accorded precedence in a military alliance. Rattray's report was nevertheless not heeded by subsequent administrators who repeatedly tried to create 'super-states' in the 1930s, by bringing together a number of Divisions under one of the more prestigious ones. They thus formed "the Peki (i.e., Kpeki) State under Peki, the Asogli State under Ho, the Hokpe State (sometimes called the Avatime State) under Avatime, and the Akpini State under Kpando (i.e., Kpandu)" (Kludze 1973:12). The colonial and national governments thus oscillated between an administration based on Divisions, or one based on those large 'States'. At the time of fieldwork, the States had been rescinded.

Rattray, however, arbitrarily reduced the issue to a single alternative. After all, the Germans were the first 'invaders' and their emissaries singled out the villages as the main administrative units, directly responsible to the District (**Kreis**) Governor. The German colonial officers treated the village chiefs as the traditional rulers. Was this another instance of administrative expediency, or did the Germans know something which eluded their British successors? I am inclined to believe that their first-hand contact with the precolonial groups had taught them one thing, namely that the villages were the sovereign political groups in the 1880s. Although this hypothesis departs radically from the accepted model of Ewe precolonial political organization, it seems to me a more seminal idea, and the remainder of this first part will be dedicated to demonstrating its greater plausibility.

If precolonial Abutia villages were sovereign, one would therefore expect (1) that in matters calling for legislative, administrative and judiciary action (excluding commercial and religious concerns), no group would have been formed above the village and, (2) that the membership of these groups would be restricted to villagers.

1. I have come across no evidence whatsoever suggesting that trials for **yiāwo, guwo** and **nuvɔ** were under the jurisdiction of a group above the village. I have indeed gained the firm impression that disputes involving individuals from different villages would be peacefully settled by the assembled elders of the two

villages concerned, meeting as equals to solve their problems. Confrontation was unnecessary; many of the village elders were kinsmen, and eager to reach a compromise; similarly, when discord arose between individuals of friendly neighbouring areas, a comparable method was used. Between hostile areas, no settlement was possible and, by definition, conflict between foes could only be resolved in homicide and warfare.

In legislative and administrative matters, moreover, I have found no indication that groups were formed either above or below the village level. Only village authorities could take action on matters of collective concern. Kludze quite explicitly mentions that there was traditionally no separate legislative body, but that legislation was created through adjudication of the village council of elders presided over by the chief. When unprecedented cases called for new legislation the elders would thus reach a consensus about the stance to take, and this new decision would be promulgated as law (Kludze 1973: 27).

2. Membership of judiciary councils, with some variation, was confined to villagers themselves; citizens of other villages were only called upon as witnesses if their testimony was relevant, but not as jury and judges. In legislative and administrative groups (i.e., when the Council of Elders was convened) membership was still more strictly restricted to individuals who were members of one of the village's minimal lineages.

These particular facts support the hypothesis of village sovereignty between 1870 and 1890, but others seem to negate it. Two offences, namely witchcraft and homicide, did indeed call for the presence of elders from all three villages, together with the **fiagā** or one of his representatives. Other cases could be taken to the priest of Atando, the Abutia High God.

If one equated **yiāwo** with our notion of civil offences, and **gu** and **nuvɔ** with the notion of moral offences, witchcraft and homicide could then be described as the only two **criminal** offences in precolonial Abutia. The penalty they incurred – that of exile – matched their criminal status. The seriousness of the exile, however, varied according to the gravity of the offence. As mentioned earlier, all instances of death induced by human agents using natural weapons were treated as manslaughter and the question of motivation never arose. In witchcraft, on the other hand, the means may be supernatural but the motives are clear. Deaths resulting from witchcraft are not accidental, and the penalty for such actions was found to be the most severe. The witch was completely exiled from Abutia lands. To compound this fate, elders usually add in a confidential tone that these malefactors actually met their death in the hands of the **asafo** (army), in the no man's land that separates neighbouring Divisions. They escaped public execution in the village only because Togbe Atando prohibited the spilling of human blood on Abutia soil.

A man accused of homicide or manslaughter would be ostracized in a much milder way[33]. He, together with the members of his minimal lineage, would have been compelled to leave the village and settle a few hundred yards away, in the 'bush'. The ban was only temporary and they would be called back to the village after a few weeks or months (I was unable to find any agreement about the period of time, which varied from eight days to three months according to the elders). His recall depended on a special ritual which was performed to close the case and 'seal the memory'. The ritual consisted in burying a pot with its mouth towards the earth (**zedzēdidi**), and any mention of the event after this ceremony was **ipso facto** litigious[34].

Interestingly enough, the symbolism which surrounds these two offences underlines their exceptional nature and treats them as instances of 'internal war'. The victims of both witchcraft and manslaughter were considered to have died 'accidental deaths', called 'death in war' (**ametsiavhame**), the province of the **asafo**. Wars are external threats which the Abutia symbolically regard as having to be 'pushed outside'. Exile was consequently the logical outcome of an internal war, implemented as it was by the **asafo**. This symbolic equation, furthermore, suggests that the precolonial Abutia did not have any notion of 'criminal offence'. All cases which could be handled by groups up to the village level and only involved payments were regarded as civil or religious-moral infractions. Criminal actions (which entailed exile), either voluntary or accidental, were actually construed as military offences. The council summoned for their arbitration, and to which the **fiagā** was invited, could therefore be interpreted as a martial court applying martial law. And the procedure for summoning, and the composition of this court, speak for themselves. The trial did not take place in the **fiagā's** village and council. On the contrary, it was the chief of the village where the crime had been perpetrated who convened an assembly of elders, to which chiefs and elders of the other villages were beckoned. Among them was necessarily the **fiagā**. I was not able to find out whether the **fiagā** would have conducted the proceedings (he did not in the only witchcraft case which occurred during fieldwork, since the High Priest of Agove took charge of the matter), and I have no reason to believe that he necessarily did. The facts that **fiagā** and other **dufiawo** were requested to attend the proceedings (if they were absent, they would have been represented by one of their titled office-holders, most likely their **tsiame**) points to a military **alliance**, but not to aggregation. To decide more definitely on this, let us look at the military organization.

In the conduct of warfare the Abutia say they formed one army (the last wars were fought in the early 1870s, so that no elder alive had any first-hand experience with colonial warfare) but they also claim that the three villages acted as three separate battalions, each under the more immediate leadership of its own army 'chief' (**asafo-fia**). Teti's army occupied the centre part of the military formation, it is said, Agove the right wing and Kloe the left. Every battalion seems to have operated autonomously, however, and it is highly doubtful that the Teti army chief even had any authority to coordinate the activities and movements of the three battalions.

The Abutia **asafo** was an army of citizens; the ownership of a gun automatically entitled a man to membership of his village **asafo**, and adult males were in possession of such weapons. The 'handing over of a gun' was in fact the only **rite de passage** which marked the transition to independence for men. A man thus purchased a gun for every one of his male children who reached maturity. This rifle was presented ceremonially, in the presence of the child's parents, parents' parents (if they were alive) and parents' siblings, and the rite announced his maturity and autonomy, and entitled him to get married and join the army...

The **asafo**'s internal structure appears to have been rudimentary. Its democratic recruitment also left room for individual exploits. The **asafofia** (army-leader within one village) distinguished himself from the mass of citizen-soldiers by his possession of more powerful war-medicines and his ritual knowledge. In war as in ritual performance (as, for instance, when burying people

who died accidentally, a responsibility of the **asafo**),
the **asafo** was thus led by a man who had been elected
to his superior position because of his personal qualities
and powers. The position of army leader had therefore to
be legitimated on every military occasion through a
demonstration of courage and prowess, and an army leader
could be dismissed if the soldiers were dissatisfied with
his performance[46]. In actual combat, it seems that
every man more or less fought for himself, although people
from the same village are said to have fought close to one
another. I have recorded from some elders that the
dufia followed the warriors of his own village and
that his drum served as their rallying-point; if he were
captured with his drum, the village surrendered. How one
village could capitulate apart from the other two was not
clear to anyone. I personally suspect that the Abutia
never fought any major war on their own, but always joined
with neighbouring areas when hostilities were afoot.
Small skirmishes might have called for the coordinate
action of a single Division but fully-fledged wars could
hardly have done so, if one considers that some Divisions
were composed of one village only and that the smallest
Division, in the 1930s, numbered only 300 inhabitants
(Kludze 1973: 13).

Furthermore, any **asafofia**, that of Teti like that
of Kloe or Agove, derived his authority from the council
of Elders of his village, of which he was automatically a
member. He was not therefore empowered to initiate any
military action on his own, nor on the **dufia's**
recommendation, since both would only act on the whole
council's instruction. Since the village Councils of
Elders seem to have been the ultimate legislative bodies
and were not aggregated in the Division, it is difficult
to envisage how the village armies could have been
aggregated into a Divisional army. The very mode of
recruitment to army leadership and the 'individualist'
methods of fighting rather support the thesis that the
armies were autonomous, but allied. I would thus regard
the three Abutia villages as allied, but not aggregated,
in military matters. And the same holds for the religious
organization[36].

Togbe Atando, the Abutia High God, stood (and still
stands) at the apex of the pantheon of Abutia divinities,
and his power exceeded (and still does) by far that of any
other god (stools included). His priest behaved **ipso
facto** as the High Priest of Abutia, although he operated
completely independently from the **fiagā**. Indeed,

there existed no connection whatsoever between Togbe
Atando and the stools, and the spiritual prestige of the
High Priest far surpassed that of the **fiagã**.   Some
lawsuits could therefore be withdrawn from the secular
courts and submitted to the High Priest.   These were
actually tried according to religious law in a religious
court but, in this instance once more, there was no
aggregation of any group.   Togbe Atando was simply the
highest ranking God to whom supplicants could turn when
other pleas failed, but there was no system of religious
courts aggregated into that of Togbe Atando, or of
religious 'parishes' aggregated into Atando's 'diocese'.
It is simply that, as the most powerful god in Abutia,
Atando's prohibitions extended to all Abutia citizens or
those residing on Abutia lands; to this extent, all three
villages could be described as allied in his cult.

In external trade, furthermore, every Division formed
part of a rotating market system integrating four
neighbouring Divisions.   I was told by some elders that
the main Abutia market-place used to be located in Kloe,
but it now stands in Teti, where market is held every four
days.   The Abutia market-place is located outside but near
the village (and this seems to be typical of northern Ewe
markets) and is protected by a special divinity (a **trɔ**,
which missionaries and administrators have translated as
'fetish') who has its own priest.   Nowadays, this priest
plays no role in the organization of the market and, from
the little that I could gather, it seems that precolonial
markets also required little policing and organization.
The great majority of traders were women and, unlike other
West African markets, the Abutia market did not serve
either as a major cross-road, or as headquarters for
regional courts arbitrating disputes between areas which
otherwise had no means of communication.   It is therefore
impossible to speak of 'administrative aggregation' in the
case of these northern Ewe markets and, even if we could,
it would in no way undermine the thesis of the
political sovereignty of villages.

Overall, then, the meagre available evidence about
precolonial Abutia supports the view that, in legislative,
administrative, judiciary, military, religious and
economic matters, the villages were not aggregated into
the Division.   The villages were politically sovereign,
but allied in defence, religion and external trade.   We
will now investigate whether the further implications of
village sovereignty also tally with other features of the
political organization of precolonial, or even
contemporary 'traditional', Abutia.

IV. VILLAGE SOVEREIGNTY: ITS POLITICAL IMPLICATIONS

A. *Within the village*

If membership of a minimal lineage is mostly gained through patrifiliation, and matrifiliation in special circumstances (the situation which prevailed, and still does, in Abutia), and if villages are also sovereign, it will follow that a person is only a citizen in his or her father's locality, and that of his or her mother in special situations only. Outside these localities, people are 'strangers' (**amedzro**), people without any citizenship, without anybody to stand for them in times of trouble.

This corollary applies well enough to precolonial Abutia, although the matter is complicated by the political inequality of the sexes. Women were indeed excluded from membership of legislative, administrative, military and most judicial groups, whereas all men could hope to join these groups if they lived long enough. Women's political 'status' (defined in terms of the membership of groups to which they were entitled) thus rated lower than that of men. This fact made it easier for them (not psychologically, but politically) to follow their husbands when marriages took place across villages.

Including these instances of village out-marriage, a male child's domicile and citizenship could therefore be determined in one of four ways only: (a) in cases of village in-marriage, a child could not elect domicile outside his native village; he was a citizen of that village only. (b) Where the parents came from different villages but the children had been brought up in their father's village, they (the male children, let us remember) would be welcome guests in their mother's village but would nevertheless derive their citizenship from their paternal village. (c) In case of village out-marriage where the children were brought up in their mother's village, they enjoyed dual citizenship. The father could certainly 'claim' his children back as they reached adolescence, but the latter were welcome to remain in their mother's village if they so chose. (d) Children without an acknowledged genitor would automatically belong to their mother's father's minimal lineage and would only be citizens in their mother's village. The Abutia also characterize this distinction by contrasting **Kloe-vi** (Kloe-child, born to one of its women outside the village) to **Kloe-tɔ** (Kloe-citizen, belonging to the village, that is who was born to one of its male citizens).

The situation was identical for female children, except in case (b). If brought up in their father's village, women might in fact be married back into their mother's; a woman, if reared in her mother's village would thus have little incentive to move back to her father's when he claimed her. Women also refused to be married into villages where they had no matrilateral kin; for, as complete strangers, they could only have counted on their husband's support in case of disputes, and this uncomfortable situation made sucn marriages almost impossible. To force a girl into a union in a completely alien village would have been tantamount to selling her into slavery, unless she had already been pawned there as a child.

Not only the past, but also the present pattern of village domicile tallies with the notion of precolonial village sovereignty. Teti indeed never acted as a capital to which individuals would flock in the hope of sharing in the windfalls of power. Whatever mobility between the villages there was and still is (when it comes to settlement and domicile) is limited to village out-marriage; apart from this connubial exchange, extremely few men have settled outside their father's or mother's village (i.e., the one from which they derived citizenship).

The above corollary also influenced the citizens' relationship to their **dufia**. Indeed, a man's domicile in a village was an intrinsic corollary of his birth into one of the village's minimal lineages. Although the village's various clans were aggregated into one locality (the **du**), the **dufia** could not be construed as a 'territorial ruler'; by being domiciled in a village, a man did not express subjection to the head of an administrative unit, nor was it meant to be a personal bond to the chief or headman of the village, as one often finds in some African chiefdoms. Nor did a man's settlement in a locality express kinship preferences, as obtained in Nuer localities (Evans-Pritchard 1951). In the great majority of cases, a man's father's village was the only place in the world whence he could derive his citizenship, so that his domicile did not spring from any type of personal commitment. Knowing about the citizens' lack of personal commitment to their **dufia**, however, does intimate little about **his** 'rule' over the village and, to elucidate this aspect, it is necessary to understand his relationship to other titled office-holders within the village.

If my conjectures are right, chiefship as presented in this monograph had only been instituted for twenty years (1870-1890) before the imposition of colonial rule. In this relatively short span, many of its constitutional problems had not yet been suitably resolved. Since then, the tenure of chiefs has been frequently disputed, and the position of other office-holders has been ignored by the colonial administration. As a result, every office-holder claims to be the 'acting chief' or 'regent' because of the obvious pay-off of occupying this position in a situation in which disputes over chieftaincy are endemic. In such a confused state of affairs, it has proved more profitable to seek enlightenment in an area where the evidence is less discrepant. As was mentioned earlier, the **sămewo** are also religious corporations, and the **fiawo** are in fact priests of a special divinity, the 'stool'. The stools are enshrined ritual objects in which dwells the spirit of a **trɔ̄** from which the chief derives his power. Like the famous Ashanti stools, the Abutia stool is carved out of a single piece of wood and kept hidden in a room, designated as the 'stool-room' (**zikpui-xɔme**). The stool is always wrapped in a sheep-skin and white calico, and kept on a table so as not to touch the ground. It is named after the god whose abode it is. The spirit in the stool is neither an ancestral soul (**togbeŋɔ̄li**) nor the soul of former chiefs, as has been recorded in some southern areas.

Every village recognizes only one of its two or three clan stools as the village stool, and the heads of two other clans carry titles defined with respect to that village stool. Such are the **tsiame** (derived from the Akan **okyeame**, or 'linguist') and the **mankraɖo** (from the Akan **amankrado**, or 'regent'). The **dufia, tsiame** and **mankraɖo** occupy the central offices in the political organization. The occurrence of other offices associated with other clan stools is utterly random, showing neither a recurrent pattern, nor any articulation between the three villages. In Kloe, for instance, one finds a Siehene (most likely derived from the Akan **gyasehene**). The position does not exist in any of the other two villages, and the Siehene never had any jurisdiction outside Kloe. In the village of Teti, one **sămefia** bears the title of **tsiriɖom** (most likely derived from Twi **kyidomhene**), an office unique to Teti and only operative within its boundaries. These 'random' stool-linked offices do nevertheless share one common feature, in that their holders claim a traditional role in war. For example, the Kloe Siehene now contends, among other things..., that his forefathers' task in warfare was to keep a look-out on the rear of the army; and again, the Teti **tsiridom** believes his forbears to have been responsible for the distribution of gunpowder and ammunition during battles.

In addition to these offices, two more are also found within stool-owning clans, namely that of **zikpi-tɔ**, or 'stool-father' (sometimes referred to as **fia-tɔ**, or 'chief's father') and that of **tsɔfo**, or heir-apparent[37]. To understand the articulation of these diverse offices, one needs to know more about the religious categories, among which the **trɔwo** are found, and their study will suggest that the key to an understanding of the structure of titled offices ultimately lies in the ritual division of labour.

The Abutia villages are densely nucleated settlements within which no horticulture is practiced. This creates a clear and visible contrast between the village as a settlement (**gbɔme**) and the surrounding bush (**gbeme**), and one which is clearly echoed in the local symbolism where the town is represented as the 'inside' and the bush as the 'outside'. In this symbolic system, the 'inside' is always associated with purely positive elements (such as life, health, growth, fertility) whereas to the 'outside' are attached both positive and negative elements. 'Outside' is therefore an ambivalent category, being at the same time a source of life - as the place where food is farmed and animals hunted - and a cause of death - as the place where hunters get accidentally killed, where farmers occasionally suffer snake bites, and where wars have in the past been fought. The Abutia therefore pray to and worship their numerous divinities to secure their assistance in order to multiply both human and animal populations, to favour and promote life, growth and propagation of the species. They also seek the power to destroy life, either through hunting or killing enemies. A substantial number of supernatural beings fulfill this dual task of life-giving and protection (through destruction), and the most important for this study are the **dzowo** (sing. **dzo**), the **legba** and **trɔwo** (sing. **trɔ**).

A **dzo** is some form of magical object that only men can purchase (although prostitutes are now believed to resort to **dzowo** to attract clients...) and which serves the exclusive purpose of its purchaser. One usually obtains these magical objects ('juju' in pidgin English, or 'medicine' in anthropological literature) from 'medicine-men' who live outside the area. Powerful 'jujumen' (or 'medicine-men') spend years travelling the length and width of West Africa to procure these objects. A **dzo** partakes symbolically of the nature of 'outside' elements; it can help or hinder, cure or kill, protect or attack. As long as it remains a **dzo**, its positive or negative influence depends entirely upon its owner's inclination. An evil man will use the medicine for evil purposes, an honest citizen for constructive ones.

This ambivalence of the **dzo** can however be neutralized through some kind of 'collective purchasing'. Villages have been known to procure powerful **dzowo** to protect themselves against outside threats (including epidemics, such as smallpox). These magical objects were ritually buried outside the village's entrances (every village has two such 'symbolic gates' along the road - formerly a footpath - that links the three villages together), as what one might refer to as spiritual sentries. They are the **legba**, easily recognizable by the phallic shape of the stone which was placed on top of the medicine's burial site. Village elders thus sought to employ the **legba's** ambivalent potential in a positive way, to destroy potentially harmful external agents and thus protect the villagers. During my fieldwork some **legba** had their priest, but none of them was the object of any serious cult.

It is the **trɔwo** which really dominate the Abutia pantheon. The **dzo** one purchases, but the **trɔwo** choose their own priest. Two dominant categories of **trɔwo** can be distinguished: the **autochthonous earth trɔwo**, and the **immigrant celestial trɔwo**, a binary distinction which Spieth had already observed for Ho and northern areas in general (Spieth 1906: 443-445).

The autochthonous chthonic gods (known also as **tɔgbe-trɔwo**, literally 'ancestors' **trɔwo'**) are under the ritual responsibility of specific clans, from which they select their priest. They elect men exclusively as their officiants, but do not 'possess' them (i.e., the gods do not enter their body to produce a trance and speak through their mouth; in Ewe, **dze ame dzi**). They reveal their choice through divination, often in the following way. A pregnant woman will have a disquieting dream which an elder will construe as an omen. The case will then be reported to a diviner (normally a foreigner living in one of the immigrants' hamlets) who will announce the god's intervention and his selection of her child (if it is a boy!) as his priest. However, many of the rituals offered to earth gods are now falling into obsolescence, and many of their priests are self-appointed. Where the god has not manifested its will, the clan head or another elder will take over the ritual responsibility. The priests of these chthonic gods are known as **trɔnua**, or 'god's leader'. According to the elders, these divinities originate from Notsie, the Ewe Babel, and have always been with the Abutia. They dwell in the surrounding natural environment - in trees, rocks, caves, streams - and their rooting in the ground gives them power over fertility and life. Their influence is only benign, they never 'trouble' (**de fu na ame**) villagers, and cannot bring harm to the population.

In contrast, the immigrant gods dwell in stools which can never touch the ground, and they are notorious for killing citizens. They are not the property of any special clan, but are inherited in female lines. Their priesthood is handed down from mother to daughter, or to daughter's daughter. They select women as their priestesses and reveal their choice by inducing sickness and through direct 'possession'. They are designated as **mamatrɔwo** (i.e., ancestresses' gods) and their priestesses are known as **trɔsiwo** (sing. **trɔsi**), or 'god's wives'.

These celestial gods are new arrivals in Abutia history. During my stay, new ones were manifesting themselves (especially Mama-Water), and most of them (like Dente Kwasi) hail from Ashanti or the northern regions. They share the ambivalence of outside elements, capable both of decimating whole families as a punishment for ritual failures, or of bringing health and fertility to those afflicted.

The Abutia also conceive of their chiefs' stools as **trɔwo**, but **trɔwo** of a somewhat hybrid nature, which may be attributed to their origin. M.J. Field has argued that the original Ga **maŋtse** (chieftain) was a 'fetish-priest' (**trɔwo** are also translated as 'fetishes' by missionaries and ethnographers) who procured a stool as a potent war-medicine in order to fight back the Ashanti (Field 1940: 72-74). Hugo Huber has reached a similar conclusion about the Krobo (Huber 1963). There is equally strong evidence that the Abutia borrowed the institution of the stool from the Ashanti, since all the paraphernalia and insignia surrounding chiefship bear a

direct Ashanti trade-mark, and all the war songs in Abutia
are in Twi. None of the Kloe stools, moreover, had had
more than six incumbents, including the comtemporary one,
since their inception (and in one case only four). Some
of the elders, finally, openly confessed that their
ancestors did not have stools, but **dzowu** (literally a
'juju-outfit', that is, some kind of attire completely
covered with **dzowo**). All these facts converge to
suggest a possible adoption of stools as **trɔwo** in the
late 1860s and early 1870s, during the last Ashanti wars.
I would also surmise that chiefship itself dates back to
the same period. As it was abruptly terminated in 1890 by
the German invasion, the life-span of this 'traditional'
political organization was only twenty years!

Whether or not the stools were actually purchased as
war-medicines or captured from the enemy, one crucial fact
remains: they were adopted and actually 'internalized',
not as **legba** in the way that collectively purchased
dzowo are, but as a new kind of **trɔ**. The stools
thus share the origin of the celestial gods, namely the
'outside', as well as their type of abode (a normal
rectangular room attached to a house) but, unlike them,
they only work towards positive ends, do not 'trouble'
people and do not possess their priest. During the
enstoolment ceremony, however (see Appendix 3) the priest
of the stool, the **fia**-designate is 'seized' or caught
by strong men **against his will,** in the same way as the
priestess of a celestial god is 'attacked' and 'possessed'
by her god. Like his female counterpart, the **fia**
cannot refuse the office without facing the immediate
threat of madness. Unlike other men, chiefs must not be
circumcized so that, symbolically speaking, they remain
more like women. Unlike his female counterpart, however,
the priest of a stool cannot fall into a trance and 'speak
the god' (**fho trɔ**)[38].

This very fact that the stool is a **trɔ** automatically makes the **fia** a priest and this appears to
be the element needed to understand the structure of
titled offices in Abutia. To substantiate this view, I
will review the manner in which labour is divided in
rituals to the **trɔwo**.

The priestess of a celestial god is only a 'medium'.
She literally acts as the 'voice of the **trɔ**'; when
possessed, she falls into a trance and 'speaks the god'.
During rituals, she behaves as an intermediary between the
assembled crowd and the god, and acts as some kind of
interpreter, listening to the questions from the audience

and uttering the god's reply. The priestess strikes the observer as the main 'actor' in the rites, but she does little to prepare the stage. This is done by her 'manager', or ritual 'attorney' (to borrow an expression from Van Velsen 1964), who is responsible for the preparation and organization of the ritual, and some of its performance. It is the priestess' real or classificatory father who acts as her ritual attorney. In secular life, this person is jurally responsible for her, a responsibility which is carried over into her ritual obligation. The ritual attorney, however, does not merely play a subordinate part; when the sacrificial meat is carved and distributed, the 'father' receives the head and the priestess is given the chest. They explain that the head controls, organizes things, whereas the chest stands for the organs of speech and seat of emotions, always subordinated to cerebral activity. Thus, as far as the worship of celestial gods is concerned, the priestess' father represents the head and she is only the voice[39].

This division of labour is mirrored in rituals to autochthonous earth gods (tɔgbe-trɔwo). Chthonic deities are 'mute'; their priest is therefore not a 'medium' but his priestly role, like that of any ritual officiant, is in fact limited to that of an intermediary between clan members and villagers who seek divine assistance, and the deity itself. The priest's main task is to pray, to talk to the god and beg for fertility. The preparation, organization of the ritual, as well as many of its activities, devolve upon another elder who also acts as a ritual attorney. He is usually the clan head, who acts as the priest's 'father'. When a priest becomes a clan head, the role of ritual attorney then passes on to another elder who stands in **loco parentis** towards him. There is indeed an infallible rule in Abutia and northern Eweland that every individual, regardless of his or her age, can always designate a person who stands towards him or her in **loco parentis,** even if that person is younger. This is in accordance with the custom that everyone needs somebody to speak on his or her behalf.

The same division of labour is repeated in stool rituals. Like other priests, the **fia** cannot act ritually on his own behalf. He needs a ritual manager, an elder who will take it upon himself to see that the ritual is performed. The **fia's** ritual attorney cannot be the clan head, since the **fia** himself represents the clan, so the task is fulfilled by the head of the **fia's** own

agbanu. Already acting as the **fia**'s father in
jural matters, the lineage head also takes up ritual
responsibility for the stool, whence comes his title of
fia-tɔ or **zikpi-tɔ** (chief's father, or
stool-father). These facts suggest a strict
correspondence between (a) the **trɔsi** and her **tɔ**
(the priestess and her father), (b) the **trɔnua** and his
sāmemetsitsi and, (c) the **fia** and his **zikpi-tɔ**
(the chief and his stool-father, or lineage head).

The **fia**, as priest of a stool, is therefore little
more than a 'medium', or an intermediary between his
people and the spirit of the stool. He addresses the
divinity in the stool, prays to it and observes its
taboos[40]. It is nonetheless the stool-father who
provides the sacrificial animal, who actually sacrifices
to the stool, and who washes and purifies it with the
blood of the animal sacrificed. It is the stool-father
who organizes the stool's yearly **tedudu** (or 'yam
festival', to which a sheep is sacrificed[41]). The
fia 'communicates' with the stool through prayers and
ritual observance, but it is the stool-father who, as head
of a religious corporation owning a stool, is actually in
charge of it. Only he, together with elders of the clan
and their **srɔnyi**, can actually see and touch the
stool. Only elderly men have **srɔnyi**, who are
described as the children of a sister who married into
another clan. By extension, the **srɔnyi** also include
those elders from other clans who are the descendants of
ancestors' sisters who married into other clans. They are
in fact cognates of the clan elders so that the group
formed in rituals to stools, like judiciary councils,
assembles cognates.

Furthermore, the stool-room is located in the stool-
father's house, and **not** the chief's, and the **zikpi-
tɔ** is entitled to enter the stool-room at any time.
Some chiefs told me that they were only allowed to enter
the stool-room on the day of their investiture. When a
stool-father or a chief dies, the stool is taken to the
new stool-father who either builds or reserves a special
room for it in his house. During the Nkrumah regime, the
Kloe stool-father fled with the village stool to Togo,
because his own candidate was forcibly removed from office
by the C.P.P., (Nkrumah's party). Such extreme action
could only be sanctioned in a **zikpi-tɔ**. It is also
quite obvious that, with the stool moving houses with
every new stool-father, one does not find in Abutia the
tɔgbefheme (or 'ancestral home', i.e., house of the

apical ancestor who settled in the place, and where his shrine is kept) typical of Anlo proper.

This responsibility over the stool itself accounts for the stool-father's powerful influence in traditional constitutional matters.   Because of his proximity to the stool and his ritual attorney-ship, the stool-father was (and still is, in 'normal' circumstances) expected to select the candidate for chiefship; he alone wielded (and still wields) the ritual authority necessary to 'enstool' a chief, and is consequently empowered to 'destool' the person he has ordained into office.   To repeat the description used by the Abutia themselves, the stool-father is the 'king-maker'.   This interpretation also agrees with the facts adduced by Kludze.   He mentions, among other things, that the Ewe-dome chiefs had no control over the 'stool-lands' (Kludze 1973).   The lands, indeed, were **agbanu** property and the **agbanu**, as a corporation, was represented by its **ametsitsi.**   It is thus he who had the power to dispose of the proceeds accruing from the stool lands, since he was the one responsible for the expenses incurred by sacrifices to the stool.   Since he had to carry the financial burden of rituals to the stool, he enjoyed the meagre benefits from the stool lands.

The stool rituals have now shed some light on the relationship between **fia** and **zikpi-tɔ**, but they seem to cast no light whatsoever on the other offices. The **tsiame** and **mankradɔ** positions, it will be recalled, are not defined with reference to a divinity of their own clan, but vis-à-vis the village stool.   The principles of this articulation are therefore to be sought at a different level in the religious symbolism.

The immigrant gods both assist and 'trouble' the villagers, and both their shrine and spirit are found within the settlement.   Autochthonous gods, on the other hand, can only act in a positive fashion, but their aid is restricted to fertility and growth - indeed, they are powerless against outside threats.   Their shrines are built at the periphery of the village, but these do not constitute their real abode.   The spirit of the god itself dwells in natural sites, outside the village.

In some ways, the stools surpass other divinities (with the exception of Togbe Atando).   Stools do not kill people unless they are called upon by the swearing of an oath to avenge a victim, and they enjoy the dual power of both increasing fertility within the village (and the forest), while protecting the settlement against external dangers.

Their influence is thus mostly positive, and they operate both internally and externally. Like the immigrant deities, their spirit actually resides within their shrine, in the village.

I would be tempted to regard these cosmological factors as accounting for the facts (a) that the spiritual power of the stool exceeds that of other deities and, (b) that the spiritual power of the **fia** outdoes that of other priests. I would believe that the stool confers on its priest additional spiritual command, to the extent that the **fia** comes to be regarded as the living repository of the stool's spirit. This notion would only apply to village stools; other stools obviously do not wield the same power to defend in war and against external perils, and fail to gain the ascendancy over the village stool. This interpretation enables us to suggest a model of the relationship of **dufia, tsiame** and **mankrado**.

During the enstoolment ceremony, strong warriors catch the selected candidate by surprise and sit him forcibly on the sheep-skin which covers the stool. This 'seizure' is said to be necessitated by the individual's reluctance to become chief. The contact with the stool 'wrapping' is the critical gesture which makes him **dufia**. Through this physical contact, the spirit of the stool takes up abode in him and any human resistance to this spiritual osmosis would result in madness. As a consequence of this spiritual 'invasion', the **dufia** partakes of the stool's own nature. He is transformed into a visible, public version of the stool (the real one being always hidden from sight), the living repository of the stool's spirit. This is manifested by the fact that the **dufia**, and the **dufia** alone, is publicly addressed by the name of the stool god. The spirit of the Kloe stool, for instance, is Togbe Ayipe. The chief of that stool is consequently known and addressed as Togbe Ayipe. Priestesses of celestial gods, on the other hand, are only addressed by the name of their god when they are in trance and 'speaking the god'; and the priests of earth gods and other clan stools are not addressed by the name of their divinity at all.

Villagers have to treat the **dufia** as an incarnation of the stool, somewhat as they would have to treat a **trɔ**; as a public and secular (and therefore much weaker) version of the divinity, however, the **dufia** only requires a secular priest and attorney. Consequently, if we represent the **dufia** as a 'secular incarnation' of the stool, the roles of **tsiame** and

mankraḍo could then be defined respectively as those of 'intermediary' (i.e., secular priest) and 'attorney' between the **dufia** himself and the mass of citizens.

The **tsiame** is indeed the 'priest' of a human divinity, he is the very 'voice of the chief', as the **dufia** himself represents a 'verbal intermediary' between the stool and his people (the **tsiame** is a 'priest' twice removed....). The **tsiame** (or 'linguist' in administrative English) acts as an 'interpreter' between the villagers and the chief when the latter is addressed in his capacity of **dufia**. A village chief, **qua dufia**, cannot be greeted or addressed directly, nor does he converse directly with his interlocutors. The linguist functions as an intermediary (like a priest), repeating requests and replies between chief and audience. He also works as the chief's messenger, a function which is ritually institutionalized through the 'linguist-staff' (**tsiame-ti**). A third replica of the stool, the linguist-staff represents a material public version of the divine object. In the chief's absence, the linguist carries the linguist-staff and herein lies his authority, derived ultimately from the stool. The ritual care of this sacred pole also devolves upon him; he sacrifices to it in the same way, although on a smaller scale, that the chief sacrifices to his stool. The selection and investiture of the linguist are also reminiscent of those of the **dufia**, and he shares the latter's ritual observances.

If the chief is a weak, public incarnation of the stool (thus being infinitely less 'divine' than the Anlo Awoamefia or the Yoruba Oni, who were not allowed to be seen by their 'subjects') and the **tsiame** his public and 'secular' priest, the **mankraḍo** is therefore the attorney, the key organizer in secular matters pertaining to chiefship. Cases to be heard by the chief were channelled through him, as he was meant to administer all dealings between villagers and village chief. As attorney to strangers and citizens wishing to deal with the chief, the **mankraḍo** also worked as their representative, as the one who spoke on their behalf.

Unlike the **tsiame**, the **mankraḍo** lacks any ritual embodiment of his authority. He possesses neither stool nor staff, nor any other cult object. A 'manager' of chiefly affairs, his authority does not emanate from any special association with spiritual entities; it springs from the fact that he is backed by the whole community, as the citizens' representative.

It is thus the dual dimension of the village stool which connects these various offices. As a clan property, it remains concealed in the stool-room, like any other deity (although, unlike other cult objects, it is brought out once every three years to be washed in a river). This represents the clanship or 'private' dimension of the stool, with the **fia** as its priest and the **zikpi-tɔ** as its ritual attorney. As a war-medicine, on the other hand, it gave its priest pre-eminence within the village and became a community concern. In the process, the stool's **fia** himself came to represent a public and 'secular' version of the stool, with the **tsiame** as his 'voice' (priest) and the **mankrado** as his 'attorney' (see Diagram VII).

This interpretation has nevertheless left two questions unanswered: (a) what was the place of the **tsofo** in this structure and, (b) who was most likely to be the 'legitimate' acting chief during the chief's absence, and regent during interregna?

The office of **fia** rotates between all the lineages of a clan, since the stool is a clan, and not a lineage, property. But such purely demographic matters as the excessive longevity of two successive chiefs could seriously jeopardize this principle in a society without literacy (as recollections of past reigns would be blurred, or even distorted), and some sort of safety mechanism had thus to be evolved. This would seem to account for the existence of a **tsofo.** An heir-apparent is indeed chosen during the life-time of a chief, allegedly to live close to the **dufia** and learn about village affairs. This, however, contradicts the notion of secrecy surrounding the selection of candidates and the nomination of a **tsofo** would seem to me to be a simple mnemonic device. When a chief dies, the **tsofo** is a possible candidate, but not necessarily the designated one. His very existence, however, reminds the elders which lineage is next in line for the chiefship. If a chief from lineage A dies, the **tsofo** from lineage B would either be enstooled if accepted as candidate, or his presence would indicate to which lineage the chiefship now belonged. Upon enstoolment of the new chief from lineage B, a new **tsofo** from lineage C would be nominated, thus ensuring the smooth rotation of chiefship when the chief from lineage B came to die. If the office of **fia** is to rotate, a reminder is necessary.

The two offices of **zikpi-tɔ** and **tsofo** thus represented the more 'private' face of chiefship. As

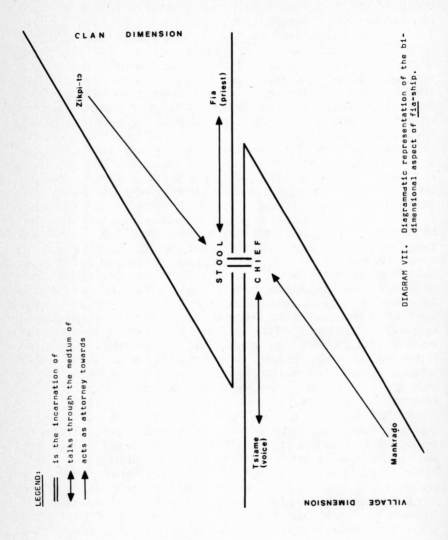

CLAN DIMENSION

Zikpi-tc

Fia
(priest)

STOOL

CHIEF

Tsiame
(voice)

Mankraḍo

VILLAGE DIMENSION

LEGEND:

|| is the incarnation of

↕ talks through the medium of

↑ acts as attorney towards

DIAGRAM VII. Diagrammatic representation of the bi-
dimensional aspect of fia-ship.

clansmen and sometimes close kinsmen of the chief, these two office-holders were expected to share his everyday life, almost as members of his household. As such they acted as private counsellors and their influence counter balanced that of the chief's more public office-holders, the tsiame and the mankrado.

On the matters of regency and acting chiefship, however, the solution is more conjectural. The two tasks diverge significantly; an acting chief only attends to the secular matters of chiefship (judicial and administrative) whereas a regent would have been called to perform the stool rituals should the interregnum last long. During a chief's absence, the mankrado could certainly function by himself, since the chief wields no special legislative, judiciary or executive powers separate from those of the whole council, and since his authority was more or less limited to that of summoning those councils. As a person, he might have used his personal charisma or persuasive skills to enforce certain decisions, but these would not form constitutional privileges. Nothing could therefore impede the mankrado from putting the whole judiciary machinery into action.

A regency, on the other hand, requires the ritual capacity of sacrificing to the stool. In the yearly rites to the other gods, the ritual attorney is always entitled to replace the priest, in the event of the latter's incapacity to perform the ceremony. Only a stool-father could therefore substitute himself for the chief to accomplish the stool's annual 'yam festival'. From the logic of this ritual model, I would thus conclude that the mankrado seemed the designated person to behave as acting chief, while the stool-father was probably the only one to take over as a regent.

Admittedly, I do not claim that the sovereignty of villages would account for the peculiarites of this system of titled offices, but it does seem to explain one key feature of this organization, namely the dufia's lack of any real power. Large settlements aggregated on the basis of territoriality and sovereign, for instance (and here I would be tempted to include, perhaps rashly, the Tswana, or Yakö, or Tonu towns, or ports of trade like Ouidah), have evolved centralized forms of government. Small sovereign settlements composed of various descent groups not aggregated on the basis of territoriality like those of precolonial Abutia[42] - and here I have in mind, perhaps wrongly, the Mbembe, Dida, Pueblos or Yanomamö - seem, on the other hand, incompatible with

centralized authority and despotic rule, for reasons as
yet not satisfactorily clear to me. Abutia's diffuse
power base and the dufia's concomitant lack of real
power, I would therefore regard as a corollary of village
sovereignty, whereas his relationship to other title-
holders, I view as peculiar to Abutia and Ewe-dome
polities.

B. Between villages

If precolonial villages were sovereign, furthermore, the
village chief was then a citizen and ritual custodian in
hiw own village only, his ritual functions being confined
to the very boundaries of his locality. This situation
seems indeed to have prevailed in the Abutia of 1870-1890,
where no dufia appears to have had any jurisdiction
outside his own village, and where no village chief could
vie with the chiefs of other villages for political
allegiance. Any competition between chiefs of different
villages was thereby precluded. Every office or position
of authority was closed in on itself, and did not lead to
a higher one. A clan chief was indeed confined forever to
clan chiefship; he could never aspire to become village
chief, as only the 'chiefly clan' gave the village its
dufia. No village chief ever nursed any hopes of
being enstooled as fiagā, since the title belonged to
the Teti dufia. The offices were all 'terminal';
there was no upward mobility from office to office through
the interplay of political allegiances and manipulations.
The size of any political group, therefore, depended
entirely upon natural increases; movements of population
between villages were practically ruled out. To put it
briefly, the relationship between titled officers, and
between dufiawo and fiagā, was eminently static.

A stranger outside his own village, the Paramount Chief
was forbidden to interfere in the politics of other
villages. When his presence was required, he would
actually come to the village where the case was tried,
instead of assembling a council in his own village. Of a
Paramount Chief, the Abutia fiagā thus possessed very
few of the features! Paramount Chiefs usually stand at
the apex of what Service has labelled 'redistributional
economies' (Service 1962:44). Such economies operate over
a territory which is ex definitione larger than one
single locality, and which is unified through this
particular mechanism. Abutia clans were not united within
the villages through accumulation and redistribution,

since they all equally shared in government, nor were the villages thus united within the Division. Neither the **fiagā** nor any of the **dufiawo** were ever in a position to attract followers to their village, nor were they authorized to eject a citizen. Only witches could be banished, and this had to be decided by a council of Elders of the whole Division. The chiefs could not, **a fortiori**, emerge as the apices of a redistributional economy.

This would explain why no tribute of any kind was ever paid to the Paramount Chief or any of the village chiefs. None of them could accumulate wealth by virtue of their position. As a corollary, the **fiagā** did not have any obligation of hospitality towards his people, nor did he have any trading or economic privileges, in contrast to the Anlo Awoamefia who could exact corvée labour and was also expected to provide hospitality (Nukunya 1969:11). Incapable of exacting tribute, the Abutia **fiagā** or **dufiawo** thus lacked the means of entertaining a court or a retinue, as one witnessed in Anlo proper. They could never build a 'palace' nor afford any special retainers, and their houses and households were indistinguishable from others both in architecture and in size. They had no special rights to more wives or to special brides. Like any of their fellow-citizens, they simply married whom they could afford to marry and whoever was willing to marry them.

The **fiagā** and **dufiawo** did not own slaves by virtue of their position, and no special status or special aristocratic privileges were ever attached to their clan. The Abutia chiefly clans never constituted the embryo of a rank society, as is reported in the case of Polynesian chiefdoms.

The village, finally, was the highest level of grouping where offices were defined with respect to someone else's stool. The chiefs of Kloe and Agove never defined their respective positions with respect to the Teti stool, and never acted as subordinates or functionaries of the Paramount; even the **fiagā**'s own **tsiame** and **mankrado**, who defined their titles with reference to the **dufia**'s stool, always behaved as independent figures in their own right[43]. Within their own village, the chiefs were even excluded from the affairs of lower councils unless they were directly involved or expressly invited, and they were liable to prosecution like any other citizen.

Consequently, not only did the **dufiawo** lack any real power, but so did the **fiagã** who, as ritual custodian of his village, and direct descendant of the man who originally led the Abutia during their migrations to their present territory (according to the legend), was given precedence and treated as **primus inter pares**, or First Citizen of Abutia. This preeminence did not imply that he 'ruled' at the top of a hierarchy, since he had no subalterns. Indeed, other office-holders were meant to instruct the **fiawo** rather than be instructed by them. Even the Abutia **fiagã** had more in common with the Ga **mantse**, whom Field described as a 'fetish-priest' (Field 1940) than with the Anlo Awoamefia whose 'divine' features displayed a closer affinity to the Yoruba Oni (Bascom 1969:31).

The precolonial Abutia thus lived in sovereign villages represented by a ritual custodian but governed by a Council of Elders recruiting from every constituent clan, which were united in a tight system of multiple military, religious and economic alliances, with their foci in different villages. The **fiagã** lived in Teti, the High Priest in Agove and the precolonial market was located in Kloe. By disconnecting the different foci of power within this alliance, the Abutia managed to retain the sovereignty of their villages within a loose confederacy which gave the villages what they needed, namely protection against slave-raiders and other enemies. They were further allied for defence with neighbouring confederacies, when greater perils threatened them.

Abutia villages thus differed from the 'townships' of the Tswana or Tonu Ewe, and from the Ashanti **oman** in which various villages were aggregated (Field 1948). The Igbo 'village-groups' would provide a more plausible model, were it not for the fact that their villages are composed of one clan only, and are organized on the basis of age-sets. The villages of the forest area of south-western Ivory Coast and south-eastern Liberia (and here, I would think of the Kissi, or western Dida - Paulme 1954; Terry 1966), although comparable in some ways, differ too much to provide a valuable analogy. I have found the closest parallels in the Cross River area, not so much in the large settlements like Umor which ought really to be compared to Tonu settlements, but in the sets of allied Mbembe villages (Harris 1962;1965). To find an appropriate locution to designate these polities I have used an historical example which will also help to account for some of the differences between Abutia and Anlo proper.

Fifth-century Greek cities, in fact, were sovereign but many of them allied for defence against the Persian threat. The association became known as the Delian League and, on this model, we could represent the alliance of Abutia or Mbembe villages as a 'village league', formed for similar purposes. In the Delian League, however, Athens gained military command, and with it came the expectation of taxes levied for military purposes, and the religious supremacy of Athenian deities. As Athens became the only focus of this military, economic and religious association, it also employed funds and the newly-acquired power to promote its own interests. The League thus served as a stepping-stone for the Athenians to create their own empire.

Similar processes might have operated in Anlo proper. Religious and military command came to be united in the same town (Anloga) which emerged as the capital of a small 'empire' extending over villages and towns which were formerly sovereign. The presence of a Danish fort and the large immigration from Ga-Adangme areas following Ashanti forays (see Greene 1981) might have contributed to this development but, whatever the circumstances, the result is clear: the relationship between the Awoamefia and other title-holders and group-representatives within and outside his capital bore little resemblance to that of the Abutia **fiagā** to other title-holders. In my opinion, the dissimilarities in their political organization flows directly from the fact that sovereignty was attached to different levels of grouping in the two polities.

As a corollary, Anlo's style was much more aggressive; like the Ashanti with whom they did in fact ally against the northern village leagues, the Anlo were slave-raiders and traders whose operations extended to the north. Northern alliances, by contrast, were protective and defensive. Furthermore, the decentralization of military, religious and economic power in the northern polities thwarted the growth of a capital which might have used the league to foster its more limited interests; and this decentralization favoured the sovereignty of villages.

From 1734 to 1833, the Abutia suffered Akwamu domination, making it difficult to speak of village sovereignty during this period. The **fia**-ship as it still existed (but in a disputed way...) in the 1970s seems to have been borrowed in the late 1860s or early 1870s only and, from that period on to 1890, we can truly speak of a league of sovereign villages. No evidence has surfaced for the period 1833-1870 but, had the villages been aggregated into the Division (or into a 'chiefdom-like' polity), it is impossible to explain why they should have lost this aggregation with the introduction of **fiawo** which, logically, should have strengthened their centralization. I would thus surmise that Abutia villages have enjoyed their sovereignty since they overthrew the Akwamu yoke in 1833.

V. VILLAGE SOVEREIGNTY: ITS DEMOGRAPHIC IMPLICATIONS

A. Village reproduction

Abutia and Anlo proper also display other contrasting features. If Anlo was a 'kingdom' - and the available information seems to corroborate this impression (Amenumey 1964, 1968, Nukunya 1969) - the sovereign political group was therefore not the village, but the group of villages under the Awoamefia. The level at which group aggregation stopped in political matters thus differed between Abutia and Anlo, and this difference ought also to be observable in other features.

If the village represents the maximal political group, it should be the case that any group wishing to leave the village to create a new **permanent** settlement will be claiming independence as a separate sovereign group (since, by definition, every permanent local group is sovereign). In such circumstances, the village elders (from the mother-village) are not likely to tolerate easily the formation and departure of such a splinter group. If, on the other hand, the Division (or group of villages) represents the largest extension of the body politic, the creation of a new permanent settlement will not necessarily constitute too great a threat to the established authorities. In this last instance, the new locality will simply form one more component group of the sovereign entity, without claiming sovereignty for itself. The only internal menace to a kingdom's sovereignty is the secession of a whole group of villages which would then assert its separate independence.

Ceteris paribus, the creation of new villages should take place more easily in a kingdom than in polities where villages are sovereign. This idea seems to be corroborated by the ethnographic facts. Anlo (and the coastal Divisions on the whole) number many more villages than the northern village leagues and this discrepancy can directly be attributed to the rate of village proliferation. For instance, Spieth reported eight villages for Adaklu (a southern Division, although not a coastal one) and I counted sixteen at the time of fieldwork (1972) (Spieth 1906). Nukunya also reports that "traditionally, the Kingdom (of Anlo proper) was reputed to comprise 36 different towns and villages, but in 1960 no less than 116 localities were shown in the census returns" (Nukunya 1969:9).

There is no reason to suspect a dramatically divergent annual growth rate between northern and southern villages, or any significant difference in immigration/emigration. In contrast to Anlo proper, Rattray enumerated three villages for Abutia in 1915, and these were the same three that the Germans had found at their present site in 1888; there was also no indication in 1888 that they had moved recently. To this day, there are still only three Abutia villages, and no evidence of any kind that another locality will be formed in the foreseeable future. In all the neighbouring northern areas of Ewe-dome (and non-Anlo) extraction not bordering the Volta, one finds an identical copy of the 1915 and 1960 enumerations, regarding the number of localities. If their number in fact increased by one, it is generally due to factors such as Christianity, chieftaincy disputes or the presence of immigrants. I have personally noted a 'Christians' village' in Sokode, and Kludze reports that a chieftaincy dispute in Gbi triggered off the formation of a new village (Kludze 1973:169).

In a sovereign village, any endeavour to move out and create a new permanent locality is a bid for independence. It thus seems logical that elders in such a polity will refuse permission to settle to any group with secessionist aspirations. For a separatist group to succeed in its bid for autonomy, it would have to satisfy two conditions, namely, to be of sufficient size and to settle on its own land, as it would normally be expelled from lands of other groups in the mother-village. Lineages (and some minimal lineages) in Abutia are land-owning corporations, but secession would ruin them. Only large lineages or many small ones, or part of a clan could ever hope to achieve secession.

It follows from these conditions that a new locality would have to be completely mature and independent from the very beginning. In other words, I believe that Abutia villages (or sovereign villages in general) can proliferate through a process of mitotic fission only, or 'instantaneous reproduction'. This mode of reproduction

is indeed not peculiar to Abutia.   In the polities with
sovereign villages known to me, such as the Mbembe,
Pueblos, Dida or Yanomamö, for instance, reproduction does
take place in this mitotic fashion.   Among the Dida or
Yanomamö, however, one could argue that villages must be
mature at their very inception because of the constant
threat of inter-village warfare.   Inter-village warfare,
however, normally presupposes village sovereignty, so that
it becomes difficult in those instances to extricate the
two variables.   In Abutia, on the other hand, the lack of
inter-village warfare and the ecological conditions do
permit the separation of the two and seem to support the
hypothesis that the mitotic fission of villages is
attributable to village sovereignty.   Overall, then, I
would contend that village sovereignty does entail
instantaneous village creation but that the mitotic
fission of villages does not necessarily imply their
sovereignty.

Because of their dramatic nature, moreover, such
mitotic fissions should occur after long intervals of
time.   If sovereign groups do not easily grant sovereignty
to their own component groups, it is quite likely that
many years will pass before new villages are created, if
villages are sovereign.   The information gathered bears
out this conclusion.   The inauguration of a new village is
a very rare occurence indeed in Abutia, since none has
been recorded over the last one hundred years or more,
despite a fivefold increase in population since
approximately 1885 (see Appendix 1).   The present sites
were occupied when the first missionaries arrived in 1888,
and the eldest citizens do not recall that their own
fathers or grandfathers ever lived in different
localities.   This indicates that the present Abutia
villages have been settled at their present location
possibly since 1865.   Since the formation of the last new
settlements in Abutia antedates by at least one generation
the oldest of the present elders, it has been impossible
to investigate the real causes of fission (as distinct
from the legendary ones, to be analysed below).   There are
nevertheless indirect ways of supporting the hypothesis of
mitotic fission.

First of all, I have never heard an elder suggesting
that one of the minimal lineages or lineages moved out to
found a new village, or that a small group has seceded to
establish a new settlement.   The comparable size of all
three villages adds to his evidence;   if some groups were
clearly offshoots of others, one would expect greater

variations in size.   But, above all, the lack of clan
dispersal in Abutia may have been caused by mitotic
fission.   To find clans completely confined to one
locality (i.e., lack of 'dispersal'), I believe that one
of three things must have happened - (a) whole clans
seceded to form new villages, (b) different groups
(lineages or minimal lineages of different clans) seceded
and severed all their genealogical links to their previous
clans, or (c) part of a clan seceded and erased any memory
of common clanship.

If new villages were always created by the secession of
whole clans, the original number of clans in Abutia would
tally with the present number, and this is a most unlikely
proposition.   If groups from different clans (situation
(b)) moved off to settle elsewhere and sundered their
clanship links with the mother-village, they would
automatically form new clans in their new locality.
Situations (a) and (b) both presuppose territorial fission
and lack of clan dispersal.   In the third possibility,
clans can split but can also remain in the same locality.
Conditions (a) and (b) would be the most conducive to
territorial fission, and condition (c) less so, although
all three possibilities suggest the removal of a large
number of individuals all at once, and the immediate
creation of a mature and independent community.

Anlo provides an interesting contrast.   With a
population considerably smaller than that of Anlo proper,
Abutia has twenty clans.   There are only fifteen clans in
Anlo proper, and they are dispersed throughout the one
hundred odd villages in the kingdom.   If the creation of
new localities in Anlo proper does not threaten the
sovereignty of the political group, there is no reason why
new settlers (i.e., splinter groups) should have to create
new clanship affiliations.

Finally, the new villages recently founded in other
Ewe-dome village leagues suggest the same mitotic fission
- the secession is precipitated by chieftaincy or
religious disputes (the Christians being forces to move
out, for instance), and it assembles individuals from
various clans who 'spontaneously' create a full-fledged
and independent village.   The new village is mature from
its very beginning, as Kludze himself reported about the
Gbi (1973:169).

Mitotic fission also precludes any developmental cycle
of village growth (outside the mother-village, that is).
Settlements on lands outside the village can only be
temporary, since permanent ones represent such a radical
break.   In other words, I would contend that no group can

settle on farmland and slowly grow into a new locality, in sovereign villages. This last corollary appears critical when we assess the evidence regarding the **kɔfhewo** (sing. **kɔfhe**), or small settlements on farmlands outside the village nucleus.

Nukunya, writing about Anlo proper, contrasts the **kɔfhe** to the **du** as the 'village' to the 'town'. He regards the two as different levels of socio-political integration and there is indirect evidence that the **kɔfhe** is formed by a group of emigrants who have detached themselves from the **du** and will eventually develop into a **du** if the ecological and demographic conditions permit (Nukunya 1969:12). This interpretation is made quite explicit in Westermann, who wrote about the Glidyi Ewe - another coastal group east of Anlo proper, in southern Togo (Westermann 1935:170-172). Westermann translates **kɔfhe** as 'hamlet' and depicts it as the embryo of a new village, a seceding group which will itself grow and evolve into a separate **du**.

This was also Spieth's interpretation, although in his case he was writing about Ho, an Ewe-dome village league to the north of Abutia (Spieth 1906:365-367), and not about the coastal areas. Spieth's thesis may be quite consistent with Anlo political organization, but I would dispute the view that **kɔfhewo** are permanent settlements representing an early phase in the cycle of village growth in northern village leagues. Spieth argued that **kɔfhe** is derived from **ko**, a word meaning 'extended family' (German **Grossfamilie**), or what I would probably call a 'minimal lineage'. Although his etymology may have been right (I have no way of checking since, in Abutia, the same word does not designate any group; it takes on different meanings, such as 'people', 'neck' or 'ant-hill'), his inferences are more open to question. He concluded that the **kɔfhe** was consequently (because of the etymological reconstruction) an extended family (let us say 'minimal lineage') which established itself away from the original settlement and formed the nucleus of a new village. This extrapolation, though seductive at first sight, is unfortunately mistaken. Spieth's reliance on etymological evidence seriously confused the issue. Writing on Ho, Spieth was regrettably unable to mention a single instance of a **kɔfhe** which matured into a village in the Ho village league. My personal experience also supports this fact. All the Ho villages (which merged into an administrative town of more than 20,000 inhabitants) have been rooted in their present location since the end of their migrations - so their legend of origin says - and there is no evidence to the contrary.

Incapable of producing an example from Ho, however, Spieth substantiated his claim with an illustration from Adaklu Woaya, where such a case is allegedly reported. But it so happens that the Adaklu are of Anlo extraction, and not Ewe-dome. In this unique case alluded to, Spieth fortunately specified that it occurred as a result of manslaughter, after which incident the 'family' of the slayer was banished. This illustration only exaggerates the general confusion. As we have seen, the Abutia also used to banish those guilty of manslaughter, together with their minimal lineage. These forcible removals however, never yielded a kɔfhe.

Some may wish to argue that things have changed in the seventy years since Spieth's writings. By comparing Rattray's 1915 list of villages to contemporary ones, it emerges clearly that the number of villages is substantially the same throughout much of northern Eweland. In the northern village leagues known to me, none of the 1910 kɔfhewo had expanded into villages by 1973, and none were about to, but I would believe it possible that such occurrences were witnessed in Anlo. Against Spieth's assumption about the nature of the kɔfhe, I would rather contend that permanent settlements outside the village would negate the latter's sovereignty. Granted the hypothesis of local sovereignty, it seems erroneous to compare the northern Ewe kɔfhe to a budding village.

My own fieldwork revealed that the Abutia kɔfhe, or 'hamlet', rarely includes more than two mud houses. Farmers build their hamlets in the middle of the farmlands, some miles away from the village. One man alone, or a man with his family will take up residence in a hamlet, sometimes accompanied by a married daughter and her children. A married son, however, will not follow his father to the kɔfhe, nor did he in the past. It is also only relatively recently that married daughters have started living in their father's hamlet. Hamlets are few: there were approximately ten in Kloe, and hamlet-dwellers build their farm-houses with temporary materials. Most villagers spend most of their wealth on building permanent housing in the village, using cement and corrugated iron in the construction. Only the poorer citizens will resort to dry mud, but they will plaster it with cement. Cement and corrugated iron are never brought to a hamlet. Nobody in Abutia would ever dream of investing money on a kɔfhe house; it is simply nonsensical.

The Abutia hamlet does not contain the seeds of an eventual village. Some lands are located furthest from the old settlement, and farmers adjust to his pattern of land tenure by staying on their farm land in the agricultural season. Instead of commuting every day, a farmer might decide to build a shelter on his farm and sleep there. If he wishes to extend his stay for the whole farming season, he may decide to bring his wife and children with him. This is not simple, however, since love-making is strongly prohibited in the 'bush' (i.e., outside the nucleated settlement). The prohibition can nevertheless be lifted if domestic animals (chickens or guineafowls are sufficient) are brought in. Nowadays, a man's married daughter may join him with her children, with or without her husband (only husbands who married in would accompany their wife to her father's hamlet) so that a hamlet may ultimately consist of up to twenty persons, but mostly children. Every adult male hamlet-dweller also owns a house in the village, regardless of the amount of time he spends in the hamlet. Women never build houses in hamlets.

Even if it outlasts the death of its founder (and I know of few such cases in Abutia), the hamlet always remains a 'domestic affair', an agricultural outpost of some residential group from the village. Its growth and composition are those of residential groups and, like any such group in Abutia, it only continues to exist because of its links with the village. Severed from the village, it would be a group in exile. In brief, then, the Abutia kɔfhe is only a 'residential group seasonally stationed on its farmland'.

This situation is not peculiar to Abutia but also characteristic of the Mbembe who, like the Abutia, appear to form leagues of sovereign villages not systematically involved in inter-village warfare. Of their hamlets, Rosemary Harris writes:

"The most significant difference between a village and a hamlet is that the latter is ritually subordinated to the village. This is normally obvious since a hamlet is almost without shrines . . . This obvious ritual difference between the two types of settlements stems from the fact that they occupy entirely different ritual statuses; unlike the village, the hamlet has no direct communication with the world of the dead; it has the ritual status of the bush . . . It is therefore impossible to bury anyone in a hamlet and it is a serious misfortune to die there . . . Some even hold that the entry of a spirit child into a woman's womb, which is as necessary as sexual intercourse for conception to take place, cannot occur in a hamlet." (Harris 1965:61-62).

These beliefs and prohibitions have the obvious result that hamlets remain hamlets, and do not gradually develop into new sovereign villages. If no permanent settlements can be established outside the village, the creation of new villages can only be 'catastrophic', as it is in Abutia.

In contrast to Abutia, I do believe that the Anlo **kofhewo** are permanent settlements which, in due time, can ripen into full-fledged villages. In other words, one ought to detect in Anlo proper a slow and gradual developmental cycle of village growth and reproduction, and not a mitotic or catastrophic one as in Abutia. The figures show that villages are more easily created in Anlo, and the time interval between the creation of new villages is consequently significantly shorter than in Abutia. This being so, there is also a much greater demographic variability in the size of Anlo villages. Indeed, the present population of Anlo villages varies from one hundred to many thousands, whereas that of Abutia villages displays little variation.

These facts all help to substantiate the hypothesis of mitotic village fission (or reproduction) in Abutia (it remains an hypothesis because no living Abutia citizen knows anything about the manner in which the last village was created), which in turn lends greater plausibility to the hypothesis of village sovereignty. If legends of origin recount the way groups were created and went about proliferating until their present distribution is explained, they might perhaps reflect the very process of mitotic fission as it seems to have taken place in the precolonial past (as it does in the present), and support further the initial hypothesis.

I have collected numerous versions of the legend of origin, but I have selected only four of these testimonies for the following presentation. I have constructed the following account from the most common and plausible elements of the four sources. The more mythical part of the story remains approximately the same in all versions.

The Abutia point to Ketu as their ancestral home but they, together with the two other Ewe branches (Tonu and Anlo) derive their more recent origin from Notsie, a village in south-eastern Togo. Notsie is the Ewe Babel. In it all the ethnic groups surrounding Abutia - the Akan, Krobo, Ga, Ada and Ewe - lived together. Each one occupied a different ward of the town and their respective languages, already differentiated, were nevertheless mutually intelligible (something which is no longer true). The town was walled and lay under the oppressive rule of a wicked chief named Agokoli.

One day, Agokoli ordered his subjects to make a rope with pounded clay. Faced with such an extravagant request, the elders of the town debated upon the strategy to adopt. They finally advised their people to ask Agokoli himself to show them how to make such a rope, as they had never seen one before. Upon hearing this, Agokoli exploded with anger, and he ordered his mercenaries to mix broken glass and thorns with the clay to wound the insolent ones who were going to pound the clay with their feet. Horrified by this cruelty, the townspeople planned a flight from Notsie. To put their plan into effect, the elders told the women to always throw their dirty water at the same place on the wall, in order to soften it. At this juncture, the different versions fail to agree as to how the wall was broken and which group fled first. Most narrators agree that the Ho were the first to make their escape through the hole in the wall. The sword used to carve the hole in the fortification is still displayed as evidence by the Ho chief.

Some elders say that the Abutia absconded with the Ho, Sokode and Adaklu; others contend that they fled with the Agomes. Another version mentions that they escaped with the Bator (a Tonu people) and reached the River Volta. The Bator crossed the river and settled on the southern bank (where they still live at the present time) but the Abutia moved back inland. This part of the tradition is the most obscure, but most reports converge after that. The Abutia were then led in their migration by a man called Agbeme. They followed him and settled on a mountain, some five miles south-east of the Abutia Hills. Some time after their settlement on the mountain top, the Abutia split in two groups. One of their scouts left to explore the northern lands and died away from home. For some unknown reason, his corpse was not brought back to the mountain, so his relatives went to bury him where he

had died, but they failed to return.   The deceased was
called Foli (a first-born) and his followers were named
after him, and called Fodome.   They are presently located
east of Hohoe, some thirty-five miles north-east of
Abutia.   Fodome and Abutia acknowledge a common origin,
but have severed their links for many generations.

One elder reported that the Abutia originally formed 35
villages.   Six major tribal wars with their neighbours (in
the south) took their toll, leaving them with only eight
villages (or **duwo**).   Five of them followed Foli, and
three remained on Agbenu, the mountain south-west of the
Abutia Hills.   During their stay on Agbenu these three
villages allegedly occupied one common settlement (or
locality), despite their separate identities as distinct
duwo (villages).   For unknown reasons, perhaps because
of the lack of land, or the excess of water on the
mountain as some elders suggest, the Abutia left their
mountain site.   They migrated to what are now the Abutia
Hills, and built their settlements at the foot of the
Hills, somewhere south of their present location (it is
not specified how many different sites the three **duwo**
then occupied).   Another slave-raid from the Akwamu
compelled them to move northward, where they formed two
localities: Teti on the one hand, and Agove-Kloe on the
other.   Agove and Kloe formed a twin village on the
present site of Agove.   Quarrels broke out between the
women of the two villages over the use of water resources,
and the Kloe people resolved to part from the Agove.   They
moved back southward to their present location.   This last
migration must have occurred some time before 1865.

The Abutia possibly migrated from the Agbenu to the
Abutia Hills at the time they freed themselves from the
Akwamu (1834).   It was indeed quite common in West Africa
to find people taking refuge on mountain tops to protect
themselves against slave-raiding.   As their 'rulers', the
Adwamu should have promoted peace in northern Eweland, but
they failed to, and indulged freely in 'panyarring', or
kidnapping people to sell them into slavery.   After their
successful rebellion under the Kpeki lead, the Abutia
might have wished to settle closer to the Kpeki and move
to the Abutia Hills (but they never settled on the Hills
themselves).   If this is right, they would have migrated
to the Abutia Hills around 1835.

None of the Abutia legends of origin ever mentions that
a village arrived first in the area, or that a clan
settled first on a village site.   All arrived together,
but **led** by a man.   When they came, there were no

autochthonous people already settled on the land, and thus
they were not obliged to conquer or chase away a native
population. This legend of origin puts the emphasis
directly on **historical** events, particularly the flight
from Notsie and the long odyssey to the present location.
It does not invoke any genealogical charter, nor does it
mention any apical ancestor. If anything, the Abutia
legend of origin is certainly not 'apical'. In legends
that I have collected in Tonu, on the contrary, the first
settlers of different villages or towns are recollected as
being genealogically related, as one also finds in Anlo
proper. The Abutia story, however, lacks a mythical
description of the genesis of the different groups found
in their known world, and it contains no idea of group
development.

Indeed, theirs is some kind of pre-formationist theory
of social evolution. All the groups now observable were
already differentiated and pre-contained in the Ewe Babel,
the mythical womb[44]. There is no story of their
development. No group ever gave birth to another group.
The Fodome simply detached themselves, already organized
into five **duwo**. The present and precolonial social
order ('abstracting' the national organization
superimposed upon the present one) have existed since
mythical times; it reflects the social order that existed
in Notsie, save for its scale and geographical
distribution. All future groups were preformed in the
original **ovum** (Notsie); they were already distinct and
differentiated, only awaiting to emerge, to migrate and
finally settle. Their legend only recalls the
geographical spread of groups which have always existed,
it hints of no 'biological' time of inner development. It
only recounts the 'spatial time' of geographical
distribution.

A pre-formationist theory nevertheless supposes
filiation, and even this is absent in the Abutia legend.
No village is said to have engendered another village, no
clan another clan, no lineage another lineage. The groups
only nest like Chinese boxes or Russian dolls: all clans
were pre-contained in their respective villages, the
villages in Abutia, Abutia in the Ewe people and
surrounding ethnic groups in Notsie. The only link
between clans, villages and divisions is the recollection
of a common historical experience - the long migration and
the alliance in their struggles against common enemies.
This 'migratory report' is the only ideological validation
of the unity of the villages, of the village leagues, and

of the identity of the Ewe people (apart from their common language).

Clans and villages were certainly born out of one another, and fissions there were, but the tradition only alludes to three major ones: (a) the Fodome departure, (b) the creation of two localities at the foot of the Abutia Hills, from the only one on Agbenu and, (c) the Agove-Kloe separation. Kloe, for instance, was not 'created'; it already existed side by side with Agove, as an independent du within the same locality or site and, to emerge as a separate and independent political entity, it only moved away. The new settlement did not progress gradually out of a few original families; it started life grown-up, mature at the very start. And the same applies to the other instances of territorial fission in this legend. All groups which sought a separate territorial identity were already complete and sovereign as they detached themselves.

I consequently regard this legend of origin as a clear and direct reflection of a process of mitotic, or 'catastrophic' village reproduction. It tells a similar story, recounting that villages are born, not through a long reproductive cycle involving gradual emigration and slow growth outside the mother-village, but through the secession of a large group, already mature and sovereign at the moment of its separation. If, in the legend, Kloe has always existed, I take it that Kloe was sovereign from the very moment that it settled apart.

The initial notion that group aggregation in political matters stops at different levels in Abutia and Anlo proper serves to explain a number of features which contrast the two areas. The level of grouping to which political sovereignty is attached does have serious implications for the manner in which the component groups reproduce themselves. The Anlo create new permanent settlements more easily, and at shorter intervals than the Abutia. This is reflected in the relative size of their different localities (almost equal in Abutia but with great variations in Anlo proper), in the nature of the hamlets (kɔfhewo), in the 'localization' or 'dispersal' of the clans, as well as in their number. It is also echoed in the traditions of origin which are less 'geographical' and more 'genetic' in Anlo proper.

B. Descent group reproduction

If the level of grouping to which sovereignty is attached affects the manner in which new villages are created, we should further expect it to influence the manner in which new descent groups are created. To substantiate this hypothesis more fully we would need a detailed study of descent groups in Anlo proper which, unfortunately, is not available. With the information that Nukunya offers in his monograph, however, it is still possible to sketch the rough lines of a significant contrast.

Nukunya writes that compounds:

". . . are usually grouped into larger residential units, which may be called 'clusters of families' (. . .). A cluster consists, in the main, of the compounds of full and half-brothers, and sometimes parallel first cousins, under the authority of their eldest living member. The family cluster is not a static group. It undergoes a cycle of growth and segmentation, and sometimes even declines and fuses with other within the lineage . . . But whatever its size it is defined by the possession of an elder. He is responsible for the settlement of minor disputes within the cluster." (1969:32).

From this statement and from an examination of the genealogy of a family cluster presented (p. 34), I do not hesitate in comparing the Anlo 'family cluster' to the Abutia **fhome**, or minimal lineage, although the high incidence of polygyny in Anlo proper may influence the proliferation and size of the family clusters. Indeed, I would not be surprised if Anlo family clusters were 'ideally' descended from ancestors in G+2, and were therefore larger than Abutia minimal lineages. These family clusters, or minimal lineages, are further aggregated into lineages (**afhedo** in Anlo proper). Nukunya also mentions that young people from crowded lineages are encouraged to build and settle **permanently** outside their native settlements in **kɔfhewo** which often grow into full-fledged towns, as evidenced by the history of Anloga (the capital) and Woe, two large coastal towns (p. 28). The emigrants, claims Nukunya, do not sever their links with the mother-settlements and retain their membership of the mother-lineage. This claim, however, manifestly rests on a synchronic appraisal of the phenomenon; this is evidently the way things look like for the first generation of emigrants. But a diachronic, or 'developmental' reading of the facts would certainly disclose a different reality. Let us indeed imagine a hypothetical reconstruction of the process.

Initially, young men from various lineages move out to a new settlement, but remain members of their native lineages. After three to five generations, however, and especially if they have been blessed with reproductive success, large 'family clusters' will have developed from these original settlers. The larger ones, which may indeed be larger than the native lineage itself, will obviously wish to redefine their relationships to their ancestor's native group. The original settlers may have all originated from the same lineage in the mother-settlement. In this case, the descendants of those who came from the same family clusters may use their common ancestry to form a new **afhedo** by erecting a shrine to the first ancestor who came to settle; alternately, the original settlers could have belonged to different lineages of various clans. Three to five generations later, those family clusters descended from forbears of the same mother-lineage will invent new collateral genealogical connections to form a new lineage, their size permitting, while other family clusters descended from settlers from another lineage would create yet a different lineage of a different clan.

I am thus quite positive that, after a few generations and successful reproduction, the families of original settlers will develop into family clusters and eventually into new lineages altogether. Otherwise, it is impossible to explain how lineages of the same clan are dispersed over many settlements, and how one settlement may contain many lineages of a single clan (1969:25). The number of lineages in Anlo proper is not fixed so that lineages must proliferate, however slowly (but necessarily faster than in Abutia), and they must achieve this partly by building and settling permanently outside their native settlement. As new lineages sprout the precise genealogical connections linking them to their former lineage are forgotten, but a vague recollection of common descent remains, keeping them together within the same clan. Because Anlo localities are not sovereign, people from one village can create small, new, **permanent** settlements outside their native locality and these settlements, over the generations, can gradually develop into full-fledged villages or even towns; for these same reasons, the emigrants do not have to relinquish their clan membership

as they settle apart and even achieve new lineage status,
so that clans are 'dispersed'. In Anlo proper, lineages
can therefore multiply within the same clans by being able
to settle at various places; it is therefore the creation
of new clans which is inhibited[45].

These facts, in my opinion, give us the clue we need to
account for the statics of lineage reproduction in Abutia.
The main difference from Anlo proper, as we have so often
emphasized, lies in the sovereignty of Abutia villages.
In sovereign villages, overpopulated lineages cannot
invite their members to emigrate and create new, permanent
settlements.   Incapable of 'dispersal', the Abutia
lineages cannot proliferate. By implication, the clans
are neither 'dispersed' and new ones are formed only when
new villages are created. Now, why lineages come three
per clan is a different question, and one which can be
answered in terms of either symbolism or 'Realpolitik', or
both. On the one hand, the number 'three' symbolizes life
and fertility to Abutia and northern Ewe. Farmers always
plant three seeds together to ensure fertility, and men
aim at inseminating their wives three times in a row to
ensure impregnation...; to include three lineages may thus
have meant growth and fertility of the clan.   Three
lineages, moreover, make it more difficult to polarize
issues, there being always a third party to tip the
balance one way or the other, or to act as mediator.

Overall, then, although the exact number of lineages
per clan may have been decided for symbolic or political
reasons, their inability to multiply is directly
associated to their inability to disperse, which stems
from the villages' sovereignty. If clans are not
dispersed but their number increases significantly every
time a new village is created, it is easy to understand
why the Abutia have more clans than the Anlo proper,
although they are much smaller in size.

Anlo proper and Abutia descent groups do share some
features.   Both are composed of minimal lineages
aggregated directly into lineages without any intermediate
level of aggregation. The lineages are further aggregated
into clans, an organization in fact quite common to many
West African and Melanesian societies; indeed, I have come
to believe that lineages with intermediate levels of
aggregation are the exception rather than the rule, even
in Africa. But Abutia and Anlo descent group vary in
their size, number and mode of reproduction. These
features are easy to detect and describe, and their
variations seem to derive from the fact that political

sovereignty is attached to different levels of grouping in the two societies. Other traits of Abutia and Anlo descent groups are also discrepant: Anlo lineages are religious corporations and their clans own land. Admittedly, one could account for every minor deviation at the end of an exhaustive comparative analysis which would require a wealth of both ethnographic and historical data which are unfortunately not available. It remains reassuring, however, to see that the initial hypothesis of village sovereignty does account for so many of the features of Abutia social organization, and for so many of the dissimilarities between Abutia and Anlo proper.

This brief survey concludes the somewhat conjectural analysis of the precolonial polity, and of the traditional political groups observable nowadays. Much of this reconstruction remains hypothetical because of the extent to which new political circumstances have completely disrupted the precolonial machinery of government and fostered a definition of 'traditional' jurisdictions and practices which bears little resemblance to the precolonial past. Between the precolonial past and the traditional present, a vast number of external interventions have pushed the Abutia into unforeseen political arenas. To retrace this political history, to probe in depth the transformations of the precolonial polity after the impact of colonization, as the past becomes a contemporary 'tradition' within a nation would call for a different type of enquiry, and one which my own data would not enable me to accomplish.

From the minimal lineage to the Division we have delineated the political organization but completely overlooked the 'domestic organization'. And yet, many a student of social organization views domestic groups as the lowest level in the political hierarchy; Nukunya states it explicitly and Fortes, while acknowledging that the two only overlap, roots lineage segmentation in the organization of the polygynous household. These views imply a connection between descent and the composition of domestic groups, one of the fundamental assumptions of classical descent theory. A careful analysis of domestic groups in Abutia, on the other hand, will reveal that political and domestic organizations have little in common and that descent plays no role in the composition of domestic groups.

SECTION 3

Residential and Domestic Groups

I. RESIDENCE IN AN OPERATIONAL PERSPECTIVE

In an earlier publication (Verdon 1980d), I surveyed the theoretical literature on residence and domesticity and suggested that the various approaches could be subsumed under three models: normative, rational, and structural-functional. In the normative model, anthropologists have identified a norm of post-marital residence and described societies in those terms (patrilocal, matrilocal, neolocal, and so on). In the rational model, residence is viewed as a strategy. Inspired by Goodenough's plea for an emic understanding of residential behaviour (1955) and by Leach's pronouncement that groups (or social structure) are only the 'statistical outcome of multiple individual choices rather than a direct reflection of jural rules' (Leach 1960:124), the 'rationalists' assume that only a scarcity of resources (i.e., houses in this particular instance) makes residential choices necessary. If everyone could possess a house of his or her own, residence would be unproblematic. Residential choices, prompted by scarcity, serve therefore as means to an end (the allocation of scarce resources) and must consequently be rational.

Both the normative and rational models are ego-centered, and assume that a knowledge of either the norms or the various strategies which guide individual behaviour is sufficient to reconstitute the actual residential groups and therefore to account for their composition. This assumption I do not share, and I rather concur with Harris (1974) in believing that even a perfect knowledge of the rules cannot help us to predict behaviour (and hence to predict to which groups individuals will belong)! I do not believe that one can derive group composition from rules regulating individual behaviour. In short, the study of domestic groups should rest on a group-centered approach.

This is exactly what the structural-functionalists aimed at doing by shifting the focus from the residence of marital pairs or individuals to whole, constituted groups. In its classical form (especially Fortes 1949a, 1949b), the model implies that the various types of residential groups recorded in a given society represent different stages of a developmental cycle. To account for a particular cycle, Fortes identified certain 'principles' (such as affinity, motherhood, agnatic or uterine descent, and so on) which allegedly operate with a differential strength throughout individuals' life-cycles and pull them together into diverse residential associations at various times. This approach, however, denies any relevance to **residence** itself, speaking rather of **domestic** groups or **family** structures, thereby reducing residence to an epiphenomenon of kinship and descent.

Goody (1958) went very far towards an operational solution of the problem by distinguishing various 'units' (what are here called 'groups') subsumed under the umbrella-concept of 'domestic'. There is no collection of individuals which corresponds to a 'domestic group', he argued, but various subgroups involved in different domestic activities, namely production (including production proper, distribution of products, food processing and consumption) and reproduction. 'Domestic', he concluded, denotes the zone of overlapping membership of these various units but, he added, residence is only the spatial projection of groups of production and reproduction. Residence, once more, was denied any reality in its right.

In sum, the 'rationalists' approach residence from an ego-centered perspective and treat it as an epiphenomenon of economics and politics; the 'normativists' regard it as a phenomenon **sui generis** but still to be approached from an ego-centered point of view; the 'structural-functionalists', finally, do study constituted groups but treat residence as an epiphenomenon of kinship and marriage. In an operational perspective, one would ideally like to combine a group-centered approach with a non-reductionist treatment of residence.

But, one may ask, why be so concerned about treating residence as a phenomenon **sui generis**? Because, on the one hand, Bender's classical distinction between family, domestic functions and coresidence must be upheld (Bender 1967)[46]. On purely empirical grounds, moreover, residence must also be distinguished analytically.

Indeed, what are 'domestic activities'? - They are the activities organized aroung the **domus,** either performed **in** the house (such as copulation, food processing - in cold climates - or food consumption) or performed by individuals living in the same house (such as maintenance and socialization of children, distribution of food, production, and so on). The groups formed around these activities do have overlapping membership in many societies but they never coincide entirely.   But, more importantly, one finds instances where the several units are almost completely dissociated.   In some West African populations (the Ga and the Ashanti being among the better known - see Field 1940, Fortes 1949b) husband and wife live in separate houses.   Among the Abutia, the dislocation goes much further.   Some adult women sleep in one house (alone or with some of their children), cook in another, have intercourse with their husband in yet another house, and finally receive foodstuffs from and feed people scattered over several houses.

In some extreme instances, moreover, the individuals occupying the same house do not collaborate in any of the 'domestic activities'!   In a census, why should we then include these individuals in the same group? - Because they are all engaged in the performance of one activity, namely the occupation of a dwelling-place for the purpose of sleeping.   This activity is **residence,** and specific groups - residential groups - are formed in its performance.   In fact, residence has often been misinterpreted because anthropologists have posited eating, or cooking, or residence itself, as criteria of membership[47].   One   must   therefore   distinguish residential groups from the groups formed in production and reproduction; operationally speaking residence is an activity, and not the spatial projection of groups created for other purposes.   Without this distinction, a clear anthropological analysis of Abutia 'domestic groups' would be impossible.   Before examining the composition of residential groups, however, we must have a clear understanding of what the dwelling-place is and how it is occupied, from an emic point of view.

II.   DEFINING THE ABUTIA DWELLING-PLACE

The Abutia designate their habitations as **xɔnu,** some kind of 'residential complex' which comprises three types of buildings, namely (a) a rectangular building **(xɔ)** internally divided into bedrooms (sing. **xɔme)** which are not interconnected, since their only door opens on the outside; (b) a kitchen (**avame**) which faces the **xo** across an open space and shelters one to three hearths and, (c) a 'bathroom-cum-urinal' (**tsilefhe**) which stands behind the kitchen or next to the bedrooms. These three buildings are disposed on both sides of or around an open space (**xixe**) which also forms an integral part of the **xɔnu**, rather like an open room. When at home, women spend most of their time in the **xixe**, either busy with the care of young children, or absorbed in the preparation of meals. The **xixe** is diligently swept every day and kept as neat and tidy as the floor of an actual room, since it is in fact the place where food is processed.

Three main types of houses can be observed in Abutia, their sizes directly reflecting the wealth of the builder. The smallest ones, with thatched roofs, are one-room buildings with a kitchen facing towards the house. Larger **xɔnuwo** boast of a larger number of bedrooms in their **xɔ**, whereas the largest comprise two separate **xɔwo** (sing. **xɔ**) built at a right angle to form an L-shape, and each divided into three or four bedrooms (the largest number of bedrooms I recorded in Kloe was thirteen). A large kitchen faces one of the wings, thereby giving the whole residential complex a U shape.

A **xɔnu** rarely has more than one kitchen. Kitchens in the largest houses can be mistaken for a **xɔ**, because of their cement walls; kitchen floors, however, are never cemented. Large kitchens house two or three hearths, without any dividing walls, whereas the poorer ones simply consist of a hearth sheltered by a palm-branch roof, supported by four poles.

The Abutia dwelling-places are not enclosed by either fences or walls, but they are arranged in such a way as to be half-enclosed by the back walls of surrounding buildings. The intervening spaces between **xɔnuwo** are mainly made up of the network of paths used to reach them, or of the ditches into which dirty water is thrown. The **xɔnu**, however, is not a 'compound'. Once built, the owner rarely adds a room or another building to it. 'Building' means erecting a completely separate and distinct **xɔnu**, not adding to an already existing one. Two houses may have adjacent kitchens and their respective **xixe** may form one continuous floor. Merged houses like these seem to form a compound, but are in fact referred to by their dwellers as distinct **xɔnuwo** with their separate kitchens and bathrooms, despite the

exchange of services which may take place between the two.
Such situations tend to arise when brothers build their
houses with the rooms facing one another across the open
space (**xixe**) and not back to back, as is the normal
practice; I have recorded only four such cases in Kloe.
These facts thus suggest that the Abutia dwelling-place is
a discrete and clearly delineated unit and that it can
best be described as a 'house', despite its layout around
an open space.

The desire to build a house dominates economic pursuits
in Abutia. As with the cattle among the southern Bantu,
horses among the Plains Indians or even automobiles among
rural French-Canadians..., one encounters somewhat of a
'house-building complex' in Abutia! When asked the
reasons why they wish to emigrate to the city, young men
always mention the need to amass enough cash to build a
beautiful house in the village. Houses, and not the
number of wives, are the main symbols of status and
economic achievement. In essays which they were asked to
write in class, young boys did not mention polygyny as one
of the more interesting premiums of wealth, but the
building of a huge and magnificent house. A major form of
ostentatious spending, house-building is nevertheless not
a kind of capital investment, since men do not build to
rent but to head larger residential groups. The bigger
the house and the more numerous its occupants, the greater
the head's prestige in the community. The few lodgers
that I found in Kloe (they numbered approximately twenty
five) all lived in five enormous houses which could not be
filled even with the whole minimal lineage of the late
owner. Their builders died without leaving many children
behind them, and their heirs resolved to let the rooms
instead of leaving them vacant.

Abutia houses were formerly built out of dried mud and
thatch, and apparently lasted, with occasional repairs,
for the lifetime of their owner. Few of these can be seen
nowadays, cement having replaced the traditional building
material. The new concrete houses can last for many
generations with only minor repairs, but are relatively
expensive to construct; in 1971, their cost ranged from
¢400.00 to ¢1,000.00 (i.e., from U.S. $400.00 to U.S.
$1,000.00 at the 1971 rate of exchange), an expenditure
which represented from one and a half to four times the
annual wages of an unskilled labourer working in
Accra, or between one and three times the annual earnings
of a small-scale cocoa farmer. This capital outlay, of
course, is all the more onerous in a situation where
house-builders do not have access to mortgages.

Modern houses are personally owned by the person who pays to have them built. Houses are not yet purchased from their previous owner, and there was no evidence at the time of fieldwork that such a practice would soon develop. When the original builder-owner dies, however, who inherits the house? According to Kludze, a man's personnally-acquired immovable property (including houses) devolves by right to his children, among whom it is shared. The **agbanu-metsitsi** and his elders oversee the sharing, but the house does not become **agbanu** property (or property of the **dzotinu**). In the devolution sons have priority over daughters, but this priority does not extend to their rank in the sibling group. Traditionally, Kludze reports, personnally-acquired immovable property became 'joint entitlement' of the set of siblings under the trusteeship of the oldest living male; this system, he claims, has broken down under the impact of a complex economy. Here, I respectfully disagree with Kludze's otherwise thoroughly researched an extremely learned book on the northern Ewe law of property. What I have observed in Abutia does not concur with his assertions, for the simple reason that he treats personnally-acquired immovable property as a homogeneous category, thereby failing to distinguish houses from lands planted with. perennial tree crops. It should be noticed, however, that houses often comprise numerous rooms and that various siblings may claim a right to occupy at least one of them, whereas several farms can be distributed to separate individuals. This, in my opinion, explains why houses are still bequeathed according to the 'traditional' rule in Abutia. When the original builder-owner dies the house devolves to his eldest living son if the owner was a man, but this heir only acts as a trustee for his group of siblings who retain a 'joint entitlement' in the house and, therefore, secure an inalienable right to occupy one of its rooms if there is one available. In other words, the set of siblings forms a house-owning corporation represented by its oldest male member. In the absence of a son, the house will descend to the original owner's oldest surviving daughter.

When the trustee-holder dies, the devolution is then influenced by two additional factors, namely (a) whether the next oldest brother alive has already built his own house and, (b) whether the deceased trustee is survived by a grown-up son. If the trustee-holder dies before his own son has reached maturity, the house will revert to his brother next in line, whether the latter has already built

a house or not. If the trustee is survived by a grown-up
son, the latter will inherit his father's house if his
father's eldest surviving brother has already built his
own. Otherwise, the house will devolve to this brother,
and later revert to the original trustee's own son when
the brother-trustee dies (assuming that there is no other
brother to inherit), and this son himself will own the
house as a trustee for his own set of full siblings.   If
the trustee-holder is survived by sisters only, the house
will pass on to them if his own son is too young to head a
residential group, or if he has no son; if he leaves a
grown-up son behind, however, the house will automatically
devolve to the latter.   If the sons are still children,
one of the sisters will act as trustee until the oldest
son reaches maturity, at which time she will hand the
house over to her nephew. When the original holder or
trustee-holder has no male sibling or children as heirs,
the sisters or daughters will take possession of the house
and gain complete 'right of purchaser' (i.e., full
personal ownership) over it. Women who inherit from their
agnates have to pass the house on to their own sons, if
they have any. When women build houses, however, the
devolution follows a different path, since a woman's
oldest daughter will inherit and treat the house as
personally-acquired property. Houses built by women are
thus bequeathed along female lines.

Women are thus entitled to inherit their father's house
and other personally-acquired immovable property as
epiclerates (i.e., as residual heirs in the absence of
brothers - the word is Goody's 1976:10). As members of a
set of full siblings, they also belong to the house-owning
corporation (enjoying however less rights than their
brothers, in that they are last in line to inherit) and
share an inalienable right of residence (henceforth
designated as 'domiciliary' right) in the paternal house.
If women can inherit houses, it goes without saying that
they are also entitled to build their own.

Movable property, on the other hand, falls in two broad
categories, namely (a) the less valuable (including a
man's clothing, sandals, stools, knives, plates, cups,
hoes, cutlasses, or women's articles of clothing,
headkerchiefs, sandals, stools, plates, pots and cooking
utensils, less valuable beads and earrings (Kludze
1973:266) and (b) the more valuable property: animals
(goats, sheep), clothes, valuable beads, money.
Inexpensive movable property is distributed to paternal
and maternal relatives of the same gender as the deceased.

Valuable movable property, on the other hand, together
with lands planted with perennial tree crops, is divided
among the **domenyilawo** who, above all, include the
owner's own children. In the absence of children, this
type of property follows a very specific 'agnatic' path
(see Kludze 1973:295). (Very little space will be devoted
to inheritance in this analysis; the reader interested in
this topic should ideally refer to Kludze's excellent
monograph).

In brief, three key principles operate in the
transmission of personally-acquired property in Abutia:
(a) devolution along sexual lines to both paternal and
maternal relatives of less valuable movable property, (b)
distribution to children of both sexes, with priority
given to males, of the more valuable movable property and
of immovable property, and in the absence of children,
distribution to agnates. Since daughters can inherit
their father's movable and immovable property as
epiclerates, there is consequently a certain amount of
'diverging devolution' (Goody 1976). (c) Finally, no
property of any kind can be bequeathed to spouses or
affines; in no case can devolution cross the affinal
divide. Affines and spouses can exchange gifts between
themselves, but they cannot bequeath property. The wife
does not inherit anything from her husband; I have even
heard some elders claim that the wife was herself equated
with property in days of yore, and was inherited, together
with the man's house. There is no granary, no crop even,
left by the deceased husband, of which the wife could take
possession. A man's children, moreover, do not derive any
right in his property from their mother, but simply from
the fact that the man they call 'father' has acknowledged
their paternity. Matrifiliation does not play any role in
defining eligibility to a woman's husband's property, a
fact which may account for the lack of ranking of
co-wives. Once patrifiliation has been established, the
type of link between the genitor and the child's mother
does not give the child rights of membership of any group.
The simple fact of filiation suffices (see Kludze 1973:
43-44 and Appendix 4).

Consequently, men never build houses for their wives,
nor do they give houses to their brothers; I have recorded
two instances only, of men who built a house for a sister
in Kloe. Two other men have built for their father, and
two women for their mothers. In all these instances, the
house will revert to their builders when the present heads
die.

Returning to houses and their occupation, we also notice that bedrooms are occupied in a patterned fashion. Each adult male enjoys a separate room which he mostly occupies alone - a man rarely shares a bedroom with his wife, and never with another adult. A man's room is a very private, almost secret place where only women enter at night, and only if invited to make love. During daytime, women and children keep away from men's rooms, because men keep their 'medicines' (**dzowo**) in their room. Young men, however, do share rooms, depending on the availability of space. Women's rooms, on the other hand, enjoy very little privacy since children use them during daytime, either to fetch things or to rest. Old women sometimes prefer to occupy their room alone, if they can, although most adult women share their bedroom with their young children or grandchildren, and often with an adult daughter and her own children. Adult sisters, however, very seldom occupy the same bedroom. There is thus a cycle in the occupation of bedrooms. Children sleep with their mother or mother's mother until their teens, by which time they share a room with peers of the same gender. Teenage girls sleep together until they bear children, whereas adolescent boys eventually move into a room which they occupy alone.

Finally, the **xo** is not complete without a verandah, used by the men as a 'reception room'. A man expecting guests will wait for them on his verandah where they will sit to greet him. The verandah is reserved for formal public meetings, when a serious topic has to be discussed between a few men. Otherwise, men tend to spend their leisure time at the different social centres in the village - the palm-wine bar, the general store, or simply the streets, where they sit on rows of large stones set out like seats. Men thus meet each other outside the house, in one of the many public places, unlike women who rather congregate in the open spaces around their kitchens. Men only use houses to eat and sleep, and they occupy the time not spent eating or sleeping on their farms or in public places. This fact underlies the very secular nature of Abutia houses, which shelter neither shrines nor ritual objects, and are not protected by any special spirits, no more than are Abutia farms. There are no special ceremonies which precede the choosing of a house site, nor any to accompany building or removal. A new owner contents himself with pouring libations to the 'collective ancestors' before moving into his new dwelling-place, but never performs any other ritual connected with it. The only activities prohibited within the **xɔnu** are the **guwo**. No taboos or prohibitions about stored food or storage places were recorded, nor any special interdictions regarding the separate buildings which lodge domestic animals. Only houses of powerful medicine-men – houses known as **afhegame** – must be protected from menstruating women because of the prohibitions attached not to the house but to the medicines. Yet, despite their 'openness' and extremely secular nature, houses are not occupied in a random fashion.

III. DESCRIBING AND CLASSIFYING RESIDENTIAL GROUPS

Houses are not only places to be occupied (or in which other activities, such as copulation or cooking, are performed) but, as we have seen, they are property to be owned. Residential groups and house-owning corporations thus overlap, without necessarily coinciding entirely, and we can therefore in most instances identify a person who 'owns' the house either personally or as a trustee, through building or inheritance[48]. He is the **afhe-to** in Abutia, and the group occupying his house is designated as the **afhe-me**. A standard method of description has evolved, which consists in tracing all the genealogical (or other) connections of every individual occupying the house to its 'owner' who is 'head' of the residential group (Laslett 1972, Hammel and Laslett 1974). A diagram depicting these links will then give a precise and graphic description of the group's composition, and this method has been adopted in this monograph although the groups thus described will not be referred to as 'households', but 'residential groups'.

The sketching of these pictograms often reveals a bewildering diversity in the composition of residential groups and this diversity must be reduced without distorting the data. In other words, the analysis cannot proceed without a **classification**, but the value of a classification is purely heuristic and its greatest value lies in its simplicity. The danger of any simplifying procedure, however, is that important facts may be obscured in the analysis. Ideally, one should therefore try to combine a classification with a set of ethnographic footnotes or comments which would rescue the important facts veiled by the classification. This notion of a 'ethnographic addenda' to the classification will be used below, in the presentation of Abutia data.

I have devised a classification on the assumption that children are under the jurisdiction of adults, and normally coreside with the adults who have taken up the responsibility of their maintenance, socialization and education. In other words, I do not believe the coresidence of children with adults to pose any problems, but only that of adults with adults. Young children and young siblings of the head will thus enter the classification in the absence of secondary members only; otherwise, their presence or absence will be recorded in the ethnographic addenda.

I have also selected the 'head' as the point of reference, both in the classification and description of the groups' composition, a decision which cannot be accepted, however, without some specification. In many populations (and in Abutia particularly) the group's head is often absent from the house for long periods of time, if not indefinitely. An absentee head may be a migrant or may occupy different dwelling-places at different times of the year but, insofar as his or her existence (or that of any other absentee person) affects the occupation of the dwelling-place (i.e., other people refrain from occupying a given space which is reserved for that person), I have counted the absentee as a full member of the group and included him or her in a description of its composition[49]. If absenteeism affects the composition in any other special way, it must be included in the ethnographic addenda and accounted for in the analysis, but it should not enter the classification. In instances where one person owns several houses but occupies only one or some of them (but never all of them), he or she is not involved physically in the occupation of all the houses he/she owns, and is correspondingly **not** a member of the residential groups formed in the houses which he/she owns but does not occupy. In houses not occupied by the owner, two situations may then arise: either (a) rent is paid to the owner, in which case the person who pays the rent stands as the head and the residential group's composition is defined with reference to him or her; or, alternatively, (b) no rent is paid, and people are allowed to occupy the dwelling-unit without payment because of their relation to the owner. In this latter instance, the owner stands as the head and the group's composition is defined with reference to him or her. Individuals are then entitled to occupy this dwelling-place because of their relationship to a person who does not himself or herself reside there (and who is thus external to the group, since not engaged in the activity or residence).

Where the composition of a residential group is defined with reference to someone (the owner) who resides elsewhere, we find an activity (residence) and criteria of membership, but the criteria are defined with reference to an individual not himself or herself engaged in the activity (i.e., the 'head' does not occupy the same house). In the Introduction, I have referred to such collections of individuals as 'exo-groups', and I assume that the factors operating in the formation of exo-groups differ from those at work in the formation of groups[50].

Having indentified the head, one must next distinguish between the group's **core** and **incorporated members**. The core members consist of (a) the head himself or herself and (b) the group's **secondary members**. The secondary members comprise the head's father, mother, **adult** siblings, **adult** children, and spouse. Members of the group who are neither head nor secondary members I have grouped as 'incorporated members', with two important qualifications. The spouses and lineal descendants of secondary members will be classed as incorporated when the secondary member to whom they are married or from whom they are descended is **not** himself or herself a member of the group. If he or she is, they will then be counted as secondary members themselves but only included in the classification if simplicity permits. If they do complicate the issue, I will only mention their presence in the ethnographic addenda appended to the classification (see Table 4   ).

On the basis of these definitions we may therefore suggest a new classification. We will first separate residential groups **with** secondary members (henceforth designated as 'nucleated groups') from those **without** secondary members (and hence, 'non-nucleated groups'). The sex of the head further distinguishes male-headed groups from female-headed ones and the sex of the secondary members differentiates 'cross' groups (when the secondary member belongs to a gender different from that of the head) from 'parallel' groups (where head and secondary members belong to the same gender) and 'bilateral' groups (when the group includes secondary members of both sexes). Finally, the kind of secondary member (spouse, sibling, child, parent) enables us to classify the groups into 'conjugal', 'extended', 'expanded', or 'extended upward' types. (See Table 5 for detailed classification). Admittedly, any classification which seeks to include as many of the pertinent differences as possible conceals a paradox, as the number of possible permutations is so great as to defeat the classification's very purpose, namely its simplicity.   If we were to complicate the classification by specifying the **number** of secondary members also (i.e., whether the head is accompanied by only one, or two, three . . . adult siblings, or children, and so on) we would complicate matters to the point of rendering the classification useless.   To offset this proliferation of types, one must introduce 'ethnographic addenda'.   It is in fact left to the analyst, basing himself or herself on numbers mostly, to decide whether a particular permutation should appear in the classification or the ethnographic addenda.   If an observer found numerous residential groups composed of a female head, her mother, her adult brother, the latter's wives and young children, he should label this type and include it in the classification.   If he encounters only one such group in the society studied, the anthropologist will be well-advised to mention its existence in the ethnographic addenda only, and account for its idiosyncratic existence later in the analysis, without encumbering the classification with unusual combinations. Fortunately for anthropologists, only certain permutations appear possible.

Strictly speaking, no two residential groups in Kloe displayed exactly the same composition but I have tried to handle this diversity by applying the above classification (see Tables 6-7 and Diagram VIII) and adding the following ethnographic comments.

Ethnographic addenda to the classification of Abutia residential groups:

1)   In Kloe, spouses of secondary members are generally excluded from residential groups.

2)   Since Kloe women share bedrooms, I have treated the coresidence of (a) a woman, (b) a woman and her young children (i.e., a 'matricell') and (c) a woman, her adult daughter and the latter's young children (or a 'matriline') as equivalents.

3)   The Abutia practice polygyny but co-wives rarely coreside (only two instances in Kloe).

4)   Kloe half-patrisiblings do not coreside.

5)   Five male-headed conjugal expanded groups conceal the presence of a married daughter of the head with her young children (groups are both expanded and extended).

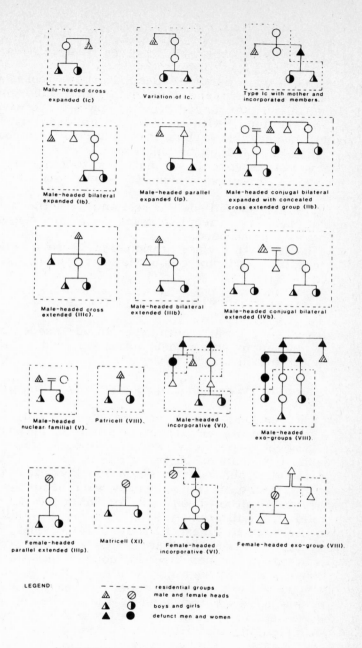

DIAGRAM VIII.   Pictograms of some common residential groups in Abutia.

6)   In male headed pure cross extended groups, only one adult daughter coresides with the father.

7)   In male-headed conjugal cross or bilateral groups, two adult daughters sometimes coreside.

8)   In male-headed parallel expanded groups, coresiding brothers are sometimes found with their young children; in male-headed bilateral expanded groups, however, coresiding brothers are not found with their young children.

9)   Adult males seldom live in female-headed groups, either as spouses, siblings or children.

10) Many married people do not live together in the same house, a practice which is known as duolocal residence.

11) I have classified coresiding mothers as incorporated members, except in cases where the mother is the only coresident member.

On the basis of this classification and these ethnographic comments, we can now begin the analysis proper.

IV. THE ANALYSIS OF RESIDENTIAL GROUPS

Male-headed groups greatly outnumber female-headed ones, and I have chosen to study their formation first, starting with the nucleated groups[51].

A. Understanding male-headed nucleated residential groups

As I stressed earlier, Abutia houses are not only 'slept in' but also constitute an important form of personally-acquired immovable property which is bequeathed, and around which corporations of full siblings are formed.   I have thus found it pertinent to begin the investigation by looking at the manner in which houses were acquired.   All Kloe houses have either been built or inherited by their owners, and this difference is related in a significant fashion to the various types of groups (Table 8).

Indeed, many nuclear familial groups and the greatest majority of extended ones live in houses built by the present owner, whereas the majority of expanded groups are found in houses they have inherited.   Leaving nuclear familial groups aside for the moment, the manner in which the house was acquired does seem to provide an important clue to understanding the differences between extended and expanded groups.

A male heir, let us recall, acts as trustee on behalf of his full siblings who enjoy inalienable rights of residence in the paternal house; this fact underlies the association between expanded groups and inherited houses. Note that this privilege extends to half-patrisiblings **de jure** but is limited to full siblings **de facto** because half-patrisiblings do not coreside (addendum No. 4). The reason behind this peculiarity may be found in the separate residence of co-wives. As the following pages will reveal, polygyny is not widely practiced, co-wives are not ranked and women often have domiciliary rights in their father's, brother's or mother's house. These facts combine to deprive them of any incentive to tolerate the presence of co-wives in their residential group, and sets of full siblings are brought up by their mother in various houses (whether polygyny is contemporaneous or serial). The heir to the house (who acts as trustee) is their husband's eldest surviving son, regardless of the time at which the mother had been married (or even is she had not been married). In most instances, this child and his mother live in the father's house. The heir's half-patrisiblings, being already dispersed over different residential groups, will not move to live with the heir for an obvious reason: if they never resided in the father's house in their life, they will not do so, **a fortiori**, under a half-brother's authority. The coresidence of half-patrisiblings is thus extremely rare, and occurs in special circumstances to be elicited below.

A man's siblings, on the other hand, cannot claim any domiciliary right in a house which he built himself; those rights are reserved for his wife and children. If coresiding siblings are found in a house built by the head, they are therefore merely tolerated because of extenuating circumstances. Overall, then, the manner in which the house was acquired, and the differential rights accompanying it, do make sense of the distinction between expanded and extended groups. But do they also account for the coresidence, or lack of it, of the head's spouse(s)?

A closer scrutiny of conjugal expanded groups discloses two important facts, namely that either (1) the house in which they live has been inherited by a younger son because the older one is socially maladjusted and therefore never married (but has remained in the house) or, (2) the house has been built by a man who has older male siblings still alive, one of whom (the eldest) has inherited the paternal house. The younger sibling has nevertheless invited a sister to live with him, for purely circumstantial reasons. In yet a last case of conjugal expanded group, an eldest son moved out of the paternal house to take possession of his own, and bequeathed his father's house to the oldest son of a group of half-patrisiblings. By abandoning his rights of inheritance in the paternal house, he was forced to confer domiciliary rights in his own house to his full siblings who had been deprived of their rights in their paternal house (since half-patrisiblings do not coreside **de facto**). In view of the very special circumstances which surround the existence of conjugal expanded groups, I regard those groups as the outcome of abnormal and idiosyncratic conditions, and I would in fact view them as aberrations from the extended type, of which they share the basic characteristics since five of the conjugal expanded groups conceal extended ones (addendum No. 5).

These facts thus show that affines are excluded from inherited houses because siblings are given preferential treatment. The rules of devolution of houses endow the heir's full siblings with domiciliary rights in the paternal house, but deny them to his spouse. As the heir must favour siblings over wife and the wife does not share her husband's bedroom, the heir's wife does not coreside with him, except in the exceptional circumstances already noted. However, if there was nothing more to the coresidence of the head' spouse than domiciliary rights, we should then expect either (1) heads of both expanded and extended groups to be married in comparable percentages with the first ones living duolocally, and the second ones living with their spouses, in which case pure expanded groups would greatly outnumber pure extended ones, or (2) duolocal residence to foster divorce, in which case one would find a greater number of divorcees than widowers among heads of pure expanded groups, and the converse among the heads of extended groups.

In fact, we do observe a greater percentage of 'pure' groups among the expanded ones (69% against 44% among the extended groups), but the sheer number of pure extended groups requires explanation. Furthermore, we find that by far the greatest majority of heads of both pure expanded and extended groups are divorcees. In other words, the occurrence of non-conjugal groups (i.e., 'pure' ones) among the male-headed nucleated ones cannot be attributed solely to the manner of acquiring a house, since they also result from an unquestionable marital instability in the lives of their heads (Table 9).

Now, if most heirs head expanded groups, should we conclude that most builders head extended groups? The fact that most heads of nuclear familial groups have built their own dwelling-place belies this assumption. One could nonetheless possibly explain the difference between nuclear familial and extended groups by describing them as various 'phases' in the groups' 'developmental cycle'. Heads of nuclear familial groups might otherwise from extended groups, if they only had adult children. This possibility, however, is not supported by the facts, as only 7/15 heads of nuclear familial groups do not have adult children. A further two lack the physical space to house them, so that 6/15 heads have both the adult children and the physical space but have failed to form extended groups. Demographic and physical constraints are therefore not sufficient to account for the formation of nuclear familial groups.

One might nevertheless contend that such constraints do account for the existence of the other types. It could be argued that all groups, given the same demographic and physical opportunities, would reach the same ultimate composition, irrespective of building or inheritance - in other words, that expanded groups are only formed because the heads do not have adult children, and extended groups are headed by those men who do not have adult siblings; therefore, men with both adult children and siblings would form a composite expanded-extended type of residential group. Let us test this hypothesis with the expanded groups first.

We have already seen that five of the twenty-three expanded groups conceal the presence of a married child (addendum No. 5). Of the remaining eighteen exclusively expanded groups, nine heads do not have any married children (and could not therefore form extended groups, even if they so desired), and a further three lack the physical space to house a married child. There nevertheless remain six heads who, in the absence of any demographic or physical constraints (i.e., they have adult children and the room to shelter them) coreside with their adult siblings but **without** their adult children. Let us now see whether extended groups are more easily reducible to demographic or physical constraints.

Seven out of the 34 heads of extended groups do not have any living siblings and could not therefore create expanded groups, even if they so wished. As we shall explain below, adult men in Abutia are reluctant to coreside, so that the existence of living sisters would constitute a more reliable index of the hypothesis. Fourteen heads of extended groups have no living sisters and, if we restrict ourselves to those heads of extended groups who have built their own houses, we find that twelve do not have any living sisters, and a further two occupy premises too exiguous to allow such coresidence. This leaves us with a total of 14/28 heads of extended groups who have both the sisters and the rooms to house them, but who nevertheless abstain from doing so.

The formation of extended and expanded groups cannot consequently be reduced to demographic and physical parameters, and I would therefore conclude that the manner in which the house was acquired does account satisfactorily for the coresidence of adult siblings, adult children and spouses (but the latter to a lesser extent only, since it is complicated by the fact of marital instability) among male-headed nucleated groups in Abutia, but it fails to explain why members of a given sex, eligible according to the criteria of membership, may or may not join.

The difference in political status between men and women may provide an answer. Elderly women are often highly respected, but they are normally excluded from membership of political groups, unlike men who are assured of such membership as they become elders. Eldership does not come with age only, and the ownership of a house is one of the necessary prerequisites for the achievement of this status in Abutia. In a house of which they are not the head, adult men find themselves in a subordinate position and their children do not have domiciliary rights. In other words, a man cannot become an elder if he cannot give his children domiciliary rights and this he can only fully accomplish in a house he owns, and preferably one he has built. Every self-respecting man wishes therefore to build his own house above all, and even heirs sometimes build to give their children fuller domiciliary rights. Adult men consequently shy away from coresidence, and this accounts for a clearly 'neolocal' trend in Abutia residence. On the other hand, women are always politically subordinate and coresidence in a house they do not head does not jeopardize their political status. There are nevertheless some instances of male coresidence, and we must look at them more closely.

Adult male siblings, first of all, coreside in unusual circumstances only. In four cases the coresident brother has remained celibate and is socially maladjusted. In another case, the coresiding brother teaches outside the village and rarely occupied his room. In all the remaining instances, the siblings' mother originated from outside Kloe, and her sons may be trying to compensate for the lack of local matrilateral tries through coresidence.

Now, what can we say about coresiding sons? On the whole, heads of parallel extended groups are older - 8/13 were born before 1900 (and were thus more than seventy years of age at the time of fieldwork) and the five others before 1914. In 8/13 of the cases, the coresident son is relatively young (less than 35 years of age), leaving a wide gap of approximately forty years between father and son (a large gap in Abutia), and this somehow erases the stigma attached to subordination. Of the five remaining instances, one is an extremely successful man who rarely lives in Kloe and has built a large house for his ageing father (who was approaching eighty at the time of fieldwork[52]), and the others are social misfits who will never reach the status of elder. The coresidence of adult brothers and sons in male-headed groups thus occurs in uncommon circumstances, and I have not been able to detect similar evidence where women coreside with male heads.

These two sets of factors, namely the various domiciliary rights attached to the different types of house-ownership and the achievement of eldership, account satisfactorily for the formation of male-headed cross expanded and extended groups, but they have completely left aside the questions of nuclear familial groups. In fact, the latter have not extended because the head's daughters are either newly married, successfully married and living with their husband, or away in search of employment. These groups are nevertheless exposed to the same influences as the two other types and will possibly develop into either extended, expanded or extended upward groups as the daughters will divorce or return to the village, or they may possibly remain nuclear familial and evolve into solitary residence if the young children leave and the wife dies. Residential groups admittedly grow, but it is impossible to predict in which direction; to that extent, there is no discernable 'developmental cycle' (see appendix 5).

The factors which affect the composition of male-headed nucleated groups would nonetheless leave some features unexplained if they were not viewed in a time perspective. The great majority of expanded groups, for instance (i.e., 21/23) belong to the two largest and richest lineages of the two largest clans, Akpokly and Gulegbe! In fact, the modern type of concrete house was introduced in the 1920s, and the richest citizens from the village, who apparently came from these two lineages, were the first to build.

They have long since died and their houses have been inherited by their eldest surviving sons. Those who built later are still alive, and this time lag in the building of concrete houses accounts for the fact that most heads of both expanded and extended groups are oldest children of their group of siblings, as it accounts for the age distribution of the heads (Table 10). The heads of expanded groups (i.e., heirs) belong to a younger cohort - only one of them born before 1901 - whereas 15 heads of extended groups were born before this date. This time perspective will also elucidate other features of Abutia residence but, before dealing with it in any greater detail, let us first identify the factors at work in the formation of other types of residential groups.

B. Understanding female-headed nucleated residential groups

Most female-headed nucleated groups are in fact parallel extended (Table 11). The two expanded and cross extended ones have been formed in very unusual circumstances[53]. Indeed, if adult men abstain from living in houses headed by women (addenda No. 9; and the reason for this fact is obvious: if men avoid residential subordination to other men, they will a **fortiori** avoid residential subordination to women who are politically inferior) female-headed groups should only develop to be parallel extended or expanded. But, despite their political inferiority, Abutia women prefer subordination to men (who are politically superior) than to women, and therefore avoid coresidence with a sister who heads her own residential group. As a result, female-headed groups are predominantly parallel extended.

Does this mean then, if we take our clue from male-headed groups, that most women heads have built their own house? This is partly true, as Table 11 suggests. From 32 female-headed groups for which I gathered the information, the number of those living in houses built by the head was double the number of those who did not. Only nine women inherited houses - seven from agnates and two from their mother - and one woman has inherited two houses. Out of the seven who obtained their house from male agnates, only four were epiclerates, and the remaining three all have brothers who forfeited their rights in the paternal house. This, at least, would seem to be the case, since these brothers had already built their own house before they inherited the paternal home.

They might not have completely relinquished their claim on the paternal abode, however, since their sister cannot bequeath the paternal house to her own children if her own brother had children (and they all have). This might account for the brothers' apparently generous gesture. A man who already possesses his own domicile can leave the paternal house to one of his sisters without fear, knowing that it will return to his own son. Fortunes may change, however, and the female heirs may eventually come to treat the house as their personal property, but this is left to the lineage council to decide.

The pattern which emerged from the study of male-headed groups does repeat itself. Women-builders generate extended groups whereas female heirs head incorporative groups including their siblings' young children and sometimes an adult daughter of one of their siblings, together with her young children; their siblings themselves shun coresidence, for the reasons mentioned above. In other words, adult siblings avoid coresidence with a female head but nonetheless send their children to be fostered by her. Female builders, on the other hand, do not foster their siblings' progeny. Female-headed nucleated groups (including the incorporative in this instance are consequently governed by the same sets of factors as the male-headed ones. But who are those female heirs and builders?

We have already seen that women have inherited houses either as epiclerates (5/9 cases) or because their brother had already built a house. What, on the other hand, prompts women to build? One could surmise that the lack of domiciliary rights might provide a strong motive. Women whose father never built a concrete house, on the one hand, and women not currently married to a man who has built his own house, on the other, would belong to this category. Altogether, 20/22 female builders are deprived of domiciliary rights, but other women share the same fate and do not build. What, then, has enabled these women to build? The answer, in a word, is their wealth. It is indeed remarkable that all wealthy women without domiciliary rights have built houses, although this wealth has generally been acquired at the cost of marital stability - 17/23 women-builders have been or still are (in 1973) prostitutes in Ghanaian cities, and 16/23 have children who will never be in position to gain domiciliary rights through their genitor. By building, these women both express their jural autonomy and give their children inalienable rights of residence which would otherwise be denied to them until they built their own house, and indeed, these are the very reasons why men build. These woman stand as **pater** towards their children, whose genitor is either unknown or living far away. Four barren women have also built houses (from the proceeds of a similar trade), preferring an independent life, and also in order to redress somewhat the unenviable social position resulting from their lack of fecundity.

I would conclude then that wealthy women normally build houses but that wealth attracts a special type of woman, namely those who do not care about attachment to a man and give up matrimonial stability in favour of trading and/or prostitution.   Now, what of non-nucleated groups?

C. Understanding non-nucleated residential groups

Patricells are formed when heads of nuclear familial groups lose their wife, through death or divorce. All but one of the male solitaries are men who built or inherited a house very early in their life, who were previously married and had formed nuclear familial groups but who were divorced by their wives, who took the children with them. When their daughters start bearing children they will eventually rejoin their fathers and these solitaries will then form male-headed cross extended groups. Finally, male-headed cross upward extended groups arise when heads of nuclear familial groups inherit the paternal house, where their mother resides alone. They move in with their mother because of the small size of their own house, initiating duolocal residence with their own wife.

Matricells are formed around women who either built or inherited earlier than other women, whose children are still young and whose daughters are unwed, and who will potentially form parallel extended groups when their daughters eventually marry and have a children. Female solitaries, however, can be regarded as abnormal cases. Of the four instances recorded on is blind, another epileptic (epilepsy is believed contagious and greatly feared), and a third is reputed to be the most fractious and grumpy woman in Kloe. The fourth solitary woman is a priestess whose god ordered that her house should be built on the outskirts of the village. Female solitaries apart, these non-nucleated groups simply result from the earlier timing of normal events in the process of formation of residential groups.

Incorporative groups, however, are somewhat different. I have already examined the female-headed ones (they are headed by heirs who foster their siblings' children). The male-headed incorporative groups, on the other hand, essentially comprise the remaining members of a dying minimal lineage (Diagram VIII). The survivors of these minimal lineages try perhaps to group themselves residentially in order to assert a separate identity, to avoid submersion in other larger collateral minimal lineages. Incorporative groups can take almost any form but, as a rule, neither families nor groups of siblings are incorporated, and only individuals, matricells or matrilines are.

Of the non-nucleated groups, finally, residential 'exo-groups' should constitute a test case, since the permanent absence of the head from the group should ease some of the constraints about adult coresidence. If the head does not occupy the dwelling-place which he or she owns, the coresiding adults will not stand in a subordinate position to anyone within the house. As can be expected, most instances of coresidence of collateral adult kin do take place in such exo-groups (coresidence of sisters, brothers, half-patrisiblings, first cousins, and so on). The conceptual distinction between groups and exo-groups thus corresponds to important variations in reality.

This brief survey of non-nucleated groups has not revealed any set of factors different from those at work in the formation of nucleated groups. Can we say the same thing about individual incorporation?

D. Individuals incorporated to nucleated groups

Nucleated groups incorporate individuals whose presence was neglected for the purposes of classification. Most individuals incorporate themselves in a residential group because of circumstances too personal and idiosyncratic to enter the analysis, although the incorporation itself is not a random process.

Among male-headed groups, the nuclear familial and expanded ones have the greatest share of incorporated members. The conjugal groups among them incorporate kinsfolk of the head's wife, another group includes a mother who stayed with her son after her husband's death, and a last one was formed around a son who inherited a house of such a size that it would have remained virtually empty had he not extended his hospitality to his distant kin. In the four isolated instances of incorporation in extended groups, the incorporated members are very distant relatives with genealogical links traced through both

patrilateral and matrilateral sides.
Seen differently, all incorporated members in male-
headed nucleated groups fall into three categories: (a)
affines linked to a coresident wife of the head, (b) a
mother who used to coreside with her husband and stayed
with her son and heir after she was widowed and, (c)
distant agnates with closer matrilateral ties. In female-
headed groups, members incorporated to nucleated groups
also fall into three categories: (a) a mother invited to
coreside with her daughter, (b) a son's wife and her young
children and, (c) young children who may be related in a
number of ways and who are fostered by the head. In all
these cases, however, it is clearly the type of group
which determines the categories of individuals who can be
incorporated; it is not the process of incorporation which
influences the formation of residential groups.   Indeed,
despite its seemingly erratic occurrence, incorporation
does not contradict the basic factors operating in the
formation of residential groups.   Mothers and agnates are
assimilated to inherited houses (except in cases where
women build) and affines incorporate themselves in the
groups headed by men who are stably married to their
kinswoman, and live in houses build by themselves. There
is consequently nothing in the process of incorporation of
individuals in nucleated groups which refutes the previous
findings about nucleated groups.

Clearly, two features of Abutia residence should draw
out attention, namely (1) the fact that we find both
extended and expanded groups and, (2) the fact that is is
mostly women who coreside and contribute to the formation
of these expanded and extended groups.   The manner in
which houses were acquired (and, by implication, the laws
of devolution of houses) accounted for the existence of
expanded and extended groups and the 'neolocal trend'.
The prerequisites of eldership moreover, explained why we
found almost exclusively women coresiding with male heads
(and none coresiding with female heads).   Two more
questions, however, remain to be answered:
    (a) why do women actually coreside with their fathers,
brothers, or even mothers (when the latter has built) and,
    (b) why do we find such a 'neolocal proclivity'? The
first question calls for an analysis of change whereas the
second, relegated to the end of this section, needs a more
comparative perspective.

Why do women coreside? Elders claim that young men used to move out of their father's house as soon as they married, and used to build their own separate house near the paternal one. Divorces were substantially less frequent and brides followed their husbands. But, above all, traditional houses were built communally; the newlywed would gather his peers to build him a house in return for a beer party, and they used the material which was freely available in the environment - namely, dried mud and thatch. Traditional houses also seem to have been smaller, doubtless because they were designed to house smaller residential groups.

The introduction of cement as a new building material completely disrupted this traditional pattern. Dried clay and thatch were available to all; but cement could only be purchased with cash. The very task of building lost its communal character to become the new profession of a specialist, the mason. Trained in an urban centre, the mason demanded cash for his services, and thus house-building developed into an investment. The new concrete houses could also outlast the life of their builders by many years and could be built as large as the owner could afford. Their sizes came to reflect differences in wealth and houses became one of the most important forms of property.

Money and masonry came from the outside and sons had to emigrate in order to procure them. Some went to cities in the Gold Coast in search of a trade; others had more flair and acquired cocoa farms or planted cocoa and coffee on their own land in Abutia. Over the years, most of the sons left the village in search of employment, as the statistics on emigration eloquently testify (Table 12). The very cost of a concrete house also prolonged the time spent on migrations, so that emigrants extended their labour migrations for up to thirty years, coming back to the village only occasionally, during their holidays or for burials and funerals of close relatives (a type of migration Gonzalez has termed 'recurrent'; see Gongalez 1961). These recurrent labour migrations directly affected the marital relationship.

In the precolonial society men built as they got married, and one might think that a delay in the age at which a man could build would have also retarded the age at marriage. This, however, it failed to do. The age at marriage seems to have remained more or less the same (approximately 18 to 20 years old for women, and 25-30 for men) and in the early days, the wife simply followed her husband to the city. Her presence added to the husband's financial burden, further postponing the time of his definitive return to the village. The 'neolocal trend' remained so powerful, however, that young married couples did not attach themselves to the residential groups of older relatives in the city, but tended to create separate residential groups.

A migrant husband could hardly provide for two or three dependents in the city and so he would sent his wife back to the village after his second or third child. Back in her native village, the wife would join her father's residential group since her husband had not yet built. Her father's house, according to customary law, was the only place where she had domiciliary rights. Since women share bedrooms, the returning daughter could simply move into her mother's bedroom. After a few years of physical separation (or duolocal residence), the migrant husband could hardly resist occasional affairs with other women, and many a husband then elected to marry a second wife in the city. Being eventually obliged to provide for two families, he would send less and less money to his 'village wife' (counting on the fact that she would be farming for herself) and the latter would in turn accept lovers to compensate for the loss of cash! Such situations could only lead to divorce.

Having hoarded up the desired mony, the migrant would eventually return. If not divorced, his first wife might then move in with him (but might prefer to stay where she was). If divorced and re-married in the city, his 'city-wife' would not accompany him and he would eventually welcome a married daughter to share his house. Some of the daughters who coresided with their father would remain in the house after his death and live with the brother who inherited.

From the point of view of conjugal sets, these recurrent labour migrations thus prompted (1) duolocal residence, often followed by divorce, (2) marriage with individuals from different Divisions and (3) female emigration. Indeed, some brides who proved infertile and were divorced remained in the city and practiced prostitution or trade. Sometimes, the wives who emigrated with their husbands requested that one of their teenage female relatives join them to assist with child care. Through their husbands and other relatives, scores of women thus experienced city life for various periods of time. Some lived alone but others found husbands from outside Abutia. These out-marriages only lasted as long

as the cohabitation did and ended in divorce.   In the last
ten to fifteen years, however, women have not even
associated themselves with other females relatives in
their migrations.   Many of them simply imitate the men,
and one of the effects of recurrent labour migrations has
been to level off much of the social difference between
men and women (about female emigration initiated by women
themselves, see Brydon 1979, on Avatime).

The introduction of cement thus delayed the age at
which a man could build his house, it contributed largely
to forcing young people into lengthy recurrent labour
migrations and was responsible for duolocal residence,
out-marriage, increased divorce and female emigration.
Women who were thus divorced or forced into duolocal
residence tended to move in with their fathers or
brothers, or built their own houses, later to be joined by
their own daughters.   I would thus regard this
technological innovation as the main factor which
stimulated the creation of both cross expanded and cross
extended residential groups, as well as the creation of
female-headed ones.

It is worth stressing once more that the group
delineated in the classification and discussed since the
opening paragraphs of this section are residential groups,
i.e., groups formed around the occupation of houses for
sleeping purposes.   Although the facts presented have
justified the analytical isolation of residence and
residential groups, one cannot claim that the formation of
residential groups is influenced by factors pertaining to
houses only.   Insofar as we can ascertain, precolonial
conjugal groups overlapped with residential ones (i.e.,
spouses coresided; I do not know what obtained then in the
case of polygyny) so that the changes which have disrupted
conjugal sets have also been echoed in residential groups.
As divorce rates have soared, conjugal or familial
residential groups have decreased in number, to be
replaced by extended and expanded ones.   Changes in
house-building and marriage have thus interacted
reciprocally to produce duolocal residence and the
residential groups we observe nowadays.   Residential
groups, however, also overlap with groups of production
and the groups involved in the other 'domestic'
activities, and we must therefore understand their mutual
articulation before concluding a study of residence.

V.   PRODUCTION IN ABUTIA

A.   *Agricultural production*

Abutia straddles two ecological zones which mould its agricultural practices.   The particular requirements of both forest and savanna farming have dictated not only the crops to be grown, but also the technology needed.   Badly irrigated and devoid of any tree cover, the savanna is arid, dry and lateritic in places [54].   The ideal way of clearing its tall perennial grasses is to set fire to it, a task which is normally carried out in February, although this practice is not subject to any precise regulations.   The fire destroys the stems but leaves the roots unscorched, and ready to be uprooted.   Baked by the flames, the dry February soil resists easy tilling, and only the deep incisions of a hoe can pierce the surface and sever the roots.   In the treeless savanna, under the hot sun, hoeing is laborious but it is a task which falls within the capabilities of women and children.   It is the back that bears the brunt of it, not the biceps.

The Abutia start sowing in March, and plant mostly cassava and yams in the savanna.   Cassava can be planted during both farming seasons - the 'major season' which extends from March to July, and the 'minor' one which lasts from September to December.   The planting of yams, on the other hand, is restricted to the major season.   Cassava, which can grow in soils with varying degrees of moisture, possesses ideal qualities of ecological adaptation.   It reaches maturity in one and a half years but, once ripe, it can stay in the ground for two more years without decaying.   Yams, on the contrary, must be harvested in the following September although, once stored, they remain edible for a further year.

Yam and cassava farms rarely exceed one and a half acres, and the biggest yam farmers cultivate up to three hundres tubers.   The cultivation of yams and cassava is also extensive; the same field is rarely tilled for more than two consecutive farming seasons, and it is then left to fallow for five or six years.   Women rarely cultivate yams, and men seldom grow cassava.   Cassava and yams are either directly consumed, or marketed at the traditional market-places; to that extent, they can be called 'subsistence crops' in contrast to cocoa, coffee and partly maize which are sold directly to Buying Agencies which distribute them nationally and internationally and can be described as 'cash crops'.

Maize is grown in woodland savanna or the forest patches in the plain. Cocoa and coffee, however, are cultivated in the mountain forest only - or the part of it available for cultivation. In fact, most of the Abutia Hills were withdrawn from cultivation in the late 1940s when the colonial government designated it as a Forest Reserve, but the unrestricted parts have remained under cultivation. The forest tree cover directly affects the soil's degree of insulation and moisture retention. It isolates it from the rays of the sun, and retains its humidity, rendering it so much softer and more humid than in the savanna that combustion is impossible. Plants growing in this moist and thin humus are easily uprooted with a hoe, but trees can withstand tougher handling, so that their felling dominates production in a forest environment.

Kloe farmers fell trees with matchetes. Cutting down one acre of gigantic tropical trees is a task which needs collaboration, which nowadays can only be obtained through the hiring of labour. In 1971 a farmer had to invest around $20.00 to fell one acre of forest trees, a sum which proved prohibitive to most farmers at the beginning of the farming season, with the few credit facilities at their disposal. Between 1971 and 1973, all those who started farming on the Hills were aiming at growing perennial tree crops, namely cocoa and coffee, which are distributed to Buying Agencies for cash, and all these Hill farmers were men. For reasons that I failed to elicit farmers abstain from growing maize in the Hills and from cultivating coffee and cocoa in the scattered forest patches in the plain. Palm-trees are not cultivated (as one finds in southern Benin, for instance) but are left to grow wild in the forest patches, amid the banana and plaintain farms. Maize which is planted in the forest patches requires both the felling of trees and the 'slash and burn' cultivation typical of forest cultures. But tree growth, generally thinner in the peneplain, also demands less labour. Even if women do not plant perennial tree crops, both sexes nevertheless engage in maize cultivation. The maize grown by women is destined for cooking pots, whereas the men's harvest is directly sold to Buying Agencies.

The environment, the type of techniques it imposes on cultivation, as well as the pattern of crop distribution compel farmers to specialize. Men farm yams, cocoa, maize and very little cassava, while women cultivate mostly cassava, maize and other 'condiments' (onions, tomatoes, beans, garden-eggs, and so on). In this production, however, both sexes have their own farms, and individuals mostly work alone. Some phases in the production - especially clearing, or tree-felling - may demand some degree of co-operation, although on a temporary and extremely limited scale. In exceptional cases, young men and women may help a grandmother, and an old couple may sometimes be seen working jointly (only those couples coresiding and stably married would thus cultivate together); in a few instances, a mother and daughter may also farm the same plot. In the vast majority of cases, however, husband and wife, parents and children, as well as individuals of alternate generations have their separate farms and till the land individually. Every cultivator also decides individually which crops to cultivate, and which piece of land to clear. All adults work for themselves and personally own the products of their labour. Crops are not accumulated in common granaries. Indeed, the Abutia have not adopted any method of common storage in which a household's production is centralized.

The settlement pattern also exacerbates the division between the sexes in matters of production. In addition to farming, women are expected to execute most of the domestic chores; they fetch the water, sweep the house and prepare the breakfast before setting off for their farms, and they also have to return home early to cook the evening meal. These additional tasks would considerably shorten their farming hours if they had to walk many miles to farm. Thus, women tend to till the land nearest to the village, whereas men commute daily to their distant farms, sometimes located six or seven miles away. For both sexes, however, and for men above all, agricultural production absorbs most of the productive time, taking up four to five days of every week.

B. Other productive activities

The Abutia do not keep any cattle, and only a few sheep, goats and poultry. Sheep and goats are not tethered, but left entirely free to roam about. They feed partly on the leaves of the trees (banana, plantain and coffee) growing in the immediate vicinity of the village, and partly on kitchen scraps (cassava skin, maize cobs, and so on), but they seldom venture into the farm areas, which are not fenced. Their occasional raids into cultivated plots, however, do not fail to arouse bitter complaints. The owners of these animals build small huts attached to their own house for them to shelter in during the night. The settlement pattern somehow deters the keeping of a large number of domestic animals, so that the largest flock of sheep and goats in Kloe only numbered some thirty-odd animals. Their owner lived at the edge of town and had been forced to fence his animals in. At a rough guess, I would estimate the total number of sheep and goats in Kloe to approximate one hundred, tended only by five to ten individuals since people with few animals tend to leave them in the care of others. No special groups are formed around the ownership or the care of domestic animals[55].

Hunting was, and still is, a very prestigious male activity, but the mindless slaughter of game over the last two centuries has decreased its importance, and the planned creation of a Game Reserve in Abutia will certainly (if it has not already) deal a fatal blow to this tradition. Bush Cows, Bongos, all species of Duikers and Bucks, antelopes, kobs and Western Hartebeest, as well as smaller animals like the Forest Genet, the African Civet and various species of mongoose thrive in the Abutia hunting grounds. Extremely few species of monkeys are left and all the big game (leopards, elephants, giraffes) has been extinct for almost a century. The tradition of hunting is all the more respected since the Abutia believe their forbears to have been exclusively employed in hunting.

After the savanna has been set on fire, most farmers try to kill some of the Cane Rats and other small mammals which try to escape, but this does not count as real hunting, and carries no prestige. The real hunters cross the farmlands to the large forest area which separates Abutia from Adaklu. The bravest and most respected warriors hunt alone, confident in the power of their medicines, as their mythical ancestors used to do. The majority, however, only join the communal hunts which are organized once or twice a year to track down large game. Only male adults are qualified to take part, and they are divided into two groups - one to beat the bush, and the other to ambush and shoot the fleeing animals. The Abutia do not fish, because of the lack any sizeable river on their territory.

Within the village, few other economic activities are open to men. Most of them emigrate in their early twenties to find employment in one of the Ghanaian cities. They often remain in the city for periods of up to thirty

years, only coming back occasionally during their main
holidays and for important events (such as funerals of
relatives), and finally returning to the village when they
have amassed enough money to erect their own dwelling-
place.   The migrants engage in a great variety of
employment but fail to form groups of production or even
create 'colonies' in their places of emigration.

In the village itself, two tailors and store-owners
have succeeded in eking out a living from their trade, but
only one of them (the main store-owner) has managed this
without farming. All of them own and run their businesses
individually. Siblings or friends sometimes associate to
tap palm-trees and sell palm-wine but their association,
although extremely lucrative, is only temporary.   Some
farmers have also found part-time employment with the
Local Authorities.   One blacksmith still practices the
traditional art, although the villagers' requirements are
mostly met by hardware stores in Ho. The blacksmith does
not enjoy the assistance of an apprentice but works alone,
and in his leisure time.   Despite Bukh's claim that the
northern Ewe mined their own iron ore, I have not recorded
any evidence that the Abutia exploited any mines and,
although blacksmiths certainly fulfilled a most necessary
function for both warfare and farming, they have never
enjoyed the prestigious status that they were accorded in
other parts of West Africa.

Next to farming, trading is the most important economic
pursuit of the women.   Elders claim that women used to
market their husbands' agricultural products. If this was
true, the practice has now vanished. Men now sell their
cash crops directly to the Buying Agencies in the village
and hand over their subsistence crops to the woman who
cooks for them. Women, on the other hand, market the
products they produce individually, and generally trade
for their own personal benefit. Trading is not limited to
agricultural products, as some women traders travel to
Accra to purchase clothes and hardware which they then
resell in the village.   These female traders sometimes
secure their capital from their husband, but they retain
the proceeds, and successful women-traders often amass
more wealth than men (for greater details on northern Ewe
women traders, and economic activities of women in
general, see Bukh 1979).

In order to earn cash, young women in the village also
'break stones' and make gravel used for road maintenance.
Others sell the food they cook to people going to farm.
Indeed, most farming wives only have time to cook one main

meal a day, in the evening, and they keep the left-overs
for the following day's lunch.   If the left-overs are not
sufficient to make a meal, people will then buy their
cooked food from these various 'caterers'.   One woman also
owns a palm-wine bar and hires other women to fetch the
palm-wine from the bush.   These are the only economic
activities available to women in the locality and, in all
these, women do not form groups.   The more educated women
work outside, as teachers, civil servants or secretaries.
Many can sew, but seamstresses would not earn a living in
the village.   Many of the women who emigrate eventually
take up part-time or full-time prostitution, and a
relatively substantial contingent of Abutia women practice
it.   I have failed to make a detailed count but, in Kloe
alone, I know of at least thirty women either actively
engaged in it, or retired.   The problem certainly dates
back to the 1940s as I have found archival evidence of
petitions sent to the then District Commissioner in 1947,
by one Ewe-dome Division, begging him to stop this trade
by restricting the mobility of women.   Prostitutes are
inactive in the village, but flock to the main Ghanain
cities - Aflao, Koforidua, Accra, etc.   Some of them
assemble in brothels which have their own 'queen', but
others work singly; pimps, however, are unheard of.   The
prostitutes rank among the richest women in the village,
and many of them have built their own houses.

    The overwhelming impression one gains even from such a
cursory survey of production is the deep individualism of
economic life in Abutia.   Very few conjugal sets till the
land together, and fewer groups still, comprising mother
and daughter, collaborate in production.   These few
exceptions apart (all of which imply coresidence), every
individual produces alone.   This individualism is made
possible by the pattern of land tenure (see Appendix 2)
since the main means of production, namely land (and
marginally hoes and matchetes) is neither distributed nor
allocated, but available to every adult.   As a general
rule, consequently, individuals who occupy the same house
do not work together.   Production, reproduction and
residence are thus utterly dislocated.   If spouses avoid
coresidence and members of the same residential groups
avoid collaboration in production, what do they do in the
other 'domestic' activities?

VI. OTHER 'DOMESTIC' ACTIVITIES AND THEIR GROUPS

The groups formed in the distribution of cooked food are the most complex of all. To study them adequately, one should ideally have traced the composition of all the groups of distribution, and analyzed their distribution according to the types of residential groups. Having collected a sample of 50 groups of distribution only I was therefore unable to study their overlap with every residential group; furthermore, such an investigation would have complicated and lengthened the analysis considerably, and with greatly diminishing returns, since one could not conclude much more than the obvious. On the one hand, women will distribute cooked food (1) to men who have given them foodstuffs for cooking, (2) to children under their care and (3) to children under the care of the other women (i.e., mother or sister, or both) with whom they form a cooking group, if they form one. On the other hand, an adult must contribute part of the raw foodstruffs if he/she wants to have a right to a woman's cooked food, although the woman is under no obligation to accept this foodstuff, except from her husband (in other words, a woman must cook for her husband, if he gives her either cash or raw foodstuff). Since women cook themselves but few men do, it is mostly men who take their raw foodstuffs to women for them to cook. A man will thus give his foodstuffs to his wife, if she lives in the same locality, whether they coreside or not; lacking a wife, he will ask his mother to cook for him; lacking a mother, he will request a coresident sister to do it. If none of his sisters live with him, he will call upon a sister who lives nearby, or a more distant kinswoman. If the man has a grown-up daughter living with him, she will obviously cook for him if he is divorced.

Male farmers thus produce individually and distribute part of their harvest to one or two women – a wife, a daughter, a mother or a sister. Beyond these, they are completely unaware of the ultimate destination of their products. Consequently, Abutia men do not apportion their harvests to women with the explicit purpose of feeding a well-delineated group of people; the relationship is restricted to the man and the woman. He gives her the raw food, and she allocates the cooked food. A man who is dissatisfied with this arrangement can always take his food elsewhere! But men do not tend to worry about this type of distribution; if every adult who benefits from a woman's cooking must also contribute cash or foodstuffs, the distribution eventually balances out equitably; if I feed my wife's siblings or siblings' children today, her brothers will feed me tomorrow, and so on...

As I mentioned earlier, few men cook their own food, and these are mostly solitaries. Women are responsbile for processing the raw foodstuffs, which they usually cook in the kitchen attached to the house where they sleep so that, to a great extent, we may consider residence as a condition for access to the hearth attached to a house. A few women cook in more than one house and men often obtain their cooked food from houses other than the one where they reside.

The largest kitchens contain up to three hearths. The adult women in a residential group all have access to one of the hearths, and women related through filiation often utilize the same hearth but take turns at cooking. Most cooking groups thus comprise either a single woman, a matricell or a matriline, but collateral female kin (sisters, half-sisters) avoid using the same hearth unless their mother is also a member of the same cooking group. In other words, adult sisters co-operate in food processing or coreside when their mother forms part of the same group only (addenda Nos 6 and 7). Otherwise, they live and cook apart. I have failed to elicit any reasons behind this fact, but I would see it as a weakened version of the 'neolocality' typical of adult males.

In the consumption of their food, finally, the Abutia do not assemble randomly, and the manner in which eating groups are formed reflects by and large the way in which individuals share bedrooms, since people mostly eat in the house where they sleep (teen-agers being a notable exception). Most adult men eat alone, in their bedroom or on their verandah, although some allow a child, usually the youngest of their grandsons, to eat with them; just as women keep away from men's rooms except for love-making, men and women avoid eating together. Adult women from the same residential group habitually eat together (unless they cook in separate houses), accompanied by their coresiding children. Only elderly women copy male behaviour by eating alone, although most of them eat with their daughters and grandchildren. Women eat in the kitchen, a practice strictly avoided by men who believe that eating in the kitchen will endanger their virility.

The residential distribution of the individuals involved in those groups of distribution, cooking and consumption may be quite limited (mostly in conjugal groups, and extended ones) but it may also be quite complex, as Appendix 8 illustrates. Whatever may be the case, it is quite clear that their composition does not influence the formation of residential groups; quite to the contrary, it is rather coresidence which affects most directly the composition of these 'domestic' groups.

If we had not isolated residence analytically and had only concentrated on the 'domestic' groups, we would have gained a strong impression of 'matrifocality'. Indeed, women manage their own production and choose their own residence, therefore deciding with whom they cook and eat. They are also responsible for the distribution of cooked food so that an analysis in terms of 'domesticity' would have revealed a different picture. Women, to all appearances, live independently and dominate the domestic scene and the men, inconspicuously toiling on the land or idling in the streets do seem, to a casual observer, to depend upon women. Some men spend so little time in the house - only to sleep and eat - that their very residence might appear to be at the women's command. If one failed to probe the dynamics of residence, one could easily depict a Caribbean-type household for Abutia, in which men would appear to attach themselves casually to a stable group of femal kin. By studying residence under the umbrella of 'domesticity', we could thus project an inverted image of reality and portray matricells and matrilines as the constant elements in residential groups. When we separate residence from the other domestic activities, however, the picture is radically different, as the previous analysis has shown.

This lack of fit between residential and other domestic groups accounts for the apparent fluidity of Abutia social organization. Houses are physically and socially open; food travels to and for, entering raw and coming out cooked. Before their teens, children often sleep in one house and eat in another food which has been cooked in a third one, from foodstuffs supplied by a man who resides in yet another house. The impression of domestic 'detachment' is so strong that I needed more than a year to discern to which houses individuals were attached, despite the fact that I had taken a census. Neighbouring houses seem to live 'communally', especially insofar as women and children are concerned (see Appendix 8 for a vivid illustration).

Such impressionistic feelings as 'openness', 'fluidity' or even 'solidarity' are better understood in terms of the overlapping of domestic groups. As I reviewed the few households celebrated for their unity, the closeness of their members, their general 'solidarity' and mutual support, I found them to consist of residential groups which coincided more or less exactly with the 'domestic groups', and in which some of the members (husband and wife, or mother and daughter) sometimes produced together. Such overlappings tended to make groups introverted and fostered a unique sense of identity. These closed-in groups, however, are uncommon features in Abutia because people constantly move in and out of residential groups. There is even no concept in northern Ewe to designate the 'family' as a unit of reproduction (consisting of a conjugal set plus the offspring born to them) apart from the notion of residential group, the **afheme**. **Afheme** possibly designated a group of reproduction when residential groups were more familial in character but it no longer means this, since contemporary families are scattered over many different residential groups as a result of divorce, duolocal residence and labour migrations.

Indeed, the figures on fostering eloquently show this dispersal (Table 13 - the figures presented in this table are aggregate ones. For a finer numerical breakdown, see Appendix 6). To my knowledge, no compensation is paid to the relative who fosters one's child, since fostering itself often represents a service rendered to the foster-parent. A foster-child is often of great assistance (and may have been invited for this very purpose) to a working mother with young children, who lives in the city. The foster-parents may thus derive indirect benefits from the arrangement because their foster-child will help with the domestic chores. Also, parents on migrations often send their children back to Kloe for them to receive an Ewe education and, sometimes, even to learn the Ewe language.

Large-scale labour migrations are directly responsible for fostering in Abutia. In the sample (N=1,037), only 477 children or (47%) live either with both parents, the father, or patrilateral relatives. All the others (53%) live with the mother or matrilateral relatives. If one singles out the children born of extant marriages, only 53% live with both parents and, over the whole sample, only 296 (or 29%) coreside with both parents. On the whole, children tend to be distributed equally among patrilateral and matrilateral relatives. If they live with the father, they are probably brought up by a step-mother; if they live with the mother, they are presumably part of their mother's brother's, mother's father's or mother's mother's residential group. When mothers live outside the village, they will send their child back to be fostered by its grandparents, in preference to uncles and aunts.   Non-migrating Kloe mothers, on the other hand, have no incentive to have their children fostered unless one of their siblings living in the city asks for one of his or her nieces or nephews to come and live with him or her to help with various domestic chores.   Finally, couples currently married and living together rarely resort to fostering.

The persons involved in the socialization of children, moreover, do not form well delineated groups.   In the first one and a half to two years of its life, a child will be reared by its mother mostly, although various members of the same and neighbouring residential groups will play an important role in its socialization.   From the second year onward, the responsibility of socialization diffuses to a much larger group, almost impossible to map out. The peer-group plays a very active role, as children play in large bands. Neighbouring kin and friends continue to exert some influence, and the school takes over when the child reaches six.   Nowadays, parents even threaten to take an erring child to the Police Station, to be punished.   On some occasions the threats are carried out and I have often witnessed policemen imposing minor penalties on rebellious children who had been dragged to the Station by their desperate mothers.

I have not found any simple criterion (such as the right to punish, or the duty to pay for education) which could be applied mechanically to delineate a group of socialization.   In a densely nucleated village of open houses where families are dispersed residentially, where children often move from house to house and where they are left to play in groups from age two onward, it is futile to try to define a group of socialization apart from the mother (or foster-parent), the peer-group and the school. This diffused socialization only amplifies the general impression of openness and fluidity.

Unlike other African or Eurasian residential groups, Abutia residential groups overlap only partially with the groups formed in the performance of other domestic activities.   In some extreme cases, the members of a residential group are not engaged in any activity other than coresidence.   To unravel and analyze this complex domestic organization the operational approach has proved most fruitful but does it also measure up to the comparative goal of social anthropology? To answer this, we can now turn to a question that was asked earlier, 'Why do we find this neolocal trend in Abutia?'

VII. RESIDENCE IN A COMPARATIVE PERSPECTIVE

At first glance, an operational approach seems a poor alternative when comparison is at stake. After all, comparative analysis thrives on simple classifications of societies, and there is nothing simple in the classification proposed earlier. There is no reason, however, to be pessimistic.

I have avoided the notion of 'developmental cycle' because I was unable to discern any such cycles in Abutia; other anthropologists have had the same experience elsewhere (Gonzales 1969, Korn 1975). One could perhaps try to derive a developmental cycle from the synchronic distribution of types (a cycle progressing from nuclear familial to extended to expanded) but such an endeavour would be futile because:

(a) Some people started building concrete houses around 1920, and others only fifty years later.

(b) Both men and women migrate, and each individual for different periods of time. Most of them do not have permanent jobs and, if they do not enjoy exclusive access to a room in a house, they will return to live in various houses every now and then, when out of work.

(c) The stability of marital relations is highly variable and no two couples are married for the same period of time, nor do any two individuals remain divorced for the same period of time before remarrying.

(d) Every individual, man or woman, may decide to build at any period in his or her life. Having built, moreover, people do not necessarily decide to move in at the same of their life-cycle.

(e) Men often choose to build a house even after having inherited one, and the ages at which people die and at which heirs take possession of their father's house also vary greatly.

These factors combine in such a way that residential groups can develop in almost any direction - from nuclear to expanded or extended, back to nuclear, directly from extended to nuclear, and so on (see details in Appendix 5). Whether or not developmental cycles exist in a given society, I would nonetheless contend that residential

groups rarely exceed a certain level of complexity in
their composition. When they do exceed it, the anomaly
can normally be attributed to specific and singular
circumstances by the actors themselves. In every society
with residential groups, one thus observes a certain limit
of internal complexity in their composition, some kind of
'breaking point' which is only exceeded in uncommon
demographic, economic or physical circumstances.
Residential groups do not commonly grow beyond this level
of complexity. This level represents a 'ceiling' to their
formation. Some groups, however, will never reach that
ceiling because of demographic, economic and physical
conditions which have a restraining effect upon them. But
all groups, the circumstances of which are subject neither
to restraining nor to singular circumstances, will reach
that level and that level only. This limiting composition
may be called the group's 'limit of growth'. Where
developmental cycles are discernable, the group's limit of
growth corresponds to the last stage in the cycle, before
the residential groups break up to form new ones. Some
populations may have more than one such limit of growth to
their residential groups, but rarely more than three or
four.
    The fact that 'limits of growth' are few in number
makes the concept an interesting alternative for
comparative analysis. Societies with comparable limits of
growth in their residential groups may be classified
together (when the evidence is available; unfortunately,
the relative neglect that anthropologists have displayed
on the topic of residence does not make this task easy for
the moment) and the general conditions which give rise to
such limits can then be investigated cross-culturally.
The fruitfulness of this approach can be assessed from its
application to stem families (Verdon 1979a). In the case
of Abutia, I would regard the **conjugal cross extended**
type as the limit of growth of male-headed groups in which
the head has built his own house, and the **pure cross
expanded** type as the limit where the head has inherited
his house. These limits are exceeded in unusual
circumstances only.
    Female heirs in Abutia usually head incorporative
groups, and this lack of secondary members does not allow
one to infer a limit of growth. Groups headed by female
builders, however, can grow to the **pure parallel
extended** level. I consequently see these three types as
representing the ultimate composition (or internal

complexity in composition) that Abutia residential groups can reach without either restraining or singular circumstances. From the evidence we have gathered about contemporary groups and the transformations they have undergone, we can also claim that Abutia residential groups did not formerly grow beyond the nuclear and polygynous familial types; because of the changes in house-building and large-scale labour migrations the age at building has been delayed, conjugal pairs divorce more frequently and, as a result, we find the new limits of growth that we observe today. This, interestingly enough, invites comparison with Anlo proper. Indeed, Nukunya writes:

"Anlo young men become independent of their parents at marriage. This independence is emphasized by the Anlo ideal that a young man should have a house of his own before thinking of marriage. Invariably he does" (1969:123) and "In fact the household consisting of a man, his wife and unmarried children was regarded by the Anlo as the ideal, and this is still largely the case today, though it is not always realized in practice" (128).

Among the deviations, we find some already detected in Abutia, namely a large percentage of female-headed groups, and the inclusion of secondary members other than spouses:

"Kinsfolk in the household who were not members of the head's own single family seemed to fall into four main groups: head's siblings and their children, head's parents, head's children's children, and affines" (1969:128).

Of the coresiding siblings the majority are sisters and all but one of the coresiding adult children are daughters (p. 129); duolocal residence is also more common than ever (p. 130). Nukunya also reports about female-headed groups that "it would seem that dependants of female household heads were predominantly females" (p. 133).

Admittedly, the Anlo proper practice polygyny on a much larger scale than the Abutia, so that their precolonial residential groups presumably grew to polygynous familial types in greater percentages. Moreover, Nukunya remains silent on the topic of house-inheritance and of changes in the method of house-building. We learn of labour migrations, but not of their scale, and the Anlo proper seem to be less prone to divorce. When we take these variations into account, we can then understand most of the difference between residential groups in Abutia and Anlo proper.

Our analysis has nonetheless left one question open, namely the reason why the Abutia should favour neolocality. Indeed, why should Abutia young men wish to form separate residential groups as soon as they marry? I will answer this question on the basis of aprioristic assumptions, by contending that adult males will normnally avoid coresidence with other adult males and opt for coresidence with adult females, preferably those with whom they can mate, in a situation where the sexes are unequal and men dominate political matters, as one finds in Abutia. I would therefore posit the existence of nuclear or polygynous familial residential groups (granted that polygyny is practiced) as unproblematic, and assume that residential groups would naturally tend towards this type in the absence of contrary conditions. When they diverge from these 'natural' types (i.e., when married sons or siblings coreside, for instance), their 'natural' formation is consequently altered.

In other words, married sons or brothers would only coreside when compelled to do so, when the heads have the power to exact residential dependence and subordination, and I would see this power as emanating from the types of sanctions available to the older generations. If fathers and older siblings officiate as priests of an ancestral shrine, for instance, the subordination and coresidence of adult males should be more easily exacted. By enabling elders to threaten religious reprisals, these institutions endow fathers and older siblings with a greater power of coercion.

The little we have seen of Abutia religion makes it clear that the Abutia do not practice any type of ancestral cult. Abutia ancestors are not reputed to haunt the living and demand ritual worship; as a matter of fact, they are almost absent from the local cosmology. The **afheto**, the **fhome-metsitsi** or the **agbanumetsitsi** are devoid of special ritual or spiritual powers; the only ones who wield such powers are the 'fetish-priests' or 'medicinemen' but to coerce people by invoking their fetish or magic would be tantamount to wizardry. In other words, Abutia citizens cannot coerce their children with the invocation of supernatural sanctions.

Alternatively, fathers and elders could demand
coresidence and collaboration if they controlled the
allocation of the main resources needed for production and
reproduction. But land is abundant in Abutia, and large
parts of it are 'communal' property and available to every
adult living in the locality. Everyone can therefore
start a farm by himself or herself, although advice may be
sought. The lineage heads, despite their responsibility
over their corporation's land, do not allocate the various
plots for cultivation. Elders, fathers, oldest siblings
or husbands do not control either the distribution of
land, or the acquisition of the other means of production.
Both the hoe and the matchete, the only implements
required in cultivation, can be procured cheaply from
stores in Ho. Men in general, and elders in particular,
cannot rely on their economic domination to exact
subservience or subordination from either women or the
younger generations. Abutia farmers are not compelled
economically to produce under the direction or management
of someone else, and only associate by good will, when the
quality of a relationship makes collaboration attractive.
Kinsfolk whom one dislikes, one can also keep at arm's
length; they do not receive any assistance and have no
means of any kind to enforce co-operation, whatever their
age, generation and genealogical proximity. Finally,
fathers and elders also lack control over women, since
marriage payments are not substantial (and now have
completely disappeared), and since adult men do not
necessarily need the intercession of their fathers to get
married. Overall, then, the Abutia elders lack most of
the means of coercion found in other African societies, a
fact which may account for the fiercely and proudly
independent individualism of both male and female Abutia
citizens, and their low threshold of tolerance of
subordination, residential or other.

I would thus regard the economic and religious
circumstances of the Abutia Ewe as the factors most
directly responsible for determining the limit of growth
of their residential groups. In other words, the lack of
economic and religious sanctions at the command of Abutia
elders has promoted a 'neolocal' tendency and favoured the
formation of nuclear and polygynous familial residential
groups. The economic changes which emerged around the
1920s (and perhaps earlier) then account for the
transformations of these familial types into the cross
extended and expanded types we recorded in the 1970s.
Since comparable evidence is not at hand for Anlo proper,

the hypothesis cannot be tested but it goes without saying that I would expect conditions similar to those found in Abutia to prevail in Anlo proper.

These last conclusions prompt us to re-think the relationship between residence and descent. In an article which greatly influenced my own views on the topic, Goody related variations in the composition of residential and domestic groups among the LoWilii and LoDagaba to their varying rates of reproduction which, in turn, he linked to differences in the inheritance of movable property (whether through the mother, or the father) (Goody 1958). Despite a remarkable breakthrough in the study of domesticity, Goody phrased his conclusions in the old language of descent, re-asserting their perennial conjunction.

It so happens that Goody was not writing about patrilineal or matrilineal descent, but about patrifiliative and matrifiliative corporations. I would not deny that the criteria used in the formation of corporations and other elementary groups (which are not **aggregated** groups, let us re-emphasize) may have a bearing on the formation of residential groups but I would assume the connection to be complex. Goody's LoDagaba were distributed over residential groups, the members of which also collaborated in reproduction, production, and other domestic activities, so that the inheritance of movable property (especially rights over crops) did have an impact on the formation of residential groups because it acted upon the rate of reproduction of groups of production. But let us take Abutia, where most of these groups are unconnected. Minimal lineages and land-owning corporations (i.e., **agbanuwo**) recruit predominantly on the basis of patrifiliation, so that we should have perhaps expected the residential groups to be 'patrilocal', or male-headed parallel extended at their most complex. Such is not the case, however, and the inheritance of crops or land influences residence only indirectly; indeed, I have surmised that the very abundance of land, and its corporate ownership by the **agbanu** may have promoted neolocality among Abutia men (and women to a lesser extent). Admittedly, Abutia residential groups might have been different if personally-acquired houses had devolved to the **agbanu** after the original owner's death, and not to his children. What residential groups would then have been like I dare not conjecture.

In contemporary Abutia, the inheritance of houses therefore plays the dominant role in the formation of residential groups. If its mode of devolution changed, or if the articulation of residential groups to other domestic groups were transformed, residential groups would also change in their composition and limit of growth. But to claim any association between 'patrilineal' or 'matrilineal' descent and residence without serious qualifications, even if we retain the definition of descent of previous authors, seems mistaken. And, a **fortiori**, it is still more so if we try to link residence to descent as defined operationally (i.e., as an element of group aggregation). Indeed, if we were to postulate such a link we should also assume a connection between territoriality (another mechanism of aggregation) and residence. One only has to think of the immense variety of residential groups in any nation-state to realize that any theory trying to link the two in the present state of our knowledge would be premature.

In other words, scores of detailed analyses of residence will be needed before we can ascertain with some degree of confidence how the criteria of membership in various corporations and groups affect it, how the articulation of residential groups to other domestic groups renders it sensitive to various sets of factors and, finally, how elements of aggregation such as descent and territoriality can ultimately have a bearing on the composition of residential groups because of their influence on other groups. After years of painstaking comparative research, if the data on residence come forth, I am confident that anthropologists will not dream up an all-encompassing theory linking all types of residential groups to one predominant parameter (such as descent), but that they will probably put forth a series of modest connections between the formation of residential groups and a vast array of pertinent variables. It is quite ironical that our theories are the boldest when our data is the poorest and our concepts the most muddled!

If descent has little to do with residence, we can better understand how the domestic organization can be independent from the political organization. Both of them, however, may have a bearing on reproduction and marriage. To ascertain this, we must now look closely at Abutia conjugal sets.

SECTION 4

Matrimonial Practices

I. DEFINING MARRIAGE

To study marriage preferences, divorce or the origin of spouses we need, first and above all, the heuristic tools which will enable us to decide whether particular couples are 'married' or not; this has been made extremely difficult in Abutia because of changes in their definition of marriage.

Before 1920, I was told, most Abutia parents 'arranged' the first marriage of their daughters, many of whom were betrothed in infancy[56]. The initiative usually came from the boy's parents who, after lengthy procedures involving an intermediary, would be told whether the girl's parents and their respective **fhomewo** had agreed upon the betrothal or not (for details, see Appendix 9). The approval would then initiate a long series of services and prestations on the part of the prospective groom. Over a number of years, the future son-in-law would clear farms for both his father- and mother-in-law and would give them, and their daughter, presents. Many of the prestations to the future bride would be symbolic (such as firewood, kitchen utensils, mat and loin-cloth) and would emphasize the various duties expected of her after the wedding.

The groom would also contribute to his fiancee's puberty rites (the latter were individual, not collective), after which the final 'wedding' ceremony could take place. The latter ceremony involved payments[57] which were made by the groom (helped by his father if it was his first marriage) to the bride herself, and the 'wedding' essentially consisted of a 'blessing ceremony' during which elders from both sides would pray with palm-wine and expatiate on the virtues and tribulations of matrimony. After this 'wedding', bride and groom were properly 'married', although the woman would return to live with her parents until her husband had built his own separate house.

The 'traditional' Abutia marriage thus involved services and prestations to in-laws and to the fiancee, a wedding ceremony and small marriage payments which were 'terminal': after the wedding formal services, prestations and payments stopped. The children of such marriages gained membership of their father's **fhome** and **agbanu**, although it would be exaggerated to regard the relatively small marriage payments as a means of acquiring rights **in genetricem**. Indeed, if a 'properly wed' wife became pregnant because of adultery, it seems that the husband could either claim the child, or repudiate both mother and child; the latter then belonged to its genitor. If a woman initiated divorce procedures, furthermore, she was expected to repay the money which she had received at the wedding but refusal to comply did not mean that the children she bore after the separation belonged to her former husband. They belonged to their genitor.

Until about 1920, most women seem to have undergone this sequence for their first marriage (matters were different for the secondary ones); until the end of the Second World War, a decreasing fraction still complied with the conventional procedure. Since the 1950s, however, it has completely vanished!

In fact, parents could arrange marriages and exact services and prestations from their future sons-in-law because they controlled their daughters' sexuality. This was easily achieved because villages were nucleated and much smaller (one-fourth to one-fifth their present size), while the prohibition against sex outside the settlements (i.e., in the 'bush') was and still is supported by the strongest religious taboos. Also, daughters lived with their parents until their marriage, and in the smaller houses of precolonial Abutia teen-age boys did not enjoy the privacy of a separate room to themselves, where they could entertain girlfriends.

Around the turn of the century, and especially after 1914 when communications with Gold Coast cities were made much easier, Abutia men started their long-term labour migrations which, as we have seen, provoked duolocal residence and spread both families and conjugal sets over different residential groups, encouraging the practice of large-scale fostering. As we shall see, it also precipitated sharp increases in the number of divorces.

Duolocal residence and extensive fostering have now withdrawn most children from direct residential contact with both parents, a trend which has been greatly amplified by the spread of schooling. The school removes children from parental care and supervision for the greater part of their time and exposes them to various influences. School work now serves as alibi for teen-age girls to visit their lovers in the evening, and some of the teachers abuse their position of authority to blackmail some of the teen-age girls into sexual intercourse [58]. From the school, the children have learnt a new code of sexual permissiveness based on individual attraction and self-determination, in which infant betrothal no longer has any part to play.

With the young men working away as early as their late teens and early twenties and the loss of control over the sexuality of daughters, parents have also lost the power to arrange marriage and exact services and prestations from future sons-in-law. As a result, the sequence of events which constituted the traditional Abutia marriage and which culminated in the wedding ceremony have now **completely disappeared.** In other societies, these rituals have been simplified or postponed; young couple may start cohabiting and, if their relationship endures and is sealed by the birth of children, may eventually decide to 'get married'. In Abutia, the traditional marriage has utterly and entirely vanished, and has not been replaced by any special sequence of events or rituals. Despite Abutia's long exposure to Christianity, Church weddings are extremely rare; none occured during my two and a half years of fieldwork and, in the Kloe genealogies, I recorded three only, two of them children of a local pastor.

The traditional practices did not seem to raise any serious problem in the definition of marriage. Those who had undergone the wedding ceremony were automatically 'married' and could be counted as conjugal sets. Nowadays, as the younger members of the population have dispensed with services to in-laws, payments and ceremonies, it is more difficult to decide which couples to regard as 'married'. On this question, we can expect little help from the actors themselves, whose categories share the ethnographer's disarray! When collecting genealogies for the younger generations, I often winessed the elders disputing among themselves whether a couple was married or not, without any other criterion than their own experience of traditional practices. The individuals concerned may call one another **srɔ̃** (spouse) but, when asked if they were 'married' (**de srɔ̃**), often denied their conjugal status because the vernacular expression implies transactions and rituals no longer performed.   At best, the new couples may feel strongly that they are married without being able to suggest anything that justifies their assumption, apart from the fact that they act like married people.   This, in itself, suggests a solution.

Where one draws the line is indeed critical; according to the traditional definition of marriage, nobody has been married in Abutia since 1950!   To rely on the emic catego- ries of the younger generations and their 'feelings', on the other hand, does not take us very far analytically. But to base oneself, not on their reflexions, but on their actual practice, does enable us to formulate a heuristic, operational definition upon which the study of Abutia marriage could solidly rest.

If to use common anthropological jargon, we assume that men and women in Abutia were traditionally married when, after a series of events culminating in a wedding ceremony, they assumed new statuses (those of husband and wife) in order to legitimate their reproduction, we can safely conclude that this purposive component has been lost from contemporary practice. Nowadays, young men and women simply get together for sexual enjoyment and suddenly 'happen' to have children! It is the fate of these mating pairs after the pregnancy has made the relationship public which can be used to decide what kind of unit the man and woman form.

In other words, the initial decision is rarely one of 'getting married'.   The process normally begins with the formation of a mating pair, an event which now takes place relatively early in the boys' life-cycle because of schooling.   Indeed, I have reason to believe that men formerly married for the first time between the ages of 25 and 30, and that they rarely had the occasion of forming mating pairs before marriage, because of the parents' tighter control over their daughters' sexuality.   During the period of fieldwork, teen-age boys had their first sexual experience as early as 18 or 19.   For the girls, the age of first sexual experience does not seem to have varied significantly (it still is around 17 or 18).

Sexual involvements are nonetheless not as easy as boys would like to make out, since shoolgirls fear a pregnancy which would automatically terminate their education and seriously hamper their chances of finding employment outside the village.   They also want to avoid giving the impression that they are awaiting the first opportunity to jump into bed.

Boys avoid talking publicly to the girl they wish to befriend, for fear of betraying their intentions to their friends or peers. They prefer to solicit the assistance of a matchmaker who will mediate between themselves and the object of their attentions, a task which requires the go-between to be a close female friend of both the boy and the girl. Informed of her suitor's intentions, the girl will immediately refuse, but her relationship with the boy will be immediately transformed. Any casual public encounters they formerly had will abruptly cease, as the girl's knowledge of the secret advances of her would-be lover makes her shun his presence. The boy will certainly renew his advances with offers of gifts and promises, but eighteen months may elapse before anything happens. Some girls shorten this period of avoidance by accepting one of the boy's gifts, a gesture which unequivocally signifies her acceptance of meeting him in his bedroom. Large funerals are often conducive to this initial involvement, because of the dancing and drinking which go on all night. Otherwise, a meeting must be arranged in the greatest secrecy. It is the girls who come to the boys' rooms, a fact which complicates the arrangements, since the girl's absence from her bedroom will be noticed if she sleeps with her mother, grandmother, or younger siblings. At this juncture, the matchmaker steps in with a convenient alibi. On the appointed evening, the girl tells her parents that she is going to study with her girlfriend (the matchmaker), but instead she joins her lover.

At their first encounter, intercourse does not usually take place. The girl's position is fraught with paradox – by coming to the boy's room she has expressed her consent to sexual involvement, but she nevertheless is apprehensive of the actual experience, through fear both of physical pain and of the unpleasant consequences of an unwanted pregnancy. In the boy's bedroom for the first time, the girl will literally fight off his approaches, and a determined boy will see his manoeuvres succeed upon the second or third attempt only. One notable lad has nonetheless systematically failed and has been maliciously nicknamed **'nadɔ-loo'** ('Goodnight') since he invites girls to his bedroom only to wish them good night...

With this sexual involvement begins a mating group and, if one of the lovers hears of the other's sexual affairs with another partner, the group dissolves immediately. Young lovers try to keep their affairs confidential, and disclose their secret to their closest friends only, although parents soon develop strong suspicions about their daughters' attachments.

Many, if not most of the teen-age mating pairs break up after a short time, with or without any parental pressure, but some see their liaison unwittingly publicized by an unwanted pregnancy. Despite the strong taboos against abortion, teenage school girls now resort to it commonly and, in a period of six months when such confidences finally reached my notebooks, I recorded no less than twelve successful attempts (others obviously escaped my notice). Those who fail to abort cannot conceal their clandestine love life and are forced to confess the name of the child's genitor.

The girl can name one boy only; to mention a second name would amount to admitting promiscuity and the boys named would certainly deny their responsibility in the conception. Boys often reject the paternity, especially when the girl is still attending school because of the heavy compensation they would have to pay for the girl's loss of schooling. If their flirtation was an open secret to their peers and the girl was known not to be promiscuous, even an unwilling genitor could be forced to accept the paternity and would then be requested to pay a bottle of Schnapps and 10.00 Cedis ($10.00 at the 1971 official and even unofficial rate of exchange) to the girl's parents, and up to 200.00 Cedis in compensation (in 1972) if the girl had to leave Secondary School, or even Middle School (because a girl expelled on the grounds of pregnancy could never resume her studies). By acknowledging the paternity the genitor becomes automatically the pater, whether or not he ever sees the girl again. Marriage payments have disappeared and have been replaced with paternity payments (which, however, do not imply marriage).

In the greatest majority of young loves the pregnancy completely disrupts the mating pair, since the girl's parents will forbid further encounters. If the girl's infatuation outweighs parental pressures and she resumes the relationship, she may be beaten into submission or sent away to live with a relative in a distant town. Some forceful girls, however, win the battle.

Empirically, we thus find the following situations: (a) young couples involved in secret entanglements, whose association will be terminated by a pregnancy; for this reason, they can be counted as 'mating pairs' only. (b) Older couples involved in clandestine affairs. If the woman has not passed child-bearing age, the older couple may (a) wish their intrigue to remain secret, in which case the ethnographer ought not to know..., and will regard them as mating pairs if he stumbles upon their secret; alternatively, they may (b) see their amours publicized, willingly or not. To make the romance public, the woman will openly visit her lover at night, and cook for him. By so doing, the couple asserts that its union will not be disrupted by a pregnancy, and is treated as a 'conjugal set'. A sudden pregnancy may also render the liaison public; if it intrinsically disrupts the relation-ship, the pair cannot be treated as a conjugal set.

When women have passed menopause or are known to be barren, the situation is different. If they make no effort to conceal their affairs, especially when they cook for their lover, their relationship is treated analytically as marriage. These considerations have led me to propose an operational definition of marriage (Verdon 1981, n.d.1).

When individuals who are sexually involved use this involvement as a criterion of membership (i.e., to exclude others, with whom they have no sex), I will write of a 'mating group', or 'pair'. A mating group, however, is not a conjugal unit. Only marriage can create a conjugal pair but marriage, according to sociological and anthropological definitions, implies statuses and reproductive goals, both of which are lacking when young Abutia men and women get involved sexually.

Instead of starting with the purposive behaviour of individuals and the manner in which society endorses it, I start with constituted groups or sets and focus, not on 'final causes' (i.e., reproductive goals) but on an **effect**, namely what the birth of a child does to a partnership responsible for the birth of that child. If it disrupts or transforms it (because of social pressures to kill or ostracise the child, to punish or separate the parents, or force them to 'get married'), there is consequently no marriage and conjugal unit; if it does not disrupt it, on the other hand, we can then assume that their partnership was potentially created around the reproduction of a woman and that they constitute a conjugal set[59]. The element used in the formation of this conjugal set has this one effect, that the birth of a child does not disrupt the set, and I call this element 'marriage'[60]. Since many elements can be used in any given society to create conjugal sets, there are therefore various types of 'marriages', as in Abutia. It should be noted, moreover, that this effect (namely, that the birth of a child does not disrupt the union) occurs if, and only if, the new-born belongs to the group of its genitor or genitrix.

In many societies, this placement is automatic (i.e., independent of marriage) so that a child, whatever the conditions surrounding its birth, always enters the group of either its genitor or genitrix; in other societies, however, this placement is not automatic, and whatever serves to form conjugal pairs (i.e., marriage) must, by definition, act as a mechanism for social placement. Marriage thus presupposes social placement, but determines it in some societies only; the two must therefore be separated conceptually.   This operational definition, unlike previous ones, is non-teleological (see Verdon 1982c).

The 'family', then, can be defined as the 'conjugal set plus the offspring born and/or adopted to it' (i.e., the biological set formed around the actual or fictitious reproduction of a woman) but the family, it should be emphasized, **is not engaged in any activity** (because reproduction is internal to women; see footnote 59).

The very fact of 'being married' (i.e., membership of a conjugal set) may also serve to provide membership of other groups. In Abutia, for instance, marriage entitles a woman to residence in a house that her husband has built. Furthermore, a woman's marriage (or the particular type of marriage she contracted, if the types are many) may also affect the range of groups to which her children will later be able to claim membership.

In contemporary Abutia, however, marriage does not entitle a women to membership of many other groups beyond the husband's residential group (and only when he built the house in which he lives). Otherwise, marriage does not make a woman a member of her husband's **agbanu** or group of production. Nor can she inherit his wealth or position [61]. Moreover, the marriage of a woman does not regulate the social placement of her children. The simple facts of patrifiliation (when acknowledged) or matrifiliation (when paternity is denied) give the child membership of all the relevant socio-political groups in the society. Matrifiliants suffer one handicap, since they cannot hope to assume chiefship of their **agbanu**; this, however, has nothing to do with marriage and does not mean that they are less members of the **agbanu.** They are equal members of the corporation, but do not fulfill the criteria of eligibility to the corporation's trusteeship. Whether a woman was married to her child's genitor or not (and in whichever way she was married,

according to the traditional marriage or in the modern
fashion) does not change anything about the child's status
(status being here defined in terms of the number of
groups of which an individual can become a member): "The
Ewe law is that marriage is not necessary for paternity or
legitimacy of a child", writes Kludze, speaking of the
inland village leagues (Kludze 1973:43; for a vivid
illustration of this principle, see Appendix 4).

Formerly, Kludze informs us, the genitor designated by
the mother was forced to accept the paternity, but this no
longer obtains. Children not recognized by their genitor
are treated as their mother's father's child and do not
suffer any loss of status (operationally defined). With
respect to their mother's father's personally-acquired
property, however, they do not rank as equal to their
mother's father's other male children (who are their
mother's brothers) and can only hope to inherit part of it
if their mother herself inherits, although they may
receive gifts **inter vivos**. Since most children
inherit little from their father, this can hardly be
regarded as a handicap. Conditions differed slightly in
the past, in that children born out of wedlock, like
contemporary children without recognized genitors, could
not inherit their father's personally-acquired property
(unless he had no other son). The sanction, then as now,
seems to have been a very weak one.

In an operational perspective, marriage is a criterion
of membership in conjugal sets and therefore contributes
to the formation of conjugal sets and families, it is to
be studied, not through the 'rights and duties' acquired
at marriage, but through the objective features
characteristic of the sets it forms, such as the origin of
the spouses, the lifespan of the set, the mode of
termination of the union, the numbers of spouses married
at the same time, and so on. It is to these features that
we now turn our attention.

II. MARRIAGE PROHIBITIONS AND PREFERENCES

As we shall see, marriage is permitted between individuals
of the same lineages and clans, but of different minimal
lineages. Moreover, (1) a man cannot marry within his
father's and mother's minimal lineages; (2) outside his
minimal lineage he cannot have intercourse with and, **a
fortiori**, cannot marry two sisters or two women from the
same minimal lineage; (3) two or more men from the same

minimal lineage, marrying outside the prohibited minimal lineages, cannot marry two or more women belonging to one minimal lineage and, finally, (4) a man cannot marry the wives of the male members of his mother's minimal lineage. Elders also claim that cognates descended from common grandparents are too close to marry.

These prohibitions rule out sororal polygyny but permit widow-inheritance. Widows, however, were rarely inherited; I have recorded four cases of brothers inheriting widows in the complete genealogies of Kloe. All of these cases had occurred before 1940. Furthermore, I came across only one instance of a son inheriting one of his father's younger wives, before the 1920s. Widows are now completely free to remarry according to their own choice, and this seems to have been the practice for the last hundred years. They could also choose not to remarry. If a widow chose a husband outside her late husband's minimal lineage, no special compensation had to be paid.

The prohibition against marrying two women from the same minimal lineage is not uncommon in Africa (the Taita, Gonja and Dida practice it, among others - see Harris, G. 1972, Goody, E. 1969, and Terray 1966) but it is less often found with the only positive preference expressed in Abutia, namely that every woman has a right over one of her daughters, whom she should marry back to her own people (only the Eastern Dida, of those mentioned, share the same combination of features). If she has many daughters, the woman will marry one to her own brother's son (or the closest equivalent); in such unions, the daughter marries her MBS and the boy his FZD (this belies the elders' claim that cognates descended from common grandparents do not marry). Some women, however, only bear sons and others have no brothers. Whether she engenders daughters or not, the in-marrying wife retains a claim on a woman of a younger generation from her husband's minimal lineage, whom she will send back to her own minimal lineage to marry. Because of the small size of minimal lineages, in-marrying women can only claim their own daughter, their husband's daughter by another wife, their son's daughter, their husband's brother's daughter and, **in extremis**, a husband's brother's son's daughter, who will be married back to her own half or full brothers' sons, or parallel cousins (Diagram IX). Other variations do occur, but these types of alliance encompass the greatest majority of recorded marriages in which women were betrothed in infancy (I have failed to record the

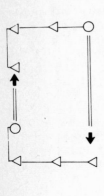

1) Immediate exchange in the first descending generation:
patrilateral cross-cousin marriage.

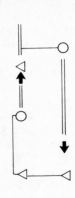

2) Exchange in the second descending generation:
tonga-todevi marriage.

3) Exchange between collaterals in the first
descending generation.

4) Exchange between collaterals in the second
descending generation.

5) Some variants of the pattern of exchange.

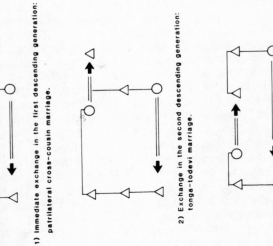

IX.   Marriage preferences.

relative percentages of the various types because I did not feed my genealogies into a computer for the analysis of marriage alliances). Since a woman has a claim over a woman of a younger generation of her husband's minimal lineage, we can analytically translate the process as a delayed exchange between minimal lineages and treat the Abutia minimal lineages as exchanging units in matrimonial alliances[62].

In Abutia, nevertheless, the exchange is 'sealed' or terminated after a daughter has been 'returned' and the 'returning daughter' cannot normally claim her own daughter or another woman of her husband's minimal lineage unless she bears numerous female offspring. In other words, women possess such claims over 'daughters' only when they initiate an exchange. Otherwise, the marrying back and forth of women to their real or classificatory MBS would soon weave a dense web of genealogical connections which would inhibit further exchanges between the two minimal lineages for many generations because, with the exception of the FZD marriage, individuals descended from a common set of grandparents do not intermarry. Some minimal lineages nonetheless go on exchanging over many generations but they are all larger groups, possessing more collateral branches, and they all space their alliances both in time and in genealogical span so as to avoid genealogical 'short-circuiting'.

This model of marriage preferences was derived from a detailed study of the complete genealogy of the inhabitants of Kloe, but I have no reason to suspect that my findings do not extend to the other two villages. The pattern of marriage preferences revealed by actual practice did in fact bear out the only stated preference, namely that daughters of women who initiated an exchange ought to marry back into their mother's minimal lineage. In other words, the Abutia never state their preference in terms of either genealogical or terminological categories. But I did ask them which categories of kin ought to marry preferentially. After an initial puzzlement and some reflection, people would risk an opinion. No consensus emerged, but there was enough general agreement to enable us to abstract the following preferences: (1) the best marriages among kin are those between **tasivi-nyirevi** (cross-cousins, without specification of the side); (2) it is good, but not preferred, for **tɔnga-tɔdevi** (patrilateral parallel cousins) to marry, and finally, (3) **nɔga-nɔdevi** (matrilateral parallel cousins) should not marry because they are too close.

The slight preference for the terminological category of patrilateral parallel cousins first surprised me because minimal lineages are exogamous so that first, second and third degree parallel cousins cannot inter-marry. However, I found the answer in the genealogical distortions brought about by the kin nomenclature.

Indeed, one finds a flagrant discrepancy between genealogical and terminological specifications. Terminologically speaking, individuals are categorized as cross-cousins (**tasivi-nyirevi**) when they are related genealogically through individuals of different sexes in the **first** ascending generation (see Appendix 10 for kinship terminology). When a daughter is sent back to marry her MBS or MFBSS, genealogical and terminological specifications do coincide and both refer indeed to cross-cousins. It must be noticed, however, that the **tasivi-nyirevi** preference does not operate in both directions. Since a man cannot marry in his mother's minimal lineage, he is prohibited from marrying his MBD. Marriage with the real MBD is impossible, and no instance was found in the genealogies. I have not checked for marriage with classificatory MBD's because the question is too complex. Indeed, according to the Ewe kin terminology, such kin as Ego's MFFZZSD are designated as MBD, so that it would have been meaningless to try to elucidate marriage preferences on the basis of classificatory terms.

When FZD marriage (defined from the point of view of a male Ego) is impossible because of demographic or other reasons and the woman arranges for her son's daughter to marry back into her minimal lineage, the bride and groom are genealogically related as 'cross-cousins once removed' but are **terminologically** designated as patrilateral parallel cousins (**tɔŋga-tɔdevi**) because they are related through fathers in the first ascending generation. The confusion had thus arisen only because I had asked questions in terms in which the informants do not normally conceptualize their practice.

In other words, if the 'delayed' exchange is completed in the first descending generation (woman sending her own daughter back), the bride and groom stand as **tasivi-nyirevi** and this is the ideal marriage among kin. If the exchange is delayed a further generation and the woman can only send a son's daughter back, the bride and groom stand as **tɔŋga-tɔdevi**; this remains a good union, because the 'return' marriage has been completed. Since women have claims over women of their husband's minimal lineage only, there is no room for marriage with the matrilateral parallel cousin in this system of delayed exchange, especially if cognates descended from the same grandparents are forbidden to intermarry. On the whole, then, the preferences as stated in terms of kin categories did tally with the explicit predilection for delayed exchange.

III. THE ORIGIN OF SPOUSES

Within both Abutia villages and their component descent groups in-marriage does take place, and on a large scale[63]. A study of all female marriages (Table 14) reveals that 64% of them were contracted within the village, and 74% of their first marriages. The figures suggest that women's secondary marriages take place proportionally more often outside the village, and they also indicate a strong preference for village in-marriage. The same tendency towards in-marriage can be observed within clans and lineages; in a survey of both first marriages and all female marriages, approximately 50% of the cases of village in-marriage conceal marriage within the clan, and a further 30% of instances of clan inmarriage also consist of marriages within the lineage. Abutia descent groups - lineages and clans - thus permit in-marriages in large numbers. These global rates are reliable indicators but they also mask two other important dimensions, namely those of (1) size and (2) time.

1. When broken down by clans, the rates disclose new facts. First of all, Wome and Atsadome, two of the smaller clans, display higher proportions of village out-marriage. The differences are numerically too small to be significant, but one would nonetheless expect the larger clans to marry outside more frequently, and the smaller clans less so. Strangely enough the converse seems to obtain, except for Etsri (Tables 15-17).

The incidence of clan and lineage in-marriage, when distributed by clans, shows that the smaller clans, Etsri included, practice descent group in-marriage on only half the scale of the larger ones (Table 14). Gulegbe nonetheless exhibits rates identical to the smaller clans, but because two of its lineages have split. Had they remained united, they would have married in on a scale comparable to that of Akpokli [64]. This same distribution by clan evinces another interesting feature. The large clans (Akpokli and Gulegbe) feed on themselves matrimonially, as it were, while the smaller clans marry outside the village proportionally more often than the large ones. This, however, applies to women's first marriages only; when all female marriages are taken into account, the proportions are very similar.

The movement of brides between clans (Tables 15-17) shows that exchanges more or less even out, except for Gulegbe and Etsri. Gulegbe's greater size may account for its excess of 'exported' brides, but Etsri's general deficit vis-à-vis other clan does not stem from its size. Some elders divulged that Etsri clansmen immigrated only a century or so ago from Teti, for reasons which I was unable to elicit. Their possible 'marginality' may explain their compulsive giving of daughters to other clans and their higher proportion of village out-marriage may simply be the outcome of a more prosaic fact, namely that in one of Etsri's lineages the women far outnumber the men, an imbalance which flow directly from the lineage's small size (see age pyramids, Appendix 11). The smaller the lineage, the greater its sensitivity to random demographic variability. This particular combination (the excess of women and a stronger desire to marry in the village) may thus account for Etsri's special position. The same tables also show that the smaller clans orbit matrimonially around the two large ones, and marry little between themselves.   Clans thus seem to close off matrimonially as they grow, and open up as they shrink, but open up to larger clans only (assuming that clans did diminish in size[65]).

The movement of brides between clans has changed little except for Wome which has essentially stopped giving brides to smaller clans since 1935.   Atsadome never supplied many brides to small clans, and Etsri's quotas have not abated. But the reasons why Atsadome, from the earliest records, and Wome since 1935 have avoided inter-marriage with other Kloe clans remains puzzling. If we discount Atsadome, both Etsri and Wome appear to have inter-married in proportion to their respective sizes. Since the 1930s, however, the building of houses has interfered with matrimonial practices. The smaller clans are on the whole the poorest and poorer men from small clans have either failed to build a house, or built a small one.   As a result, their sisters or daughters are generally deprived of domiciliary rights.   By marrying into a small clan, a woman of a small clan would only taste more of the same until her husband married; if they divorced, she would then have nowhere to go.   If this is the alternative open to them, it is quite logical that they prefer to leave on labour migrations and marry where they work. The small size of the minimal lineages of those small clans may also induce men from these clans to rely on their daughters and sisters to increase its population, by 'giving birth to the minimal lineage' (**dzi vi na fhome**). This would account for the fact that proportionally more prostitutes come from these smaller lineages. Prostitutes build their own house and, to all practical intents and purposes, act as 'father' to their own children. More powerfully attracted by labour migrations, women from smaller clans thus tend to marry more outside the area. This association, however, can only hold if the higher proportion of village out-marriage for the women of these small clans is a recent phenomenon, and only a diachronic enquiry can answer this question.

2. When the rates of in-marriage are broken down by cohorts of ten years (Table 18-19), it is clear that this higher percentage of village out-marriage in the smaller clans dates back to the end of the Second World War only, and that all clans have witnessed a similar surge of village out-marriage at two specific moments in the history of Abutia, namely in the decade following 1915, and around 1945. Both increases follow known events - the expulsion of the Germans in 1914, which facilitated migrations to and from the Gold Coast, and the new economic opportunities which followed the Second World War. The late 1940s and early 1950s also saw the opening up of new roads and the introduction of motor vehicles. Out-marriage treads on the heels of labour migrations, and its general frequency varies with the economic opportunities outside the Division.

This chronological breakdown also suggests that village in-marriage was also practiced before 1890, although possibly on a smaller scale. I nevertheless suspect that the higher rates of village out-marriage before 1875 (Table 19) result from genealogical amnesia. Ancestresses are more quickly forgotten than ancestors, to allow the freedom to marry within the locality. When women marry out, on the other hand, they do not intensify the internal web of kinship but rather enlarge the number of marriageable women, so that ancestors or ancestors' sisters who married outside the village could very well be remembered long after men and women of the same generation who married in the village have been forgotten.

Selective recollection could also account for the evolution of clan in-marriage, apparently very uncommon before 1880 (Table 18). The similar but belated

development of lineage in-marriage nevertheless rules out
the influence of selective genealogical recollection in
this case and suggests that the figures obtained for clan
in-marriage may more or less reflect the real situation
and not be greatly affected by genealogical amnesia. I
therefore believe that clan in-marriage was rare a century
ago, but increased drastically in the late 1880s and
1890s. This hypothesis is all the more plausible since
the dates correspond to the waning of Ashanti-Akwamu
expansion in the Volta Region, and the imposition of the
Pax Germanica. Clans may thus have sought to inter-marry
to create and strenghten alliances in times of war, but
preferred to close in on themselves with the coming of
peace. Precolonial clans were undoubtedly smaller, and a
policy of clan in-marriage would have spelled doom in
troubled times.

Clan in-marriage reached a peak around the 1930s and
then declined, especially in the two decades before 1972,
perhaps contributing partially to the rise of village out-
marriage at the same period. The youth of the last two
decades may indeed have been faced with only one
alternative - to marry within their own clans, or marry
outside the village altogether. The figures also leave no
doubt that lineage in-marriage is a comparatively recent
phenomenon, since no instance took place before 1915,
except in Akpokli. Akpokli started to marry in early, but
is now abandoning the practice. Gulegbe copied it later,
but still practices it vigorously (in 1972). In the
smaller clans, the absolute number of lineage in-marriages
is too insignificant to warrant analysis. But the recent
emergence of both clan and lineage in-marriage, and the
fact that their incidence varies greatly according to the
size of clans, are two critical features which call for
explanation.

In my opinion, the sudden appearance of descent group
in-marriage requires both organizational and demographic
conditions. The organizational prerequisites existed
already in Abutia but were not sufficient to precipitate
in-marriage in clans and lineages. I therefore believe
that the small number and differential size of clans may
have provided the additional demographic conditions to
spark it off. In most African societies, a man does not
marry from the exchanging (or exogamous) units of his
father and mother. If precolonial Kloe clans were
exogamous and the villagers preferred local in-marriage,
the men whose parents hailed from the two large clans
would have to find spouses in the smaller clans, which may

not have been able to satisfy this demand for brides. As two of the clans greatly outgrew the others, they may have seen no alternative to marrying within the clan.

Differentials in size do not account so well for lineage in-marriage because of the larger number of lineages. At least fifteen of them existed in the 1910s, when the first lineages started marrying in. The larger lineages did initiate the practice but their size alone, although necessary, was not sufficient to stimulate the practice. I would rather invoke economic causes. Abutia **agbanuwo** are also land-owning corporations, and the Abutia used to give a piece of land to daughters who married outside the clan or the village 66. Some elders claim that these gifts of land had to be returned to the women's **agbanu** after her death, but others contend that it passed on to the woman's sons, if she had any; if she did not bear any sons, the land would then revert to her **agbanu.** Whatever the case may be, the gifts did incite disputes over land and some elders suggested that the practice of marrying within the lineage grew as an attempt to avert such litigations. The practice once started, there were no serious grounds to stop it. Lineage in-marriage also began in the richest lineages of Akpokli and Gulegbe, and it may also be that rich individuals wished their children to marry their equals (following Goody's association between stratification and endogamy, Goody 1976). I have unfortunately been unable to probe deeper into the problem. Of the six earliest cases of lineage in-marriage recorded, two did take place between the children of unusually rich individuals, but I lack the information for the other four cases.

The global rates for in-marriage with which I opened this section thus concealed two critical facts, namely that descent group in-marriage in Kloe is associated with the groups' sizes, and that it only dates from the turn of the century. But did the precolonial descent groups show the same differentials in size and, if not, what has happened since? Precolonial lineages could not have been much smaller than present-day Type I lineages, and the differentials may have been exagerated in the last seven decades or so. Smaller clans have certainly increased in size in the last century, but their rate of growth was possibly lower than that of Akpokli and Gulegbe. On the basis of a demographic retrojection (Appendix 1) Kloe could not have numbered more than 300 inhabitants in the

1870s.   If these were divided into five clans and every clan into three lineages, the differentials had to be much smaller.   The smallest lineages would have had a population of 15-20 people, including children, so that small clans composed of such small lineages only could have been 45-55 strong.   The three smallest clans could thus have accounted for close to 150 individuals, leaving between 150 and 200 members for the other two clans, or 75-100 souls each.   The differences could have hardly been much more than a ratio of 2:1.   Alternatively, there could have been one less clan, although this is more disputable. With four clans the two largest clans could not have numbered much more than 100-125 individuals each, or a ratio of 3:1 with the smaller ones.   But the differences between large and small clans have now doubled this ratio, so that the large clans must have increased more rapidly than the small ones.   If this has happened, commonsense suggests that the purchase of slaves and/or polygyny would best account for those differentials in the rate of growth.

IV. POLYGYNY IN ABUTIA

Before presenting the rates of polygyny themselves, a few words ought to be said about the sample from which the data was collected.   I gathered the complete genealogy of Kloe and further collated it to a census of the village. From this source, I distinguished four 'populations', namely (1) the set of men engaged in extant marriages at the time of fieldwork (1972), (2) the set of individuals not married during the period of collection of genealogies but who had been married in the past and who, together with (1), form the category of all men 'ever married' and still alive, to be distinguished from (3) all men ever married, but dead. (2) and (3) combine further to give (4), the 'global' male population ever married, both dead and alive.

A.   Polygyny: incidence and intensity

What first strikes the observer is the great proportion of individuals alive, married at some point, who were nonetheless not currently engaged in any matrimonial union at the time of fieldwork (Table 20).   To match the numbers of marriageable men and women would yield a ratio of 156 women to 100 men, a figure greatly discrepant from reality; indeed, we presently find 165 monogynists, 28 polygynists married to two wives, and eight married to three. Altogether, there are only 119 currently married women per 100 currently married men; the incidence thus amounts to 1.19 only. Kloe thus possesses a potential for polygyny which is only partially exploited and, in both absolute and relative terms, the village exhibits a very low incidence of polygyny.

All the available rates convey the same impression. Only 222 women, for instance, are married to 100 polygynously married men, yielding an intensity of only 2.22. All the 81 'one time' polygynists alive have been married polygynously to a total of 200 women, thus yielding an intensity of 2.47. This might suggest that polygyny has declined in recent years, but this would be an erroneous conclusion if one wanted to measure the intensity at any given point in time. Some men married a first, then a second wife, only to divorce the second later and marry a third one some time after. They consequently practiced polygyny more than once in their life, but never with more than two women at a time. We can therefore divide the set of 81 'one time' polygynists alive further according to the maximum number of wives to whom any of them were married simultaneously. 57 men did not marry than two wives, and did this only once in their life, and nine others never engaged in polygynous unions with more than two wives, but did so twice in their life. Consequently, 66/81 (or 81%) of the living 'one time' polygynists were never married to more than two wives simultaneously. Three were involved in four unions at one point in their life, but none was ever remembered to have been married to more than four wives at the same time. The remaining cases (12/81) married different combinations, ranging from two to three wives. Altogether, then, the intensity of plural marriage of these 81 polygynists remains very weak.

I have chosen a different ratio, namely the proportion of polygynous marriages to all male marriages, to discuss the rates of polygyny for the deceased and global populations (Table 21). A certain number of 'uncertain cases' are encountered in the computation of these rates, when it is known for certain that a particular man has married more than one woman, but impossible to decide whether it represents a case of real or serial polygyny. Two different percentages have therefore been presented: (a) a lower rate, which treats all uncertain cases as instances of serial marriage and, (b) a higher rate, which

regards them as occurrences of real polygyny.   The truth
lies somewhere between these two frequencies.

In 1971-72, I recorded a relatively low percentage of
extant polygynists in the population of males who were
currently married (31 extant polygynists out of 201
extantly married males, or 16% - see Table 21). Of all
living men, 81 have been reported as polygynists at one
time or another in their life, with one uncertain case.
25% of the total male population ever married had thus
experienced polygyny, and only 44% of the 'one time'
polygynists still enjoyed the status at the time of
fieldwork.   Similar ratios were calculated for the dead
population, selecting only the cohort of those whose first
marriage was celebrated on or after 1895, to increase the
reliability of the conclusions[67].   Among the deceased,
155 married their first wife in or after 1895 and, of this
number, approximately 27% experienced polygyny (Table 22).
Of both the defunct and live male populations, the
polygynists constitute only 25%.   All these rates concur
to indicate that, at any given point in the last hundred
years or more, less than 30% of the male population has
ever experienced polygyny. Such percentages nevertheless
include young men who have not yet terminated their
matrimonial career, and the data must once more be divided
into cohorts to account for the time perspective and to
correct this bias (Table 23).

Among the live population who were first married in or
after 1895, and for whom the date of first marriage is
known (N=301), the proportion of polygynists increases as
we go back in time to the point where the only survivor of
the earliest cohort is a polygynist (Table 22). But when
mortality is also taken into account (in the 'global
population'), the figures attest an increase in the
incidence of polygyny (expressed as the ratio of
polygynous marriages to all male marriages - Table 23). I
do not believe the data before 1875 to be reliable, but it
nevertheless reveals a dearth of polygynists among the
ancestors who are recollected.   I construe this as a
further indication of low polygyny rates, since societies
with a high frequency of plural marriage do remember their
ancestors as having been more polygynous than the living
population.

From what I know of the marital behaviour of Kloe men,
the men who contracted their first union before 1935 will
not re-marry so that rates of polygyny for these cohorts
will not change.   They reveal a probable increase in the
1870s (after the Ashanti wars) and a second, smaller one,

at the turn of the century (Table 23). The comparatively
smaller percentage of polygynous marriages for the
1915-1925 cohort, however, goes against this trend and
even the relative imprecision of dates or the possibility
of cumulative errors would not explain it away. I believe
religion to be largely responsible for this lower
incidence. The German missionary and educational effort
reached its peak from the late 1890s to 1914, and the
children brought to their missionary schools were the most
successfully indoctrinated in the Presbyterian faith; they
formed the first generation of staunch Christians (and
perhaps the last..., as the British educational methods
were not as 'forceful' as the German ones!) and the first
ones who systematically shunned polygyny.

Overall, then, the diachronic distribution of plural
marriage (Tables 22-23) safely supports the following
conclusions: (a) that the proportion of polygynous
marriages has probably increased by a factor of 10% since
the beginning of the German colonial rule (early 1890s);
(b) that those educated by the Germans, who started their
matrimonial career after 1915, have tended to shy away
from plural marriage; (c) that approximately 40% of the
men who marry have experienced polygyny by the time they
die; most of them will have experienced it only once, and
with two wives only. Finally, (d) before 1875, one may
assume that scarcely more than 25% of any given cohort of
men who married would have practiced polygyny by the end
of their life. When added to the contemporary 16% of
married men who are currently (1972) polygynous and 25% of
all living males who have ever experienced polygyny
(selecting adult males only, by the very definition of
polygyny), these various rates confirm the impression that
the incidence and intensity of polygyny in Abutia are low
for sub-Saharan Africa. Dorjahn has indeed calculated, on
an area basis, that the lowest sub-Saharan incidence
approximates 25% of all married men (compared with 16% in
Abutia) and both he and Clignet accept 20% and less as a
'limited' incidence of polygyny (Dorjahn 1959, Clignet
1970). But even if its practice is not widespread, some
individuals do practice it. Who are they?

B. The Abutia Polygynists

Anthropologists have portrayed the classic African
polygynist as either a chief, or a tribal elder
accumulating wives as he gets older. The age distribution
of extant Abutia polygynists immediately belies this

assumption (Table 24). 81% of them have not celebrated their fiftieth birthday, and all elders aged 61 and above, save one, are presently monogynists. The extant polygynists are thus in the main young (between 30 and 50 years old) and do not stand in any privileged position in the political organization (very few of the **fiawo**, for instance, are polygynous). In most other respects, the observer can hardly distinguish them from other individuals of the same age group.

The number of years for which they practice polygyny is also relatively small (Table 25). From a sample of 77 individuals (or 58% of the known cases of polygyny) who married only two wives only once in their life, and for whom the duration of marriage was known, the average span of polygynous life slightly exceeded six years for those who had at some time been polygynists (dead and alive), and eight years for the extant ones. The many uncompleted unions make the sample slightly inaccurate, but the small number of cases in the sample made it impossible to convert extant into completed marriages (following Barnes 1967). If such transformations were possible, they would certainly show that the great majority of polygynous unions did not outlive a decade and that most polygynists have divorced at least one of their two wives by their early fifties, and do not remarry thereafter.

Divorces also take place with increasing frequency (see following section). The 'overall' incidence of polygyny was presumably lower before the implantation of German colonial rule, but I would surmise that the duration of polygynous unions was longer, with the result that, at any given point in time, the incidence of polygyny would have equalled, if not surpassed that observed nowadays[68]. The main difference lies in the fact that men who were then engaged in polygynous unions probably represented 90% or more of the men alive who ever experienced polygyny, and the 10% or less who had been polygynists but were no longer so probably owed their fate to mortality, and not divorce. If divorce has replaced death as the dominant means of terminating marriage (and it has, especially since mortality rates have also declined) it consequently decreases the proportion of current to 'one time' polygynists.

The contemporary Abutia polygynists are also fairly representative of men of their own age cohort in their residential behaviour. Most of them tend to reside outside their native village, although domiciled in the latter (Table 24). Conversely, all but one of the older polygynists (50 years old and above) live in their native village, and the only exception to this rule is a man prevented from living at home by illness.   Extant polygynists thus display a life-cycle identical to other men of their own age: they emigrate to Ghanaian cities in their early twenties, with the ultimate aim of making enough money to build themselves an impressive house in Kloe to which they will retire twenty or thirty years later.   Not all are equally successful in their labour migrations, nor are they all equally committed to this quest.   In this respect, the young polygynists stand out as deeply Westernized and economically successful.   They are among the best educated and among those who have found lucrative and permanent employment in teaching or administration.   This finding corroborates those of Clignet and Sween (1974), who discovered in African cities a strong correlation between polygyny on the one hand, and successful integration to national or urban life on the other.

During their migrations, most of these younger polygynists do not yet own a house in the village or, if they do, they await retirement before settling in.   One of their wives shares their residence in the city, and the other lives with her own father, mother or brother in Kloe or in her own native village.   The husband's coresident wife is often newly-wed or infertile.   The status of infertile wives, kept despite their sterility when a co-wife is much more prolific, is expressed by the Abutia as **kɔdinu**, or 'play-thing'; such women are not divorced because their lack of fertility does not subject them to the post-partum taboos on sexual intercourse. Also, their freedom from child care enables them to be gainfully employed.   Such situations often provide men with a real bonus, while the sterile women, for their part, are sometimes satisfied to remain married (until they become rich enough to build their own house in the village...).

Contemplated from the point of view of individuals, and as a form of matrimonial behaviour, Abutia polygyny could hardly be called a 'productive' strategy.   Polygyny certainly thrives on wealth but many, if not most, rich men remain monogynous. Men also acknowledge the financial deficits that plural marriage often incurs.   Married women may ask their husband money to trade, often at a loss, and no economic 'success story' ever associates plural marriage with accumulation of capital.   If rich people sometimes indulge in polygyny, their wealth is never seen

as flowing from their matrimonial circumstances; the line
of causation is rather inverted. It is the younger men on
their labour migrations who engage the most in polygyny,
and their wives keep all the money or profits they make
from trading in the city (even if the initial capital
outlay was supplied by the husband). Women work for
themselves, and the pattern of residence underlies this.
If Abutia men desired polygyny for economic reasons, they
would   presumably   attempt   to   control   their   wives'
production. Such control is next to impossible because
co-wives do not coreside either with their husband of
affines, but with their own kin. While wishing to avoid
burdening the reader with more numerical information about
the polygynists' 'etic' coordinates, I can nevertheless
assert that a thorough examination of these economic
coordinates has not revealed any substantial evidence to
justify the labelling of Abutia polygyny as a productive
strategy. The Abutia recognize that money attracts women
and   that   part   of   the   polygynists'   matrimonial
circumstances stem from their economic achievements, but
no Abutia would claim that many wives attract more
money...
     If we look at other demographic coordinates of the
extant polygynists, we find more evidence to support the
view that Abutia polygyny is a reproductive strategy.
Indeed, all extant polygynists fall into one of the
following three, and only three, categories: (a) men whose
father came from another village, who were raised by their
mother in her village, and who have elected domicile
there, (b) men whose father was the only surviving adult
male of his minimal lineage to beget male children and,
(c) men whose father was not the only reproductive male of
their minimal lineage, but who are themselves the only
fertile sons of their father.
     The minimal lineage is the minimal political group in
Abutia. Although the Abutia are not obsessed with the
idea of becoming an ancestor (as one finds in many
societies with the worship of individual ancestors) and
begetting progeny numerous enough to create eventually a
new lineage, men do nevertheless prefer not to see their
minimal lineage disappear completely, and it is quite
normal that those threatened with extinction should seek
to redress the demographic fate of their minimal lineage.
Therefore, men in categories (b) and (c) can see a real
danger that their minimal lineages will be short of males
to perpetuate it. But why individuals with alien fathers
(i.e., fathers hailing from outside Abutia) aspire to

polygyny is less obvious, and I would surmise that they want either to compensate for their lack of patrilateral relatives with a greater number of affines and children, or that they hope to create their own minimal lineage in time.

As a form of matrimonial strategy, Abutia polygyny may thus be regarded as a direct response to the precarious position of either individuals or minimal lineages. The Abutia polygynists can consequently be characterized as young men from dwindling minimal lineages or without local patrilateral relatives, who have become both Westernized and economically successful on their labour migration. To apprehend it as a reproductive strategy, however, does not explain why it should occur with such low frequency. This problem will be taken up at the end of this chapter.

C. Polygyny, wealth and demographic increase

By concluding that polygyny is a reproductive strategy, one could wrongly infer that all Abutia lineages can correct their demographic imbalance through plural marriage and are all comparable in size. In fact, all extant polygynists are more less clustered in the largest lineages (Table 26)[69]. Between 50% and 70% of the male members of Types II and III lineages, alive and 'ever married', are extantly engaged in a matrimonial alliance, and between 10% and 20% of the latter are polygynous. On the other hand, between 70% and 90% of the male members of Type I lineages, alive and 'ever married', are extantly married and one finds among these lineages an extraordinarily high percentage of polygynists, or none at all. Where wealth permits, the smaller lineages seem to frantically desire plural marriage, while the more impecunious ones must refrain.

When all polygynists, dead and alive, are distributed by lineage (Table 27), the association between wealth, plural marriage and a large size still holds. Some lineages (Avexo, Gu and Akam) have enjoyed a relatively large share of polygynists but have failed to grow in proportion, because not all polygynists are equally prolific. Other small lineages (Dotse, Agodzo) have only recently started practicing plural marriage, and their small size will be somewhat redressed in the next generation. For the majority, however, a small size betrays the absence or quasi-absence of polygyny, whereas a large size bespeaks of large-scale polygyny. The two can only be connected if plural marriage, in contrast to monogyny or serial marriage, augments the number of offspring born to men. Tables 28-31 reveal that it does, since the polygynists, on the whole, have engendered twice as many children as monogynists - the latter have sired an average of 3.33 children per man, whereas the former, an average of 6.68. Men who married serially score higher than monogynists, with an average of 4.41 children per man, but still lag far behind the real polygynists. In fact, the majority of polygynists have also divorced some of their wives so that, when the number of their children is calculated for the total number of their wives, it climbs up to 8.05 children per man[70]. It is thus clear that polygyny does promote demographic increase, and its clustering in the largest lineages is not accidental[71].

The richest lineages have thus enjoyed the highest incidence of polygyny since the 1890s and have considerably surpassed the others in size. They probably started life with a demographic advantage which was soon amplified by their polygynous inclinations. Their wealth perhaps served also to buy slaves, but the taboo surrounding the subject made it impossible to isolate slave descendants; I am convinced, however, that differentials in wealth, and therefore in the access to slaves and women, does account for most of the differences in the sizes of lineages and clans. Nevertheless, significant differences in divorce rates could have also influenced the rate of demographic increase, and the hypothesis must be tested.

V. DIVORCE IN ABUTIA

Our computation of divorce rates and understanding of divorce depends entirely upon our definition of marriage. In the present context, there is divorce in Abutia when there is a public acknowledgement that sexual relations between a conjugal pair have stopped and that the woman is openly available to form a new mating pair or conjugal set. As a matter of fact, the matter is somewhat more complex, since a woman may decide to form a new mating pair or conjugal set at any time. If the former husband had not made any of the traditional marriage payments (and the majority have not), there is nothing he can do if his wife decides to leave with another man. If the traditional payments have been made, he is entitled to claim from her that part which is reimbursable, but no court order can enjoin her to return to her former husband, even is she refuses to repay the wedding payments.

Because we cannot make a distinction between the legal aspect of marriage and **de facto** separation of spouses in the Abutia cases we cannot distinguish divorce from conjugal separation (Goody, E. 1969:28). If the situation were different and children born to a separated woman before the payments had been reimbursed belonged to her former husband, or if a court order could enjoin her to return to her husband for failing to give back the marriage payments, we could speak of conjugal separation (as distinct from divorce) because the woman's new partnership with a man could not be called a marriage. According to my definition, their children would not belong to the groups of either the mother or the genitor. But because a woman can enter a new marriage the very minute she walks out on a man, there are only divorces in Abutia!

In fact, younger Abutia men and women leave conjugal sets as they enter them, without any fuss or ceremonial. The man or woman simply 'walks out', often without giving any reason. When grounds are mentioned, the two spouses often give different versions of the events. I have not systematically researched the reasons adduced by men and women for divorce, but two complaints always predominate; men claim that their wife has 'flirted' (i.e., slept) with other men, whereas women accuse men of not looking after them properly. The two are causally related since men often stop providing their wives' monthly allowances (between 5.00 Cedis and 10.00 Cedis in 1971-73) and spend the money on a mistress instead, while women react to this masculine irresponsibility by finding lovers who are willing to 'spend on them'. Beyond these dominant themes, the range of reasons invoked is truly astounding - some women cite sickness (epilepsy, venereal disease, or fits of madness), old age, impotence, poverty, or the marriage of a co-wife as the motives which incited them to divorce their husband, while men allege bad character, ugliness, infertility, polydactyly, insults or whatever else as the reasons which prompted them to leave their wives. Many others simply do not recall what caused the divorce. From the individuals' point of view, therefore, any reason is as good enough a reason to divorce as any other, and no reason at all is as good as any reason! Before searching for the factors which have precipitated this state of affairs, let us first assess the frequency of divorce in Abutia.

A. *Divorce frequencies; some methodological problems*

With Barnes's excellent study of divorce rates (1967), we now possess useful and clearly defined analytical tools, granted that our data lend themselves to these computations. The basic divorce ratios only require a decision about the type of union (whether there is a 'marriage' or not), and about the manner of its termination. In Abutia, the first decision is fraught with problems, as we have seen earlier, but they are minor in comparison with the knowledge necessary to compute tables of divorce risks, which cannot be calculated without information about the **duration** of the unions concerned. In preliterate societies, as all ethnographers know, problems of dating are almost unsurmountable, and I do not claim to have solved them. In fact, under the new 'matrimonial regime' it is difficult enough to know when a 'marriage' started, let alone when it terminated!

The ethnographer wishing to study marriage quantitatively is thus uncomfortably seated on the horns of a dilemma. On the one hand, he now has within his grasp powerful analytical tools but, on the other, he can rarely hope to collect data good enough for mathematical treatment. He or she must either remain silent on the topic, or live with imprecise, if not outright, sloppy data. I have opted to live with the sloppiness! Through lengthy cross-examinations and demographic extrapolations (not to mention the simple fact that some individuals did know the precise dates of their marriage), it was possible to 'guess' approximate dates for the beginning and end of a conjugal set. A great deal of my information is certainly wrong but there is no necessary direction in which it errs so that, not naive enough to believe that errors cancel out, I nevertheless trust that they do not all accumulate in the same direction. I would therefore suppose that, at their worst, the aggregate durations estimated could vary by up to two years either way. I have thus decided to build divorce risk tables on such shaky data because the only alternative was to bury them. Since rough approximations can always give us a fairly good idea of the order of magnitude I have decided that approximate knowledge, in this area, is better than no knowledge at all, and I have gone ahead with the computation of the divorce tables.

Furthermore, I also had to make minor adjustements to Barnes's rates because he based his definitions on the marital experiences of live informants only, whereas my sample includes those of both live informants, and the deceased recollected by the living. In the calculations of some rates, I have therefore distinguished global rates, applying to the total population of individuals both dead and alive, from the rates applying to the live population only, and from those applying to the defunct exclusively.

B. Present and cumulative marital status

Tables 32-34 clearly bring to the fore the great number of adult individuals who have at some point been married but were not extantly so in 1972, whose marital status betrays the predominance of divorce over deaths as a means of terminating unions[72]. The cumulative marital experience (Table 34) reinforces the impression of high frequency of divorce. Of the global sample (both dead and live populations), 37.5% of the men and 41.1% of the women have divorced at least once. In the live population alone, the rates are even higher: 46.5% of men and 44.9% of women. These rates vary between men and women, and between live and dead populations. By definition, the frequency of divorce for village in-marriages should be equal for both sexes. The variation between frequencies of divorce for male and female populations therefore suggest that the factors which stimulate divorce in out-marriage do not operate with the same strength for the two genders. Similarly, the disparity in the rates between live and dead population intimates that different generations were not exposed to the same degree of external pressures.

One could nevertheless argue that both deceased and live populations would exhibit comparable rates of divorce had not the defunct peoples' marriages been terminated by their death. However, the hypothesis does not stand the test of reality, since mortality alone could not yield variations as large as those observed between the two populations. Among the living, almost 45% of male and female marriages have ended in divorce, and approximately 83% of the **completed** male and female marriages have been concluded by a divorce. On the other hand, all deceased have completed their unions, but only 24% of their male, and 30% of their female unions have terminated in divorce (Tables 35-37). Barnes has however emphasized the inadequacy of rates which do not discriminate between the effects of divorce and mortality, and he has developed a method of calculating survival tables for marriages in order to compensate for this difficulty (Barnes 1967).

C. Risks of divorce

Applying Barnes's measures to our global sample yields interesting results (Table 38).   According to these computations, both male and female marriages last an average of eleven years, with a median of eight to nine years, and both male and female marriages which end in divorce endure an average of seven years, with a median of four to five years.   Also, 67.43% of male marriages would have ended in divorce without mortality, the effect of which is estimated at 16%.   Both rates are surpassed in the female marriages - 80.55% of them would have been concluded by a divorce without the effect of mortality, estimated to be 21%.   Such figures compare well with the ones Barnes collected among the Ngoni and thus classify Abutia among the African societies with high divorce rates.

As suggested earlier, the cause of the discrepancy between male and female divorce frequencies is to be sought in village out-marriages. Among men and women who married outside the village, 8% more women than men have terminated their union by a divorce (Table 39).   When divorce is calculated as a ratio of all completed marriages, the disparity is still more striking: 55% of male, and 76% of female out-marriages have ended in divorce.   I have not been able to identify the causes of these differential rates, although I suspect that the testimonies of informants vary according to their sex.   A man married to a woman who lives in a distant village may contend that he is still married, while the woman thinks otherwise.   Women who have been sent back to the village would thus initiate divorce or act in public as if they were divorced, while the husband in the city still maintains the fiction of a marriage.

The tables of divorce risks and survival (Tables 40-45) show that divorce does not only occur in the early years of matrimonial life; many divorces indeed take place after thirty or forty years of wedlock, and are often initiated by the woman who decides to coreside with a daughter or brother, as practiced among the Gonja (E. Goody 1969). Divorce risks reach their peak within the first five years of marriage.   If a conjugal set survives the birth of a second child, that is, if it survives the duolocal residence imposed by the woman's return to the village, its risks of divorce are slightly reduced for another ten years, and if it survives this decade, the risks are further reduced by two-thirds.   These percentages are subject to caution, however, since the couples married for five or fifteen years have been exposed to different circumstances.

Once divorced or widowed, men and women do not hurry into re-marriage, and women tend to wait longer than men before re-marrying (Table 46). Indeed, 32% of the female divorcees and widows who are not extantly married have treasured their freedom for more than twenty years, as opposed to 20% of the men in similar situations. Kloe men and women do not hasten to re-marry because they gain little in forming conjugal pairs that they cannot obtain in forming mating groups (although the mating groups of older individuals are practically conjugal pairs, insofar as a pregnancy would not disrupt their relationship). This difference, Esther Goody has suggested (personal communication), could be partly explained in terms of age at separation. Since the Abutia also know of the 'terminal separation' which Esther Goody identified among the Gonja, and since men do not want to marry women of 45 and above, these instances would increase the mean duration of remaining unmarried among women. Since I failed to tabulate the data in that form, I can only offer this a plausible hypothesis.

The size of descent groups does not appear to influence the frequency of divorce (Tables 47), as most clans display comparable rates. Etsri males and Wome females seem to form more stable sets, but their number is too small to be significant. The greater tendency of Etsri males to form durable conjugal pairs would in fact be consistent with their policy of integration in the selection of spouses. Finally, the origin of the spouses does not seem to affect the lifespan of conjugal pairs, or the mode of their termination. Couples married outside the village seem to stay together for a shorter period of time than those married in, but I have already suggested a cause for this variation. Instances of inter-clan village in-marriage and clan in-marriage also exhibit equal frequencies of divorce, namely 50% of all marriages. The most 'unstable' alliances, it would appear, are those uniting individuals from the same lineage. This is rather puzzling, in view of our earlier explanation of lineage in-marriage; indeed, if lineage in-marriages did arise as a consequence of socio-economic differentiation, we would expect their risks of divorce to be lower, whereas they display the highest rates recorded, namely 80% of all lineage in-marriages[73]. These higher frequencies should, however, be placed in a proper time perspective.

Lineages initiated in-marriage around 1915 only, and women married since have been exposed to changing conditions which have been more disruptive of marital stability.

D.   Divorce over time

To assess how much divorce rates have varied over time, the same rates have been re-computed by cohorts (Tables 48-49). Both ratios A and B, but most especially B, give a clear picture of this variation. Ratio A embraces extant marriages, and thus tends to dwindle in the younger cohorts, but ratio B only assesses the importance of divorce for completed unions (i.e., expresses divorce/ divorce + death) and reflects the upward trend admirably. In the light of these figures, I would certainly expect between 90% and 95% of the marriages of the younger cohorts to end in divorce, since the bride and groom on the day they form a conjugal pair have a life expectancy exceeding thirty years (see Appendix 1) whereas unions rarely last more than twenty years.

A diachronic picture of divorce risks echoes the same trend (Tables 50-52). The cohort of individuals first married between 1901 and 1920, and who had completed their matrimonial life by the time of fieldwork, was first selected. These conjugal pairs lasted an average of 17 years, with a median of 18 years, and those of their unions which were concluded by a divorce had nonetheless endured an average of twelve years, with a median of eight to nine years. Of the male marriages of this cohort, 51.28% would have ended in divorce without the effect of mortality (as compared to 67.43% for the global sample), and 58.37% of the female marriages would have known a similar fate (in contrast to 80.55% for the global sample).

To sharpen the contrast, the cohort of individuals first married since 1946 was then singled out. Unfortunately, Barnes's method cannot be applied satisfactorily to such a sample because few of the individuals have completed their matrimonial career. Despite these serious limitations, the table of marriage survival provides a striking contrast with the previous cohort. The mean duration of all their marriages, and also of their unions terminated in divorce barely exceeds seven years, no doubt because of the young age of the cohort. Had they finished their matrimonial engagements the mean duration might climb up to ten years but, in my opinion, not much higher. The same table shows that 100%

of the younger generation's marriages would terminate in divorce without the effect of mortality. This last figure is again slightly exaggerated, but it almost tallies with ratio B calculated for the younger cohorts, which reveals that between 90% and 95% of the completed marriages of the younger generation have ended in divorce (Tables 48-49). With a spiralling frequency of divorce, much longer life expectancy at birth (now approximating 60 years for women, and 55 for men) and diminishing risks of mortality, we can safely assume that virtually all the Kloe marriages would cease through divorce without the effect of mortality and that, given the influence of mortality, more than 90% of the conjugal sets will indeed be disrupted by divorce.

We can thus safely conclude that Kloe has witnessed a drastic increase in the occurrence of divorce while other factors (medical, hygienic, nutritional or other) have lengthened the life expectancy of spouses. The tremendous escalation in divorce rates graphically expresses the impact of the changes discussed earlier.

The men and women who married for the first time before 1885 knew of different circumstances, in which life expectancy at birth was probably fifteen years shorter and divorces more difficult to obtain. Assuming that the elders did not recollect with complete accuracy the manner in which ancestral marriages terminated, we can nonetheless assume that between 15% and 20% of precolonial conjugal sets broke up because of divorce, although the latter figure might be relatively implausible. This, in my opinion, is a finding much more interesting than the predictable increase in divorce rates, and it calls for an explanation.

VI. EXPLAINING ABUTIA MATRIMONIAL PRACTICES

I have hitherto described, but not explained, the main features of Abutia marriages: the simplicity of 'getting married' and the concomitant high divorce rates, the fact that the type of union between the biological parents of a child does not affect its status, the type of marriage payments, the marriage prohibitions and preferences, the preference for local in-marriage, the existence of descent group in-marriage and the low rates of polygyny. This particular constellation of features must now be explained, and we can conveniently start with the question of divorce.

If we take 1890 as our dividing line, we can easily see how schooling, labour migrations and duolocal residence have pulled couples asunder and created condition in which divorce is endemic. Before 1890, in a population where the difference in age between spouses was possibly greater and life expectancy significantly lower divorce rates were probably six to seven times lower than in the early 1970s, but approximately 15% of the completed unions nonetheless ended in divorce. Other conditions being equal, this percentage would in fact be higher in the present demographic situation (with shorter age intervals between spouses and longer life expectancy) so that it is legitimate to speak of divorce as having been relatively common in the late nineteenth-century Abutia when, intuitively, we would expect it to have been much rarer. Indeed, if couples then lived and produced together, if marriages were arranged, ritually sanctioned and sealed by the transfer of marriages payments, and if the type of union between the biological parents did slightly affect the status of children (whereas it does not any longer), how was divorce possible then?

For many decades, classical descent theory provided an array of factors to account for variations in divorce rates, such as the types of descent, the amount of marriage payments, the types of rights acquired at marriage, polygyny, and so on, all of which concurred to determine the amount of absorption of the woman into her husband's or father's lineage (Gluckman 1950, Richards 1950, etc.). At the same time, other anthropologists were probing another avenue, by looking at divorce in terms of the strategies opened to women (Schneider 1953, Stenning 1959, Cohen 1961), an approach which culminated in a fresh understanding of divorce in terms of the social features which ease for women the exit from conjugal sets, or facilitate the transition from being married to being a divorcee (E. Goody 1969, 1972, Cohen 1971, Potash 1978). Potash has provided the best illustration of this approach by showing that because married Luo women cannot retain the custody of their young children (or any of their children, in fact), and because they lose all rights to their father's houses and lands, they have very few choices but to resign themselves to their marital fate, and bear the brunt of the adjustment to the status of being married (Potash 1978). The factors that Esther Gody, Cohen and Potash have identified now stand out as the most pertinent in any account of divorce. Indeed, in many West African societies known for their high divorce rates (such as the Kanuri, Gonja, Kpelle or Abutia - see Cohen 1971, E. Goody 1969, Bledsoe 1980), women who divorce their husbands can retain the custody of their young children, or find adequate fostering for them (Abutia, Gonja, Kanuri). But, above all, female divorcees in those societies (especially Gonja, Kpelle, and Abutia) do not have to act as runaway slaves and survive in the interstices of legitimate groups if they leave their husbands, because they have somewhere to go.

Indeed, Abutia women retain domiciliary rights in the paternal house, as well as rights over both their **agbanu** and village lands. They can cultivate almost anywhere, at any time, without asking anybody's permission, and could do the same in the past. They can now, as they could in the past, survive easily without a husband since they were always actively engaged in trading or agriculture and derived their subsistence from it. A woman could become rich through trading and the making of pottery and, although houses were then smaller and possibly less available to shelter a married daughter or sister, women could easily have their own house built if they had the money.

This, I believe, is the light in which we must view the 'conservative role' of marriage payments. Where women have strong **bargaining powers** because they retain rights in their father's house and land, and also have independent means of making money, the amount of marriage payments may affect the rate of divorce but not that of conjugal separation, as the Nuer case eloquently shows. In the traditional Abutia marriage ceremony, the prospective husband performed services to his in-laws and made presents which were sometimes distributed to his fiancee's paternal and maternal relatives; he also provided his bride with 'women's things' such as a wooden chest, clothes and a kitchen stool but goods were never transmitted from the elders of one minimal lineage or corporation to the elders of another. As such, neither the minimal lineage nor any larger group was responsible for the matrimonial transactions. Fathers were expected to contribute toward their son's first marriage but the payments were within any young man's reach. Sons accepted their father's contribution because it saved them delaying the age at marriage and also was a sign of filial subordination, but the size of payments never precipitated the formation of a gerontocracy controlling the movement of brides. In fact, sons did not depend on their fathers economically to get married.

If a man divorced his wife, nothing had to be repaid; if the woman initiated the divorce and won the case, she had to repay the amount that the husband had given in cash, an amount not exorbitant by any standards, and which a lover or a father could have easily supplied if the woman herself did not have enough money of her own. Thus, because the marriage payments were not prohibitive but, more essentially, because Abutia women, unlike Luo women, retained strong bargaining powers, divorce was always rife in nineteenth-century Abutia. This, however, does not explain why we find this particular type of marriage payment.

Despite Jack Goody's remarkable efforts to advance our understanding of the question (1973, 1976), anthropologists cannot yet answer such general questions because we still lack a general theory of marriage payments. In the absence of a general model I can therefore only offer tentative hypotheses to account for the type of Abutia marriage payments. To achieve this, we first need to characterize these marriage payments.

Jack Goody has already defined bridewealth as a transaction involving two minimal lineages or corporations which exchange large marriage payments against the reproductive powers of their women. These payments are not consumed immediately but are 'circulated' and 'stored' to enable the wife-giving groups to obtain wives for themselves. The dowry, on the contrary, channels property to the couple, who can own property jointly[74]. The rules of property devolution in Abutia rule out the possibility of dowries. The Abutia marriage payments are distributed to the brides' bilateral relatives, or conveyed to the bride herself. The goods and money which the relatives receive, on the other hand, are not stored or retained to serve as marriage payments to obtain wives of their own. If we assume that bridewealth, in order to be circulating, must be large and that it connects various marriages through the circulation of payments, we can then conclude that Abutia marriage payments are relatively small and do not serve to connect various marriages. To this extent, an Abutia marriage is an 'individuated event' and the payments are 'terminal'[75]. To understand these features, let us look back at the idea of village sovereignty.

In their last wars east of the Volta (1869-1873), the Ashanti razed the Abutia villages, burning huts and people inside them, and taking as many slaves as they could. In the general confusion that followed their passage, many refugees must have joined the indigenous population in rebuilding the villages. Even before the last Ashanti wars, many of those villages must have recruited many refugees. The villages they then formed were not large, numbering more or less 300 inhabitants around 1875, and perhaps even fewer (see Appendix 1). The sovereignty of villages, moreover, favoured in-marriage, and their sizes permitted it. Among similar polities (Mbembe, Eastern Dida, or even Pueblos) one does observe a similar inclination towards local in-marriage. Out-marriages were used to underwrite and strengthen political alliances, and sometimes resorted to for purely demographic reasons, but they were not preferred. To maintain in-marriage in relatively small localities, furthermore, the exchanging units themselves must be small. As I explained earlier, the original clans were probably small enough to exchange but, as some of them outgrew the others, clan and eventually lineage in-marriage evolved so that, in the long run, minimal lineages (which are on the whole fairly small) emerged as the exchanging units. I would thus see the small size of exchanging units as a prerequisite for village in-marriage in smallish sovereign localities. Furthermore, as we have seen, the political organization precludes any mobility between offices. More than that, it precludes the ranking of groups, and any form of clientelism[76].

Recent research has demonstrated the clear links between bridewealth and clientelism, or the ranking of groups and the building up of clienteles (Holy 1979, Kuper 1982). Consequently, one can no longer share Goody's views that bridewealth is to egalitarian societies what dowry is to stratified ones. Dowries do seem to evolve in stratified societies, but bridewealth is practiced in those polities where cattle or wealth can be used to create clientship. Bridewealth also makes possible large-scale polygyny, a practice which also clashes with Abutia social organization. Because the sovereignty of small localities precludes ranking of groups and clientelism, and because bridewealth is conducive to both practices, bridewealth does not seem compatible with the Abutia constitution[77].

If the Abutia discourage ranking and clientele-building, why should they not simply resort to sister-exchange? Once more, one would need a greater understanding of sister-exchange in Africa to answer the question satisfactorily but we can try to do so negatively. From the instances known to me (Komo, Tiv,

Mbuti, Amba), it seems that sister-exchange presupposes that the exchanging groups be scattered geographically. In other words, no one has yet recorded any instance of sister-exchange coupled with a preference for local in-marriage. Why this is so is not clear to me but the answer may be found in some of the implications of sister-exchange. First of all, sister-exchange seems to occasion a detailed accountancy which often leads to disputes; the level of hostilities encountered among the Komo or Tiv, for instance, would completely disrupt a polity like Abutia. The Komo, Tiv and Mbuti, moreover, have no descent groups (I have not analysed the Amba in sufficient detail to warrant any such conclusion about their social organization). It may be that the answer is to be found at a different level. Indeed, both bridewealth and sister-exchange influence clearly the affiliation of children. If bridewealth is not paid, the children belong to the mother's group; if a sister is not exchanged, the children belong similarly to their mother's group. Both types of transactions discriminate clearly between the groups to which the children belong. In a sovereign locality relatively closed-in matrimonially, such distinctions are meaningless; Ego's patrilateral and matrilateral relatives are close neighbours and neither failure to make the necessary payments nor failure to 'return a daughter' ever affected the group affiliation of children in Abutia. This, in my opinion, would militate strongly against bridewealth and sister-exchange and would go a long way towards explaining their absence. Failing these types of matrimonial alliances, it would seem that the delayed exchange between minimal lineages, coupled with the payment of small sums of money, was most appropriate. It more or less guaranteed a wife for every man without creating ranking or clientelism, and did not connect the group affiliation of children to any specific transaction; the simple recognition of paternity by a man ensured that the children were his.

Conversely, the marriage prohibitions serve similar purposes. Indeed, they preclude the formation of unions which, if they took place, would give two or more groups of full siblings the same paternal and maternal **fhomewo** (as minimal lineages). These bans imply that the children of female siblings, or the children of women from the same minimal lineage should never share a common paternal minimal lineage. The interdiction of marrying within one's own minimal lineage enjoins every individual to keep his children's paternal and maternal minimal lineages separate, and the ban on marrying two related women ensures that every woman of a minimal lineage creates a separate paternal minimal lineage for her own children. The prohibitions thus operate to prevent the formation of exclusive exchanges. To receive two or three women from the same minimal lineage could indeed have 'mortgaged' completely the daughters of the receiving group for one or two generations, as most of its women would have to be returned to the same wife-giving group. Such a debt could not fail to subordinate the receiving lineage for at least one generation, because of the small size of most minimal lineages. The size of groups and the time-span required to complete exchanges are too often overlooked in studies of matrimonial exchanges. Many minimal lineages have known intervals of up to twenty years between the marriages of two of their daughters and would understandably resent having their women 'mortgaged' to one group for so many years (see age pyramids in Appendix 11 for illustration). When marriage is viewed chronologically and against the small size of the exchanging units, it is clear that the prohibitions against sororal polygyny and the marrying of many closely related women combine to prevent a situation where groups would act as wife-takers or wife-givers over long periods of time, as they also ensure that wives are circulated widely.

The size of the villages, their sovereignty and lack of ranking or stratification thus seem to account for the preference for local in-marriage, the small size of exchanging units, the terminal marriage payments, the FZD marriage and its variants, the marriage prohibitions and the irrelevance of marriage in establishing the legitimacy of children. These same factors, and especially the sovereignty of villages, have further implications. We saw earlier that village sovereignty inhibited the reproduction of descent groups (lineages and clans) and that this was achieved by aggregating minimal lineages on the basis of descent alone. In other words, the maternal origins of ancestors and their generational levels did not operate in aggregation. If the generations to which ancestors belonged are not accurately remembered and irrelevant, and if genealogies are shallow, the recollection of individuals' ancestors is not important, and neither is their worship. There is therefore no religious incentive (as in ancestor worship) for a man to become the apical head of a new descent group, and therefore no stimulation to indulge in excessive polygyny.

Furthermore, descent groups can only be successfully prevented from multiplying if men are discouraged from inordinate reproduction. Polygyny and the purchase of slaves were the two main means of leaving a large number of descendants. We have direct evidence that polygyny was indeed discountenanced because both its incidence and intensity are weak and because Spieth reports about Ho that polygynists were scorned as lustful and incontinent men (Spieth 1906:64). I personally construe the low rates of polygyny as a direct means of preventing the excessive growth of some minimal lineages, which would then want to assert their separate identity as full lineages, if not clans. From the oral tradition, moveover, the purchase of slaves seems to have been rather uncommon.

If polygyny was not practiced on a significant scale, and mostly indulged in by younger males, husbands and wives would be almost coevals, and so most were. Of the living couples in Kloe, I did not find one single instance of an elderly man married to a teen-age girl, and the evidence from the genealogies supports this. Differences of twenty years are sometimes found but only rarely, and most husbands are only five to ten years older than their wives. In societies where young girls marry elders they soon face widowhood and immmediately re-enter the 'marriage market'; in other words, large-scale and gerontocratic polygyny is often accompanied by large-scale widow-inheritance. But where the age differences between husband and wife do not often exceed ten years, young widows are uncommon; women are widowed later in life, often after having terminated their reproductive career, and widow-inheritance is correspondingly less frequent. Past their child-bearing age, widows may indeed choose not to remarry, or marry whom they wish to have as a conjugal partner.

Finally, the fact that maternal origins do not operate in group aggregation has two serious implications: (1) it makes divorce a less disruptive practice from the point of view of descent groups, and removes one of the many obstacles to its occurrence and (2) it provides the organizational prerequisite for the emergence of descent group in-marriage. If minimal lineages in Abutia were aggregated like those of the Namoos of Taleland (Fortes 1945), that is, on the basis of descent from the wives of ancestors, descent group in-marriage would be ruled out. Otherwise, agnatic descent would no longer operate, since individuals could trace their connections to the apical ancestor through women as well as men. When this impediment is removed (i.e., aggregation on the basis of maternal origins), the greatest organizational obstacle to descent group in-marriage is automatically removed. This does not imply that descent group in-marriage will evolve there and then but that, given new demographic and economic conditions which will make it advantageous, it will be organizationally possible.

These various factors, directly, or through their reciprocal reinforcements, combine to shape the matrimonial practices of the Abutia (or at least of Kloe) as they were recorded (see Diagram X). Admittedly, many of these explanations are only tentative and may very well be invalidated on the basis of serious comparative analysis. On the limited scale that this monograph permits, however, comparative analysis seems to confirm most of them. The Eastern Dida, for instance, who together with the Abutia practice village sovereignty, also share many of the features described in the foregoing pages: they prefer to marry within the locality, have small exchanging units as well as relatively modest marriage payments which look terminal, their women send a daughter back to their own people (FZD marriage and its variants), sororal polygyny is prohibited and men from one exchanging unit are also forbidden to marry many related women of another exchanging unit, matrilateral cross-cousin marriage is banned, divorce rates are high, the status of the mother (whether married or not) does not seem to affect that of the child (status being defined in terms of group membership, always) and the polygynists are also men in their mid-thirties to mid-fifties (Terray 1966). I have noted only one discrepancy: rates of polygyny, although not described numerically, are said to be high. But we do not know anything about the manner in which Eastern Dida descent groups are aggregated and reproduce themselves so that this deviation is not disturbing, in contrast to the astounding number of features which Eastern Dida and Abutia share. It would have been interesting to know more about the matrimonial practices of the Mbembe (apart from their preference for local in-marriage) but Rosemary Harris confined her study to the political organization (Harris 1962, 1965).

Anlo proper also provides a point of comparison. Anlo descent groups, we know, can proliferate. We can therefore expect them to tolerate polygyny more freely and its incidence (and perhaps intensity, which is unfortunately not mentioned) is indeed higher than in Abutia (Nukunya 1969:157). Large towns, or even wards of towns tend to

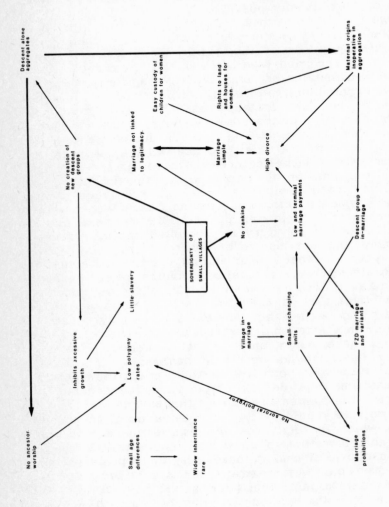

DIAGRAM X. Causal linkages between village sovereignty, descent, and the various features of Abutia matrimonial practices.

marry in but smaller (and newer) settlements certainly have less incentive to do so, and we can expect the size of exchanging units also to be larger than in Abutia; they are, since the Anlo lineages have remained exogamous (although not the clans). The larger size of exchanging units removes the imperative of sending a daughter back, and we do find a predominance of MBD marriages over FZD ones (a ratio of 4:1 - 1969:72-73), but we do observe the same kind of marriage payments that we recorded in Abutia. A more thorough comparative analysis would be needed to account for the predominance of MBD marriages, but the answer would not be difficult to find. Indeed, the sister's son inherits the mother's brother's personally-acquired property in Anlo and this major difference in the laws of inheritance is bound to affect matrimonial alliances. We do not find either levirate or widow-inheritance in Anlo; the absence of levirate follows from the type of marriage payments but the low incidence of widow-inheritance is surprising in view of the high frequency of polygyny. Polygyny is indeed more frequent, but its intensity is not reported and, furthermore, there is no evidence of great discrepancies between the ages of husband and wife. If it is the younger men who marry polygynously, as among the Eastern Dida or Abutia, higher polygyny rates would not automatically entail a greater incidence of widow-inheritance. Finally, the Anlo do not divorce easily but, as Nukunya remains silent about women's rights to paternal houses and lands, and about the custody of children and the extent of fostering, it is difficult to compare the two societies on this topic. On the whole, consequently, the features observed in Anlo proper bear out most of our hypotheses and, on some topics, the information is too scanty to warrant comparison.

There are some important divergences between the explanations offered in this chapter and the views of more classical writers. By defining marriage in terms of status, i.e., in terms of rights and duties, classical descent theorists and many social anthropologists have concentrated on the manner in which rights in brides were transferred from one descent group to another, and how much this transfer allowed the absorption of the bride in her husband's descent group. By defining marriage operationally we are led to focus on the constituted groups themselves, i.e., the conjugal pairs and exchanging units but, like previous theorists, we examine the manner in which they are related to other groups. This, however,

is where our affinity ends. In classical descent theory
descent has a bearing on marriage because marriage is a
status, because statuses are owned by corporations
(Radcliffe-Brown 1935), and because descent groups are
corporate groups. In other words, descent groups were
defined in a way which encompassed what we distinguish as
aggregated groups, simple groups, corporations and
categories (see Section 1.I.). These corporate groups
'pulled' individuals together, tearing women between
conflicting fields of gravitation, namely that of her
father's descent group and that of her husband's descent
group. The features of the matrimonial 'system' were thus
accounted for in terms of this transfer of rights, this
acquisition of a new status, in the general background of
the corporateness and solidarity of descent groups.

In an operational perspective one abandons the **pro-
blématique** of solidarity, and regards the association
between descent and marriage as, at best, indirect.
Truly, the membership of corporations (and especially
house-owning and land-owning ones) does bear on the
frequency of divorces, not because of conflicting 'pulls',
but because it determines how easy it can be for a woman
to abandon membership of conjugal sets, or to become a
divorcee. But corporations are not descent groups (see
Section 1.I). The level of grouping to which sovereignty
is attached does influence the manner in which descent
groups (operationally defined) reproduce which, in turn,
affects the manner in which they are aggregated. Both
factors have an impact on physical reproduction and,
consequently, on the main agency responsible for this
reproduction, the conjugal pair. This association is
expressed most directly in the fact that the organization
of descent groups allows their marrying in, and that the
inhibition on descent group multiplication discourages the
large-scale practice (and particularly intensity) of
polygyny. But, in my opinion, this is the extent of the
implications of descent for matrimonial practices in
Abutia. In other words, the classical association between
descent and marriage no longer holds; conjugal sets are
not so much affected by the manner in which rights over
women are transferred from one group to another, than by
such facts as the sovereignty of villages, their
egalitarian constitution, the size of exchanging units,
the type of land tenure, and so on.

An operational approach thus severs the time-honoured
links between descent and domesticity, descent and
marriage, and even descent and kinship behaviour because

it severs the sacrosanct connection between groups and statuses, or groups and social relationships. At the end of this altogether brief meander through the groups formed in adjudication, legislation, administration, warfare, residence, production, distribution of products, food processing, socialization of children and reproduction, we have shown that one can study the social organization of one society in some detail without ever making reference to social relations, without mentioning relationships between agnates, neighbours, fathers and sons, mothers and children, and so on. This is not to deny their analytical relevance; they form a legitimate subject of study, but so does the study of groups, and I hope to have demonstrated that groups are better studied in themselves, independently from social relationships.

Before concluding this operational analysis of Abutia groups, however, we ought to tidy up the analysis by presenting a coherent picture of the changes that have transformed Abutia in the last hundred years [78].

SECTION 5

Social Change in Abutia

If an anthropologist had visited Kloe in 1875, what kind of social organization would he have found?

First and above all, he (or she; but let us assume that a nineteenth-century anthropologist would have belonged to the male gender...) would have discovered a society trying to recover from the ravages of a war which had decimated or enslaved part of its population, and ruined its settlements. Its people would have been busy re-building their tight, nucleated villages and would have teamed up to build their houses; only the wealthier could have insisted on larger abodes. The majority would have contented themselves with a two- or three-bedroom house. On bedroom would shelter the husband while the wife (and, for a few among them, the wives) would sleep in the other bedroom(s) with her (their) children. Teen-age boys might have moved out of their mother's bedroom to sleep with some of their peers, either in the father's house or in that of a close relative. Most residential groups would have been composed of nuclear or polygynous families, and the co-wives of a polygynous man might perhaps have coreside with him. The low incidence of polygyny, however, would make such occurrences rather uncommon.

Rights over houses might have been the same as in contemporary Abutia but the devolution of houses would not have played the same critical role because houses did not represent a large investment, being built collectively from materials found in the environment. If a son inherited as a trustee for his siblings, he might then have no spare bedroom for his sister. As houses were built collectively the heir might have gained rights of purchaser over the paternal domicile, and would therefore not act as trustee for his siblings. Whatever may be the case, the anthropologist would not have found many expanded or extended residential groups. Divorce was nevertheless possible and occurred with some frequency so that female divorcees must have had access to houses other than their husband's. Some of them might have been epiclerates who inherited the paternal house, and others could have had brothers who inherited larger houses. But some, I believe, were rich enough to build their own house unless they hurried into re-marriage soon after their divorce, or divorced because of their involvement with a lover. But there is no evidence to suggest such a tradition. The female divorcees would have then formed female-headed residential groups, and we might also have found some male-headed cross expanded and extended ones, but in proportions far more modest than those found in contemporary Abutia.

Most women would have been betrothed in their childhood and, some time between their fifteenth and seventeenth year, would have undergone a puberty rite financed and organized by their parents (and sometimes with contributions from their prospective groom), but involving no more than two or three sisters or cousins. This rite would make them nubile and accelerate the customary marriage procedures. At the end of the marriage prestations and ceremonies, the bride would join her husband in a house which he had built near his father's. Once married, the children she bore, whoever their genitor may be, belonged to her husband but, outside wedlock, the children she conceived belonged to the genitor she designated, who could not deny the paternity. Children born of married mothers would enjoy all the normal rights to her husband's personally-acquired property (which more often than not meant very little) while those born of a divorcee, although legitimate in every other respect, could not inherit the property that their genitor had amassed during his lifetime (unless, obviously, the genitor did not leave any other children; if he did not sire any sons, his 'illegitimate' son might have inherited his property).

As soon as a father felt that his son was old enough to start a family, he would buy him a gun and hand it over ceremonially, thereby announcing that his son was independent. It is not clear if the sons worked on their father's land until this declaration of their independence but, after the residential separation from the paternal abode (which followed their marriage), the sons cultivated their own plots separately, and singly most of the time. Men then bore the brunt of agricultural production, which consisted of yams mostly, intercropped with the vegetables which are used as condiments. Women helped at certain stages in the agricultural process but otherwise withdrew

from it.   Land was more abundant then, because of the
smaller size of the settlements, and rights to land were
held corporately by the **agbanu**.   The savannah was open
for cultivation to any villager of any gender and men
could cultivate, without asking anybody's permission, the
forest land that belonged to their **agbanu** and which
was not claimed as fallow (see Appendix 2).   Men then
farmed for subsistence only and gave their foodstuffs to
their wives for consumption;   the groups of residence,
production, consumption and distribution of products thus
overlapped.   To acquire foreign goods the men would weave,
a craft practiced by all adult men.   Kloe was located on a
major salt trade route and the Abutia would exchange their
clothes for European goods imported from the coastal
forts, or for salt dried on the coastal lagoons.   Some
Abutia traders even ventured as far as Cape Coast or Lome,
buying European articles which they traded on their
return-trip.   Some amassed considerable wealth, part of
which they could lend to others against 'human pledges'
who worked on their farms or wove for them, thereby
allowing them to trade on yet a greater scale.   But very
few achieved such affluence and they could not easily
convert their riches into political capital because their
pledges were mostly children.   During fieldwork, I found
one nonagenarian only, who had been a pledge in his
childhood.   But pledges could always be redeemed and
sometimes land, and not people, was pawned.   'Big men'
there were, but the political organization precluded their
growing into powerful patrons or petty chiefs;   like
today's 'big men' in local politics, they only wielded the
power of their wits, or wisdom.   Wealth could not serve to
build clienteles.

If man tilled the land, and wove or traded in their
leisure time (although some engaged in full-time trade),
women discharged their domestic duties, looked after the
children, occasionally helped in the husband's farm(s),
but they also practiced complementary crafts, such as the
making and dyeing of the thread needed in weaving, or
pottery.   Skilful craftswomen could thus amass some wealth
and gain the kind of economic independence which enabled
them to build houses and divorce without too many
difficulties.   Women also marketed their husbands'
agricultural products in the local market places, and
retained that part of the proceeds only, which served for
domestic consumption.   Husband and wife thus coresided in
separate and autonomous residential groups, occasionally
produced together (and increasingly as the women were

freed from child care) and engaged in complementary activities. Their collaboration, the smaller houses, the transmission of skills from fathers to sons and mothers to daughters, all these gave them a greater control over their children, and especially the sexuality of their daughters. Pre-marital virginity does not appear to have been an overwhelming concern as Nukunya registered in Anlo, where a bride had to prove her virginal state after the consummation of her marriage, but Abutia parents presumably wanted to ensure that their sons-in-law would perform the necessary services and give the customary prestations before being allowed to take their daughters away. The customary marriage procedure was slightly elaborate and adhered to in most cases of first marriage, and there were specified marriage preferences (FZD and variants). Although possible, divorce was less common because of the combination of these factors (greater parental control, greater meaningfulness of marriage and of 'being married' for group membership and access to property, coresidence and co-production, and so on). Despite 'infant betrothal' and marriage arrangements, the age discrepancy between husbands and wives does not seem to have been great, so that widows were not frequently inherited. Some widows or divorcees would not re-marry but find lovers and retain semi-independent unions with men.

If one abstracted the Christian Church of today, the anthropologist would have found religious practices very similar to contemporary ones. Divination was not an Abutia art, and ancestors were not worshipped. Witches did not haunt the land, but 'medicine-men' were certainly to be found in greater numbers. The cults, on the whole, would have been much the same: cults to the **trɔwo**, **ade** and **legba**. The cults surrounding these latter two types of deities, now relatively obsolescent, would then have been quite alive because of the great prestige accorded to hunting, and because of the constant menace of war. The many rites of passage, now mostly abandoned (such as the outdooring ceremony, the puberty rites for girls, the handing over of a gun, the marriage rites and rites of widowhood) were then practiced assiduously.

In 1875, the anthropologist would have found Kloe a small settlement of approximately 300 souls, and divided into four or five exogamous clans, two of which owned stools and were already larger than the others. Despite the attempt to imitate some Akan institutions, Kloe was then essentially egalitarian, governed as it was by a

Council of Elders assembling elders from all clans, as
well as the **asafofia**, the **sohefia**[79] and the
nyɔnu-fia ('queen-mother', or rather 'woman
representative'). All citizens were constitutionally
equal, and the **fiawo** acted as ritual custodians only;
in fact, many citizens would have been more influential
and powerful than the **dufia**, since the avenues to
power were many. I would be tempted to speak of a society
with true 'equality of opportunities' since those who did
not inherit a legacy of any susbtance (i.e., the greatest
majority) could nevertheless 'climb up' socially through
industrious farming, warring prowess, the possession of
powerful medicines, weaving or long-distance trading. But
prestige and influence, I wish to repeat, did not imply
the creation of dependants and clients. Unlike other
polities which could be described as chiefdoms (and here I
have the Kpelle, or some Bamileke chiefdoms in mind),
precolonial Abutia did not operate politically on the
basis of 'wealth in people', to use Bledsoe's expression,
because no one wielded political power beyond his ability
to convince others in public debate. The inequalities in
wealth were not matched by inequalities in political
status and power. The rich Abutia traders might acquire
more wives, build larger houses and sire more children as
well as acquiring a few pledges, but the poorest of their
neighbours never depended on them for protection and could
challenge them at any public meeting. All citizens were
constitutionally equal, and equal soldiers in the
citizens' army. No rich man could buy his way out of
participation in the **asafo**, and those who led the army
did so because of their former achievements.

These small nucleated settlements were sovereign, but
joined in multiple alliances with two neighbouring
villages from whom they might have split in times past,
and with whom they recollected a tradition of common
migration. In legislative and administrative activities
the villages thus formed the supreme authorities but, in
judicial matters, the political organization was more
complex. According to the types of offences and the
social origin of the disputants, there were various levels
of groupings (minimal lineages, lineages, clans and
village) with group representatives empowered to convene
judicial courts.

Much of this reconstruction is obviously conjectural,
although founded upon plausible and sound inferences from
contemporary practices and traditions, and it provides us

with a convenient yardstick to measure the distance between precolonial and contemporary institutions (i.e., as observed in the 1970s).

In the political realm the precolonial organization has preserved many of its features but has mostly suffered from the superimposition of, first, a colonial and, then, a national political organization.   Precolonial minimal lineages, for instance, shared today's criteria of membership but were more exclusively patrifiliative because the 'special circumstances' which warrant the use of matrifiliation as a criterion of membership occurred less frequently.   As divorce rates climbed up, village out-marriages multiplied and the practice of duolocal residence spread, these 'unusual circumstances' (i.e., children without genitors, or children brought up in their mother's village) have become so common that matrifiliants now crowd minimal lineages, which have taken on a more cognatic appearance as a result.   Eligibility for positions as group representatives is still dictated by precolonial criteria (except that the **fiawo** now have to be literate) and the contemporary 'traditional' courts recruit the same cognatic spread of relatives that precolonial ones did, and follow the same legal procedures.   With the superimposition of a national judicial organization, however, some of the cases formerly adjudicated by the Kloe courts (such as theft, homicide or adultery) have been withdrawn from the traditional authorities.   Lineage and clan elders have not lost much of their jurisdiction over traditional offences, but the new national legislation has altered the customary classification of offences.   Indeed, most contemporary infractions entail transgressions of national laws or logal government by-laws. Refusal to pay taxes, drumming without permission, failure to pay back government loans, insulting a police agent, and other such breaches could not have counted as misdeeds in precolonial days.   The colonial and national states have therefore created these new offences, and their adjudication devolves upon the state's representatives.

The colonial and national authorities have also misunderstood the 'system of offices'.   The Germans regarded the village as the minimal administrative unit, represented by its **dufia**.   They singled out the **dufia** from the village council and treated him as the lowest colonial administrator, directly responsible to the District Governor stationed in Misahoe (now in Togo). 'Chiefs' who failed to implement the Governor's policies were promptly removed from office. The Governor thus took over the role of 'king-maker' and neglected the other title-holders and elders in general. After 1914, the British reversed this general policy; they selected the Divisional Chiefs both as the lowest administrators and the lowest magistrates in their Divisions, which were merged into Local Authorities, Districts and Regions. After 1957, Nkrumah strove to separate the administration from the judiciary and deprived Divisional Chiefs of their judiciary functions. Local government councils (ancestors of the Village Development Committees of the 1970s) were then implanted in the villages, but the lowest magistrate's court was raised to the District level. During the same period, the intrusion of party politics further complicated village politics. 'Chiefs' who did not support the C.P.P. (Nkrumah's party) were deposed and the Government set up rival candidates who displayed loyalty to the party.

This governmental interference wrought havoc in village politics. Factions emerged and those who backed the deposed chief refused to acknowledge the 'party chief's' authority. As mentioned earlier, the Kloe stool-father even went so far as to flee to Togo with the stool! The 'traditional' **dufiawo** who were not deposed in this fashion were the only ones to retain some degree of efficiency in their administration; the other ones were simply ignored. Elected according to 'tradition', village **fiawo** nonetheless received their instructions from the colonial (and now national) authorities; by electing them, their co-villagers were not choosing a true group representative, but a minor civil servant. The administrative group over which the new kind of village **fiawo** preside, moreover, does not coincide with the precolonial Council of Elders. It does include some elders but not all, but also recruits younger literates who eventually by-pass their elders by climbing up the administrative hierarchy outside the village. Those who reach the upper echelons are ultimately responsible for formulating the very policies which their own local 'chiefs' and elders are expected to implement.

By grafting these national institutions onto the pre-colonial ones, the new authorities completely overlooked the traditional title-holders other than **dufiawo** and **fiagã**. Misunderstood and neglected by both colonial and national governments, these office-holders found no other recourse than claiming the roles of regents and acting chiefs. As colonial administrators, the

dufiawo or **fiagā** receive a salary, but the constant disputes left their positions vacant for most of the time. So the **mankrado**, the **zikpi-tɔ**, the **tsiame** and **tsɔfo** now vie with one another to fill in those vacancies by presenting themselves as the **dufiawo's** traditional replacements. The traditional **asafo** and its leaders have not been spared. The colonial government banned traditional armies, and left them a purely ritual role. The village armies were later not merged in the national military organization; instead, the national army and Police Force recruit on their own, independently of traditional organizations. All police stations in Eweland, for instance, are manned by officers and men who are strangers to the village where they are stationed (and to the Division as well). Despite its military inactivity, the **asafo** has nonetheless preserved its criteria of membership and its criteria of eligibility to the position of **asafofia**.

Precolonial jurisdictions (which even then were perhaps not clearly defined) have now been completely confused, and the precolonial political groups have been absorbed into a national legislative, administrative, executive and judiciary organization. This assimilation has given rise to sporadic flurries of protest and palaver. Every new law or by-law, every new administrative decision and policy creates new issues which in turn generate more manipulations between the various organizations, and more complex factionalisms. If the traditional polity hampered mobility between political offices, the national one promotes it.

These political changes have been paralleled, and have in fact been partly precipitated by, the spread of schooling and literacy. Christianity was implanted in Kloe before the first administrators arrived (always the cross before the sword...). As early as 1888, the German Evangelical-Presbyterian Church had founded a Mission with a primary school attached. Ever since, the Abutia schools have remained closely associated with the Church - as Mission schools, instead of Local Authority Schools - and their curricula bear heavily the mark of their religious orientation. All three villages now boast of both a Primary and Middle School. Children study for six years in the Ewe language in the primary school, and spend an additional four years in the Middle School, where all the teaching is done in English. After a first or second year in Middle School, the pupils can sit for an entry examination for one of the Secondary Schools. If they succeed and can find a sponsor to support them through the seven years of Secondary School, they then have to leave Kloe. Secondary education is expensive, but both primary and Middle school education were free in the 1970s, and compulsory for ten years. Only pregnant girls are expelled from schools, and prevented from re-entering. Most of the teachers are recruited from outside; they have their own quarters at the periphery of the village and take little part in village life beyond their school commitment.

After ninety years of contact with Western-type schools, the Abutia have reached a high degree of literacy. They have produced 21 trained teachers stationed throughout Ghana, and other highly qualified professionals, civil servants, or even academics (including a Ph.D. in economics from M.I.T. and one in sociology from a Canadian University!). Young men and women between the ages of 17 and 25-30 have on average completed nearly ten years of schooling and speak reasonably good English (Table 53). Most men between the ages of 30 and 40 have attended schools for periods ranging from 4 to 10 years, whereas a far higher proportion of women in the same age-group have had no schooling at all. Since the sample was taken among those who resided in the village (excluding the emigrants) it may include a higher proportion of less educated people for those aged 20 to 50. Most women above forty have had less than seven years of education, and many had no formal schooling at all.

The Evelangelical-Presbyterian Church has not known any serious challenges in Abutia since its foundation. Changes were forthcoming, however, as members of an Ewe syncretic Church - the Tondome White Cross Society - were starting to make converts in Abutia and to compete successfully with the established church. From its very beginning, the Mission and E.P. Church in Kloe have been associated with certain families, mostly from the Akpokli clan. The Church, like party politics, also fostered factionalism between the Christians (**sukutowo** - literally 'those who belong to the school') and the 'fetish-worshippers'. The families which controlled the Church enjoyed a better education, and eventually formed a wealthier group. They also used the Church as a new platform to gain political power. Because of these nepotic tendencies in the administration of the church, accusations of malpractice were hurled against its representatives, thus causing a split among the Christians themselves. In the 1960s, a devout Christian took the lead in these denunciations and called for change; his exhortations went unheeded, and he found a purer form of worship in the Tondome Church which he introduced to the village. In 1973, he was already holding bi-weekly services in his house, which succeeded in drawing an attendance of approximately twenty individuals.

The E.P. Church owes part of its success to its method of recruitment, first through the schools, but also through Bible Classes and other groups which rely heavily on singing in their activities. Local forms of musical entertainment (and dancing) are uncommon since Local Government by-laws forbid traditional drumming and dancing, because of its 'heathen' and arousing character. This lack of musical expression, so popular in the past, is thus compensated by the singing groups of the church.

Every village has its church, but only one resident E.P. pastor ministers to the Abutia villages, in addition to ten other villages. The Pastor himself does not originate from Abutia. The individuals responsible for the administration of the village church (the **hamegāwo**), however, are recruited locally, and serve for a limited number of years. Pastors are appointed to an area for a period of approximately five years, and they are answerable to a superior resident in Ho, where the Church's District diocese is located. Administratively speaking the villages are the minimal religious groups in this organization, and they are aggregated into 'parishes' on the basis of territoriality. A vast number of Kloe citizens declare themselves to be Christians (I have failed to make exact calculations, but I would suspect that at least 70% of the Kloe population proclaims itself Christian, although far fewer than that attend services). Women and older men, together with school children, form the great majority of church-goers.

'To be a Christian' is nonetheless rarely an exclusive category. To most people, it simply entails involvement in two sets of religious practices - those initiated by the church, and those initiated by the traditional religious leaders. There is however a strong core of staunch Christians, mostly from the Akpokli clan, whose uncompromising attitude has engendered much friction between families. Barely a week goes by without a clash between Christians and non-Christians over the performance of traditional rituals, and the bitterness on both sides is not easy to placate. Christianity constantly interferes with traditional practices, as even chiefs have

to renounce their faith before accepting the **fia**-ship.
This high degree of literacy certainly played an
important part in the labour migrations. In this respect,
the Ewe somewhat resemble the Igbo, in that many of them
occupy clerical posts throughout Ghana. But schooling was
not the only impetus behind the vast emigration to the
Gold Coast cities. Cocoa played an equally critical role.
Introduced to the Gold Coast in the 1870s, cocoa did not
spread to the British Mandated Togoland until the 1920s.
In Abutia particularly, its impact was further curtailed
by a Government edict, in the 1950s, which declared the
Abutia Hills (or most of them) a Forest Reserve. Since
most of the coca was farmed on the Hills, its farming came
to an abrupt end. A few farms can stil be seen, but the
richest Kloe citizens owe their fortunes to cocoa farms
which they purchased outside Abutia, in other Ewe
Divisions or in Ashanti. Education and cocoa-farming thus
combined to spur emigration, after the Germans were
ousted. One or two generations later, secondary education
or work in the city remain the greatest attractions of the
outside world.

These wage migrations, together with the introduction
of cash crops, had the most important economic effects.
Colonial governments collected taxes in money, and forced
the farmers to sell for cash. The men who did not
emigrate and who were not able to farm cocoa or coffee in
Abutia (and barely ten farmers enjoy this privilege)
nonetheless specialized in the cultivation of cash crops,
and especially maize. Yam farming was thus slowly phased
out and was practiced only marginally at the time of
fieldwork. The men thus stopped producing for subsistence
and many of them worked away for decades, so that women
were forced to take over the agricultural production for
subsistence and abandon their traditional crafts (as the
men themselves have completely abandoned weaving, which
nobody now practices in Abutia). Because women were not
freed from child care and domestic chores and had to take
on this new productive role, they found it ecologically
and economically more rational to specialize in cassava
farming, so that cassava has now almost completely
replaced yams as the main dietary element (for an
excellent exposition of the rationality of cassava farming
for northern Ewe women, see Bukh 1979: 83-86). But
contemporary Abutia women, like precolonial (and
contemporary) men, produce alone; they do not assemble in
large groups of production, although mothers and daughters
(and sisters) sometimes farm contiguous plots and help one

another in times of need. In one way, the fate of women has thus worsened, although the same process has also brought them complete freedom from men (which is the best of the two evils?!). The labour migrations have thus exaggerated a tendency towards individual production which already existed in precolonial Kloe, and it has also altered the marketing system. Women now trade for themselves and keep the proceeds, whereas male farmers distribute the greatest part of their production to external buying agencies which pay for them in cash, and circulate the products nationally and internationally. The economy's dependence on cash is now complete, but the methods of cultivation themselves have not changed.

Prostitution has flourished with the emigration of women, who now leave not only as wives of migrants but on their own initiative. Their mobility has substantially increased since the 1940s and 1950s, with the extension of the road systems and the multiplication of motor vehicles, and prostitution even reached home when the Government opened a "State Farm" on Abutia lands in the 1960s. Collective farms were Nkrumah's answer to the problem of unemployed and potentially explosive youth, by keeping them away from urban centres, occupied in agriculture. This sudden influx of wage-earning immigrants, barely five miles south of Kloe, did give the local women an opportunity to exercise their spirit of free enterprise... and to keep the youth busy! This eagerness to capitalize on new resources at their own door nevertheless alienated many of them from their local mates and the wounds had not yet healed in the 1970s.

The use of Abutia lands for the State Farm was not altogether accidental, since the Abutia had sold land to the Bator people as early as the 1860s. But the introduction of cash crops and the demographic increases of the last century (Kloe has multiplied approximately five times in this period) have hastened the evolution of individual property in land. The precolonial **agbanuwo** owned the land corporately, but the farmers retained their rights over their fallows, as long as they did not revert to forest. When a farmer died, his children inherited his claims over specific fallows. When planted with perennial tree crops such as cocoa or coffee trees, however, the farms no longer revert to forest, so that the individual claim to cocoa or coffee farms last the lifetime of their owner, to be inherited in the following generations by his children. For all practical purposes, the few farms of prerennial tree crops are now owned individually but the

new prospects of land sales have worsened the trend.
Minimal lineage heads now try to claim as theirs the
portion of lineage land farmed by their fathers and
forbears, and by acquiring this land, sometimes succeed in
creating conditions conducive to the creation of new
lineages, as the Abutia elders themselves recognized (and
as Bukh recorded in Tsito - 1979:30). **Agbanu** lands
are thus shrinking, while individuals and minimal lineages
are carving out larger and larger shares for themselves.
But minimal lineages split over the generations, and the
process can only accelerate the individualization of land
ownership (when the minimal lineages do not sell their
newly-acquired land, that is). Land sales, individual
ownership of land, cash crops, all have also contributed
to the exaggeration of differentials in wealth. In the
1970s, the wealthiest contented themselves with the
building of larger and larger houses, but were not yet
forming 'classes'. Their wealth did not give them
privileged access to their own lineage or minimal lineage
land, and no class interests brought them together. They
spent most of their lives outside Kloe and, upon their
return, aligned themselves on traditional patterns and did
not try to form special lobbying groups with their new
colleagues in affluence.

But the insertion of Abutia into a cash economy, the
individualization of the ownership of land, the greater
differentials in wealth, or even the integration into a
national political organization, are not the factors which
have precipitated the greatest transformations since
precolonial Abutia. I would rather regard schooling,
together with large-scale emigration in search of wage
earnings, as the two main agents of change which have
yielded the new features as we observed them in the 1970s,
namely the transformation of the composition of
residential groups and their dislocation from other
domestic groups, the individualism in production and the
women's greater share of agricultural production, duolocal
residence, soaring increases in divorce rates and village
out-marriages, and the complete loss of parental control
which has rendered redundant infant betrothal, marriage
preferences and customary marriage procedures themselves.
It has introduced the quasi-universal experience of
premarital sex, frequent abortions, the selection of
conjugal partners by individuals themselves on the basis
of mutual attraction, and a high rate of fostering. These
very features, however, have evolved because of many
characteristics of precolonial society, notably its

neolocal residence, its land tenure, the possibility of divorce, individual production among men, economic opportunities for women as well as their access to land and houses, the egalitarianism which made it impossible to 'demote' socially children born out of wedlock, the important involvement in trade, and the individualism which gave everyone an equal opportunity to make it socially, to become a 'big man' or be patient and wait for eldership. In the new path that Abutia has followed it has created little **ex nihilo**, but it has developed along a line partly traced by its precolonial features, by its past. In this respect contemporary Abutia, like the operational approach to descent and social organization which has inspired this monograph, does not represent so much a denial of tradition as tradition re-interpreted and re-shaped in the face of changing circumstances.

Conclusion

Looking back at this ethnography, social anthropologists committed to non-operational models will undoubtedly exclaim 'So what? What is so different about this ethnography?' Differences are best measured by contrasts and I have tried, all along, to emphasize where and how the operational model diverges from the more classical ones. It is easy to grasp conceptual differences, but much less so to relate them to phenomenal reality; the ideal answer to the anthropologist's skeptical sally would be to demonstrate how our perception of reality is directly shaped by our conceptual tools and theoretical frameworks. To achieve that, I will try to show what Abutia would have looked like had I described and analyzed its social organization in the light of classical descent theory.

Inspired by classical descent theory I would have presumably depicted villages composed of agnatic descent groups (clans, lineages and minimal lineages). I would have noted, however, that women retained membership of their father's 'descent group' (by which term I would have encompassed what are distinguished in this monograph as elementary groups, corporations, and aggregated groups) and that, by extension, they were not absorbed in their husband's descent group. I would have taken this crucial fact as an indication that the agnatic descent groups in Abutia were weak and, from this observation, I would have attempted to derive most of the features of Abutia's 'social system'. The fact that women remain full members of their father's descent group would explain why marital ties are weak, why divorces are frequent, a feature which would find further support in the low marriage payments. Because the conjugal bond is frail, the cross-sibling ties are very strong; this would further account for duolocal residence and the existence of male-headed cross expanded and extended 'domestic' groups, since the strong 'pull' towards the father's or brother's descent group would bring female divorcees back to their fathers or brothers. Furthermore, weak descent groups would not encumber themselves with deep genealogies and would also tolerate matrifiliants, gaining therefore a somewhat cognatic appearance; this cognatic composition would be reflected in the cognatic system of kinship behaviour and the beliefs about conception (children are said to take either after their mother or father, depending upon their physical resemblance).

A butia agnatic descent groups would be weak, moreover, because their members strive to preserve the unity and solidarity of the village. If agnatic descent groups were strong and commanded powerful loyalties, their centrifugal pull would generate strong disruptive forces in village life, and tear the villages asunder. To keep alive their unity amidst a diversity of descent groups, the villages would also have adopted a centralized political organization, which further integrated the villages into a chiefdom ruled by a Paramount Chief. This centralization of power would further erode the strength of descent groups, exaggerating their weakness still more.

This monistic approach has much to commend itself. Only one parameter, the strength of descent, can explain most of the features of the social organization. The simplicity and the coherence are overwhelming and alluring and why, trained in the tradition of classical descent theory, did I resist its seduction? Two major reasons have dictated my dissension. The first one, already clearly formulated by Schneider (1965), relates to the question of the 'strength' of descent: how can we measure it, and therefore compare it? The answer is, we cannot. The second reason involves some contradictions in the monistic approach. If the model yields any explanatory value, we should expect all societies with 'weak agnatic descent' to have comparable 'domestic' groups, or comparable percentages of matrifiliants, but they do not. We would also expect low marriage payments to accompany marital instability and weak descent but anthropologists have shown that it does not (Fallers 1957, Leach 1957); even in Anlo proper, the same low payments co-exist with high marital stability or 'strong conjugal ties', which further allow the expression of even stronger links between mother's brother and sister's son! In other words, the monistic model does not stand the test of comparative analysis, and epicycle upon epicycle have to be added to make the system function. For instance, the 'weakness of agnatic descent groups' does not easily

explain the low polygyny rates, the descent group in-
marriage or the marriage preferences of Abutia, any more
than it does the changes witnessed in the last century,
such as the transformation from familial to predominantly
male-headed cross expanded and extended residential
groups, or the recent emergence of lineage in-marrriage.
One may argue that the 'weakness' has increased over the
last century, but I would reply that we should logically
expect the contrary: with the imposition of colonial rule
and the political emasculation of traditional chiefs, the
centrifugal tendencies of descent groups no longer had to
be held in check and descent groups in Abutia should then
have strengthened their agnatic component.

The picture I would have drawn in the light of
classical descent theory would have therefore been at a
loss to explain some of the contemporary features and the
evolution of the last century, it would score low on
comparibility and, above all, it would present a distorted
image.   By describing Abutia as a chiefdom, or a
centralized polity, it would have to disregard a large
number of facts which fly in the face of such a
hypothesis.   Finally, I must confess a certain unease with
monistic views of the world (and these include alliance
theory, or marxism, among others) because they usually
operate to the detriment of conceptual clarification (in
the early stages of a discipline, I should perhaps add).
In 'classical descent theory', for instance, Abutia
'descent groups' would include groups aggregated on the
basis of descent, elementary groups, corporations and
categories.

It seems futile to go on enumerating these shortcomings, many of which have already been stressed by
previous writers.   But am I flogging a dead horse?   Not at
all!   The assumptions of classical descent theory are
still very much alive, under the guise of transactionalism
and the other 'culturalist' models which have sought to
supersede it.   Indeed, what have the new models really
said?   They advocate a divorce between ideology and
practice, between representation and action, between
culture and society.   Descent belongs to the cultural, or
representational, or ideological realms, they claim, but
deviates from practice or action.   To the
transactionalists, descent represents only one of the many
rules which organize social behaviour.   They do not
doubt that the 'rule of descent' affects residence,
marriage or kinship behaviour, but they deny that it acts
alone and they contend that the other rules are to be

detected, not in culture or ideology, but in the direct observation of peoples' actions. They deny the monism of classical descent theory, to replace it with a pluralistic view of social behaviour. With this substitution I utterly concur, as I also do with their shift of emphasis onto 'what people really do' but I nonetheless diverge on some of the essentials, especially their assimilation of descent to value, and the search for the **values** which govern social behaviour, when they write about group organization. The critics of classical descent theory have therefore failed themselves to discriminate conceptually between groups and social relationships, and consequently share many of the most fundamental postulates of the very theory they question. They still believe, for instance, that descent in intrinsically relevant in the organization of politics, residence, marriage and kinship behaviour because they regard descent as a value, and one of the most important ones at that. Classical descent theory still lurks in the back of transactionalist thought and, by questioning its underlying postulates, by redefining descent in the light of a radical distinction between groups and social relationships, and by severing the sanctified association between descent and the various manifestations of social life in 'descent-based societies', we are flogging a horse that is alive and kicking!

By separating groups from social relationships, we are also by-passing the notorious Aristotelian dichotomy between ideal and actual which has bedevilled every science at its beginning (Lewin 1931). By doing so, paradoxically enough, we can finally implement the initial programme of Fortes and Evans-Pritchard, that of studying groups on their own, but only by using a conceptual idiom largely foreign to both Fortes and Evans-Pritchard. We can finally speak of descent groups which are or are not, and cannot vary in their strength, although they can differ in their modes of aggregation and reproduction. The alternatives were simple; classical descent theorists would have represented Abutia descent groups as 'weak'. Dissatisfied with this perspective, the transactionalists would have contrasted an agnatic ideology with a cognatic practice. The problem is, there is no 'agnatic ideology' in Abutia, whatever we may mean by 'ideology'. Both solutions created more problems than they solved and, above all, would render comparison almost imposssible. An operational model has enabled me to avoid referring to the strength of descent or dissociating ideology from practice; it has made it possible to posit the unqualified existence of descent groups, and to describe and analyze them in a way which, in my opinion, makes comparison easier.

This illustrates how conceptual models can shape our perception of reality. It is because we distinguished elementary from aggregated groups, and defined descent groups as aggregated groups that we could present their aggregation and reproduction as we did. It is the definition of sovereignty as the highest level of aggregation, and the distinction between aggregation and alliance, which enabled us to hypothesize and argue with some plausibility that the Abutia villages were formerly sovereign, and finally to relate village sovereignty to the manner in which descent groups were aggregated and reproduced themselves, and to contrast them to those of Anlo proper. It is the conceptual separation of residence which inspired us to look at the occupation of houses and take into account their ownership and transmission, instead of abstracting domestic groups from the very houses they inhabit; it is the same conceptual distinction which rendered pertinent such neglected facts as the materials of construction and the size of houses. It is by circumventing the definition of marriage as a status that we managed to steer away from the problems of solidarity and of the absorption of wives in descent groups, and to explain the Abutia matrimonial practices in terms almost completely dissociated from descent.

But there is no point in repeating the analysis! I only wish to stress that it is a specific conceptual model, based on operational redefinitions of groups, corporations, descent groups, categories, sovereignty, residence, marriage, and so on, which has inspired this view of Abutia social organization. With another set of concepts, we would have depicted a different Abutia. Is the operational presentation of Abutia social organization more faithful to reality, then? I believe so, perhaps naively, because it makes sense of a wider range of facts, and seems to tally more closely with the emic perspective. But, above all, I am convinced that this operational analysis has yielded a description and analysis which are more amenable to comparison, and that it has improved upon the description and analysis that I could have offered in the light of classical descent theory or transactionalism. An improvement it may be, but it unfortunately does not constitute the 'ultimate' application and achievement of an operational approach! And there is a very simple

reason for this (apart from my own limitations...). Many
social anthropologists indeed (including myself) do their
research first, and worry about the models after, with the
result that our data do not always live up to our
theoretical expectations. This ethnography certainly does
not fulfill the ultimate ambitions of an operational
model, partly because I dedicated my fieldwork to the
study of production and symbolism. I will be forever
thankful to Professor Meyer Fortes, however, who instilled
in me the values of traditional ethnography, and who
convinced me that a 'proper' ethnographer should not be
selective in the field, but afterwards! I owe it to him
that I mechanically collected genealogies and censuses,
and the general information pertaining to social
organization which enabled me to draft this brief sketch
of Abutia social organization, as I also owe it to him
that I relinquished my concern with symbolism for an
interest in the problems of social organization (although
some might think it unfortunate that he inspired me in
that way...). Had I left for the field with an
operational model in mind, however, and with the explicit
purpose of understanding how the Abutia formed groups in
their various activities, my presentation would have
undoubtedly been richer in details, and in quantitative
data. I could have aimed, among other things, at
collecting exhaustive life histories of every adult
citizen..., and dated with the greatest accuracy every
event of their lives! I could have paid more attention to
the sizes of groups, and the time intervals between their
reproductions. I would have been more sensitive to a host
of objective and easily computable features since an
operational approach should lead to a kind of presentation
more amenable to numerical treatment and mathematical
analysis. The mathematical techniques already exist, such
as multivariate analysis (used brilliantly by Cohen 1971)
and path analysis (used widely by sociologists, and by
Goody 1976), which enable us to assess with greater
precision the relative weight or importance of the various
factors which combine to produce a given phenomenon. If
the techniques are still too crude, I am confident that
mathematicians will soon see to that and it is simply the
paucity of my numerical data and my own innumeracy which
confined me to purely qualitative model-building (as in
Diagram X).

But do not misread me. An operational approach should
strive towards the greater clarity and precision and
parsimony which will welcome numerical statements and

mathematical analysis, but is not to be confused with a kind of 'number reductionism'. It is fundamentally a conceptual tool designed to describe social organization in terms which will make its comparison easier, and more rigorous, and it will treat numbers and mathematics as servants, and not as masters. To identify and describe the groups, their criteria of membership, their internal structure, their mode of aggregation and reproduction, their mutual articulation, the level to which sovereignty is attached, whether the groups are aggregated or allied, to build models (i.e., to hypothesize about the conditions which have promoted given features), to fathom the past and reconstitute the diverse transformations which have altered the society's organization, these and other activities are and will remain qualitative, and represent the very first step of any social anthropological analysis. The numbers will complete our descriptions, strengthen our demonstrations, bring out unforeseen corollaries and implications, sharpen our hypotheses and improve the standards of our comparisons, but they will never replace the observation and intuition which directly feed our descriptions and analyses.

The very quality of these descriptions and analyses, furthermore, flows directly from the conceptual and analytical frameworks which mould them, and will be improved only if the 'social' is definitively divorced from the 'cultural'. Let us not describe an operational model in negative terms. This is not an analysis of social organization in which 'ideological factors', or symbolic and value 'systems' have been ignored; it is rather an approach predicated on the idea that groups can be isolated and described with the accuracy and clarity necessary for rigorous comparative analysis **if and only if** we succeed in setting aside symbols, values and ideologies. Admittedly, the symbolic system may enter directly into the attributions of the various tasks of an interconnected set of activities (in defining a division of labour), as it does with the Abutia political 'offices', but it does not serve to define groups. Where groups are formed around religious activities we can expect the symbolic system to operate in their structuring (but not their definition, necessarily) but this is the only extent of the interface. We should thus view the two movements as one: the invitation to mathematics is a direct corollary of a conceptual and analytical movement which seeks to repel the lure of 'ideology' or 'culture' in the analysis of groups, without thereby falling victim to a numerical obsession. The divorce from ideology and culture, from social relations and the systems of beliefs or values which shape them I view as the prerequisite for the conceptual and analytical isolation of groups.

Appendices

APPENDIX 1: ESTIMATES OF POPULATION GROWTH

Genealogies constitute an interesting source of demographic data for more recent cohorts and we should tap whatever information they contain, despite their obvious limitations. When I collected genealogies I could rarely elicit the exact age at which individuals had died, but the elders normally recollected whether the defunct ones had died before or after the normal age at marriage and first procreation. I then assumed, on the basis of observation and information for many women, that women started procreating around the ages of seventeen or eighteen and that men started later, in their mid-twenties. From this information, I could then derive a rough estimate of survivorship to age 17 for women, and to age 25 for men. By selecting those women, dead or alive, who had lived to age 44 and counting the numbers of daughters they begot, and the numbers of daughters who survived them to the age of reproduction, I was also able to calculate both the gross and net reproduction rates for various cohorts. This information enabled me to use the model life tables calculated by Coale and Demeny (1966), but not the more sophisticated ones of Lederman. The Princeton life tables were calculated for stable populations, and Kloe experienced declines both in mortality and fertility rates in the last century. Despite these further shortcomings I decided to consult them to obtain a rough order of magnitude; the alternative was to leave the whole topic aside.

Assuming further that the population of Kloe behaved demographically like those of Model East in the Coale and Demeny tables, the rate of survivorship indicated which level ought to be the most representative, and the results have been presented in Table 56. However, I have not confined myself to the Coale and Demeny extrapolations, but presented in fact two sets of calculations, namely those extrapolated from the model life tables, and those calculated on the basis of the net reproduction rate (N.R.R.) that I could derive from my own data. The two are systematically discrepant, as the Princeton N.R.R. appears consistently lower than the one that I obtained from the genealogies themselves. The same discrepancy extends to the annual rate of growth (r) and I also presented an array of possible values. I first indicated the annual rate of growth suggested by Coale and Demeny for a given mortality schedule and G.R.R. (this is shown as r 'Princeton'), which is calculated on the assumption that the mean age at maternity (m) is 29. To these Princeton rates I contrasted the values or 'r' that one obtains from the formula $r = \log_e N.R.R./T$, where T is the mean generational length and is assumed to be the same as the mean age at maternity, for different values of m (namely 25, 27 and 29). Since the value of 'r' that I calculated for m = 29 was the closest to the one given by the Coale and Demeny tables, I adopted a value or 'r' mid-way between r (27) and r (29).

The figures presented by cohorts show that the annual rate of growth is declining, a fact which tallies with the decreasing fertility rates (Table 57). Because the value of 'r' varies for women born at different time intervals, it is impossible to infer a remotely accurate annual rate of growth but the available figures would suggest an approximate value of .02 $\pm$ .002, with which we can extrapolate the precolonial population.

In 1972, I estimated the population of Kloe to number 1,900 citizens, including the non-residents. But since village affiliation is only definitely settled when the children reach maturity (i.e., many men would claim children as theirs who lived with their mother in other villages), it would be more realistic to assume the figure to be 1,700. Now, if we assume a maximum annual rate of growth of 2.2% over the last seventy years, Kloe would have had 350 inhabitants in 1900. We do have a German census of 1903 which records 285 people in Kloe. This divergence suggests caution either in the demographic inferences, or in the German census, or in both. It is a known fact that people used to escape to the bush during German census-taking because household heads were taxed according to the number of adults in their residential groups. Elders also recount how people absconded to the Gold Coast to escape the harsh German domination. Taking all this into account, and taking also into account the fact that an annual rate of growth of 2.2% may be on the high side, I would estimate the number of Kloe citizens in 1900 to have been around 400 $\pm$ 25. In the early 1870s, Kloe could have numbered between 250 and 300 souls.

If we are to believe the Princeton model life tables, the expectancy of life at birth has increased from approximately 45 to 55 years for women in the last seventy years, and from 40 to 50 for men in the same period. The lower life expectancy for men, however, may result from the method of inference, since there was formerly less variation in the age at marriage of women than men and it was therefore easier to elicit whether deceased female children had died before age 17 or not. The figures (Table 56) also disclose an abnormal behaviour for the cohort of women born between 1911 and 1920, and who were first married between 1928 and 1940. They seem to have borne far less children than earlier or later cohorts, and a far greater ratio of boys to girls. I cannot explain these peculiarities, which may be due to random variation. Overall, it seems nevertheless plausible to assume that women before 1900 gave birth on average to approximately five children, and that they now give birth on average to only four children. We also find a very high rate of barreness except for one cohort.

APPENDIX 2:   LAND TENURE

Since Kludze has already covered the topic in great detail (1973), I will confine myself to the briefest sketch. The Kloe territory presents an unpatterned patchwork of lands of different shapes and sizes, allegedly delineated by the hunters of yore and which, at first glance, fall into four categories: (1) savannah land (**dzogbe**) which is not subject to either individual or corporate ownership and which any villager can till without asking anybody's permission (as long as (s)he respects other peoples' claims over fallows) and, (2) forest lands which are owned either by (a) lineages (**agbanuwo**), (b) by 'stools' or, (c) by individuals.

By far the great majority of forest lands are owned corporately by lineages (which do not hold them from anybody else, but enjoy absolute

right of purchaser over them), under their head's trusteeship.
Parcels of lineage land can be sold, even to strangers if both the
lineage elders and their head agree to the sale. The money thus
procured remains under the trusteeship of the head, and should be used
to defray the costs of education, court cases or funerals of lineage
members although, in reality, some people claim that heads tend to
spend the money on their immediate family, and to bequeath part of it
to their own children (or give it **inter vivos**). For, quite
understandably, the lack of any formal mode of accountancy can easily
lead to minor forms of appropriation, as less scrupulous lineage heads
do not always consult their elders before spending the money.

Members of the **agbanu** do not have to ask their head's
permission to clear and till the forest land if they are not planning
to plant cocoa or coffee trees, and if they are not encroaching upon
someone else's fallow. By tradition, the person who has first cleared
the forest retains a 'claim' over the fallow plot which (s)he has
cultivated as long as visible signs remain to remind people that the
plot has been cultivated. Such a fallow is called a **flu** and
anyone can 'own' numerous **fluwo**. If the **flu** has not been
re-cultivated and is covered with secondary forest (after twenty
years, let us say), the original owner loses his or her claim and the
plot reverts to corporate ownership by the lineage and can be tilled
by any member of the **agbanu**.

These 'claims' are a form of property which can be inherited. A
man's fallow plots will devolve upon his sons and daughters, although
the daughters can only hold them for their lifetime, after which they
revert to corporate ownership. Some lineages will tolerate their
daughter's sons on the land and, over the generations, such generosity
leads to land disputes. Because of the size of Kloe's territory,
however, disputes over land do not seem to have been common in the
past (they certainly were not during fieldwork) and they mostly
revolved then around the lands 'given' to, or 'inherited' by,
daughters. In more recent times, these individual 'claims' over
cultivated plots and their inheritability led directly to the
individualization of land ownership where farmers began planting
perennial tree crops, since these new fallows would not revert to
forest and could be claimed for generations. A cocoa farmer thus owns
his farm individually, bequeaths it to his children, or can even sell
it, claiming that he is selling the trees, and not the land on which
they are planted...

Because of the implications of cocoa or coffee farming, a
prospective farmer of perennial tree crops has to ask permission from
his lineage head before clearing the forest for this purpose.

Besides these lineage- and individually-owned lands, we also find
'stool lands'. But as Kludze insists, the situation bears no
resemblance to Ashanti land tenure, where the 'stool' enjoyed a
sovereign title over all the land under the chief's jurisdiction. The
Abutia stools act like other Abutia corporations (i.e., the lineages)
in that they hold absolute title over a small tract of land only.
Over that land the chief himself has no power because the stool-father
is responsible for its management, since he is financially responsible
for the ceremonies to the stool. The proceeds accruing from the
exploitation of timber and palm-trees on the stool land thus revert to
the stool-father, to defray the costs incurred by the stool
ceremonies. Stool-lands are inalienable, because nobody has authority

to allow their sale, since the **fia**-ship rotates between the three lineages of the chiefly clan. No clan, however, owns land.

In addition to these four types of land, well analyzed by Kludze, there is a fifth one which he seems to have overlooked but which does exist in Abutia, namely minimal lineage (or **fhome**) lands. Minimal lineages as a rule do not own land, but some Kloe minimal lineages undeniably own some tracts of land. The situation is somewhat paradoxical, since minimal lineages are aggregated into lineages which are themselves land-owning corporations, and I believe that this situation has emerged only recently (in the last century at the most), and as a result of the very system of 'claims' which has promoted the development of individual ownership of land planted with perennial tree crops. In fact, the geographical distribution of lineage and minimal lineage lands in Kloe seems to bear out this assumption.

Indeed, most lineage lands are closest to the village whereas minimal lineages own lands which, on the whole, are located much further away, sometimes as far as eight miles south of Kloe, or across the Hills near the Tsawoe river. They might have originated in a number of ways. Explored by the more audacious hunters who ventured far south, in the buffer zone between Abutia and its southern neighbours, they might have been acquired after the Ashanti wars, between 1870 and 1890. This hypothesis, however, does not tally very well with the fact that large tracts of land were sold to the Duffor people (of Tonu origin) even before the Ashanti wars. Alternatively (and more plausibly) the southern and furthest portions of the territory may have been held corporately by lineages but only actively farmed after the establishment of the Pax Germanica. Over time some of these parcels of land would have been claimed by the descendants of the original farmers who opened up these lands for cultivation. The process would have been recently accelerated by the market value that Abutia lands enjoy for the Accra industrialists who wish to farm on a commercial scale. I would even regard this process of claiming a portion of lineage land because of the work which forbears had invested in this land as the prime mover in the creation of new lineages in recent years.

Whatever may be their origin (and I personally believe that they originated through the system of 'claims' to peripheral areas of little interest in earlier days) the fact remains that some minimal lineages (I have been unable to count them) now own land corporately, in the manner of lineages. Their land can also be sold if the minimal lineage's adult members consent, and the proceeds are also held corporately, although they are more often channeled for private use. The heads of minimal lineages who have no living siblings tend indeed to treat the minimal lineage money as their own personal property.

APPENDIX 3: THE ENSTOOLMENT OF THE **FIAGA**

(The following description is not based upon observation, but upon information collected during interviews with the elders of the Teti chiefly clan, in the presence of the then disputed Paramount Chief).

When a **fiagā** dies, the stool-father (**zikpi-tɔ**) convenes the elders of his clan to elect a new chief. The meetings are held in secrecy and on a Thursday, the stool's sacred day. The elders establish to which lineage the 'chiefship' now belongs, and try to

designate a candidate from that lineage.   Having reached a consensus,
they later inform the elders of other clans (from Teti) of their
decision and these elders (in theory) cannot dispute their choice.
Thereafter, the elders of Teti's chiefly clan send messengers to the
chiefs and linguists of the other two villages to apprise them of the
decision.   Upon hearing the news, the linguists of Agove and Kloe
(**tsiamewo**) pour libations to their stool with Schnapps (they
formerly used **liha**, or millet beer), notifying the spirit of their
stool of the candidate's name.

Eight days later, all the Teti elders are assembled and acquainted
with the candidate's name, but no libations are then poured.   From
this day on, the stool-father prepares the ceremony but the chief-
designate is not told of his fate.   When all is ready, the stool-
father sends one bottle of Schnapps (a gift called **vlɔtɔ**) to the
chiefs of the other two villages who assemble their elders, offer them
the drinks, and inform them of the enstoolment schedule.   The chiefly
clan's **srɔnyi** (in Teti) also prepare for the enstoolment; they
learn of the heir-designate's name and the oldest among them procures
ɣɛ from the stool-father (the **ɣɛ** is a while chalky stone which is
smeared on the body on ritual occasions).

On the enstoolment day, the Paramount Chief's big talking drums
(**vuga**) echo the sentence: **Adamankama tsrama, brompra tsrama
Ohenesi numbra** (the sentence is in Twi, the orthography of which is
alien to me.   The elders translated it in Ewe as: **Mawu be vhufhola
be, fia be newova**, i.e., 'Mawu's (or God's) drummer says that the
chief should come').   At dawn, the **zikpididila** (the **srɔnyi**
responsible for praying to the stool) performs his duty.   He can only
do so if he has abstained from sexual intercourse the night before,
and if he does not suffer from polydactyly.   He dons the **blusi** (an
indigo-dyed mourning cloth), and wears neither hat nor sandals.   When
he prays to the stool, he cannot wear his cloth (**blusi**) across the
shoulder, as men do, but around the waist (**asa do de ali**) like the
women.   Then, in the morning, the townspeople slowly congregate under
the big tree in the chiefly clan's area.

The elders of the chiefly clan all sit together, facing the group
of elders from Teti, Agove and Kloe.   The stool-father welcomes them.
The heir-designate sits among the members of his own clan, unaware of
his fate.   When all have assembled a Teti elder, or the 'chief' of
Agove or Kloe, stands up to notify the stool-father that they have all
gathered, implying that they can now catch the new chief.   The stool-
father replies that they should all wait a little.   In the meantime,
the senior **srɔnyi**, in possession of the **ɣɛ** , convokes all the
stool's **srɔnyi** and, altogether, they sing and march through the
streets of the village, in the direction of the general assembly.
Upon their arrival the 'dean of the **srɔnyi**' shakes hands with the
assembled elders and orders his men to catch the candidate.   They
seize him and sprinkle him with the stool-father's   .   Then they
carry him on their shoulders through the main streets of Teti,
eventually coming back to the general meeting area where they sit him
seven times on the sheep-skin in which the stool is normally wrapped.
On the eighth time they sit him on it, facing the stoolfather who
prepares **wotsi** (corn flour mixed with water) in a calabash to give
to the **mankradɔ** to pour libations and touch the chief's mouth
seven times with it (**akɔ wɔtsi tɔ nu me**).   The **mankradɔ**
repeats the same ritual with gin (Schnapps) and a sheep is then

slaughtered at the new **fiagā's** feet (**woatso alē de efe afɔta**). The **mankrado** then puts his two middle fingers in the sheep's blood and touches the chief's mouth seven times.

The slaughtered sheep is then eaten by the members of the chiefly clan only. The head (**ta**) goes to the stool-father, the chest (**akɔta**) to the chief himself, the waist (**ali**) to the chief's mother, the jaw to the clan linguist, a bone in the thigh (known as **tofu**) to the **tsɔfo**, the part above the tail (known as **gage**) to the **vuga** drummer, and the **akɔgui** (meat around the neck), to the chief's **tɔvi**. After the main ritual the Abutia elders tell the stool-father that they leave the chief in his good care.

The **srɔnyi** then carry the new **fiagā** to his house (or the stool-father's house, if he does not have a house of his own) where he is secluded for seven days. He is guarded, and a man has to cook for him. While secluded, the chief is forbidden to eat fish, and the **srɔnyi** are allowed to catch any domestic animals found roaming freely in the town, and to kill them to feed their chief. When going to the latrines, the **fiagā** must be covered with a cloth. During these seven days, the chief is taught about the stool, about the oath to be sworn to the elders, and about other rituals. From the very day of his enstoolment, the chief cannot share a bucket, a towel, a soap, or anything which serves for his body care. If he possessed any 'medicines' (**dzo**) he must get rid of them because the stool does not tolerate it. The stool protects him like a **dzo**, and if a medicine-man tries to kill the chief with black magic, the wizard himself will perish.

On the eighth day after his enstoolment, at dawn, before eating anything, the chief goes to the stool-room's antechamber to bathe himself with the sacred water. Before entering, however, he smears his ankles, chest and arms with $\gamma\varepsilon$, and washes himself with the herbs found in the sacred pot (**doze**). He then returns to the house. When day breaks, one of his young female **tovi** comes to tie a **gbotsri** on his right arm (i.e., a bracelet made of pineapple leaves). This is performed in the house, and prepares the chief for his public appearance. Two head-scarves (always worn by married women) are twisted like ropes, intertwined and tied on to the chief's head like a crown, with the knot on his left temple. He is then dressed ceremonially, like a **fiagā**, wearing the chief's sandals. Two young women, dressed somewhat like Krobo girls who undergo their puberty ceremony (see Huber 1963: 160 for illustration) walk ahead of him, and fan him. The chief's **tɔvi** and **srɔnyi** also accompany him to the meeting at the sound of the **kantanatu**, a special drum which belongs to the chiefly clan. The linguist also precedes him, carrying his staff of office. Upon arrival, the **fiagā** is surrounded by people from the three villages.

The elders then seat themselves in a specific order: all the Teti elders sit with the chiefly clan, and all the outsiders sit together. The Teti **mankrado** and **asafofia**, however, join ranks with the outsiders, to claim the part of the **vlotɔ** which belongs to Teti. The **vlotɔ** consists of three gourds of palm-wine, three sheep and thirty pounds sterling, to be divided between the three villages. As a sign of respect, the **srɔnyi** hold the chief and sit him gently. The **fiagā** then greets the outsiders, and the Agove chief orders his linguist to ask for their **vlotɔ**, a request which is followed by the swearing of oaths. The Teti stool-father, the Agove and Kloe

chiefs and the Teti **mankrado** swear on oath of respect and
obedience to the new Paramount, who in turn swears an oath of respect
and obedience to the other chiefs.   After that, members of the chiefly
clan sing their clan songs.   Before parting, the outsiders claim their
part of the **vlɔtɔ** and the Teti linguist pours libations before the
final departure.   After drinking the alcohol offered to the ancestors,
the people ask to leave and disband.

APPENDIX 4:   MARRIAGE AND PATRIFILIATION

I have emphasized how the type of relationship between genitor and
genitrix does not influence the children's group membership and one
instance from Foli Kwasi's life illustrates it well.   As a young man,
Kwasi had an affair with a girl-friend who fell pregnant.   Kwasi did
not want to marry her and denied the paternity so that her child
remained without a known genitor.   A few years later Kwasi married a
different woman to whom he has remained married ever since and from
whom he has had many children, but unfortunately only one surviving
son who is by common agreement very peculiar and weak-willed.
Although well in his thirties he has never married and there are
strong suspicions that he never will.   In the meantime, Kwasi is
getting older and his health is failing.   A few years ago, he realized
that he could not expect much from his son.
     Oscar, the child whose paternity he had denied more than thirty
years earlier, was however stably married and extremely prolific,
having already sired many healthy sons.   Despite the fact that Kwasi
had disclaimed Oscar's paternity for some thirty-five years, he
suddenly decided in 1966 to acknowledge him finally as his son to
ensure the continuity of his own minimal lineage.   He re-asserted his
paternity by performing a simple ritual and paying a nominal fee to
Oscar's mother's minimal lineage.   From this very moment Oscar became
Kwasi's fully-acknowledged son and **ipso facto** his first heir
because he is now his first-born.   All of Kwasi's other children,
begotten through a 'legitimate' and stable marriage which has survived
forty years, were suddenly 'demoted' in favour of Oscar, whose
paternity he had always denied.   His 'legitimate' children lost their
priority of claims to the inheritance of his personally-acquired
property to the benefit of a son begotten during a teen-age affair and
whose paternity he had disowned for over thirty years!   This belated
dicision to acknowledge Oscar did not spark off feuds and hatred;
Oscar is well accepted in his new family and is now playing his role
of first-born towards his patrisiblings.

APPENDIX 5:   THE DEVELOPMENTAL CYCLE

The hypothesis of a simple unidirectional cycle of residential growth
is attractive, but it fails to tally with the Abutia data.   When
groups do not grow in a simple unidirectional fashion, it is useful to
distinguish between their 'growth', as the process internal to one
residential group, and their 'reproduction', as the creation of new
residential groups from old ones.   In a simple unidirectional cycle of
residential growth, reproduction would ordinarily take place at the
same point in the cycle and the sequence of reproduction would always
repeat itself.   But when the cycle is more complex, the two do not
coincide, as the following case histories testify.

A. First case history: Atiekpo Lanyo

When Lanyo built his house, he was a divorcee and his daughters lived
away with their husbands. He then asked his sister Yawagbo to join
him to help with domestic activities. Yawagbo was then living with
another brother and moved to coreside with Lanyo. At that time, her
own grandchildren through her two daughters (who were then prostitutes
in Aflao-Lome) were then living with her and it was understood that
the grandchildren would follow her to Lanyo's house. Lanyo later
married again; his new wife moved in with him and was still living
there at the time of fieldwork, together with Lanyo's sister and the
latter's uterine grandchildren.

Yawagbo's daughters are now planning to build their own house, to
which they would invite their mother. If this happens, Lanyo's
residential group will grow into a nuclear familial one. Yawagbo's
grandchildren, already grown up, will not follow their grandmother
into a female-headed house and Yawagbo will probably join her
daughters all by herself. The evolution is summarized in Diagram XI.
When he built his house, Lanyo started a male-headed pure expanded
group, which later grew into a conjugal expanded one when he
remarried. When Yawagbo leaves, it will evolve into a nuclear
familial one and, later possibly into a conjugal extended one. At the
same time, if Yawagbo's daughters build and invite their mother, a
female-headed upward extended group will be created from Lanyo's
group.

B. Second case history: G.K. Kumenyo

G.K.'s father, Jakob, was an only child who amassed a fortune through
long-distance trading. He married two wives whom he never divorced
and who both coresided with him. All his children were therefore
brought up together in the same familial polygynous residential group.
G.K. was the eldest patrisibling, and he was sent to the German
school. He became a teacher as early as 1920 (having re-trained in an
English Teacher's Training College) and was first posted outside Kloe.
He was later stationed in Kloe where he formed a nuclear group with
his wife in a house built for the teachers.

During these first years of G.K.'s professional life, all his other
full and half-patrisiblings were staying in Jakob's house. As Jakob's
daughters got married some moved out to live with their husbands, but
two stayed with the father. As the other sons reached adulthood they
all moved out to become apprentices in towns and cities outside. The
paternal group thus grew from a polygynous familial one to a conjugal
cross extended one. As early as 1936, G.K. had built a huge multi-
roomed house away from his father's house; he relinquished the rights
to the paternal house to his patrisiblings, and his full siblings then
moved in with him, together with their own children, but G.K. and his
wife were themselves absent, as he was posted outside Kloe again. The
paternal group thus led to the creation of a male-headed conjugal
bilateral expanded group.

During the period of my fieldwork, G.K. moved into his house with
his wife, one of his daughters and her sons. The group now concealed
a case of cross extension! In 1970, G.K. decided to build yet another
house, because of the overcrowding which beset the first one. This

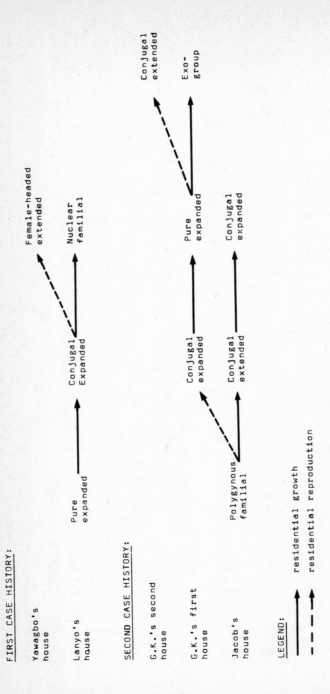

FIRST CASE HISTORY:

Yawagbo's house

Lanyo's house

Pure expanded → Conjugal Expanded

Conjugal Expanded ⟶ Female-headed extended

Conjugal Expanded → Nuclear familial

SECOND CASE HISTORY:

G.K.'s second house

G.K.'s first house

Jacob's house

Pure expanded → Conjugal extended

Conjugal expanded ⟶ Exo-group

Conjugal extended → Pure expanded

Polygynous familial ⟶ Conjugal expanded

LEGEND:

residential growth

residential reproduction

DIAGRAM XI. Residential growth and reproduction: two case histories.

was the house that I occupied during fieldwork and, after I left, G.K. moved in with his wife, daughter and grandchildren (in this new house, his sibling had no domiciliary rights). By then, his first house had grown into a residential exo-group (since G.K. did not occupy it any longer) and G.K. formed a new male-headed conjugal cross extended group (see Diagram XI).

These two cases illustrate the complexity of residential growth and reproduction in Abutia, and the impossibility of finding a uni-directional cycle. Indeed, Kloe residential groups seem to be able to grow or evolve in almost any direction!

APPENDIX 6: RESIDENTIAL DISTRIBUTION OF INDIVIDUALS

As a complement to the study of residential groups, I sought to find out the residential groups to which every individual belonged. To achieve this, the population was divided into generational levels. Such a division raised the problem of age, since two persons in G-1 could be forty years apart. On the premise that children do not decide their residence in most instances, I decided further to distinguish between 'children' (those aged up to 20) and 'adults'. This yielded a threefold classification: (1) members of G° (all adults), (2) adults from G-1 and G-2 and, (3) children (mostly from G-2 and G-3).

Every sample was divided according to sex, whether or not they were resident in Kloe. If they lived outside their natal village they were classified as 'emigrated' and no further distinctions were made (because most migrants live on their own). If adults lived in Kloe, their residence was then classified through their relationship to the house-owner; if they owned the house in which they lived, they were then considered as living with 'self'. With resident children (and emigrated ones) the case was more complicated. It was easy to find out under whose care they were (M, F, FZ, MB, and so on) but too complicated to ascertain whether their guardian headed his or her own residential group, or lived in someone else's. Children said to live with their mother may therefore be living in the mother's own house, in the mother's mother's house, in the mother's father's house, in the mother's brother's house, or in the house of an even more distant relative.

The sample was not limited to Kloe children. Kloe women who marry outside and live with their husband raise their children in his village. These children were included in the survey, as long as one of their parents originated from Kloe. On the whole, I believe this sample to encompass at least 80% of all the children born to Kloe citizens. Similarly, it includes at least 80% of the adults.

A. Residential distribution in G°

Table 58 summarizes this distribution. Let us start with the male population. Out of 93 cases, of which the residence of two is unknown, 61 (65%) are themselves house-owners and live in their own house, 7/93 live with a brother and 18 are emigrated (20%). Finally, 4 live with distant relatives and one lives with his wife in her brother's house. Most members of G° have thus built, and only 20% are still engaged in labour migrations. These migrants all come from

large groups of siblings which are part of younger cohorts, or they
are the younger members of older cohorts of siblings. In all cases,
they have older brothers alive who head their own residential groups.
The men who live with their brothers are those with alien mothers; the
cases of incorporation to the residential group of distant relatives
are all the result of demographic anomalies. The strategies for men
of G° is thus very clear: to build and head their own house if they
are old enough or, for the younger ones, to terminate their labour
migrations and build their house.

The distribution for women is obviously different. Out of 70, of
which the residence of eight is unknown, 14 only (or 20%) own their
house. Those who do not have a house have the choice of living with a
husband if they are not divorced (13/70 live with their husband in
Kloe, and 14/70 outside Kloe, altogether 40% coresiding with their
husband), with a brother if they have domiciliary rights in his house
(20/70 or 29%) or with distant relatives if they are deprived of such
rights (10/70). Two live with a sister, and four with a son. On the
whole, then, few women of this generation live duolocally. If married
they live with a husband; if they are not living with a husband, they
are widows or divorcees. Nine other women live by themselves outside
Kloe, older prostitutes approaching the end of their career. Only
three women of G° live duolocally, and eight men. Moreover, most of
the women living with brothers come from the two Type III lineages
whereas those who have built hail from Type I lineages. Finally, most
of the emigrated men of G° (75% of them) also come from the two large
Type III lineages.

B. *Residence of adults in G-1 and G-2 (Table 58)*

Out of a total of 159 men for whom residence is known (90% from G-1
and 10% from G-2) only 22 (14%) own a house and head their residential
group in Kloe, two live with a brother (forming a group with three
brothers), nine live with distant relatives, 14 live with a father
(interestingly, when the father's brothers are all dead) and two live
with a mother. All the others, i.e., 110/159 (or 70%) cases are
migrants living outside Kloe. Here again, if we took the ages into
account, we would find that only the older ones of this generation own
their house, or those who have lost their father.

The residence of women of that generation is also more complex.
Out of a total of 199 women, the residence of 189 is known. Only 5
own a house and five others live with a brother. One lives with a
sister and three live with a son. Eleven live with their mother but
37 (19%) with their father, but this classification conceals the fact
that some live with both parents. In fact, 11 are living with a
father only, and 26 coreside with both parents (the members of G° who
are not divorced). In this generation in Kloe, 25% of the women thus
reside with either the mother alone, the father alone, or with both
parents, but away from their husbands. Where they live with father or
mother alone they are usually the only coresiding daughter but where
they share their parent's domicile, they often do so with other
siblings (as mentioned in the ethnographic addenda). 18 (or 10%) of
these women cohabit with distant relative and 40 (21%) live all by
themselves outside Kloe, either as traders and/or prostitutes.
Finally, only 75 women of that generation declared residence with a

husband, 35 of them in Kloe, and 40 outside. The married women of that generation who live with their husband in Kloe are those who married older men, or the older women of that generation, but many not residing with the husband are nonetheless married and living duolocally.

C. Distribution of children in G-1, G-2 and G-3

According to the type of conjugal group, I distinguished (a) children of extant marriages from (b) children of terminated marriages, from (c) children born of mating groups from (d) children without an acknowledged genitor from, (e) orphans. I divided them further according to the origin of their parents, whether both came from Kloe (village in-marriage or in-mating), whether the father only originated from Kloe (male village out-marriage or out-mating) or the mother only (female village out-marriage or out-mating). The spouses were further classified according to their settlement (residing in Kloe or outside) and their residence (parents coresiding, or duolocal residence) (Table 59-75).

APPENDIX 7: INDIVIDUAL RESIDENTIAL HISTORY

Comfort's mother divorced her father when she was three, and the father insisted on taking her with him. She was then brought up by a step-mother in Ho who, after two years, started treating her harshly and beating her; she still bears the scars of these beating nowadays (she was eighteen at the time of fieldwork). Her father reacted by beating his wife for the punishments she inflicted on his daughter, and eventually repudiated her. He then sent his daughter to live with her **tasi** (his own maternal half-sister) in Kedjebi (in the northernmost part of Eweland, near Jasikan). Of her **tasi** and life in her house Comfort remembers little, except that the food was plenty. For many years she never saw her mother and never missed her, because she had forgotten who she was. But one day, she fell seriously ill and her mother came to see her. A few weeks later, when Comfort's mother returned to Kloe, Comfort started missing her for the first time in her life. When her father's father died (she was approximately twelve by then) she attended the funeral in Kloe and later refused to go back to Kedjebi. She insisted upon staying with her mother (who herself lived with her own mother), and she succeeded. Since then, she has not moved.

Kodjo lived with his mother for the first three years of his life only. She then divorced his father and re-married a man who worked in Tema. Kodjo was then left to live with his father's mother, who took him with her to Koforidua (an Akan town). To this day, the woman literally worships her grandson and satisfies his every whim and desire. But his father wanted him to receive an Ewe education and he sent him back to Kloe, to live with his (Kodjo's) mother's mother, a woman from Wusuta who had married in Kloe. Kodjo claims that she treated him in a 'military' fashion and never allowed him to indulge in any of his fancies. If he refused to accompany her to farm she would refuse to feed him and would even spank him the next day for the previous day's misdeeds. During all his stay in Kloe then he saw his

mother only rarely, perhaps twice a year, and she never came expressly
to see him. Nor did she invite him to visit her in Takoradi, where
she had moved. Later on, his father requested him to follow him to
Bawku (the extreme north of Ghana) where he had been stationed as a
teacher. Kodjo was then under his step-mother's care and was very
badly treated. He came back to Kloe one Christmas and refused to join
his father back in Bawku. He hid in the bush and came secretly to eat
at his father's mother's place (who had then returned to Kloe). His
father had to return to his post without his son, who then joined his
father's mother in Kloe. One year later his father was transferred to
a southern Ewe village, and he asked Kodjo to follow him since he had
divorced his previous wife. He lived then without a spouse for a
while, and treated Kodjo well enough but he eventually remarried and
Kodjo's misfurtunes started again. Kodjo was eventually sent back to
Kloe to attend Middle School (there was none in the village where his
father taught), where he lived with his father's mother again. But,
as he reached his late teens, he moved in with his father's brother
who had inherited a house from his father (i.e., from Kodjo's father's
father). He slept there, but ate at his father's mother's place. He
later quarreled with his father's brother because he invited his
girlfriends home when his father's brother was in the house and he
decided to move to a new house, at the edge of the town; the house
belonged to his father's father's brother. There he lived during my
fieldwork.

APPENDIX 8: DOMESTIC ACTIVITIES AND THEIR RELATED GROUPS

The domestic activities of the Nkubia lineage (Diagram XII; note that
this is an edited version of the lineage) illustrates well how
domestic groups can overlap. In 1971, this lineage numbered 37 people
only and in 1975, it totalled 40. Foli's minimal lineage owned three
houses and the members of Neku, only one.

In 1970 Kodjo and his mother lived in the same house, together with
his daughter Mansa who slept with her grandmother. Gbo was then
married and living with her husband in Hodzo (north of Ho). Kodjo's
tasi (FZ) Attaya was living with her husband in Podue (in Tonu,
south of Abutia) and two of Klu's children (not specified in the
diagram) also resided in Kodjo's house, presumably in the grandmother's room (the actual distribution by rooms was not investigated
during this first census). Kodjo lived in a house he had build but,
as the eldest son he had also inherited his father's domicile which he
nevertheless left to his brothers to occupy, since he had built before
inheriting. In the paternal house (built by Folitsie) Mensa used to
live with his wife Patience, his daughter Charity and son Kwasi, and
some of Patience's children by an earlier marriage. In 1971, Klu and
Donkor were living outside Kloe, together with their wives and some of
their children (in separate places, however) but they retained their
domiciliary rights in the paternal house.

During the time of fieldwork (in 1973) Donkor decided to move in by
himself (his children followed their mother somewhere else) but he and
Mensa's wife did not get along and the situation soon became
unbearable. Patience was thus forced to move out and she went to stay
with a distant patrilateral relative, but her child Mensa stayed with
his father. Patience used to cook for them in her new domicile, and
bring the food to her husband's home.

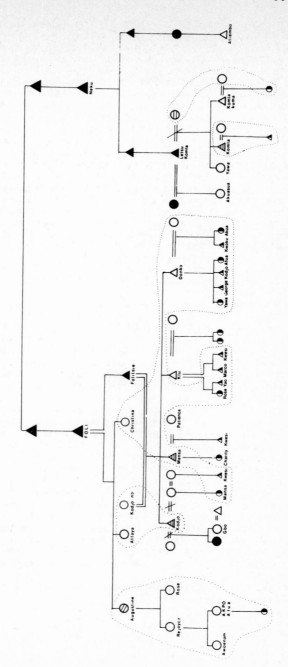

DIAGRAM XII. Edited version of the Nkubia lineage, with the residential distribution of its members.

LEGEND

· · · · · · residential groups in Kloe in 1975

△ ● boys and girls

▲ ⦶ male and female heads

When one of my assistants did a survey of the domestic situation in 1975, everything had changed. The four children who used to sleep in Kodjo's house had all moved out to sleep in Mensa's house because Kodjo's **tasi** Attaya had left her husband and had come to coreside with Kodjo, in Kodjo's mother's room. As they moved into Mensa's house, all of Mensa's children moved out to live elsewhere but Mensa is still married to Patience who cooks for him. Klu still lived in Ho with his family, but Donkor had brought his wife and children to join him in Mensa's house. Christiana still lived in a small room adjacent to their house, but her husband had left her.

In Kodjo's house in 1975, there were two hearths used indiscriminately by Kodjo's mother, his father's sister, and his children (the children who live in the neighbouring house). Aku and Adzoa (his mother) have farms which they till separately, and the food they produce is consumed by members of their own residential groups and the children of the neighbouring one. In Mensa's house Christiana has a separate kitchen at the back and the house's only hearth is used by Donkor's wife and her daughters. They cook for their own family and also for Kodjo's children, but never for the **tasi**. The children thus eat indiscriminately in either of the two houses and Mensa eats food coming from somewhere else.

Foli's three daughters do not live together. Attaya, who formerly lived in Podue now sleeps in Kodjo's house and Christiana has always lived in Mensa's (since 1971, that is). Augustine, on the other hand, built her own house, in which lives a pure matriline (or 'matrifocal' group; see Diagram XII). In 1971 she lived with only one daughter, two grand-daughters (born to that daughter) and a great-granddaughter. In 1975, a second daughter had joined the group (Rose). The head of that residential group and her two daughters often leave on long trading trips so that the six members are only occasionally together. They get their food from one farm, which belongs to Augustine but which is worked by whoever resides in the house. The food which they do not get from that farm they purchase from the proceeds of their trade. There is only one hearth in the house, and it is used indiscriminately by any of the women present, who then cook for everybody (they thus form a residential group, a cooking group and a group of consumption). They are very self-sufficient, and one of the most solidary groups in the village. Folitsie's other children and grandchildren were not in Kloe, and their whereabouts were unknown.

In the other minimal lineage (descended from Neku), Komla's wife lives in a house she inherited from her own mother. She is married but lives duolocally and cooks for her husband. Their daughter Akuasua lives with her husband in Kloe, and Yawa has emigrated all by herself. Komla has inherited his father's house (a very small one) which he occupies with his wife and their child (they are a very young couple). His brother Kuma works in Tema but his wife and child coreside with his mother (in her house) in Kloe. Of the forty people of this lineage, thirteen were not living in Kloe, and the 27 members who resided in the village were mostly scattered over the four residential groups described.

APPENDIX 9: THE MARRIAGE CEREMONY

I recorded divergent versions of the customary marriage procedure in Kloe and Teti but I have chosen to present the version collected in Teti because it was transmitted to me by one of the oldest, most articulate and knowledgeable Abutia elders, Tobge Okai Debra.

Before a father could find a bride for his son, he formerly had to search for a person who would act as a go-between. For this role, the father would choose a villager, friend or kin, who had been married successfully and had never lost a wife by death. This person was called the **asiyola**, and he was in charge of the negotiations which could only take place on propitious days, namely Thursday, Saturday, Monday or Wesnesday. On an auspicious day the **asiyola** would meet the girl's father at dawn and present the matter to him. The father would reply that he needed some time to think about it, and would give him an answer on another day. A few days later the **asiyola** returns to be told either that the match is impossible, or that the father now needs to consult his own brothers (in which case there is no major impediment to the union). On a further occasion, the **asiyola** is told that the father will have to consult the girl's mother's people.

Having been informed of the intention of the boy, the girl's father will indeed discuss the matter with the members of his own minimal lineage and the members of his wife's minimal lineage to ascertain whether any of the two **fhomewo** has ever been wronged by the minimal lineage of the suitor. If unsettled cases are unveiled they have to be tried before the negotiations can continue. After the **asiyola**'s third call, a woman is also chosen to act as his female counterpart; she may be chosen from any clan of the village but she must also have been married successfully and never have been widowed. The female **asiyola** then meets the girl's mother and repeats the same request, and the latter answers in the same manner as her husband. The male **asiyola** is then sent to meet the girl's mother's brother and if he agrees, the 'girl is released' (**Wo de asi le asie ŋu**). The whole process of repeated visits may take up to one year, and does not involve any prestations.

After the mother's brother's final approval, however, services and prestations begin. The boy's father buys one large gourd of palm-wine (especially designated for the occasion as **xovuvuha** which the female **asiyola** takes to the girl's father early morning. The male **asiyola** follows shortly after and informs the girl's father that the alcohol is a courtesy of the suitor's father. This alcohol is also called **saha**, i.e., the 'alcohol that binds'. The girl's father accepts it, invites members of his minimal lineage, and they drink it together. This gesture is repeated three times for the father's minimal lineage, and twice for the mother's.

After that follows the phase of services to the in-laws. After the palm-wine prestations the boy's father will send a young girl who has never menstruated with six to eight large yams to the prospective bride's father who will send one yam to his wife's brother, informing him that they have started **savi**. He keeps the rest of the yams for himself and his wife. After the prestations of yams the suitor must visit his in-laws in the evenings, but he must sit on the ground in their presence. For a short while the boy will send gifts of food to indicate that his wife will never suffer from hunger with him.

The prospective groom's future father-in-law then requests his eventual son-in-law to clear a farm for him. The suitor assembles 10 to 15 of his peers, who cannot take any food but only drinks to the farm. On their return, however, they eat a goat at the suitor's house, and they also receive a gourd of palm-wine from the girl's father. The boy has to clear such farms (**sagble**) three times for his father-in-law, and twice for his mother-in-law. After he has discharged these **sagble** duties the girl is more or less considered married to him although intercourse is still impossible because the girl might have not yet reached her menarche.

In the following phase, the fiancee fells a tree called l (the same word can also mean love, agreement, or weaving) which he cuts into four logs. He removes the bark to make the wood appear as white as possible and presents it as **dzoti** (i.e., firewood, see footnote 22) to his betrothed, thereby indicating the duties that she will be expected to fulfill at her husband's house, namely to cook and fetch firewood. Later on the bride and groom choose a day when the bride, together with some of her friends, will accompany her groom to his farm. There they will light a fire, fetch six to eight yams from the farm and roast them until they are well cooked. The burnt ones are left out but the others are pealed and made to look white and attractive. They then split six of these yams open, sprinkle palm oil on them and give them to the woman who takes them back home to show her parents how good a farmer her husband is. After this episode, the husband performs the **savi-kpukpɔ** (the bride's stool). He will order a carver to make him a kitchen stool, will buy a mat and a loin-cloth and send them to the betrothed's father by the female **asiyola**. They are the very stool that the bride will use in the kitchen, the mat upon which she will sleep, and the loin-cloth which she will wear. After these prestations, the groom would then be allowed to sit on a stool when visiting his in-laws.

Some time after her menarche the woman would undergo her puberty rites (**kadodo** or **avɔtata**) to which the groom would contribute meat and yams. Before the rites, however, the groom would have also provided his bride with clothes and a chest in which to keep her clothes, as well as five pounds sterling. The money was distributed to the girl's paternal and maternal minimal lineages, but she would keep all the rest. After the puberty rites (time interval unknown) the bride and groom would undergo the last important ritual, the **tsituha**. Having chosen the day the groom's father would procure two large gourds of palm-wine, which had to be consumed on a day without rain. The bride's and the groom's relatives, together with some elders from the town, would all assemble in the bride's father's house and they would drink the alcohol until only the sediments remained. At that point the bride's father's **srɔnyi** would pour libations with the sediments and blow the remainder of the alcohol on the persons present three times (**wo tutsi zi etɔ**). They would then dip their two middle fingers in the sediments poured on the ground and touch their forehead, chest and feet. The **srɔnyi** responsible for this ritual would then pour water on top of the sediments on the ground, stir the water so as to make mud and smear that mud on the gourd that contained the palm-wine. He would then step aside and the bride's father and mother would repeat the ritual (known as **tsifafa**, or the 'making of peace'). Upon this, one elder would then expatiate on the tribulations of conjugal life...

after which the meeting came to an end and signified the beginning of the conjugal pair (or the end of the wedding).

The groom could then claim his wife but he would wait a little. The bride's mother understands that her daughter must now sleep with her husband, and she connives with her son-in-law for her daughter's 'capture'. The groom cannot capture his wife in front of her parents and he has to wait until she comes out of her house. He convenes some of his friends and they hide, ready to elope with the woman. Once seized she shouts and cries but they remove her to her husband's bedroom and lock her in there. The next day, after having slept with her husband, she is allowed to return to her father's house, and this mock capture is repeated three or four times, after which the girl comes to sleep of her own free will. She stays with her parents for a long time, but spends all her nights with her husband, until the boy has built a house for her. Once he is ready to receive his wife in his house he informs his mother-in-law who has by then supplied her daughter with all the necessary cooking utensils. The mother-in-law then invites her son-in-law to come and teach her daughter how to cook. The groom buys yams and meat, and sends it to his mother-in-law where they cook **fufu** and divide the food into twelve portions. The **fufu** and the meat are taken to the husband's house, and the procedure is repeated on three consecutive days. On the third day the wife goes to sleep with her husband and does not come back home the next morning.

APPENDIX 10: KINSHIP TERMINOLOGY

The Abutia 'kinship terminology' or nomenclature actually mirrors that of Anlo (Nukunya 1969:53-62). Ego calls his or her father **t** , a word which also indicates 'possession' when suffixed or affixed to a person's name or a personal pronoun. The father's brothers are designated on the basis of compound terms built from the same root (**t**) to which is suffixed either 'small' or 'big' according to the birth order. Ego's father's older male siblings (full siblings, patrisiblings or matrisiblings) are **tɔŋga**, or 'big father' whereas the younger male siblings are **tɔde**, or 'small father'. Ego's father's sisters, regardless of their rank in the group of siblings, are known as **tasi** (etymology obscure; it could come from **tasi**, or 'father's hand').

The mother is designated as **nɔ** (no other meanings known to me) and her sisters are designated on the same principles as the father's brothers; the younger sisters are **nɔde** ('little mother') and the older ones are **nɔga** ('big mother'). The mother's brothers, regardless of their rank in the group of siblings, are known as **wɔfa** (**wɔfa** is borrowed from Twi; they also know the 'proper' Ewe term, **nyire**). In Ego's first ascending generation, therefore, patrilateral and matrilateral kin are terminologically distinguished.

In Ego's second or third ascending generation sex only is differentiated and all four of Ego's grandparents, whether maternal or paternal, are **tɔgbe** if males, or **mama** if females. These terms apply in fact to all individuals who stand as 'fathers' to Ego's own 'fathers', or as grandparents to Ego's full or half-classificatory siblings (**tɔgbe** is also a compound of **to**, and means 'ancestral father').

In Ego's own generation, sex, birth order or parent through which the relationship is traced are all irrelevant. All relatives of Ego's generation who are considered as relations (i.e., with whom a genealogical connection can be traced) are designated as **n vi** (literally 'child of mother') although Ego can distinguish his full and half-siblings, on the one hand, from his classificatory siblings (or cousins) on the other (but no terminological distinction can differentiate full from half-siblings, whether paternal or maternal). Ego's full and half-brothers are designated according to their relative rank in the group of siblings: an elder brother is **fo**, and a younger one **tsie**. No terms separate younger from older sisters.

For all of Ego's descending generations, the terminology operates as in his or her own generation. He or she calls all kin in descending generations, whether first, second or third descending, **vi** (literally child) but can always differentiate precisely with the use of descriptive terms. Thus, to his true sisters' sons he will apply the term **wofayɔvi** (child-who-calls-me-mother's brother). He can use such specifications to contrast classificatory children to his own children. Finally, spouses in the first ascending generation are not designated by a special term, but simply as **tasisrɔ**, **wɔfasrɔ** (spouse of **tasi**, spouse of **wɔfa**).

Because it is simple, the Ewe terminology extends to include heterogeneous groups of people (when considered from the point of view of minimal lineage or corporation membership). To classify his/her kin in the first ascending generation, Ego needs to know four things: (a) the parent through which the relationship is traced, (b) the sex of the person, (c) the generational level of the person and (d) the person's relative birth order with respect to the parent through which the relationship is traced. Beyond that, the particular genealogical connection is irrelevant. Ego's FMZD, for instance, does not belong to Ego's father's minimal lineage (and often not to his lineage or clan) and yet she is terminologically assimilated to Ego's father's sister (**tasi**) because (a) the relationship is traced through the father, (b) she belongs to the father's own generation and, (c) she is a woman (the birth order does not matter in this case). Being **nɔvi** to Ego's father, she is automatically **tasi** to Ego. Terminologically, Ego thus assimilates his or her FZ and FMZD, but also FFBD, FFZD, FMBD, FMZD, and so on, who are all **tasi** to him or her. The same applies to the FB, MB and MZ.

Incidentally, the use of **nɔvi** (child of mother) to designate one's siblings and cousins is not contrasted to **tɔvi** (child of father) as matri- to patrisiblings. **Tɔvi**, as we have seen (footnote 27) applies only to individuals of the same generation and of different lineages of the same clan. When people want to dissociate full from half-siblings they specify it by saying **tɔ ḍeka nɔ ḍeka** (one father - one mother) for full siblings and **tɔ ḍeka nɔ vovo** (one father - different mothers) for patrisiblings, and so on.

In the classification of affines, most terms are reciprocal. Mother- and daughter-in-law reciprocally designate themselves as **lɔxo**, and father- and daughter-in-law as **to**. A wife calls her husband's grandparents **togbe** and **mama**, but is not designated by any special term by them. A woman calls her husband's sister **tasi** because her own children designate her so. Brothers- and sisters-in-law mutually address and designate themselves as

srönye tsitsi (my older spouse) and **srönye tukui** (my younger spouse) depending on their respective ages. Brothers-in-law call one another **akunta** or **nyö**, and I failed to elicit how sisters-inlaw designated one another.

APPENDIX 11:   AGE PYRAMIDS

The following age pyramids (Diagrams XIII - XVII) have been included to give a graphic description of (a) the age structure of the resident population and, (b) the age structure and sex ratio of all the members, both residents and emigrants, of selected minimal lineages. The age pyramids of minimal lineages clearly reveal the discrepancies in sex ratios for given age intervals.   This, as I have suggested, affects matrimonial exchanges because the men of some minimal lineages may find themselves in the situation of giving their women in marriage only once every ten or twenty years, while others can give women in marriage every five years or less.   This timing of exchanges, determined by the sex ratio and age structure of the exchanging units, probably affects marriage prohibitions and preferences.

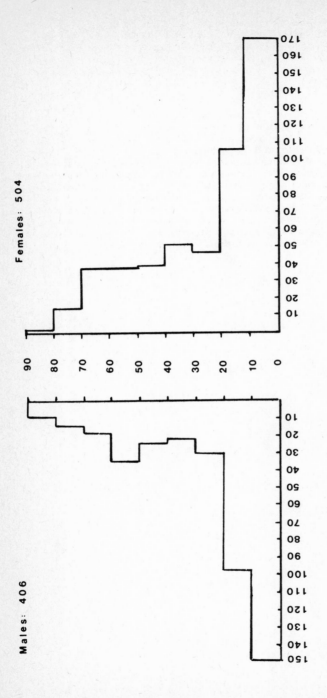

DIAGRAM XIII.   Age pyramid of the resident Kloe
population, collected in census.

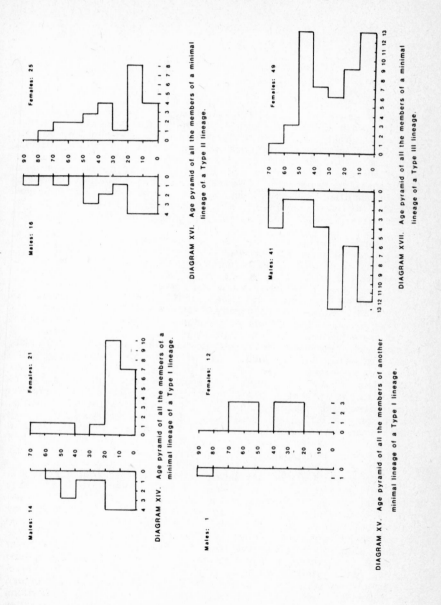

DIAGRAM XIV.   Age pyramid of all the members of a
minimal lineage of a Type I lineage.

DIAGRAM XV.   Age pyramid of all the members of another
minimal lineage of a Type I lineage.

DIAGRAM XVI.   Age pyramid of all the members of a minimal
lineage of a Type II lineage.

DIAGRAM XVII.   Age pyramid of all the members of a minimal
lineage of a Type III lineage.

Footnotes

1. To speak of 'classical descent theory' is as problematic as speaking of 'classical economics'. Both are somewhat artificial constructs, namely sets of mutually coherent assumptions derived from the writings of various authors who diverged significantly among themselves. Our picture thus presents similarities, not differences, because there is no room for a detailed history of descent theory in an ethnographic monograph. We have therefore to satisfy ourselves with a simplified paradigm which will serve, not for polemical purposes, but as a convenient term of contrast for the elaboration of an alternative paradigm upon which this whole ethnographic description rests.

2. Fortes viewed the contrast between interpersonal and intergroup relationships as one between kinship and descent (Fortes 1945, 1949). This fact would seem to gainsay the assertion that descent, in one respect, is defined as a set of norms regulating interpersonal behaviour. The contradiction vanishes, however, when one remembers that classical descent theorists distinguished two levels of interpersonal relationships, namely those **within** corporate groups, and those between individuals of various corporate groups. Descent only operates **within** groups and, as such, it is a sub-set of kinship. For those who would doubt that classical descent theorists viewed descent, **inter alia**, as a set of rules organizing interpersonal behaviour, see Fortes 1979.

3. The locution 'principles of social organization' is simply a euphemistic way that social anthropologists have of denoting 'normative mental representations'. When they write of kinship, descent or marriage as principles of social organization, they actually mean that kinship, descent or marriage are normative mental representations which function to pull individuals together and regulate their interpersonal behaviour, to enable them to form groups.

4. Some would argue that Marx's philosophical writings assume man to be an essentially social animal, thereby postulating the unproblematic nature of solidarity (or sociability). To this, I would reply: (1) that Dumont has recently demonstrated that Marx's sociology and economics were premised upon 'individualistic' assumptions, the very same which inspired Hobbes and classical economics (Dumont 1977); (2) that, although he may have viewed solidarity as unproblematic at the level of interpersonal relationships in his philosophical writings, Marx viewed it as problematic at the intergroup level (because of his assumption of class conflict) and, like other Western social theorists, he had to invoke normative mental representations (ideologies) with a power of alienation to keep class societies together; and (3) that, whatever Marx's own assumptions may have been,

it remains a fact that marxist anthropologists writing in the last decade or so have uncritically borrowed most, if not all, the concepts defined by earlier anthropologists (and most notably the concepts of group, descent group, lineage, segmentation, and so on). To that extent, my critique applies equally to them.

5.   In anthropological writings, 'function' takes on various meanings, one of which is synonymous with 'type of activities'. When anthropologists or sociologists describe the family as having a function of socialization (Murdock 1949), they mean that the family is involved in the activities of socialization.

6.   There is nothing mysterious about the label 'operational'. It does mean that groups are defined through their activities, but this is hardly new.   In fact, all the other labels - functionalist, structuralist, structural-functionalist, etc. - had been used, so I had to opt for 'operational'!

7.   Corporations are not the same as 'corporate groups', for which there is no room in an operational perspective. I call corporation a collection of individuals who differentiate themselves from the rest of the world in their relation to an estate. Corporations have a corporate identity, but so do many other types of collectivities (such as elementary groups, and aggregated groups) and even some types of alliances. To group them together and write of 'corporate groups' can only invite analytical imbroglios.

8.   Groups thus defined resemble mathematical subsets; they can be 'fuzzy' because the axiom(s) allow for some probability in the occurrence of events, but the axioms themselves remain axiomatic and are not 'fuzzy'. In other words, the existence of 'fuzzy sets' in geometry (or 'fuzzy geometry') does not in any way contradict our assumptions about the necessity of rendering groups ontologically insensitive to principles of social organization.   Neither fuzzy geometry, nor probability theory, nor indeed any branch of mathematics has ever defined a sub-set in terms of 'probable axioms'. Sub-sets, of both definite and probable events, are always defined in terms of axioms which do not tolerate one single exception.   Nowhere in mathematics do we find 'probable axioms' (like our agnatic descent, or marriage 'preferences') defining 'probable sub-sets'; there are only axioms which define sub-sets of probable events.   There is consequently a fundamental difference between a law of probability and a   'probable   law'.   What   the   structuralists   and structuralfunctionalists (and the marxists, insofar as they borrow their notions of descent, domestic and other groups from the other schools) alike are proposing is a rule (i.e., a 'law', or an axiom) which would sometimes operate, but at other times would not. Such a rule would only operate with probability. A probability law, on the contrary, predicts with absolute certainty the probability of an event taking place. The law itself is not probable, but only the events that it predicts.

9.   An operational notion of group should not be confused with Malinowski's 'theory of institutions' (Malinowski 1944). Malinowski was among the first to define social anthropology as the study of 'organized behaviour'. In order to account for the latter, he was led to posit the existence of a 'charter' partly made up of norms which ordered the relationships of individuals. In other words, Malinowski was dealing with interpersonal behaviour, its purpose, its regulation and organization by norms, and its lack of conformity with ideal behaviour.   An operational model, on the contrary, ignores

interpersonal behaviour, its purpose, its regulation and organization by norms, and its lack of conformity with an ideal charter.

10. Asamoa himself, trained in East Germany and of marxist persuasion, acknowledges that Friedländer's interpretation in terms of classes does not agree with the empirical reality (Asamoa 1972).

11. It is only since 1973, with Kludze's publication, that the inland Ewe have been specifically designated as Ewe-dome. In earlier texts, they were sometimes referred to as 'Krepi'. This usage, however, is confusing, as it actually derives from Kpeki, the Division which was empowered to administer the northern region on behalf of the Akwamu.

12. Jette Bukh, writing about Tsito, a village of the Awudome Division which shares Abutia's south-western boundary, claims that the "population density of this part of the Volta Region varies between 100-199 people per sq. mile" (1979:22).

13. Many elders now confuse this 'traditional' legal classification with the British distinction between 'civil' and 'criminal' offences, as some of these offences (especially theft, manslaughter and sometimes adultery) now escape their jurisdiction.

14. I wish to emphasize at the outset that **fhome** designates many different types of groupings, among which are 'all those related to Ego through genealogical connections' (his 'relations', so to speak). Nukunya and Kludze have insisted that this is **fhome's** only meaning and that, referring to such a 'bilateral' category of kin, it could not be used to designate patrifiliative groups, or agnatic descent groups. I must respectfully disagree; in Abutia, **fhome** is clearly used to designate what I call the 'minimal lineage' (for demonstration, see Section 2.II A). Young people are even ignorant of the traditional word to designate lineages (**agbanu**, or **dzotinu**) and use **fhome** to designate this level of grouping as well.

15. **Ametsitsi** literally means 'elder', and any man who lives to a ripe old age may be called **ametsitsi**; an **ametsitsi** is addressed as **togbe**, i.e., 'grandfather' (whether or not he has achieved this status). Age alone should ideally suffice to confer eldership but, admittedly, it is better achieved when accompanied by other attributes as well, such as parenthood (and preferably grandfatherhood), and by some dignity in behaviour and demeanour. In one respect, then, **ametsitsi** is contrasted to those who '**wometsi o**', i.e., are not 'grown up', are mere youth. In another context, it may be contrasted to **amegã** as ascribed versus achieved status; **amegã** literally means 'big man', and it is applied to younger men whose achievements, especially in financial matters (or, nowadays, in the national administration) have earned them such prestige and influence that they surpass many of their elders in those qualities. In other contexts, still, **ametsitsi** is contrasted to **fia**, as two different types of group representatives. **Ametsitsi** is here used in this political context, as the representative of a political 'group of reference'.

16. When we say that a matter falls under the jurisdiction of a lineage head, we do not imply that all the individuals in the lineage are actually involved in the activity (here, adjudication). In such instances, it is more accurate to write of 'groups of reference'. A 'municipal matter', for instance, is not a matter in which all the members of the municipality take part; we can therefore speak of a

municipality, in the context of certain activities, as a group of reference.

17. The method of genealogical notation deserves comment. I have defined G* as the 'oldest living generation', in the framework of a **fhome**. By this I mean the generation of which one still finds one living person, male or female. When a whole line of siblings dies out, that generation is then designated as G+1. G+1 is thus the first generation above the eldest living one (G*), G+2 the second generation above, and so on. Correspondingly, G-1 is the first generation below the oldest living one, G-2 the second one, and so on. By definition, all people in G+1 and above are dead, and at least one person in G* must be alive. In G-1 and below, most people are alive. Consequently a dead elder, even if he left grand-children or even great-grand-children behind, belongs to G* as long as one of his siblings is alive.

18. Many such terms are polysemic because they designate the over-lapping zone of memberships of diverse groups, and this applies eminently to the concepts presented in this study, namely **fhome, agbanu** and **sāme**. Our own concept of 'family', for instance, denotes, **inter alia** (a) a residential group and (b) a biological set defined around reproduction. Although the two coincide, their membership is often overlapping. Non-related individuals living in the same residential group with a couple and their children will be said to 'belong to the family', whereas children who have left the house are still 'members of the family' as a biological set defined around reproduction. But the family also means (c) a group of mutual aid and visitation. One may thus hear of a child who has emigrated and cut off all communication that he is 'no longer a member of the family'. The same term is used, but the groups or sets it designates vary according to the context, or the activities involved.

19. We mentioned that an upper genealogical boundary in G+1 created some problems because some individuals were too young to assume the role of **fhome-metsitsi** when the first ascending generation of their elders died out. If **fhomewo** were shallower, i.e., if they emerged as soon as one's father died, this particular shortcoming would be only aggravated and would increase political conflict. It would thus have to be discountenanced because of its disruptiveness.

20. Most individuals know their parents; in many instances, they also know their parents' parents and siblings, if the latter were alive during their childhood. Above and beyond these relatives, however, the details of genealogy are subject to individual recollection and invention. Several factors, such as the mode of genealogical transmission, naming and teknonymy, come into action to facilitate these genealogical alterations.

The Abutia do not manipulate genealogical knowledge in order to improve their status, to seek particular alignments during a factional encounter, or to win a dispute. Genealogical knowledge is, and presumably was from the time of the Ashanti wars, mostly irrelevant beyond the immediate recognition of patrifiliation. Elders are consequently not concerned about transmitting it. They do not regard it as a 'sacred' body of knowledge to be passed on religiously to following generations, and one upon which a man's achievements in life may depend. Only the vaguest notion of common descent is sufficient to aggregate minimal lineages into lineages; the rest can be excogitated if necessary, and the genealogical connection of one's ancestors vis-à-vis the ancestors of other villagers is therefore relatively unimportant. Genealogies are seldom, if ever, discussed.

A man's genealogical knowledge, then, tends to be 'picked up' casually throughout his lifetime. Whatever genealogical knowledge is learnt is transmitted collaterally. As peers grow up and share the same activities, they eventually benefit from one another's knowledge, but it is possible that the oldest and youngest patrisiblings may have different representations of their own pedigree. As individual elders pass away and whole generations die out, their genealogical knowledge dies with them, and thus genealogical constructs are renewed every generation (as Salisbury recorded among the Siane - Salisbury 1956).

The naming system and mode of address both combine to produce the same effect. The Abutia names are not 'agnatic' or patronymic in the least, but rather 'patrifiliative'. Surnames or family names do not exist; no patronyms last over the generations. Every individual is known as his or her father's child, as in Western Europe during the Middle Ages. A first born, for instance, is called Foli. If Foli begets Kodjo, the child will be designated as Foli Kodjo (literally Foli's Kodjo). When Kodjo fathers Kwasi, the latter will be known as Kodjo Kwasi. This naming system simply ignores agnation, and Kodjo Kwasi will be so named even during the lifetime of his grandfather Foli, nothing in his name indicating his lineal kinship to Foli.

Geertz has already demonstrated how teknonymous address also yields the same result (Geertz 1968). Tecknonymy is also widespread in Abutia, although mostly applied to women. Sometimes, however, men are also addressed by their peers or individuals of ascending generations as 'father of so-and-so'. As with patrifiliative names, this stress on descending generations does nothing to promote an accurate recollection of ancestral figures. The result can be seen in the transformations wrought upon genealogical representations.

If an individual knows who his parents and his own siblings are, I would regard Abutia genealogies as reliable up to specific ancestors in G+1. I would thus accept the genealogical representation of a minimal lineage as a likely picture of true genealogical connections (except where they are bounded above G+1). In many instances, however, the links between two siblings in G+1 may be distorted since surviving elders in G° may not know all of their parent's siblings, or may not know the exact links between those they addressed as their parents' siblings. Elders may thus recollect two half-patrisiblings as full siblings in G+1, or vice versa.

I would therefore believe every individual recollected in G+1 to have existed, and his links to individuals descended from him or her to be accurate. The links **between** ancestors in G+1, however, I would treat as being subject to interpretation and distortion by the surviving elders, especially if they are the younger ones of their generation. From G+2 upward, I would expect genealogical representations to bear little resemblance to reality.

21. I am acutely aware of the contradiction involved in writing of lineage or clan 'members', since I have defined descent groups as 'groups of groups'. Strictly speaking, I should write of 'the members of the minimal lineages which compose the lineage' but, for the sake of convenience and parsimony I will live with this contradiction and refer simply to lineage or clan 'members'!

22. The terms employed to categorize these groups (**fhome, agbanu, sāme**) are also endowed with a separate semantic

content. **Fho-me** literally means 'in the belly', or simply 'belly', and could be translated as 'those linked through the womb', a meaning which tallies well with its other referents. **Agba-nu** (literally 'plate-mouth'), i.e, 'those who eat from the same plate' is less evocative than its synonym **dzotinu**, or 'those organized like a **dzoti'**. The **dzo-ti** (literally 'fire-tree') is the main log used in the hearth, onto which dry twiglets are fed to kindle a hot fire. As such, it evokes very graphically the fact that minimal lineages feed into one lineage. **Sāme**, literally a banana-stem, suggests a similar symbolism. The Abutia sometimes use **hl** to designage clans, but this usage was borrowed. The German missionaries translated the Bible into the Anlo dialect and used this southern dialect as the written Ewe language.

23. In Kloe, for instance, people from Akpokli do not kill the python (their only prohibition), those from Gulegbe neither kill nor eat their 'totemic' bird, nor do they eat a type of bean called **gbona**. People from Wome also refrain from eating a different type of bean, whereas people from Atsadome do not seem to have any prohibitions; they only claim not to re-marry women they have divorced. People from Etsri, finally do not kill either the leopard or the monitor lizard and, when wives give birth, they and their husbands must sleep directly on the ground, and not on a mat or mattress. The mother of a new-born child in Etsri is also forbidden to eat salt for three days.

24. Most clans distinguish themselves through their ownership of special paraphernalia. Some of these are the exclusive privilege of stool-owning clans, especially the big talking-drums (**vhukpo**), the palanquin, the oath-swearing staff (for swearing oaths to the stool, an obsolete practice nowadays) and the large umbrella which covers the palanquin. All clans, however, possess other insignia. Such are the clan drums (usually **apinti** drums) which serve to convene clan members through the drumming of a special 'sentence' which is different for every clan. These 'drum sentences' are mostly Twi proverbs with symbolic meanings, such as 'the queen-ant has left the ant-hill, and the ant-hill is breaking down', or 'we are the bananas and come before the plantain'. Other similar proverbial sentences are also 'played' on the horns owned by most clans. All clans also possess a special staff, the **dzaŋgbe**, which symbolizes their unity. It represents a curved sword, the handle of which is carved as an animal (mudfish, crab, hawk, etc.) and to which more symbolism is associated. All these symbols allegedly describe the clans' positions in the political organization (but do not!).

Paraphernalia and various cultural objects are by no means the only features which foster a distinct clan identity. Indeed, latrines are also classed among the clan properties..., and in Kloe only the most Christian clan, Akpokli, boasts of separate latrines for the different sexes! Otherwise only one latrine, built at the periphery of the village (human faeces must be ejected from the settlement...) serves all the clan's needs. For those interested in classifications, it may be interesting to know that the Abutia distinguish **adudo** (bodily dirt) from **emi** (faeces). Urine they regard as a form of 'internal perspiration', like bodily sweat, and both are classed as **adudo**. Like bodily dirt, urine is simply 'washed out' (i.e., micturated) in their 'bathrooms' (**tsilefhewo** sing. **tsilefhe**). **Emi**, on the other hand, belongs to a radically different category, and has to be voided in the latrines, outside the settlement.

25. Despite Kludze's claim to the contrary (1973), chiefs in Abutia commonly derive their membership of one of the clan's component **fhomewo** through their mother, or belong to minimal lineages descended from women.

26. As we mentioned earlier, **ametsitsi** and **fia** are contrasted as two different types of group representative, especially in terms of their criteria of eligibility and their mode of accession. This contrast between automatic succession (**ametsitsi**) and selection (**fia**) warrants the translation of **ametsitsi**, in this context, as 'head'. As to the **fia**, we will only label him later in the analysis.

27. Within the clan, the three component lineages refer to one another as **tɔviwo**, i.e., 'children from one father but different mothers'. Tɔvi, it must be emphasized, is only used in this context, and never designates patrisiblings. It is therefore a relational term and cannot be used, as Bukh as done (1979:25) to designate lineages. A lineage is not a **tovi**; it is Ego who calls **tɔvi** a member of any lineage other than his own, but from the same clan, and this category is mostly significant during burials, when the three lineages, as **tɔviwo**, follow a strict ritual division of labour.

28. Alternately, two clans may have fused to form an extremely large one. This hypothesis, however, I find difficult to uphold.

29. These comments on Tonu towns are based on fieldwork carried out in Mefe by one of my assistants, Hayford Chormey, under my supervision. We would produce a similar type of polity if we imagined that the three Abutia villages came together, each one forming a ward. The various wards would be represented by the present **dufiawo** and would be a group of reference in judiciary activities. If the wards were aggregated, we would then find a territorial group.

30. As will become clear below, I am convinced that the stools were not introduced in Abutia before the late 1860s or early 1870s and that the emergence of **fia**-ship is contemporary with these events. This reconstruction thus applies to the polity which existed after the Ashanti wars and before the imposition of colonial rule.

31. Admittedly, political and religious activities and the goups formed in their performance overlap completely in a theocracy - to wit, pre-Chinese Tibet - but such extreme instances do not warrant the conceptual fusion of political and religious sovereignty.

32. Incidentally, some military alliances may **look like** aggregation (e.g. NATO) while others eventually develop into it (the Delian League, for instance). NATO countries are indeed allied in military (or defence) matters, but their national armies are not aggregated into one pan-NATO army. The national armies of their member-nations remain sovereign but dispatch contingents which, together, form a NATO army, with its separate Commander-in-Chief. Military alliances, however, are notoriously doubled-edged and often work to the advantage of one member who thereby gains hegemony over the others and aggregates his former allies into one kingdom, or empire.

33. Women were never charged with manslaughter, as they never took part in communal hunts, but all witches were women.

34. Spieth writes of women given in marriage to the victim's family, and of money given in compensation in Ho. I have never learned such information from the Abutia elders. I was only told that

the minimal lineages, lineages or clans of the victim and his slayer
(depending upon which groups they respectively came from) were
forbidden to shake hands, to talk to one another or to marry until the
case was ritually closed. If they transgressed these taboos, they
would swell and die.

35. It is interesting to note that although the army-leader had no
stool, he was known as **fia**. This, in my opinion, may suggest that
fia refers as much to a mode of accession (i.e., not automatic) as
to the ownership of a stool.

36. It must be remembered that Abutia was also closely allied to
other neighbouring Divisions, but the alliance was strongest within
the villages of one Division, because of its multiple character.

37. The Abutia also have a representative of the women, known as
nyɔnu-fia (and **not** 'queen-mother', as they themselves
translate) who was traditionally selected (but did not have a stool
either) and was a member of the Council of Elders. Her position,
however, has fallen into complete obsolescence.

38. One of the **trɔwo** transcends all others and acts as the
Abutia High God - he is Togbe Atando. Atando is an outsider; he is
represented as a Northerner clad in a long, white batakari, and he
exhibits none of the characteristics of chthonic gods. His present
priest claims that the god accompanied the Abutia from Notsie, but all
the ritual and symbolic evidence suggests a more recent introduction
and an origin similar to that of the stools. Atando's claim to pre-
eminence and spiritual leadership stem from his alleged assistance to
the Abutia in war. Elders contend that he, like the stools, brought
victory to the Abutia against outside threats, and fertility to their
villagers. Like the stools, moreover, he only kills when called upon
to bring retribution to a wrong-doer.

Togbe Atando also has dominance over all the **mamatrōwo**,
despite the fact that he does not belong to the same category. He is
infact one of a kind, the mightiest god in Abutia and one much revered
outside, and the only god whose prohibitions extend to all residents
of all three villages. He forbids dogs on the land, whistling or
pounding of fufu at night, and homicide (including abortion). Like a
stool, Atando is the exclusive property of one Agove clan, and he
selects (but does not possess) a man from this clan as his priest.
His spiritual power abounds so much, however, that he also possesses
women who, as his **trōsiwo**, are under his priest's leadership. The
priest of Togbe Atando thereby dominates the area of religion as the
Abutia High Priest.

39. At burials, people speak symbolically of the body of the
deceased as if it represented sacrificial meat. The head is said to
belong to the father, and the chest (**akɔta**) to the **tovi**. The
t vi, as members of the departed's own generation, speak on his
behalf and are therefore given the part of the body where the organs
of speech lie.

40. The **fia** is forbidden to sit on the ground or to touch it
with his bare feet, to eat food cooked by a menstruating woman, and to
make love either on his god's weekly sacred day, or on the night
before.

41. Spieth mentioned that sheep had been brought to Eweland in the
not too distant past (certainly since Europeean contact). This fact
adds to the symbolic cleavage between autochthonous and immigrand gods
(including stools). Rituals to stools and **mamatrōwo** always

involve the sacrifice of a sheep (for which chickens can occasionally be subtituted) and the eating of yams. Rituals to earth gods, on the other hand, require goats as their sacrificial animals and are accompanied by the consumption of maize dishes. To me, this symbolic evidence coroborates still further the recent origin of stools, and suggests a similar foreign and recent origin for yams.

42. The precolonial Abutia villages, according to my calculations, would have numbered less than 400 souls - see Appendix 1.

43. The **tsiame**, for instance, often disagrees and argues with the **fia** when the latter wants to say things that the **tsiame** does not consider appropriate. He is much more an 'interpreter' than a 'translator'. He may indeed edit or embellish upon the chief's speech at his liking. Throughout Eweland, the linguist is in fact a public figure in his own right and he may play very important roles in public gatherings, according to his oratorical skills. The chief may utter two sentences and the linguist take fifteen minutes to 'repeat' what the chief said!

44. All the symbolism in this legend of origin suggests an analogy between Notsie and a womb, and between the migration and birth. The wall, the hole made forcibly with a sword, the dish water that softens the wall, are many elements which seem to equate the flight with the delivery from the womb.

45. It therefore goes without saying that I do not accept Greene's thesis of the origin of clans in Anlo (Greene 1981). Greene, who tries to apply Wilks' thesis that the Ashanti clans were actually created by the emergence of the state (Wilks 1977), argues that the Anlo clans were formed to absorb a large population of Ga-Adangme immigrants who fled Akan agressions. From my analysis, it is quite clear that I claim that the northern Ewe do have clans - a fact which Greene denies - and that I perceive their differences from the Anlo hlɔ in terms of dispersal and mode of reproduction.

46. Bender, who had worked on Yoruba 'households' and noticed that the Yoruba lacked a concept of 'family' (1971) concluded that we must distinguish analytically between family, domestic 'functions' and coresidence (1967). I do endorse the general orientation of his conclusion, but I do not agree with his particular understanding of the problem.

47. It follows from this position that residential groups do not exist everywhere. Wherever there is no identifiable dwelling unit, groups formed around the process of sleeping will not be influenced by the occupation of a dwelling unit. Let us imagine a group of shepherds moving off on transhumant migrations for one season. In this particular instance, the manner in which these shepherds will form groups for other purposes (sleeping, cooking, eating) will certainly be dependent upon the first activity (shepherding). Their 'sleeping groups' will not be residential groups. Even if they occupied specific huts during their migrations, the main criterion of membership of their 'sleeping group' would itself be membership of the group which guards the herd. Only this last group would have specific criteria of membership (filiation, siblingship, friendship, sex, age, and so on). One way of expressing this dependence is to state simply that criteria of membership of group B is in fact membership of group A. This formulation allows the analytical distinction between the different activities and groups, but shows their interdependence. It is quite obvious, for instance, that the residence of young children cannot be treated separately; they coreside with the adult(s)

who has (or have) responsibility for the child's education.   This will explain why I have eliminated young children from the 'core members' in my classification of residential groups.

This also underlies an important distinction between residence as an activity, and residence as a criterion of group membership. Membership of a residential group can indeed serve as a criterion of membership of **another** group, but not of a **residential** group! We could assume, for instance, that the occupation of a given house is a prerequisite for using one of its hearths (a situation which obtains in most cases in Abutia) and we could therefore describe residence as one of the criteria of membership of cooking groups (in addition to, say, female gender and matrifiliation). A mother could thus cook only with those daughters who coreside with her; those occupying other houses would be excluded from her cooking group.   One must thus carefully seperate residence as an **activity** around which residential groups are formed, and residence (or, more specifically, membership of a residential group) as one of the criteria of membership of group involved in other activities (such as production, cooking, or distribution of foodstuffs).   By confusing the two and viewing residence as a criterion of membership only, some commentators have concluded that my attempt to define residence operationally was a cultural illusion generated by the fact that residence is important as a criterion of group membership in Abutia!   The irony of the matter is that residence is not really an important criterion of group membership in Abutia, as the following study will show.   House-building, on the other hand, is critical because it enables men and women to give their children domiciliary rights.   If they fail to build, their children will be forced to coreside with more distant kin, being only 'tolerated' in the house they occupy.   This fact certainly influences the dynamics of residence in Abutia, but it does not undermine an operational definition of residence as an activity in which residential groups are formed!

48.   In the Section 1.I, I mentioned that some groups lacked any division of labour, and were therefore not 'structured'.   In my opinion, residential groups constitute the best example, since there is no way in which a division of labour can be defined in the occupation of a dwelling-place for sleeping purposes.   This explains why I write of the composition, and not the 'structure' of residential groups.   But because houses are also property, they are normally 'owned' by one person, who is defined as the 'head' of the residential group.   This distinction, however, is only pertinent in terms of ownership.   Because residential groups also overlap with house-owning corporations (or individual ownership of houses) and other domestic groups it **looks as if** residential groups were structured.   If we look at them operationally, that is in terms of residence only, it is then quite manifest that they cannot be.

49.   It follows from this definition than an individual can be a member of more than one residential group.

50.   In earlier publications (Verdon 1979b, 1980a), I designated such entities as 'residential **categories**'.   Since I assumed categories not to be involved in any activity, I committed an obvious contradiction, and I now correct this mistake.

51.   At the time of census-taking (between September 1971 and February 1972), there were 172 houses in Kloe, with their respective residential groups.   Altogether, 137 of them were surveyed in detail (i.e., 80%), but my intimate knowledge of the groups not surveyed in

detail enables me to assert that none of the groups omitted differed significantly from those described in this study. I therefore believe this sample to be representative of the total population of Kloe and, by extension, of that of Abutia.

The 'native population' included in these 137 residential groups totalled 914 inhabitants. All the 'strangers' (i.e., Government workers, policemen and their families, and the anthropologist himself) where excluded from the sample. They were housed as 'lodgers' and paid for their use of a room. There were 20 strangers in the 137 houses surveyed, but all were concentrated in four large houses inherited by individuals with extremely few siblings and children. On the basis of this sample, the total resident population of Kloe averaged 1,150. 'Absentee heads', although included in the composition of residential groups and their classification, were not counted as residents of the village in this computation.

52. This particular group should have been technically classified as 'male-headed parallel upward extended', were it not for the fact that the son only spends his holidays in the village. Being engaged in very prestigious and lucrative employment in Accra, he will not settle in the village before his retirement, by which time his octogenarian father will have most likely passed away. In this instance, the father calls himself 'head' of the residential group, although his son built the house.

53. In both cases of expanded groups (one parallel and one cross) the head is a barren woman who became rich through prostitution and helped her sibling by building him or her a x adjacent to her own. The two sons who coreside with their mothers have no sisters and are both very eccentric characters.

54. The watering system is very precarious. Despite the presence of an inselberg, only one insignificant spring reaches Kloe, and people fetch their water from wells and half-dried ponds. The only stream of some importance, the river Tsawoe, lies far away on the other side of the Hills and serves as a boundary between Abutia and Awudome (see map III). This absence of rivers or streams acts as an homogenizing factor in production, since yields seem to vary little from one plot to another.

55. Meat rarely enters the Abutia diet; sheep, goats and chickens are consume on ritual occasions only.

56. I was unable to collect accurate figures for infant betrothal in the early part of this century. Out of a sample of 85 women, both dead and alive, born before 1930 and some of whom, therefore, did not marry before 1948, 48 had been betrothed either by their husband himself, or their husband's father. In Abutia, infant betrothal did not imply gaping age differentials between spouses since a father often betrothed an infant girl to his young son. From the evidence I could gather, I gained the impression that women used to marry between the ages of 16 and 18, and men between the ages of 25 and 30.

57. These payments included a wooden chest filled with clothes (men wove in those days, a skill now completely lost) and a certain amount of money. I was not able to determine with any precision what this amount was in the German period or before but, since the 1920s, it normally amounts to five pounds sterling.

58.   In   absolute   numbers   the   teachers   guilty   of   these   sexual
offences   are   few   (there   were   only   two   in   the   village   where   I   resided)
but   their   influence   is   disproportionate   to   their   numbers   because   their
victims   are   more   numerous   and   they   create   a   climate   of   fear   in   their
classroom,   where   every   child   must   eventually   go.

59.   I   use   set   because   reproduction   takes   place   **within**   women
and   is   therefore   not   an   activity   in   which   individuals   can   engage   and
form   groups.   Since   there   is   indirectly   an   activity,   however,   I   would
welcome   any   alternative   to   'set'   which   would   seem   more   appropriate
(quasi-group,   for   instance?).

60.   The   'facts'   which   go   into   making   a   'marriage'   may   themselves
be   a   whole   set   of   activities   in   which   special   groups   have   to   be
formed,   as   in   a   wedding   or   a   marriage   ceremony.

61.   When   a   wife   originates   from   a   village   different   from   her
husband's   she   becomes   a   member   of   his   minimal   lineage.   However,   this
is   subject   to   interpretation   since   women   who   marry   into   other   villages
have   matrilateral   relatives   in   that   village.   They   may   therefore   be
considered   members   of   their   mother's   minimal   lineage,   of   which   their
husband   normally   is   a   member.

62.   There   are   dangers   in   speaking   of   exchange   between   minimal
lineages.   Because   they   are   bounded   in   G+1,   minimal   lineages   should
divide   every   generation   under   ideal   demographic   conditions.   They   do
not,   but   multiply   fast   enough   that   it   is   misleading   to   represent   them
as   enduring   entities   like   lineages   or   clans.   Consequently,   if
exchanges   were   not   completed   over   two   generations,   the   claims   were
likely   to   lapse   because   the   minimal   lineages   involved   in   the   original
exchange   might   have   divided.   In   other   words,   the   size   and
genealogical   depth   of   the   exchanging   units   does   influence   the
genealogical   distance   between   the   preferred   spouses.   Moreover,
'minimal   lineage   exchange'   might   suggest   'sister-exchange'   which,
although   not   formally   practiced   in   Abutia   (only   two   instances   were
recorded,   both   of   which   had   taken   place   in   the   last   forty   years),   is
prohibited   in   other   Ewe   confederacies   (Nukunya   1969:65).

63.   The   figures   presented   in   the   following   tables   were   collected
in   Kloe   only,   but   I   have   no   reason   to   suspect   any   serious   divergences
between   Kloe   and   the   other   two   villages.   From   the   genealogies   of   the
whole   village,   I   tried   to   date   the   major   events   in   the   lives   of
individuals.   I   had   certain   reference   dates   that   I   could   use   in   this
reconstruction,   in   that   some   Christians   knew   the   year   of   their   birth,
and   some   known   events   enabled   me   to   devise   a   'local   chronology'.   With
those   guiding   marks,   I   tried   to   assess   the   age   of   various   individuals,
asking   them   if   they   had   experienced   their   menarche   by   such   and   such   a
date   (i.e.,   by   the   time   an   event   took   place),   or   whether   they   were   old
enough,   when   so   and   so   was   born,   to   carry   him/her   on   their   back.   I
was   thus   able   to   estimate   the   age   of   many   individuals,   and   dated   the
other   events   on   the   basis   of   simple   demographic   extrapolations,
knowing   for   instance   that   children   are   spaced   at   least   one   and   a   half
to   two   years,   and   that   women   rarely   got   married   before   their
seventeenth   birthday,   and   stopped   reproducing,   on   the   whole,   after   44
years   of   age.   The   dates   were   thus   approximated   and   extrapolated,   and
therefore   imprecise.

On   the   basis   of   this   information   I   filled   computer   cards   for
each   individual   and   his   or   her   matrimonial   life.   The   units   of
reference   in   the   tables   are   consequently   individuals   (or   the   marital
experiences   of   separate   individuals),   and   not   marriages.   Where   both
spouse   originate   from   the   same   village,   the   information   is   duplicated,

but where Kloe men or women married outside, their marriage is only counted once.

There were 1,364 individuals for whom cards were filled. These 1,364 individuals do not represent a sample, but the total population of the living and of those deceased who were remembered by the living. Because of coding problems, it was found preferable to count only the first four unions of any individual, but only 24 individuals had been engaged in more than four unions, and most of these unions were not actual marriages, in that they were terminated as soon as children were born.

Two different kinds of measures have been selected. The individuals' unions were coded as first, second, third or fourth. One type of measure thus applies to **all** marriages, first to fourth inclusively, whereas another type is restricted to the **first** marriage of women because, until recently, the origin of a woman's first spouse was decided by her parents. It was therefore the marriage for which she was most likely to have been betrothed in infancy, and which indicated marriage preferences. The problem differs for men. A woman can only be betrothed once, and to only one man. A man, however, can select an infant bride for his second, third or fourth wife, if he has had that many. If arranged marriages expressed a preference, this could only be detected in the women's first marriage.

64. Wome is also composed of five lineages, two of which seem to have split in the last fifty years. However, their extremely small size and the low proportion of inter-marriages between the lineages which have sundered suggests that Wome's rate of lineage in-marriage would not have changed significantly had the lineages remained united. It might have increased sufficiently, however, to place it in an intermediary position between the two largest and two smallest clans.

65. The situation may also be the result of a historical process. The two larger clans may have welcomed refugees who came in various waves, and who linked themselves matrimonially to their host-clans.

66. Since the practice had died out such a long time ago, I found it imposssible to elicit more details about the women who were given such endowments, but Kludze reports a similar practice (1973:223).

67. There is a total recollected population of 270 dead males ever married and, of these, the date of first marriage is not known for 23 individuals, especially in the earliest cohorts. Since the date of first marriage is known for all polygynists, the rates of polygyny for the early cohorts (up to 1905) may therefore be higher than in reality, and would have to be lowered slightly.

68. There is no contradiction between the two statements, since they refer to different rates. By 'overall incidence' I mean the total number of polygynous unions per males married for a cohort which has terminated its matrimonial life. The incidence 'at any given point in time', however, refers to the number of men married polygynously, expressed as a ratio of all men extantly married, in any given year. In contemporary Kloe, the first rate is 27% for the dead population, and the second rate is only 16%. The second rate is influenced by the proportion of extant to 'one time' live polygynists and would thus be higher if polygynists did not divorce their wives.

69. Agodzo stands out as the only exception. In this lineage, three rich siblings, presently in their forties and fifties (in 1972), have all married polygynously. They have only recently amassed their wealth and, as a result of their polygynous practice, will double or

treble the size of their lineage in the next generation.

70.   Polygyny in Kloe has the opposite effect on women, when the number of children is taken into account. Women who spent at least fifteen years of their child-bearing life with a co-wife engendered an average of four children, whereas women who spent most of their child-bearing life without a co-wife averaged five children (Tables 54-55).

71.   I have earlier suggested that clan in-marriage arose only when size permitted. Akpokli and Gulegbe should consequently display a greater propensity towards polygyny in the generation preceeding 1875. This is not altogether contradicted by the available evidence, which is however too scanty to account for size differentials before the 1890's. This, in my opinion, suggests three hypotheses: either (a) the incidence of polygyny among the larger lineages and clans before 1875 reached much higher levels than recorded, but the information has been lost in the distortions of genealogical recollection, or (b) polygyny was practiced on a small-scale in all clans before 1875 and the differences in clan sizes must be attributed to different causes (such as differences in fertility, or mortality), or still, (c) polygyny was uncommon before 1875 and all lineages and clans were of almost comparable size; the differences observed nowadays would thus have evolved only recently.

I am at a loss to pronounce myself on the conditions which probably existed before 1875, but I would suspect situations (a) and/or (b) to have prevailed. Indeed, hypothesis (c) would require an explanation of the emergence of polygyny, of differences in descent group sizes and of clan in-marriage.   It seems easier to posit the differential size of clans to be due to random fertility or some historical process (host versus refugee groups), and to assume that these differences were later amplified by polygyny, than to explain the sudden inordinate growth of two clans over one or two decades (since the differences were present, without any doubt, by 1895).

72.   I would like to draw the reader's attention to the fact that male bachelors are almost as numerous as male widowers. At the time of fieldwork, thirty seven men over the age of thirty had not yet married. Of these, twelve were between the ages of 30 and 35 and, on the basis of my acquaintance with these individuals, I do not expect more than two-thirds of them to find a spouse in the future. As the great majority of bachelors over 35 will never marry (in the very opinion of their peers), 29/360 (or 8%) of male adults remain bachelors throughout their life, a percentage halved for women. The bachelors are also proportionally represented in every clan. Despite the obvious fact that some of them are crippled, disfigured or simply misfits who cannot find a spouse, many others could but do not. Unfortunately I cannot account for this high percentage since it only came to my notice when I compiled the data.

73.   This instability does not arise because of conflicting expectations between kin and affines, or potential conflicts over inheritance, as Jack and Esther Goody have argued for Northern Ghana (Goody, J. and E. 1966).

74.   In fact, the situation appears more complex than J. Goody has suggested, and invites a reformulation of his hypothesis. He singled out the transmission of property over generations to account for the main differences between systems of marriage payments.   If one followed this distinction literally, I would have to conclude the existence of diverging devolution in Abutia, since daughters can

inherit their father's immovable property as epiclerates. I would rather view the critical distinction to lie in the transmission of property within the same generation, especially between spouses. Where property can move from one spouse to another, parents would be extremely reluctant to endow their daughters with property, if their daughter's husband married many wives simultaneously. The flow of property between husband and wives would mingle their capital and create bitter disputes upon the death of any one of the spouses. This situation certainly militates against dowry and would explain that the 'constitution of a conjugal fund' almost precludes polygyny and favours monogamy. But where there is an 'affinal stop gap' beyond which property can never flow, the marrying of many wives does not affect the ultimate direction of the flow of property. In other words, where spouses can mutually inherit their property, plural marriage is almost intolerable; where they cannot, the number of wives a man marries does not influence the movement of capital endowments, and plural marriage is not hindered by the clashes of property rights.

75. Marriages are occasionally connected through the 'return marriages' which give rise to FZD marriage and its variants, but this is in no way linked to the transfer of marriage payments.

76. Jette Bukh has mentioned the existence of 'big men' in precolonial times who actually used their wealth to create debts and thereby acquire pawns who constituted a servile labour force at their exclusive command (Bukh 1979: 26-27). Such a situation no doubt existed, and two or three names from the past commemorate such unusual wealth in Kloe itself. But a brief acquaintance with the Kpelle literature or the literature on the Bamileke will immediately show that the Ewe polities were not predicated on this process of clientele-building. As with sister-exchange, we can record one or two cases, but this is a far cry from claiming that the polity was governed by a political dynamics of the patron-client type. Wealthy people there were, but they were more constrained in the political use to which their wealth could be put.

77. The works of Kuper and Holy (Kuper 1982, Holy 1979a), as well as this work on Abutia and my reanalysis of the Nuer (1982b) further negates Goody's theses on bridewealth. Indeed, my own reinterpretation of Nuer ethnography and Kuper's reinterpretation of the southern Bantu ethnography leaves no doubt in my mind that these cattle-herders, and perhaps most cattle herders, **do not have any descent groups**, but are the most illustrious bridewealth-givers. The Abutia, Eastern Dida, Mbembe or even some Yoruba groups, on the other hand, do have descent groups, **but no bridewealth!** Bridewealth is thus widely found in ranked societies without descent groups, and absent in many societies without ranked groups but with descent groups.

78. The following material was collected in the field, but I have found both confirmation and inspiration from Spieth (1906, 1911), Kludze (1973) and Bukh (1979).

79. Spieth reports that there existed an organization for the youth (meaning adult men not yet elders), called **sohe**, whose representative, the **sohefia** was included in the Council of Elders. I have not been able to find any evidence about such an organization in Abutia, but this does not necessarily imply that it did not exist. In the 1930s, the young literati created a group to represent their interests, and they called it **Sohe,** a fact which suggests that a precolonial **sohe** might have existed.

Tables

Table 1. Number and percentage of matrifiliants in a sample of 21 minimal lineages.

	AIII					BII				BIII				
	1	2	3	4	5	1	2	3	4	1	2	3	4	5
Members	44	51	25	37	90	29	60	25	41	73	19	70	41	59
Matrifiliants	8	6	0	4	38	2	19	0	13	8	2	20	24	24
% of matrif.	18	12	0	11	42	7	32	0	32	11	10	28	58	41

	DI				EI	EII		
	1	2	3	4	1	1	2	TOTAL
Members	39	52	38	13	35	38	61	940
Matrifiliants	1	20	7	6	6	5	21	234
% of matrif.	2	38	18	46	17	13	24	25

Legend: A = Akpoli, B = Gulegbe, D = Etsri, E = Atsadome
I, II, III = types of lineages.

Table 2. Minimal lineage sizes.

	1-20	21-30	31-40	41-50	51-60	61-70	71-100	100+	Average size	Median size
Number	16	11	12	5	5	3	2	1	34.41	31

Table 3. Clan and lineage sizes.

	A1	A2	A3	TOT	B1	B2	B3	B4	B5	TOT	C1	C2	C3	C4	C5
No. of members	370	187	50	607	366	86	151	126	71	800	53	47	32	39	31

	TOT	D1	D2	D3	TOT	E1	E2	E3	TOT	Grand total
No. of members	202	52	52	38	142	99	35	23	157	1908

Legend: A = Akpokli, B = Gulegbe, C = Wome, D = Etsri, E = Atsadome
1,2,3,4,5 = constituent lineages
TOT = Total

Table 4. Composition of residential groups

CORE:	A) Head	
	B) Secondary members:	1) father, mother, spouse(s), adult siblings, and adult children of A
		2) spouse(s) or adult children of 1, if 1 is a member of the residential group and therefore a secondary member.

INCORPORATED
MEMBERS: Members of the group who are not in the core.

Table 5. Classification of residential groups.

NUCLEATED GROUPS: Head (male or female) and secondary member(s), with or without incorporated members.

1. Head and spouse only: conjugal residential group
2. Head and spouses only: polygynous group
3. Head and spouse and young children: nuclear familial group
4. Head and spouses and young children: polygynous familial group
5. Head and adult siblings: pure expanded group (C, P or B) *
6. Head and spouse and adult siblings: conjugal expanded group (C, P or B) *
7. Head and spouses and adult siblings: polygynous expanded group (C, P or B) *
8. Head and adult children: pure extended group (C, P or B) *
9. Head and spouse and adult children: conjugal extended group (C, P or B) *
10. Head and spouses and adult children: polygynous extended group *
11. Head and one parent: pure extended upward (C or P)
12. Head and spouse and one parent: conjugal extended upward (C or P)
13. Head and spouses and one parent: polygynous extended upward group (C or P)
14. Head and both parents: co-parental group
15. Head and spouse and both parents: stem family
16. Head and spouses and both parents: polygynous co-parental group

NON-NUCLEATED GROUPS:

A. No coresiding head but secondary members: exo-group
B. Head without secondary members:
  1. Head alone: solitary
  2. Head and young children: patricell or matricell
  3. Head and young siblings: quasi-expanded
  4. Head and incorporated members: incorporative group **

Legend: C = cross, P = parallel, B = bilateral
     *   The adult siblings may have coresiding spouse(s) and/or
         young children. If the sample is large and these
         combinations are numerous enough, they should be
         included separately in the classification, as a
         different type., Otherwise, they should be mentioned in
         the ethnographic addenda only. Note also that every
         group should be described as male-headed or
         female-headed.
    **   The classification of nucleated groups could be extended
         much further, if one included all possible combinations;
         for the purpose of this study, this classification is
         sufficient.

Table 6. Classification of Abutia Kloe residential groups

MALE-HEADED GROUPS

Nucleated														Non-nucleated					
I			II			III			IV			V	TOT	VI	VII	VIII	IX*	X	TOT
C	P	B	C	P	B	C	P	B	C	P	B								
8	5	3	4	1	2	9	3	3	13	3	3	15	72	4	4	10	3	6	27

FEMALE-HEADED GROUPS

Nucleated					Non-nucleated				
I	III	V	TOTAL		VI	VIII	X	XI	TOTAL
C	P	C	P						
1	1	2	12	1	17	7	4	6	4	21

Legend: I=pure expanded, II=conjugal expanded, III=pure extended
         IV=conjugal extended, V=nuclear familial, VI=incorporative
         VII=patricells, VIII=exo-groups, IX= pure cross-extended up-
         ward, X=solitaries, XI= matricells
         C=cross, P=parallel, B=bilateral

    * Should have been classified among nucleated groups, but
      listed among non-nucleated for purposes of this study.

Table 7.   Residential group sizes.

	I	II	III	MALE-HEADED GROUPS IV	V	VIII	TOT1	TOT2	TOT3	TOT4
Sizes:										
2 - 5	6	0	7	2	8	4	3			
6 - 10	8	1	7	8	6	6	8			
11+	2	6	1	9	1	0	0			
Aver.	6.93	13.14	6.	11.05	6.06	6	6.36	8.25	5.03	7.37
Median	8	14	6	10	5	6	7			

	III	VI	FEMALE-HEADED GROUPS TOT5	TOT2	TOT3	TOT6
Sizes:						
2 - 5	8	5	12			
6 - 10	5	0	2			
11+	1	2	0			
Aver.	6.28	6.71	2.78	5.88	4.09	4.89
Median	5	5	2			

Legend: I=pure expanded, II=conjugal expanded, III=pure extended,
          IV=conjugal extended, V=nuclear familial, VI=incorporative
          groups, VIII=exo-groups, TOT1=total of non-nucleated groups
          excluding exo-groups and solitaries, TOT2=total of all
          nucleated groups, TOT3=total of all non-nucleated groups,
          TOT4=total of all male-headed groups, TOT5=total of non-
          nucleated groups, excluding incorporative, TOT6=total of all
          female-headed groups.

Table 8.   Distribution of nucleated male-headed groups according to
           the manner in which the house was acquired.

	INHERITED	BUILT	UNKNOWN	TOTAL
Expanded	17	6	0	23
Extended	3	28	3	34
Nuclear	2	13	0	15
Total	22	47	3	72

Table 9.   Distribution of nucleated male-headed residential groups
according to the head's marital stability.

	STABLE	UNSTABLE	NOT APPLIC.	TOTAL
Pure expanded	3	11	2	16
Pure extended	6	9	0	15
Conjugal expanded	6	1	0	7
Conjugal extended	19	0	0	19
Nuclear	11	4	0	15
Total	45	25	2	72

Table 10.   Distribution of the male-headed residential groups
according to their type and the age of the head.

	I	II	III	IV	V	VI	VII	VIII	IX	X	TOT1	TOT2	TOT3
1882-1891		4	2		1	1	1				9	10	9
1892-1901	1		3	6	2	1		1		1	15	15	13
1902-1911	4	3	3	3	1				1		15	19	14
1912-1921	5	1	5	5	6			2		2	26		25
1922-1931	3	3		3	3		3	5	1		21		13
1932-1941	3			2	1			1	2		9		6
1942-1951				1	1			1	1		4		3
Total	16	7	15	19	15	4	4	10	3	6	99		83

Legend: I-X: same as Table 6.
TOT1 = total number of heads, TOT2 = total number of men
still alive from that cohort, TOT3 = total number of heads
living in Kloe.

Table 11.   Distribution of female-headed groups according to the
            manner in which the house was acquired.

	INHERITED	BUILT	UNKNOWN	TOTAL
Expanded	0	2	0	2
Extended	3	10	1	14
Incorporative	5	1	1	7
Others	2	9	4	15
Total	10	22	6	38

Table 12.   Statistics on migration (1972).

Statistics on men:

- 51% of adult population away on migration;
- of the migrants, 14% belong to the oldest generation (G˘);
- of the oldest living generation, 67% own their house;
- of the younger generations (G-1, G-2), 14% own their house;
- of the whole sample, 16% of the men live in residential groups of
  other relatives;
- of the men living in Kloe, 32% live in the houses of relatives.

Statistics on women:

- 37% of adult female population is away on migration;
- of the migrants, 22% belong to the oldest living generation (G˘);
- of the oldest generation, 21% own their house;
- of the younger generations (G-1, G-2), 4% own their house;
- of the women living in Kloe, 63% live in the house of consanguines
  (parents, siblings, children and distant kin);
- of the whole sample, 36% of women live with their husband;
- of the women on migration, 51% live with their husband (and 49% on
  their own)
- of the women living in Kloe, 19% live with their husband;
- of the women in Kloe, 29% also reside duolocally.

Sample (250 men, 285 women) represents over 80% of the adult Kloe
population.

Table 13.   Statistics on fostering.

Type of union of parents	No. of children	No. & percentage fostered
Extant endogamous*	280	21 (8%)
Extant male exogamous	136	15 (11%)
Extant female exogamous	142	21 (15%)
Terminated endogamous	160	68 (41%)
Terminated male exogamous	56	19 (34%)
Terminated female exogamous	48	11 (23%)
Illegitimate endogamous	42	17 (40%)
Illegitimate male exogamous	53	11 (21%)
Illegitimate female exogamous	58	10 (17%)
Unknown genitor	39	15 (38%)
Orphans of one parent	23	11 (48%)
Total	1,037	219 (21%)

Also:

- 130 children are fostered to lineal relatives, of which 114 (88%) are fostered in Kloe; conversely, 78% of the children fostered in Kloe are fostered to lineal relatives;
- 89 children are fostered to collateral relatives, of which 56 (63%) are fostered outside Kloe; conversely, 78% of the children fostered outside Kloe are fostered by collateral relatives;
- 147 children are fostered in Kloe, and 72 outside;
- 558 children were born of extant marriages, and 296 (or 53%) of them lived with their parents;
- of the total sample 380 children (or 37%) were described as living with their mother, 142 (14%) with their father, 11 with their MB, 27 with MZ, 20 with FB, 19 with FZ and 12 with more distant relatives.

Legend: * Endogamous and exogamous refer to village in- or out-marriage.

Table 14. Percentages of in-marriage, distributed by clans.

	Women's first marriage						All of women's marriages					
	A	B	C	D	E	X	A	B	C	D	E	X
Village IM/all marriages	77	78	64	77	68	74	68	71	60	69	67	64
Clan IM/village IM	61	57	40	20	27	50	60	54	33	21	28	49
Clan IM/all marriages	47	45	26	15	18	36	41	38	20	14	19	31
Lineage IM/clan IM	46	22	23	20	12	31	46	20	24	15	18	30
Lineage IM/village IM	28	12	9	4	3	15	28	11	8	3	5	15
Lineage IM/all marriages	22	10	6	3	2	11	19	8	5	2	3	9

Legend: IM=in-marriage,
A=Akpokli, B=Gulegbe, C=Wome, D=Etsri, E=Atsadome,
X=overall percentages.

Table 15. Clan of origin of women's first husband, to 1935.

	Husband from:				
	Akpokli	Gulegbe	Wome	Etsri	Atsadome
Wife from:					
Akpokli	61	21	9	5	6
Gulegbe	29	40	11	9	10
Wome	11	13	16	5	4
Etsri	10	9	3	8	3
Atsadome	1	8	2	0	6

Table 16. Clan of origin of women's first husband, from 1935.

	Husband from:				
	Akpokli	Gulegbe	Wome	Etsri	Atsadome
Wife from:					
Akpokli	43	14	7	4	2
Gulegbe	24	75	8	7	10
Wome	9	5	9	1	1
Etsri	9	11	2	5	3
Atsadome	5	9	1	0	4

Table 17. Lineage of origin of women's first husband.

W:	A 1	2	3	B 1	2	3	4	5	C 1	2	3	4	5	D 1	2	3	E 1	2	3	AB	ED	SE	NE	TOT
A1	24	10	3	6	3	1	1	2	2	1	0	2	1	2	0	1	1	0	2	4	9	6	4	85
A2	11	13	5	5	2	1	2	0	0	0	0	0	2	0	0	1	3	0	0	2	5	1	5	58
A3	12	4	3	2	0	1	0	0	2	0	1	0	1	3	0	0	1	0	1	2	7	1	3	44
B1	4	4	5	12	6	3	7	5	0	2	2	2	0	2	1	2	3	1	0	4	8	2	5	80
B2	6	1	1	8	1	1	2	1	0	2	0	0	0	0	1	0	1	1	0	2	7	1	1	37
B3	2	4	1	7	4	3	6	4	1	0	0	2	0	1	0	0	3	0	0	1	3	2	1	45
B4	4	3	2	3	2	5	5	4	0	1	0	0	0	0	0	0	3	0	0	3	4	2	2	42
B5	1	1	0	0	2	4	2	0	0	0	0	0	0	1	1	0	2	1	1	1	0	0	1	18
C1	1	3	1	1	1	0	1	0	1	2	0	1	3	1	0	0	2	1	0	0	4	2	4	29
C2	3	0	0	2	0	1	0	1	1	4	0	2	1	1	0	0	0	0	0	1	3	0	3	23
C3	1	0	0	1	0	1	0	0	2	2	0	0	1	0	1	0	1	0	0	3	0	1	1	15
C4	2	0	0	1	0	0	0	0	0	1	1	0	0	0	0	1	1	0	0	0	3	1	0	11
C5	0	3	1	0	1	0	0	0	0	0	0	0	0	0	0	0	0	0	0	1	3	1	1	11
D1	3	2	0	5	1	0	1	0	0	0	1	1	0	1	3	1	1	0	0	1	0	0	1	21
D2	1	0	0	1	0	0	1	0	0	0	1	0	0	1	0	2	2	0	0	1	1	0	1	12
D3	5	2	1	3	1	3	1	0	2	0	0	0	0	1	1	1	2	1	0	3	3	0	5	35
E1	3	2	0	4	1	0	0	2	1	0	0	0	0	0	0	0	1	3	1	1	5	1	2	27
E2	0	0	0	1	0	1	1	1	0	0	0	0	0	0	0	0	3	0	0	0	0	0	1	8
E3	0	1	0	1	1	1	0	0	0	1	0	0	0	0	0	0	1	1	0	0	3	0	2	12

613

Legend: A=Akpokli, B=Gulegbe, C=Wome, D=Etsri, E=Atsadome
AB=from Abutia but not Kloe
ED=from northern Eweland
SE=from southern Eweland
NE=non-Ewe

Table 18. Instances of in-marriage of women's first marriage, distributed by clan and cohort.

	Akpoli				Gulegbe				Wome			
	LI	CI	VI	VO	LI	CI	VI	VO	LI	CI	VI	VO
1800-1875	0	0	2	1	0	1	7	4	0	1	5	2
1876-1885	0	0	3	0	1	3	8	1	0	1	3	1
1886-1895	0	4	8	2	0	5	6	1	0	1	6	3
1896-1905	2	8	11	0	0	6	13	2	0	2	8	4
1906-1915	3	6	13	3	0	3	13	0	1	1	4	0
1916-1925	7	15	23	3	1	12	22	2	1	3	4	3
1926-1935	10	16	19	6	3	7	12	6	1	5	7	2
1936-1945	3	7	13	2	5	22	27	7	1	2	4	2
1946-1955	9	16	22	10	5	22	30	9	0	4	9	4
1956-1965	2	6	12	8	4	9	18	11	1	2	4	6
1966-1971	0	1	3	3	2	7	14	4	0	0	1	4

	Etsri				Atsadome				Total			
	LI	CI	VI	VO	LI	CI	VI	VO	LI	CI	VI	VO
1800-1875	0	0	2	1	0	1	1	1	0	3	17	9
1876-1885	0	1	3	2	0	0	1	0	1	5	18	4
1886-1895	0	0	2	0	0	0	2	1	0	10	24	7
1896-1905	0	0	4	1	1	2	3	0	3	18	39	7
1906-1915	0	0	8	2	0	0	2	0	4	10	40	5
1916-1925	0	0	0	3	0	2	6	2	9	32	55	13
1926-1935	1	5	8	0	0	1	2	0	15	34	48	14
1936-1945	0	1	4	2	0	2	5	0	9	34	53	13
1946-1955	0	1	9	1	0	0	3	5	14	43	73	29
1956-1965	1	2	7	1	0	0	4	2	8	19	45	28
1966-1971	0	0	3	2	0	0	1	3	2	8	22	16

Legend: LI=lineage in-marriage, CI=clan in-marriage, VI=village in-marriage, VO=village out-marriage.

Table 19.   Instances of in- and out-marriage of all women's
marriages, distributed by clan and cohort.

	Akpoli				Gulegbe				Wome			
	LI	CI	VI	VO	LI	CI	VI	VO	LI	CI	VI	VO
1800-1875	0	0	2	1	0	1	8	4	0	1	7	2
1876-1885	0	0	5	0	1	3	11	2	0	1	4	1
1886-1895	1	7	12	5	0	5	7	1	0	1	8	3
1896-1905	2	8	13	1	0	7	15	3	0	3	12	5
1906-1915	4	7	15	4	0	6	20	2	1	1	4	0
1916-1925	10	19	31	6	1	17	27	9	1	4	6	5
1926-1935	12	20	24	10	3	12	19	6	1	3	9	4
1936-1945	5	11	19	6	5	25	36	14	2	2	6	6
1946-1955	10	19	29	28	7	26	42	21	0	5	11	7
1956-1965	4	11	18	15	5	14	30	25	1	2	6	12
1966-1971	0	2	4	4	3	8	16	6	0	0	2	5

	Etsri				Atsadome				Total			
	LI	CI	VI	VO	LI	CI	VI	VO	LI	CI	VI	VO
1800-1875	0	0	2	2	0	1	1	1	0	3	20	10
1876-1885	0	1	4	2	0	0	1	0	1	5	25	5
1886-1895	0	0	2	0	0	0	2	1	1	13	31	10
1896-1905	0	1	5	1	1	2	4	0	3	21	49	10
1906-1915	0	0	9	2	0	0	2	0	5	14	50	8
1916-1925	0	0	1	3	0	3	8	2	12	43	73	25
1926-1935	1	6	10	3	0	1	2	0	17	44	65	23
1936-1945	0	1	7	5	0	2	7	2	12	41	75	33
1946-1955	0	2	11	5	1	2	7	6	18	54	100	67
1956-1965	1	2	9	3	0	0	4	4	11	29	67	59
1966-1971	0	0	3	2	0	0	1	3	3	10	26	20

Legend: LI=lineage in-marriage, CI=clan in-marriage, VI=village
in-marriage, VO=village out-marriage.

Table 20. Sample of individuals ever married, dead and alive.

		Males	Females	Total
ALIVE:	Extant marriage	201	266	467
	No extant marriage	122	240	362
	Total	323	506	829
DEAD:		270	264	534
		593	770	1363

Table 21. Incidence of polygyny as a percentage of all marriages.

Extant marriages	$\dfrac{\text{Extant Polygyny}}{\text{Extant unions}}$	$\dfrac{31}{201}$	(16%)
	$\dfrac{\text{Extant polygynists}}{\text{Ever polygynists alive}}$	$\dfrac{31}{81}$	(38%)
Dead population (first married since 1895)	$\dfrac{\text{Polygynists dead (L)}}{\text{Ever married dead}}$	$\dfrac{40}{155}$	(26%)
	$\dfrac{\text{Polygynists dead (H)}}{\text{Ever married dead}}$	$\dfrac{43}{155}$	(28%)
Dead population (first married since 1800)	$\dfrac{\text{Polygynists dead (L)}}{\text{Ever married dead}}$	$\dfrac{53}{270}$	(20%)
	$\dfrac{\text{Polygynists dead (H)}}{\text{Ever married dead}}$	$\dfrac{64}{270}$	(24%)
Population alive	$\dfrac{\text{Ever polygynists alive}}{\text{Ever married alive}}$	$\dfrac{81}{323}$	(25%)
Global population (first married since 1895)	$\dfrac{\text{All polygynists (L)}}{\text{Ever married}}$	$\dfrac{118}{476}$	(25%)
	$\dfrac{\text{All polygynists (H)}}{\text{Ever married}}$	$\dfrac{121}{476}$	(25%)
Global population (first married since 1800)	$\dfrac{\text{All polygynists (L)}}{\text{Ever married}}$	$\dfrac{134}{571}$	(23%)
	$\dfrac{\text{All polygynists (H)}}{\text{Ever married}}$	$\dfrac{146}{571}$	(26%)
Unknown cases	Dead = 11, Alive = 11		

Legend: L=lowest estimate, H=highest estimate

Table 22. Incidence of polygyny for the male population alive, by cohorts of first marriage, starting from 1895.

	1896-1905	1906-1915	1916-1925	1926-1935	1936-1945	1946-1955	1956-1965	1966-1971	Total
1. Monogamy*	0	1	18	12	21	41	73	53	219
2. Polygyny	1	3	4	14	18	22	16	3	81
3. Uncertain	0	0	0	0	1	0	0	0	1
4. Total	1	4	22	26	40	63	89	56	301
5. Percent.	100%	75%	18%	54%	45%	35%	18%	5%	

Legend: *including serial marriage

Table 23. Incidence of polygyny of global male population recorded, dead and alive, by cohorts of first marriage (where date is known), starting from 1800.

	1800-1875	1876-1885	1886-1895	1896-1905	1906-1915	1916-1925	1926-1935	1936-1945	1946-1955	1956-1965	1966-1971
1. Monogamy*	40	14	19	27	24	37	28	34	52	77	55
2. Polygyny	2	5	7	13	17	9	19	19	23	16	3
3. Uncertain	2	1	0	0	1	1	1	1	0	0	0
4. Total	44	20	26	40	42	47	48	53	75	94	58
5. L		5%	25%	27%	33%	40%	19%	40%	36%	31%	17%	5%
6. H		10%	30%	27%	33%	40%	19%	40%	36%	31%	17%	5%

Legend: *including serial marriage, L=lowest incidence, H=highest incidence.

Table 24. Age distribution and residence of extant polygynists.

Age	No. of polygynists	No. resident in village
20-31	4	1
32-41	11	3
42-51	11	2
52-61	4	3
61+	1	1
Total	31	10

Table 25. Duration of the polygynous experience for sample of 'one time' and extant polygynists.

I.	0	1	2	3	4	5	6	7	8	9	10	11	12	13	14	15	16	17	18	19	20	21	22
II.	2	12	10	12	5	5	7	4	0	3	2	2	2	3	1	0	3	0	0	0	1	0	0
III.	0	0	1	6	0	2	2	2	0	0	0	1	2	1	1	0	2	0	0	0	0	0	0

I.	23	24	25	26	27	28	29	30	31	32	33	
II.	1	0	0	0	0	0	1	0	0	0	1	= 77 (58% of known cases)
III.	1	0	0	0	0	0	0	0	0	0	0	= 21 (68% of known cases)

Mean duration:	a) 'one time' polygynists:	6.2 years
	b) extant polygynists:	8.2 years

Median duration:	a) 'one time' polygynists:	4 years
	b) extant polygynists:	6 years

Legend: I=number of years of polygynous union, II=number of cases of 'one time' polygynists, III=number of cases of extant polygynists.

Table 26. Distribution of extant polygynists by their lineage of origin, together with the percentages of males extantly married, and polygynously extantly married, by lineage.

Lineage	1) Extant Polygynists	2) % of lineage males alive extantly married	3) % of 2) also polygynous
A1	5	60%	14%
A2	2	58%	13%
A3	1	63%	8%
B1	6	52%	20%
B2	1	69%	11%
B3	3	60%	20%
B4	0	67%	0%
B5	3	58%	45%
C1	0	89%	0%
C2	0	33%	0%
C3	0	83%	0%
C4	0	83%	0%
C5	0	75%	0%
D1	1	60%	17%
D2	0	16%	0%
D3	2	86%	33%
E1	3	83%	60%
E2	4	80%	100%
E3	0	71%	0%
Total	31		

Legend: Akpokli, B=Gulegbe, C=Wome, D=Etsri, E=Atsadome
1,2,3,4,5=constituent lineages.

Table 27.   All cases of recorded polygyny, including uncertain cases,
distributed by lineage.

	DEAD		ALIVE		TOTAL	
Lineage	Known	Unknown	Known	Unknown	Known	Unknown
A1	12	1	18	0	30	1
A2	8	2	5	1	13	3
A3	6	1	6	0	12	1
B1	10	0	16	0	26	0
B2	3	1	4	0	7	1
B3	2	1	7	0	9	1
B4	0	1	2	0	2	1
B5	3	0	4	0	7	0
C1	0	1	1	0	1	1
C2	0	0	1	0	1	0
C3	0	0	0	0	0	0
C4	1	0	1	0	2	0
C5	1	0	1	0	2	0
D1	2	1	3	0	5	1
D2	1	0	1	0	2	0
D3	1	1	2	0	3	1
E1	3	0	5	0	8	0
E2	0	1	4	0	4	1
E3	0	0	0	0	0	0
Total	53	11	81	1	134	12

Legend: Akpokli, B=Gulegbe, C=Wome, D=Etsri, E=Atsadome
1,2,3,4,5=constituent lineages.

Table 28.   Fertility of male monogynists.

No. of children	0	1	2	3	4	5	6	7	8	9	10	11	
No. of fathers	21	75	44	49	30	27	20	14	8	11	4	3	(=306)

Mean = 3.33

Table 29.   Fertility of polygynists, including only their children
born of polygynous unions.

No. of children	0	1	2	3	4	5	6	7	8	9	10	11	12	13	14	15	16	17	18	
No. of fathers	1	2	1	7	8	6	7	10	6	0	2	5	2	1	1	0	1	0	1	(=61)

Means = 6.68

Table 30. Fertility of serial male marriages.

No. of children	0	1	2	3	4	5	6	7	8	9	10	11	12	13	
No. of fathers	2	10	8	15	17	9	6	6	4	3	3	1	0	1	(=85)

Mean = 4.41

Table 31. Aggregate fertility of polygynists, including the offspring born of non-polygynous unions.

No. of children	0	1	2	3	4	5	6	7	8	9	10	11	12	13	14	15	16	17	18	19	
No. of fathers	0	1	1	1	5	7	7	3	4	7	7	2	3	1	1	0	1	0	1	1	(=53)

Means = 8.05

Table 32. Present marital status.

	Extant	Divorced	Widowed	Unmarried	Unwed Parent	Total
Men	201	72	12	37	38	360
Women	266	130	36	16	74	522
Total	467	202	48	53	112	882

Table 33. Present marital status of men and women first married in
or before 1935, by order of marriage.

	MALES					FEMALES				
Marriage	1st	2nd	3rd	4th	Tot	1st	2nd	3rd	4th	Tot
Extant	8	7	6	4	25	16	2	9	3	30
Divorced	4	4	7	1	16	22	8	10	0	40
Widowed	3	2	1	2	8	20	1	6	0	27
Total	15	13	14	7	49	58	11	25	3	97

Table 34. Cumulative marital experience.

	Men	Women
Number in sample	593	770
Mean number of divorces per head	.50	.45
Percentage alive, ever divorced	46.5	44.96
Percentage ever divorced	37.5	41.1

Table 35. Calculation of divorce ratio A for all three samples.

	No. of marriages	No. ended in divorce	Ratio A1	Ratio A2	Ratio A3
Male	496	218	43.9		
Female	594	269	45.2		
Male	344	81		23.5	
Female	259	78		30.1	
Male	892	299			35.6
Female	908	347			40.7
Missing observ.	52	55			

Legend: Ratio A1 = Number of marriages ended in divorce in live
population/all marriages in live population

Ratio A2 = Number of marriages ended in divorce in dead
population/all marriages in dead population

Ratio A3 = Number of marriages ended in divorce in global
sample/all marriages in global sample

Table 36.   Calculation of divorce ratio B for live and global
            populations.

	Marriages terminated	Marriages ended in divorce only	Ratio B1	Ratio B2
Male	259	218	84.1	
Female	326	269	82.5	
Male	603	299		49.6
Female	585	347		59.3

Legend: Ratio B1 = Number of marriages ended in divorce in live
                     population/Number of marriages completed by death
                     and divorce in live population
          Ratio B2 = Number of marriages ended in divorce in global
                     sample/number of marriages completed by death and
                     divorce in global sample

Table 37.   Calculation of divorce ratio C.

	Divorces	Divorces + Extant marriages	Ratio C
Male	218	455	47.9
Female	269	537	50.0

Legend: Ratio C = Number of marriages ended in divorce in live
                    population/Number of marriages extant and ended in
                    divorce in live population

Table 38.   Main conclusions from Barnes's tables applied to the
            global sample.

	Males	Females
Mean duration of marriage	11.05 years	10.7 years
Median duration of marriage	8-9 years	8-9 years
Mean duration of marriage ending in divorce	7.125 years	7.33 years
Median duration of marriage ending in divorce	5 years	4-5 years
Marriages that would end in divorce without mortality	67.436	80.55
Effect of mortality	16.806	21.23

Table 39. Divorce ratios A and B calculated for village in- and out-marriage.

| | MEN | | WOMEN | |
	Village in-marriage	Village out-marriage	Village in-marriage	Village out-marriage
Ratio A	.38	.31	.41	.39
Ratio B	.49	.55	.54	.76

Table 40. Divorces per annum per 100 marriages existing at specific durations: Ngoni, Abutia men and women.

Duration	Abutia men	Ngoni	Abutia women
0-1	3.72	4.33	4.81
2-3	5.42	5.94	7.75
4-5	7.77	13.59	9.49
6-7	7.96	5.68	5.93
8-9	5.77	3.62	6.15
10-14	4.21	5.53	6.21
15-19	1.89	2.35	2.46
20-24	1.37	.37	2.05
25-29	2.30	3.25	2.30
30-34	.68	.97	.69
35-39	1.21		0
40-44	.75		1.06
45-59	0		0
50-54	0		9.97

Table 41.   Abutia male marriages: survival table, after Barnes.

i	j	$E_{i,j}$	$e_{i,j}$	$G_{i,j}$	$M_{i,j}$	$D_{i,j}$	$H_{i,j}$	$W_{i,j}$	$HW_{i,j}*$	$F_{i,j}$
0	1	32		4.5714	45.8703	15	3	1	8	23
2	3	32		4.0476	40.6144	49	5	6	21	70
4	5	28	14	3.5	35.1197	68	9	8	32	100
6	7	18	21	5.25	52.6795	43	12	5	32	75
8	9	7		1.5	15.0513	33	8	6	26	59
10	14	31		-.85	-8.529	60	20	13	62	122
15	19	25	9	.9	9.0307	15	13	4	32	47
20	24	22	10	1	10.0342	7	12	6	34	41
25	29	15	15	1.5	15.0513	6	7	5	23	29
30	34	7	9	.9	9.0307	1	8	1	17	18
35	39	6	2	.2	2.0068	1	1	0	2	3
40	44	5	-2	-.2	-2.0068	1	5	0	9	10
45	49	8	4	.4	4.0136	0	1	1	2	2
50	54	1		.9	9.0307	0	1	0	2	2
				23.6191			105	56	302	601

i	j	$t_{i,j}$	$D'_{i,j}$	$F'_{i,j}$	R_i	$R_i + R_{i,j}$	$L_{i,j}$
0	1	1.9943	44.9145	68.8689	838	1607.1311	1205.3483
2	3	.5802	77.4298	110.614	769.1311	1427.6482	1427.6482
4	5	.3512	91.8816	135.12	658.5171	1181.9142	1181.9142
6	7	.7024	73.2032	127.68	523.3971	919.1142	919.1142
8	9	.2551	41.4183	74.0509	395.7171	717.3833	717.3833
10	14	-.0699	55.806	113.4722	321.6662	529.8602	1324.6505
15	19	.1921	17.8815	56.0287	208.194	360.3593	900.8982
20	24	.2447	8.7129	51.0327	152.1653	253.2979	633.2447
25	29	.519	9.114	44.051	101.1326	158.2142	395.5355
30	34	.5017	1.5017	27.0306	57.0816	87.1326	217.8315
35	39	.6689	1.6689	5.0067	30.51	55.0953	137.7382
40	44	-.2007	.7993	7.993	25.0443	42.0956	105.239
45	49	2.0068	0	6.0136	17.0513	28.089	70.225
50	54	4.5153	0	11.0306	11.0377	11.0377	27.5942
							9264.3725

Legend: *There are instances where it is known that a marriage
terminated by death, but impossible to know whether wife or
husband died first. $H_{i,j}$ and $W_{i,j}$ have thus been
corrected and the total of their combined mortality is
shown as $HW_{i,j}$.

Table 42. Abutia male marriages: divorce risk tables, after Barnes.

i	j	D' o,j	Q j	Z i,j	q i,j	p i,j	T i,j	a i,j
0	1	44.9145	.0536	33.6858	.0535	.9465	100	.0372
2	3	122.3443	.146	193.5745	.1006	.8995	94.65	.0542
4	5	214.2259	.2556	413.4672	.1395	.8605	85.1282	.0777
6	7	287.4291	.343	475.8208	.1398	.8602	73.2528	.0796
8	9	328.8474	.3924	352.0555	.1046	.8954	63.012	.0577
10	14	384.6534	.4590	669.672	.1734	.8266	56.421	.0421
15	19	402.5349	.4803	303.9855	.0858	.9142	46.6376	.0189
20	24	411.2478	.4907	191.6838	.0572	.9428	42.6361	.0137
25	29	420.3618	.5016	246.078	.0901	.9099	40.1973	.0230
30	34	421.8635	.5034	48.0544	.0263	.9737	36.5755	.0068
35	39	423.5324	.5054	61.7893	.0555	.0445	35.6136	.0121
40	44	424.3317	.5063	33.5706	.0319	.9681	33.637	.0075
45	49	0			0	1	32.564	0
50	54				0	1	32.564	0
				3023.3974			32.564	

Table 43. Abutia female marriages: survival tables.

i	j	E i,j	e i,j	G i,j	M i,j	D i,j	H i,j	W i,j	HW i,j*	F i,j
0	1	36		6.4285	63.5425	16	4	1	8	24
2	3	33		7.2857	72.0155	53	5	6	17	70
4	5	21		2.75	27.1823	83	7	1	13	96
6	7	22	11	1	9.8845	48	16	4	32	80
8	9	17	4	1.5	14.8267	37	7	4	17	54
10	14	38		1.25	12.3556	77	18	12	47	124
15	19	32		1.6	15.8152	16	16	4	32	48
20	24	22	16	1.6	15.8152	8	9	6	24	32
25	29	16	16	1.1	10.8729	6	7	5	19	25
30	34	11	11	.9	8.896	1	10	0	16	17
35	39	7	9	.9	8.896	0	1	0	2	2
40	44	2	9	-.2	-1.9769	2	1	0	2	4
45	49	9	-2	-.1	-.9884	0	3	1	3	3
50	54	3	-1	1.2	11.8614	1	3	0	3	4
		269				348	105	44	235	583

i	j	t i,j	D' i,j	F' i,j	R i	R,+R j+1	L i,j
0	1	2.6476	58.3616	87.5424	852	1616.4576	1212.3432
2	3	1.0287	107.5211	142.009	764.4575	1386.9062	1386.9062
4	5	.2831	106.4973	123.1776	622.4486	1121.7196	1121.7196
6	7	.1235	53.928	89.88	499.271	908.662	908.662
8	9	.2745	46.1575	68.823	409.391	749.959	749.959
10	14	.0996	84.6692	136.3504	340.568	544.7856	1361.964
15	19	.3294	21.2704	63.8112	204.2176	344.624	861.56
20	24	.4942	11.9536	47.8144	140.4064	232.9984	582.496
25	29	.4349	8.6094	35.8725	92.592	149.3115	373.2787
30	34	.5232	1.5232	25.8944	56.7195	87.5446	218.8615
35	39	.4448	0	10.896	30.8251	50.7542	126.8855
40	44	-.4942	1.0116	2.0232	19.9291	37.835	94.5875
45	49	-.3294	0	2.0118	17.9059	33.8	84.5
50	54	2.9653	3.9653	15.8612	15.8941	15.8941	39.7352
			505.4682				9123.4584

Legend: *There are instances where it is known that a marriage terminated by death, but impossible to know whether wife or husband died first. $H_{i,j}$ and $W_{i,j}$ have thus been corrected and the total of their combined mortality is shown as $HW_{i,j}$.

Table 44. Abutia female marriages: divorce risk tables.

i	j	D' o,j	Q j	Z i,j	q i,j	p i,j	T i,j	a i,j
0	1	58.3616	.0684	43.7712	.0684	.9316	100	.0481
2	3	165.8827	.1946	268.8027	.1406	.8594	93.16	.0775
4	5	272.38	.3196	479.23785	.171	.829	80.0617	.0949
6	7	326.308	.3829	350.532	.108	.892	66.3711	.0593
8	9	372.4654	.4371	392.3387	.1127	.8873	59.203	.0615
10	14	457.1347	.5365	1016.0304	.2486	.7514	52.5308	.0621
15	19	478.4051	.5615	361.5968	.1041	.8559	39.4717	.0246
20	24	490.3587	.5755	262.9792	.0851	.9149	33.7838	.0205
25	29	498.9681	.5856	232.4538	.0929	.9071	30.9088	.0230
30	34	500.4913	.5874	48.7424	.0268	.9732	28.0373	.0069
35	39	500.4913	.5874	0	0	1	27.2859	0
40	44	501.5029	.5886	42.4872	.0507	.9493	27.2859	.0106
45	49	501.5029	.5886	0	0	1	25.9025	0
50	54	505.4682	.5932	206.1956	.2494	.7506	25.9025	.0997
				3705.1679			19.442	

Table 45. Divorces per 100 marriages contracted, within specified time after marriage.

Duration	Abutia men	Ngoni	Abutia women
1	5.36	6.28	6.84
3	14.6	16.539	19.46
5	25.56	34.772	31.96
7	34.3	40.382	38.29
9	39.24	43.360	43.71
14	45.90	51.615	53.65
19	48.03	53.846	56.15
24	49.07	54.120	57.55
29	50.16	55.866	58.56
34	50.34	56.201	58.74
39	50.54		58.74
44	50.63		58.86
49			58.86
54			59.32

Table 46. Number of years since termination of last marriage, for live adults.

	≤5	6-10	11-15	16-20	20+	TOT	≤5	6-10	11-15	16-20	20+	TOT
I.	25	15	7	4	12	63	30	13	21	6	30	100
II.	1	1	1	4	3	10	9	4	2	1	11	27
Tot.	26	16	8	8	15	73	39	17	23	7	31	127

Legend: I=Divorced, II=Widowed

Table 47. Calculations of divorce ratios A and B, by clan, for the whole sample.

	MEN		WOMEN	
	Ratio A	Ratio B	Ratio A	Ratio B
Akpokli	.38	.50	.44	.61
Gulegbe	.36	.51	.41	.62
Wome	.33	.46	.31	.47
Etsri	.29	.40	.43	.56
Atsadome	.35	.54	.42	.68

Table 48. Divorce ratios of male marriages, by cohorts of first marriage.

	1800-1892	1892-1914	1914-1945	1945-1971
Ratio A3*	12.3	21.3	43.8	38.4
Ratio B3*	12.3	21.4	55.7	89.1

Legend: * See legend of tables 35 and 36 for definition of ratios.

Table 49. Divorce ratios of female marriages, by cohorts of first marriages.

	1800-1892	1892-1914	1914-1945	1945-1971
Ratio A3*	20.0	27.8	51.3	40.8
Ratio B3	20.0	28.0	63.6	93.8

Legend: * See legend of table 35 and 36 for definition of ratios.

Table 50. Completed male marriages for cohorts first married between 1901-1920: survival and divorce risk tables.

i	j	$D_{i,j}$	$W_{i,j}$	$H_{i,j}$	$WH_{i,j}*$	$F_{i,j}$	R_i	$R_i + R_{i\,j+1}$	$L_{i,j}$
0	1	1	1	0	2	3	156	309	231.75
2	3	5	3	1	6	11	153	295	295
4	5	9	2	2	6	15	142	269	269
6	7	5	2	6	12	17	127	237	237
8	9	5	2	4	9	14	110	206	206
10	14	13	2	5	11	24	96	168	420
15	19	4	2	6	12	16	72	128	320
20	24	1	2	5	11	12	56	110	275
25	29	3	2	2	6	9	44	79	197.5
30	34	1	2	8	15	16	35	54	135
35	39	0	1	1	3	3	19	35	87.5
40	44	3	0	1	2	5	16	27	67.5
45	49	0	1	4	8	8	11	14	35
50	54	0	0	2	3	3	3	3	7.5
		50	22	47	106	156	0	0	2783.75

i	j	$D_{o,j}$	$Z_{i,j}$	$q_{i,j}$	$p_{i,j}$	T_i	$a_{i,j}$
0	1	1	.75	.0064	.9936	100	.0043
2	3	6	12.5	.0326	.9674	99.36	.0169
4	5	15	40.5	.0633	.9367	96.1208	.0334
6	7	20	32.5	.0393	.9067	90.0364	.021
8	9	25	42.5	.0454	.9546	86.4979	.0048
10	14	38	156	.1354	.8646	82.5709	.0309
15	19	42	68	.0555	.9445	71.3908	.0125
20	24	43	22	.0178	.9822	67.4286	.0036
25	29	46	81	.0681	.9319	66.2284	.0151
30	34	47	32	.0285	.9715	61.7182	.0074
35	39	47	0	0	1	59.9592	0
40	44	50	126	.1875	.8125	59.9592	.0444
45	49	50	0	0	1	48.7169	0
50	54	50	0	0	1	48.7169.	0
		50	613.75				

Legend: * In some instances, it is known that a marriage was terminated by death, but impossible to know whether the wife or husband died first. $H_{i,j}$ and $W_{i,j}$ were thus corrected to take this into account, and the total of their combined mortality is shown as $HW_{i,j}$.

Table 51. Completed female marriages for cohorts of women first married between 1901 and 1920:   survival and divorce risk tables.

i	j	$D_{i,j}$	$W_{i,j}$	$H_{i,j}$	$WH_{i,j}*$	$F_{i,j}$	R_i	R_i+R_{j+1}	$L_{i,j}$
0	1	0	0	0	0	0	143	286	214.5
2	3	7	3	2	8	15	143	271	271
4	5	13	1	3	6	19	128	237	237
6	7	6	1	5	10	16	109	202	202
8	9	4	1	4	8	12	93	174	174
10	14	16	1	4	8	24	81	138	345
15	19	1	1	4	8	9	57	105	262.5
20	24	3	2	4	10	13	48	83	207.5
25	29	3	1	0	2	5	35	65	162.5
30	34	0	0	4	6	6	30	54	135
35	39	0	0	5	7	7	24	41	102.5
40	44	3	0	1	2	5	17	29	72.5
45	49	0	1	1	3	3	12	21	52.5
50	54	1	1	4	8	9	9	9	22.5
		40	12	41	86	143			2461.683

i	j	$D_{o,j}$	$Z_{i,j}$	$q_{i,j}$	$p_{i,j}$	T_i	$a_{i,j}$
0	1		0	0	1	100	0
2	3		17.5	.0489	.9511	100	.0258
4	5		58.5	.1015	.8985	95.11	.0548
6	7		39	.055	.945	85.4563	.0297
8	9		34	.043	.957	80.7562	.0229
10	14		192	.1975	.8025	77.8371	.1159
15	19		17	.0175	.9825	62.0201	.0095
20	24		66	.0625	.9375	60.9348	.0361
25	29		81	.0857	.9143	57.1264	.0461
30	34		0	0	1	52.2306	0
35	39		0	0	1	52.2306	0
40	44		126	.1034	.8966	52.2306	.1034
45	49		0	0	1	46.83	0
50	54		52	.1111	.8889	46.83	.1111
						41.6272	

Legend: * In some instances, it is known that a marriage was terminated by death, but impossible to know whether the wife or husband died first. $H_{i,j}$ and $W_{i,j}$ were thus corrected to take this into account, and the total of their combined mortality is shown as $HW_{i,j}$.

Table 52. Main conclusions from Barnes's tables applied to cohorts which have terminated their marriages.

	Males		Females	
Mean duration of marriage	17.8	years	17.2	years
Median duration of marriage	19	years	17-18	years
Mean duration of marriage ending in divorce	12.27	years	12	years
Median duration of marriage ending in divorce	9	years	8-9	years
Marriages that would end in divorce without mortality	51.28	years	58.37	years
Effect of mortality	19.23		18.518	

Table 53. Number of years of schooling for a sample of Kloe's resident population, classified by sex and cohort.

	Years of schooling:women						Years of schooling:men					
Born in:	Nil	1-3	3-6	7-10	11+	TOT	Nil	1-3	3-6	7-10	11+	TOT
1880-1914	46	2	5	0	0	53	23	10	13	4	1	51
1915-1929	43	7	9	0	0	59	22	6	4	7	2	41
1930-1945	35	1	13	13	1	63	6	2	10	21	3	42
1946-1955	4	10	44	2		60	0	8		42	1	51
Total	128	47	57	3		235	51	53		74	7	185

Table 54. Fertility of women in polygynous unions who completed their child-bearing life between 1900 and 1960.

No. of children	0	1	2	3	4	5	6	7	8	9	10
No. of mothers	5	11	13	5	11	9	8	5	0	2	2

Mean = 3.69*   Median = 4   N = 71

Legend: *Because of sampling methods, women's child-bearing history was not completely included. Corrected mean would be closer to 4.

Table 55. Fertility of women in monogamous unions who completed their child-bearing life between 1900 and 1960.

No. of children	0	1	2	3	4	5	6	7	8	9	10	11	12	13	14	15	16
No. of mothers	4	3	8	5	8	6	11	7	7	9	2	4	1	0	0	0	1

Mean = 5.789*   Median = 6   N = 76

Legend: *Because of sampling methods, a few women were neglected, who gave birth to one child only. The corrected mean would be closer to 5.

Table 56. Calculations of gross and net reproduction rates, annual rate of growth and expectation of life at birth, by cohorts of ten years.

Women born in:	N	Males Born	Surv.	Females Born	Surv.	Total Born	Surv.	G.R.R.	N.R.R.
x - 1900	58	138	92	140	104	276	196	2.41	1.79
1901-1910	63	131	92	159	121	290	213	2.52	1.92
1911-1920*	55	107	84	88	77	195	161	1.6	1.4
1921-	71	147	131	137	126	284	257	1.93	1.727

Women born in:	N.R.R.	'Princeton'	'r' Princeton	r(25)	r(27)	r(29)
x - 1900	1.509 x 1.728	.0156 r .0193	.023	.021	.02
1901-1910	1.734 x 1.805	.021	.026	.024	.022
1911-1920	1.254 x 1.315	.0095	.0314	.0125	.0116
1921-	-	-	.0218	.02	.0188

Women born in:	'r' adopted	e˘(F)	e˘(M)
x - 1900	.0205	47.5	42-45
1901-1910	.023	50	44-47
1911-1920	.012	57-60	51-54
1921-1928	.019		

Legend: G.R.R. = gross reproduction rate, N.R.R. = net reproduction rate, r = annual rate of growth, e˘(F) = expection of life at birth for women and e˘(M) = expectation for life at birth for men.
* Girls born after 1955 and boys born after 1950 have not yer survived to the age of reproduction, so that both G.R.R. and N.R.R. should be lower for the last two cohorts.

Table 57.   Fertility rates, by cohorts of ten years.

Women born in:	N	0	1	2	3	4	5	6	7	8	9	10	11	12	Mean
						Number of children									
x-1900	58	9	3	4	6	6	6	5	5	3	8	0	2	1	4.758
1901-1910	53	3	11	6	4	6	11	7	4	1	5	3	1	1	4.6
1911-1920	55	7	14	7	7	5	1	1	3	3	3	2	1	1	3.54
1921-1928	71	13	8	7	5	7	8	9	3	3	4	2	0	2	4.00

Table 58.   Residential distribution of adults in G˅, G-1 and G-2.

			MEN						
		In Kloe:						Migrated	
	Self	Fa	Mo	Br	Wi	Dk	Tot		
G˅	61	0	0	7	1	4	73	18	
G-1+ G-2	22	14	2	2	0	9	49	110	
Tot.	83	14	2	9	1	13	122	128	

				WOMEN								
		In Kloe:								Migrated		
	Self	Fa	Mo	Br	Si	Da	So	Hu	Dk	Tot	+Hu	-Hu	Tot
G˅	14	0	0	20	2	2	4	13	10	65	14	9	23
G-1+ G-2	5	37	11	5	1	0	3	35	18	115	40	43	83
Tot.	19	37	11	25	3	2	7	48	28	180*	54	52	106

* 53 of the women living in Kloe also reside duolocally.

Legend: Fa=father, Mo=mother, Br=brother, Si=sister, Da=daughter, So=son, Hu=husband, Dk=distant kin, +Hu=residing with the husband, -Hu=residing without the husband.

Tables 299

Table 59.   Sample of children, classified by their parents' type of union and the children's place of residence.

	In Kloe	Outside	Total
Children acknowledged	24	15	39
Orphans	17	6	23
Of extant marriages	281	277	558
Of terminated marriages	150	114	264
Born out of wedlock	73	80	153
Total	545	492	1037

Table 60.   Residential distribution of children born of extant village in-marriage.

	M/IN F/IN(T)				M/IN F/IN(D)				M/IN F/OUT				M/OUT F/OUT			
	In:		Out:		In:		Out:		In:		Out:		In:		Out:	
	B	G	B	G	B	G	B	G	B	G	B	G	B	G	B	G
M					19	34			20	24						
F					4	3					5	6				
F+M	44	42													29	29
MM		1											5	1		
MF														2		
MZ		1										2				
MB			1										1			
FM													1	2		
FF		1														
FZ												1				1
FB			1													
	44	45	2	0	23	37	0	0	20	24	5	9	7	5	29	30

Legend: B=boys, G=girls, In=child lives in Kloe, Out=child lives outside Kloe, M/IN=mother lives in Kloe, M/OUT=mother lives outside Kloe, F/IN=father lives in Kloe, F/OUT=father lives outside Kloe, (T)=mother and father coreside, (D)= mother and father reside duolocally.

Table 61. Residential distribution of children born of extant male village in-marriage.

	M/IN F/IN				M/OUT F/IN				M/OUT F/OUT				M/OUT F/OUT(D)			
	In:		Out:		In:		Out:		In:		Out:		In:		Out:	
	B	G	B	G	B	G	B	G	B	G	B	G	B	G	B	G
M							4	9							10	15
F						1									2	2
F+M	8	7									37	26				
MM										1						
MF															2	1
MZ				1												
FM									4	2				1		
FZ													1	1		
FB												1				
	8	7	0	1	0	1	4	9	4	3	37	27	1	2	14	18

Legend: see Legend of Table 60.

Table 62. Residential distribution of children born of extant female out-marriage.

	M/IN F/IN				M/IN F/OUT				M/OUT F/OUT				M/OUT F/OUT (D)			
	In:		Out:		In:		Out:		In:		Out:		In:		Out:	
	B	G	B	G	B	G	B	G	B	G	B	G	B	G	B	G
M											37	37				
F	6	2			17	13									1	2
F+M							5								1	
MM							1		4	3				2		
MF																2
MZ								2								
MB								1	2	1						
FM											1					
FZ							1									
Other											1					
	6	2	0	0	17	13	7	3	6	4	39	37	0	2	2	4

Legend: See Legend of Table 60.

Table 63. Children of extant marriages, distributed by the child's place of residence and the parents' place or origin

Child's residence	In Kloe	Outside	Total
Both parents from Kloe	106	54	160
M outsider	18	38	56
F outsider	26	22	48
Total	150	114	264

Table 64. Residential distribution of children born of terminated village in-marriage.

	M/IN F/IN				M/IN F/OUT				F/IN M/OUT				M/OUT F/OUT-			
	In:		Out:		In:		Out:		In:		Out:		In:		Out:	
	B	G	B	G	B	G	B	G	B	G	B	G	B	G	B	G
M	8	6			7	14					2	2			3	4
F	6	5					8	5	9	5					3	5
MM										1						
MF													9	7		
MZ		1	2				1						1		2	
MB							1									
FM	2	1							1	3				2		
FF						2							5	3		
FZ		1	1								2					1
FB			2	1			1				4		1			1
Other			1	1									1			1
	16	14	4	4	7	16	9	7	10	9	8	2	19	15	8	12

Legend: See Legend of Table 60.

Table 65. Residential distribution of children born of terminated male village out-marriage.

	M/OUT F/IN				M/OUT F/IN			
	In:		Out:		In:		Out:	
	B	G	B	G	B	G	B	G
M			9	1			6	8
F	2	2					4	5
MM			1					
MZ			1	1				
FM	1				2	3		
FF					1	1		
FZ		1				2		
FB			2		2			
Other	1				1			
	4	3	13	2	5	6	10	13

Legend: see Legend of Table 60.

Table 66. Residential distribution of
children born of terminated
female village out-marriage.

| | M/IN F/OUT | | | | M/OUT F/OUT | | | |
| | In: | | Out: | | In: | | Out: | |
	B	G	B	G	B	G	B	G
M	9	12					1	1
F			3	2			5	4
MM						4		
MF						1		
MZ								3
FM								1
FZ								1
Other								1
	9	12	3	2	0	5	6	11

Legend: see Legend of Table 60.

Table 67. Children of terminated unions, classified by their place
residence and the parents' place or origin.

Child's residence	In Kloe	Outside	Total
Both parents from Kloe	106	54	160
M outsider	18	38	56
F outsider	26	22	48
Total	150	114	264

Table 68. Residential distribution of children born of village in-mating.

	M/IN F/IN				M/IN F/OUT				M/OUT F/IN				M/OUT F/OUT			
	In:		Out:		In:		Out:		In:		Out:		In:		Out:	
	B	G	B	G	B	G	B	G	B	G	B	G	B	G	B	G
M	3	7			2	4									3	2
F	2								1						1	
MM									2	2			2	1		
MZ														1		
FM					1		1		1	1			2			1
FZ								1					1			
	5	7	0	0	3	4	1	1	4	3	0	0	5	2	4	3

Table 69. Residential distribution of children born of male village out-mating.

	M/OUT F/IN				M/OUT F/OUT			
	In:		Out:		In:		Out:	
	B	G	B	G	B	G	B	G
M			3	8			8	10
F		2	1				6	4
MM							1	1
FM					2	2		1
FF						1		
FZ		2						
FB						1		
	0	4	4	8	2	4	15	16

Legend: See Legend of Table 60.

Table 70. Residential distribution of children born of female village out-mating.

| | M/IN F/OUT | | | | M/IN F/OUT | | | |
| | In: | | Out: | | In: | | Out: | |
	B	G	B	G	B	G	B	G
M	6	16					3	2
F			4	6			7	4
MM						4		
MF					3			
FM			2					
FF								
FZ		1						
	6	17	6	6	3	4	10	6

Legend: see Legend of Table 60.

Table 71. Residential distribution of children without acknowledged genitors.

| | M/IN | | | | M/OUT | | | | |
| | In: | | Out: | | In: | | Out: | | |
	B	G	B	G	B	G	B	G	Total
M	6	9					3	6	24
MM					4	1			5
MZ			1		1	2			4
MB			2						2
OTHER	1		1				1	1	4
Total	7	9		4	5	3	4	7	39

Legend: see Legend, Table 60.

Table 72. Residential distribution of children of widowed mothers who married in the village.

| | M/IN | | | | M/OUT | | | | |
| | In: | | Out: | | In: | | Out: | | |
	B	G	B	G	B	G	B	G	Total
M	2	5							7
FB						1	1	1	3
Total	2	5				1	1	1	10

Legend: see Legend, Table 60.

Table 73. Residential distribution of children of widowed mothers who married outside the village.

| | M/IN | | | | M/OUT | | | | |
| | In: | | Out: | | In: | | Out: | | |
	B	G	B	G	B	G	B	G	Total
M	1	1						1	3
FB								1	2
FF						1			1
Total	1	1				1		2	5

Legend: see Legend, Table 60.

Table 74. Children of widowers who married from the village: residential distribution.

| | M/IN | | | | M/OUT | | | | |
| | In: | | Out: | | In: | | Out: | | |
	B	G	B	G	B	G	B	G	Total
F	2								2
MZ	2				2				4
Total	4				2				6

Table 75. Residential distribution of children without acknowledged genitors.

| | F/IN |
| | Out: |
	G
MB	2

Bibliography

Amenumey, D.E.K. 1964. The Ewe People and the Coming of the European Rule, 1850-1914. University of London: Unpublished M.A. thesis.

Asamoa, Ansa. 1971. Die Gesellschaftlichen Verhältnisse der Ewe-Bevölkerung in Südost Ghana. Berlin: Adakemie Verlag.

Barnes, John A. 1954. Politics in a Changing Society. Manchester: Manchester University Press.

_____. 1962. "African models in the New Guinea Highlands." Man 62: 5-9.

_____. 1967a. "Agnation among the Mae Enga." Oceania 38:33-43.

_____. 1967b. "The frequency of divorce." Pp. 47-101 in The Craft of Social Anthropology, edited by A.L. Epstein. London: Tavistock.

Barth, Fredrik. 1959. Political Leadership among the Swat Pathans. London: Bell.

Bascom, William. 1969. The Yoruba of Southwestern Nigeria. New York: Holt, Rinehart & Winston.

Bender, Donald R. 1967. "A refinement of the concept of household: families, co-residence and domestic functions." American Anthropologist 69:493-504.

_____. 1971. "De facto families and De Jure households in Ondo." American Anthropologist 73:223-241

Bledsoe, Caroline H. 1980. Women and Marriage in Kpelle Society. Stanford: Stanford University Press.

Bohannan, Laura. (1958) 1970. "Political aspects of Tiv social organization." Pp. 33-77 in Tribes Without Rulers, edited by John Middleton and David Tait. London: Routledge and Kegan Paul.

Brydon, Lynne. 1976. Status Ambiguity in Amedzofe-Avatime: Women and Men in a Changing Patrilineal Society. University of Cambridge: Unpublished Ph.D. thesis.

_____. 1979. "Women at work: some changes in family structure in Amedzofe-Avatime." Africa 49:97-111.

Bukh, Jette. 1979. The Village Woman in Ghana. Uppsala: Scandinavian Institute of African Studies.

Clignet, Rémi. 1970. Many Wives, Many Power. Evanston, Illinois: Northwestern University Press.

Clignet, Rémi and Joyce Sween. 1974. "Urbanization, plural marriage and family size in two African cities." American Ethnologist 1: 221-242.

Coale, Ansley J. and Paul Demeny. 1966. Regional Model Life Tables and Stable Populations. Princeton: Princeton University Press.

Cohen, Ronald. 1961. "Marriage instability among the Kanuri of northern Nigeria." American Anthropologist 63: 1231-49.

_____. 1971. Dominance and Defiance. Washington: American Anthropological Association.

Davenport, William H. 1959. "Nonunilinear descent and descent group." American Anthropologist 61:557-72.

Dorjahn, Vernon. 1959. "The factor of polygyny in African demogragraphy." Pp. 87-112 in Continuity and Change in African Cultures, edited by William R. Bascom and Melville J. Herskovits. Chicago: University of Chicago Press.

Dumont, Louis. 1977. From Mandeville to Marx. Chicago: University of Chicago Press.

Evans-Pritchard, E.E. 1940. The Nuer. Oxford: Oxford University Press.

————. 1951. Kinship and Marriage among the Nuer. Oxford: Oxford University Press.

Fallers, Lloyd A. 1957. "Some determinants of marriage stability in Busoga: a reformulation of Gluckman's hypothesis." Africa 27:106-23.

Fiawoo, D.K. 1961. Social Survey of Tefle. Legon: Institute of Education, unpublished mimeograph.

Field, M.J. 1940. Social Organization of the Ga People. London and Accra: Crown Agents for the Colonies.

————. 1948. Akim-Kotoku: an Oman of the Gold Coast. London: Crown Agents for the Colonies.

Firth, Raymond. 1957. "A note on descent groups in Polynesia." Man 57:4-8.

Fortes, Meyer. 1945. The Dynamics of Clanship among the Tallensi. Oxford: Oxford University Press.

————. 1949a. The Web of Kinship among the Tallensi. Oxford: Oxford University Press.

————. (1949b) 1970. "Time and social structure: an Ashanti case study." Pp. 1-32 in Time and Social Structure. London: The Athlone Press.

————. 1953. "The structure of unilineal descent groups." American Anthropologist 55:17-41.

————. 1979. "Preface." Pp. vii-xii in Segmentary Lineage Systems Reconsidered, edited by Ladislav Holy. Belfast: The Queen's University Papers in Social Anthropology, vol. 4.

Fortes, Meyer and E.E. Evans-Pritchard. 1940. "Introduction." Pp. 1-23 in African Political Systems, edited by Meyer Fortes and E.E. Evans-Pritchard. Oxford: Oxford University Press.

Friedländer, Marianne. 1962. Zur Frage der Klassenverhältnisse der Ewe unter dem Einfluss der Kolonisation. Berlin University: Unpublished Ph.D. thesis.

Geertz, Clifford and Hildred. 1968. "Teknonymy in Bali: parenthood, age-grading and genealogical anmesia." Pp. 355-76 in Marriage, Family and Residence, edited by Paul Bohannan and John Middleton. New York: Natural History Press.

Ghana Government. 1976. Ghana, an Official Handbook. Accra: Ghana Information Services Department.

Gluckman, Max. 1950. "Kinship and marriage amoung the Lozi of northern Rhodesia and the Zulu of Natal." Pp. 166-206 in African Systems of Kinship and Marriage, edited by A.R. Radcliffe-Brown and Daryll Forde. Oxford: Oxford University Press.

Gonzales, Nancie L. Solien. 1961. "Family organization in five types of migratory labour." American Anthropologist 63:1264-80.

————. 1969. Black Carib Household Structure. Seattle: University of Washington Press.

Goodenough, Ward H. 1955. "Residence rules." Southwestern Journal of Anthropology 12:22-37.

Goody, Esther. 1969. Contexts of Kinship. Cambridge: Cambridge University Press.

_____. 1972. "Conjugal separation and divorce amoung the Gonja of northern Ghana." Pp. 14-54 in Marriage in Tribal Societies, edited by Meyer Fortes. Cambridge: Cambridge University Press.

Goody, Jack R. 1958. " The fission of domestic groups among the Lo Dagaba." Pp. 53-91 in the Developmental Cycle in Domestic Groups, edited by Jack Goody. Cambridge: Cambridge University Press.

_____. 1973. "Bridewealth and Dowry in Africa and Eurasia." Pp. 1-58 in Bridewealth and Dowry, edited by J.R. Goody and S.J. Tambiah. Cambridge: Cambridge University Press.

_____. 1976. Production and Reproduction. Cambridge: Cambridge University Press.

Goody, Jack R. and Esther. 1966. "Cross-cousin marriage in Ghana." Man 1:340-53.

Greene, Sandra E. 1981. "Land, lineage and clan in early Anlo." Africa 51:451-65.

Hammel, Eugene and Peter Laslett. 1974. "Comparing household structure over time and between cultures." Comparative Studies in Society and History: 73-109.

Harris, Grace. 1972. "Taita bridewealth and affinal relationships." Pp. 55-87 in Marriage in Tribal Society, edited by Meyer Fortes. Cambridge: Cambridge University Press.

Harris, Marvin. 1974. "Why a perfect knowledge of all the rules one must know to act like a native cannot lead to the knowledge of how the natives act." Journal of Anthropological Research 30:242-51.

Harris, Resemary. 1962. "The influence of ecological factors and external relations on the Mbembe tribes of south-east Nigeria." Africa 27:38-52.

_____. 1965. The Political Organization of the Mbembe, Nigeria. London: Her Majesty's Stationery Office.

Holy, Ladislav. 1979. "The segmentary lineage structure and its existential status." Pp. 1-22 in Segmentary Lineage Systems Reconsidered, edited by L. Holy. Belfast: The Queen's University Papers in Social Anthropology, vol. 4.

Huber, Hugo. 1957. "Schwangerschaft, Geburt und Frühe Kindheit im Brauchtum der Bata-Ewe." Annal. lateranensi 21:230-44.

_____. 1963. The Krobo. St. Augustin: Anthropos Institute.

_____. 1965. "Totenritual einer Ewe-Gruppe des südöstlichen Ghanas." Ethnos 30: 79-104.

Jackson, Michael. 1977a. "Sacrifice and social structure among the Kuranko." Africa 47:41-49.

_____. 1977b. "Sacrifice and social structure among the Kuranko." Africa 47:123-36.

Karp, Ivan. 1978. "New Guinea models in the African savannah." Africa 48:1-16.

Keesing, Roger M. 1971. "Descent, residence and cultural codes." In Anthropology in Oceania, edited by L. Hiatt and C. Jayawardena. Sydney: Angus & Robertson.

Kludze, A.K.P. 1973. Ghana I: Ewe Law of Property. London: Sweet and Maxwell.

Korn, S.D.R. 1975. "Household composition in the Tonga Islands."
Journal of Anthropological Research 31: 235-60.
Kuper, Adam. 1975. Anthropologists and Anthropology. London:
Penguin.
_____. 1982. Wives for Cattle. London: Routledge and Kegan Paul.
Laslett, Peter. 1972. "Introduction." Pp. 1-89 in Household and
Family in Past Time, edited by Peter Laslett. Cambridge: Cambridge
University Press.
Lawson, Rowena. 1972. The Changing Economy of the Lower Volta,
1954-67. London: International African Institute.
Leach, Edmund R. (1957) 1961. "Aspects of brideweatlth and marriage
stability among the Kachin and Lakher." Pp. 1-27 in Rethinking
Anthropology. London: Athlone Press.
_____. 1960. " The Sinhalese of the dry zone of Northern Ceylon."
Pp. 116-26 in Social Structure in Southeast Asia, edited by George
P. Murdock. London: Tavistock.
Lewin, Kurt, 1931. "The conflict between Aristotelian and Galilean
modes of thought in contemporary psychology." Journal of General
Psychology 5:141-77.
Lewis, Ioan. 1961. A Pastoral Democracy. London: Oxford University
Press.
Malinowski, Bronislaw. 1944. A Scientific Theory of Culture. London:
Oxford University Press.
Manoukian, Madeline. 1952. The Ewe-speaking People of Togoland and
the Gold Coast. London: International African Institute.
Mayer, Iona. 1965. "From kinship to common descent: four-generation
genealogies among the Gusii." Africa 35:366-84.
Meggitt, M.G. 1965. The Lineage System of the Mae Enga. New York:
Barnes & Noble Inc.
Middleton, John and David Tait. 1958. "Introduction." Pp. 1-32 in
Tribes Without Rulers. London: Routledge and Kegan Paul.
Murdock, George P. 1949. Social Structure. New York: The Macmillan
Company.
Murphy, Robert F. 1971. The Dialectics of Social Life. London:
George Allen & Unwin.
Nsarkoh, J.K. 1964. Local Government in Ghana. Accra: Ghana
Universities Press.
Nukunya, G.K. 1969. Kinship and Marriage among the Anlo Ewe. London:
Athlone Press.
Paulme, Denise. 1954. Une Société de Côte d'Ivoire Hier et
Aujourd'hui. Les Bétés. Paris and the Hague: Mouton.
Peters, Emrys. 1967. "Some structural aspects of the feud among the
camel-herding Bedouin of Cyrenaica." Africa 37:261-282.
Potash, Betty. 1978. "Some aspects of marital stability in a rural
Luo community." Africa 48: 380-97.
Radcliffe-Brown, A.R. (1935) 1952. "Patrilineal and matrilineal
succession." Pp. 32-48 in Structure and Function in Primitive
Society. Glenco, Ill.: Free Press.
_____. 1940. "Preface." Pp. xi-xxiii in African Political
Systems, London: Oxford University Press.
_____. 1950. "Introduction." Pp. 1-85 in African Systems of
Kinship and Marriage, edited by A.R. Radcliffe-Brown and Daryll
Forde. London: Oxford University Press.
Rattray, R.S. 1915. Togoland: a History of the Tribal Divisions of
the District of Misahoe and of the Sub-districts of Ho and Kpandu.
Ho archives: unpublished manuscript.

Richards, Audrey. 1950. "Some types of family structure among the
    Central Bantu." Pp. 207-51 in African Systems of Kinship and
    Marriage, edited by A.R. Radcliffe-Brown and Daryll Forde. London:
    Oxford University Press.
Rivers, W.H.R. 1924. Social Organization. London: Kegan Paul, Trench,
    Trubner.
Salisbury, Richard Frank. 1956. "Unilineal descent groups in the New
    Guinea Highlands." Man 56:2-7.
Scheffler, Harold W. 1965. Choiseul Island Social Structure.
    Berkeley: University of California Press.
_____. 1966. "Ancestor worship in anthropology: or observations
    on descent and descent groups." Current Anthropology 7:541-51.
Schneider, David M. 1953. "A note on bridewealth and the stability of
    marriage." Man 53: 55-7.
_____. 1961. "Introduction." Pp. 1-32 in Matrilineal Kinship,
    edited by David M. Schneider and Kathleen Gough. Berkeley:
    University of California Press.
_____. 1965. "On some muddles in the models." Pp. 25-86 in The
    Relevance of Models for Social Anthropology, edited by Michael
    Banton. London: Tavistock.
Service, Elman R. 1962. Primitive Social Organization. New York:
    Random House.
Spieth, Jakob. 1906. Die Ewe-Stämme. Berlin: Dietrich Reimer.
_____. 1911. Die Religion der Eweer in Süd Togo. Leipzig:
    Dieterish's Verlag.
Stenning, D. 1959. Savannah Nomads. London: Oxford University Press.
Terray, Emmanuel. 1966. L'organisation sociale des Dida de Côte
    d'Ivoire. Abidjan: Annales de l'Université d'Abidjan.
Van Velsen, J. 1964. The Politics of Kinship. Manchester: Manchester
    University Press.
Verdon, Michel. 1979a. "The Stem family: toward a general theory."
    The Journal of Interdisciplinary History 10:87-105.
_____. 1979b. "Sleeping together: the dynamics of residence
    among the Abutia Ewe. Journal of Anthropological Research 35:
    401-25.
_____. 1980a. "Shaking off the domestic yoke, or the sociological
    significance of residence." Comparative Studies in Society and
    History 22:109-32.
_____. 1980b. "Descent: an operational view." Man 15: 129-50.
_____. 1980c. "From the social to the symbolic equation: the
    progress of idealism in contemporary anthropological
    representations of kinship, marriage and the family." The Canadian
    Review of Sociology and Anthropology 17:315-29.
_____. 1980d. "From the biological to the behavioural equation:
    early milestones in the anthropological representation of kinship,
    marriage and the family." Revue européenne des sciences sociales
    Tome XVIII, No. 51:41-58.
_____. 1981. "Kinship, marriage and the family: an operational
    approach." American Journal of Sociology 86:796-818.
_____. 1982a. "The dynamics of Dynamics, or the Tallensi in time
    and numbers." Journal of Anthropological Research 38:154-781.
_____. 1982b. "Where have all their lineages gone? Cattle and
    descent among the Nuer." American Anthropologist 84:566-79.
_____. 1982c. "The operational approach is as new as non-
    teleological definitions." American Journal of Sociology
    87:1169-73.

_____. 1983. "Segmentation among the Tiv: a reappraisal."
American Ethnologist, forthcoming.

_____. n.d.1. Against Culture. Operationalism explained.
Unpublished ms.

Volta, Bernard. 1972. "Survey of the wildlife resource in the Kolor
area, Lower Volta, Ghana." Ghana: Department of Game and
Wildlife, unpublished report.

Ward, Barbara. 1949. The Social Organization of the Ewe-speaking
People. University of London: unpublished M.A. thesis.

Webster, David. 1977. "Spreading the risk: the principle of
laterality among the Chopi." Africa 47:192-205.

Westermann, D.H. 1935. Die Glidyi-Ewe in Togo. Berlin: de Gruyter.

Wilks, Ivor. 1977. "Land, labour, capital and the forest kingdom of
Asante: a model of early change." In The Evolution of Social
Systems, edited by Jonathan Friedman and M.J. Rowlands. London:
Duckworth.

Index